IN THE SHADOWS OF MEMORY

I0883615

IN THE SHADOWS OF MEMORY

VALLENTINE MITCHELL
LONDON • CHICAGO, IL

First published in paperback in 2021 by Vallentine Mitchell

Catalyst House,
720 Centennial Court
Centennial Park, Elstree, WD6 3SY

814 N. Franklin Street
Chicago, Illinois
60610, USA

www.vmbooks.com

Copyright © 2016 Vallentine Mitchell
First published in cloth in 2016

British Library Cataloguing in Publication Data
An entry can be found on request

ISBNs
978 1 912676 60 6 (paper)
978 0 85303 929 7 (ebook)

Library of Congress Cataloging in Publication Data
An entry can be found on request

All rights reserved. No part of this publication may be reproduced in any form or by any means, electronic, mechanical, photocopying, reading or otherwise, without the prior permission of Vallentine Mitchell & Co. Ltd.

Dedication

Esther Jilovsky dedicates this book to the memory of her grandparents, Hanka and Kurt Jilovsky, who inspired it, and to the memory of her Dad, Martin Michael Jilovsky, who never met his grandparents.

Jordana Silverstein dedicates this book to the memories of the Stawski family of Czestochowa and the Rosenkranz family of Sosnowitz.

David Slucki dedicates this book to the memories of his *bubbas* and *zaidas*, Eda and Yakub Slucki, and Mania and Izak Diner.

Contents

List of Illustrations

11. Ella and Dani during fieldwork in Berlin, January 2014. Copyright, Katja Harbi, who has granted permission for reproduction of photography. (She can be contacted at contact@katjaharbi.com).

12. American Freedom Defense Initiative advertisement, as seen in one subway station in New York, 2012. Copyright/permission granted by Golbarg Bashi, New York, 26 September 2012, via flickr: https://www.flickr.com/photos/golbargbashi/8028520437.

13. Sofia Stawski's travel documents, 1949. National Archives of Australia [NAA]: B78, 1957/STAWSKI S. From the Collection of the NAA.

14. Wladislaw Stawski's travel documents, 1949. NAA: B78, 1957/STAWSKI W. From the Collection of the NAA.

15. Hildegard Blum Herz and Arthur Herz, Beth Herz's paternal grandparents. Copyright/permission granted by Joshua Herz.

16. Petra Gelbart's grandfather and daughter in 2007, photographed in rural Moravia. Copyright/permission granted by Petra Gelbart.

17. Aliza Gor, grandmother of Riva Godfried, Haifa, July 2013, Photograph by Riva Godfried. Copyright/permission granted by Riva Godfried.

18. David Slucki's father, Charles Slucki, as a teenager with his father, Yakub Slucki, in the mid-1960s, about a decade before Yakub passed away. David Slucki's father keeps this photo in his wallet. With the permission of Charles Slucki.

Acknowledgements

The editors would like to thank Irene Pletka, Pauline Rockman, the Australian Centre for Jewish Civilisation at Monash University, and the Jacob Waks Cultural Fund, Melbourne for their generous support which enabled the publication of this book.

We would also like to thank Heather Marchant and Sylvia Simmons at Vallentine Mitchell for their support in guiding this project.

Notes on Contributors

Danny M. Cohen (PhD Northwestern University) is a writer of young adult human rights fiction, including the historical novel *Train*. He is a learning scientist and assistant professor of instruction at Northwestern University's School of Education and Social Policy and the Crown Family Center for Jewish and Israel Studies. Concerned with collective memories of atrocity, he focuses his teaching and research on the design of community programming for social justice, memorialization and museum design, and appropriate pedagogies for educating about violence. Danny is the founder of Unsilence Project, a non-profit that brings to light marginalized narratives of the Holocaust, genocide, and human rights. Danny was a Faculty Fellow of the Auschwitz Jewish Center and he is a current Global Justice Fellow of the American Jewish World Service. He is an appointed member of the Illinois Holocaust and Genocide Commission and sits on the editorial advisory board of the journal *The Holocaust in History and Memory*. Danny is personally connected to Holocaust history through his maternal grandfather, Maurice Ziekenoppasser, who escaped Nazi-occupied Amsterdam before members of his extended family were deported to and murdered in the Nazi camps (most likely Auschwitz-Birkenau and Sobibor). Originally from London, Danny now lives in Chicago with his husband and their daughter.

Felice Cohen is the granddaughter of two survivors who were in Auschwitz, Bergen Belsen and other camps. She is the author of the award-winning book *What Papa Told Me*, a memoir about her grandfather's life before, during and after the Holocaust. Endorsed by Elie Wiesel and Yad Vashem, *What Papa Told Me* has won three Honorable Mention book awards, been ranked number one on Kindle, and is in Holocaust museums including Washington, DC, the UK and Poland. Felice has spoken to thousands on the subject of the Holocaust and has been interviewed for two documentaries focusing on grandchildren of survivors. She has written for the *New York Daily News*, *amNew York* and *Metro*, and has published stories in two anthologies: *The Truth About the Fact* and *For Daddy, With Love*. Her ninety-square-foot Manhattan apartment was a YouTube sensation with over six million hits, and she is currently working to turn her blog Living Large in Any Space into a book called *90 Lessons Learned in 90 Square Feet*. Felice graduated from the University of

Massachusetts Amherst where she was a weekly opinion columnist and the first Jewish Affairs Editor for *The Daily Collegian*. She lives in New York City.

Adi Duchin, MA, is a doctoral student in the Department of Counseling and Human Development, Faculty of Education, University of Haifa, Israel. She is a certified bibliotherapist, working in Eitanim Mental Health Center in Jerusalem. She is currently writing a doctoral dissertation on 'Memory Books as a Bridge between the Generations: The Writing of Holocaust Survivors and the Reading Responses of their Children and Grandchildren'. Her dissertation supervisors are Professor Hadas Wiseman and Professor Emanuel Berman. Her research interests include the impact of writing on trauma processing, intergenerational communication patterns in families of Holocaust survivors, and readers' responses to books written by Holocaust survivors.

Sara Karin Fisher (cover artist) was born in London, where she studied fine art. She practises as an independent artist and illustrator, creating commissioned pieces and exhibiting her work internationally. She also trained as a counsellor and has worked in the field of mental health. She is the grandchild of Jewish Holocaust survivors. Her maternal grandmother, née Susanne Flanter, arrived in the UK on the Kindertransport in 1939 at the age of 13. Her parents perished in Minsk. Her paternal grandfather, Eliezer Fisher, was imprisoned in a work camp in the Hungarian town of Szeged, from which he escaped in the autumn of 1944, just days before liberation. His parents and siblings perished in Auschwitz. Since her schooldays, Sara has continuously returned to exploring ways of communicating various dimensions of third-generation experience in her art and written work. In 2011 she delivered a multimedia presentation on 'Inter-Generational Shadow Legacies' from a Jungian psychotherapeutic perspective, at Regent's School of Psychotherapy and Counselling Psychology, in London, during her training there. It focused on how, when we acknowledge and consciously work with our personal 'shadows', we are as individuals also assuming personal responsibility for part of the burden of the collective, which can lead to an inner liberation on a wider scale.

Petra Gelbart is a Romani (Gypsy) scholar, musician and activist who is at home both in the Czech Republic and the USA. She received her PhD in ethnomusicology from Harvard University with a dissertation entitled 'Learning Music, Race and Nation in the Czech Republic' (supported by a Fulbright-Hays fellowship) and has published in several journals, including *Signs*. She is the co-founder of the Initiative for Romani Music at New York

University and has lectured at a number of universities. Her volunteer activities focus on foster families and children's rights advocacy. She is descended from Holocaust victims as well as survivors; a recording of the Romani-language Auschwitz ballad passed down in her family can be found on Via Romen's *My Two Homes* CD (available for download through Amazon), or at no cost on YouTube.

Shirli Gilbert is Karten Associate Professor of History and Jewish/ non-Jewish Relations at the University of Southampton. She received her D.Phil. in Modern History from the University of Oxford and was a Postdoctoral Fellow in the Michigan Society of Fellows. Her book *Music in the Holocaust: Confronting Life in the Nazi Ghettos and Camps* (Oxford University Press, 2005) was a finalist for the National Jewish Book Award, and has been translated into Spanish and Japanese. She is currently completing a book about a Jewish refugee from Nazi Germany who fled to South Africa in 1936. Her maternal grandparents survived the Holocaust in Warsaw and later in the Soviet Union.

Riva Aliza Godfried is a teacher at Utrecht University and a creative writer. She holds a BA degree in language and culture studies and a MRes in comparative literary studies, both completed at Utrecht University. She was born in 1988 and grew up as the youngest of two in a Dutch Jewish family. She has close ties with her grandmother, Aliza, who lives in Israel, and who was 13 when the Second World War started. Before her grandmother retired, she worked as an educator for children with special needs. Her maternal grandfather, Shlomo, survived a concentration camp. After the war, he worked as a psychiatrist specializing in treatment with young people who have post-war trauma. Riva also feels close to her grandmother's current husband, Arthur, who survived Auschwitz. She only briefly knew her father's mother, Kitty, who passed away in 1990 when she was 2 years old. Her paternal grandfather, Emanuel, passed away before she was born and she knew him only from her father's stories. After the war, Emanuel was the director of several major hospitals in Amsterdam and he served as a board member of Jewish charity organizations. As part of the third generation after the Holocaust, Riva strives to preserve her grandparents' legacy; despite suffering, they showed kindness and perseverance.

Julie V. Gottlieb has a first-class joint honours BA in English and history from McGill University (Canada), and she completed her MPhil and PhD in modern British history at Cambridge University (UK). She taught at Manchester University and Bristol University before taking up her current post at the University of Sheffield, where she is a senior lecturer. She has published widely on gender history, and the history of political extremism, including *Feminine Fascism: Women in Britain's Fascism Movement 1923–1945* (I.B. Tauris, 2000), and she is currently examining the relationship between women and foreign affairs between the wars: *Guilty Women: Gender and Appeasement* is forthcoming in 2015 with Palgrave Macmillan. Her mother, Dr Erika Gottlieb, a 'child survivor' of the Holocaust in Hungary, was a prolific literary critic, a poet and accomplished painter who died in 2007.

Beth Herz is a product of two immigrant communities in the US: her mother grew up in an Eastern European, Yiddish-speaking household with piles of *rugelach* [cookies], and her father grew up surrounded by German expressions and slices of *pflaumenkuchen* [plum cake]. Beth's paternal grandmother fled Nuremberg as an adolescent; her grandfather and his family came as refugees from Berlin. Beth grew up with her sister in Rochester, New York. While a student, she spent eight months practising German and studying public policy in Berlin. She holds a bachelor's degree from Wesleyan University and a graduate degree in natural resources and environment from the University of Michigan. Her organizing and advocacy work has spanned a range of social justice issues. In her role at the Surdna Foundation, she develops grant-making strategies to foster just and sustainable communities in the United States. Beth lives in New York City.

Jaye A. Houston, PhD, has a BA in religion from UC Santa Barbara (1995), an MA in religion from Florida State University (1998) and a PhD in women and religion from Claremont Graduate University (2005). She teaches religion at Mount Saint Mary's University and the University of La Verne in the Los Angeles, California, area. The igniting spark that led to her research interests was earning a minor degree in global peace and security from UC Santa Barbara. Those research interests include women and religion, genocide studies, eco-theology, and sociology of global issues. Her scholarly research has resulted in numerous conference papers and keynote presentations. She serves on the advisory board of Women on the Move, Rancho Cucamonga, California.

Esther Jilovsky is an academic and writer. She currently lectures in German studies at the University of Melbourne, where she is also part of the affiliated faculty of the Program for Jewish Culture and Society. She has a BA (Hons) in German from the University of Melbourne, a master of studies in Jewish studies from the University of Oxford, and was awarded her PhD by Royal Holloway, University of London, in 2011. Her book *Remembering the Holocaust: Generations, Witnessing and Place* (Bloomsbury Academic, 2015) traces how survivors and subsequent generations write about visits to Holocaust sites. Esther has published articles and book chapters about Holocaust memory in the second and third generations, the role of place in Holocaust memory, and German-Jewish identity. She is the granddaughter of Holocaust survivors Hanka (née Hirschbein) and Kurt Jilovsky, who were from Poland and Czechoslovakia respectively.

Dalit Kaplan is a lawyer, radio host/producer, and occasional writer. She received her bachelors of law and arts from the University of Melbourne and her masters in law at the University of Chicago. She is originally from Melbourne, but has lived, worked and studied in Sydney, Jerusalem, Chicago, and New York. As a lawyer, she worked with immigrant populations predominantly from Africa and the Caribbean and provided advice and representation in a range of legal areas including refugee law, domestic violence and family law, benefits and housing law and general human rights law. She produces and hosts her own radio show on community radio called The Gender Agenda, where she covers Jewish life in Australia and beyond from a gender perspective. Dalit is the granddaughter of four remarkable Holocaust survivors: her late maternal grandparents spent time in the Lodz and Krakow ghettos and were then deported to a number of concentration camps including Auschwitz. Her late paternal grandparents fled from Poland to Russia, where they were imprisoned in labour camps. Dalit now lives in Melbourne with her husband and son.

Dani Kranz, PhD, is a social anthropologist, specializing in the anthropology of migration, legal anthropology, and inter-ethnic (couple) relationships. She has been conducting long-term ethnographic research work on Jews of German descent in Israel as well as Jews/Israelis in Germany. At present, she is mainly researching the socio-legal situation of present and former non-Jewish, foreign spouses of Israeli Jews in Israel, and she is part of a team that researches the emigration of Israeli Jews to Germany since 1990. She had refused to write anything biographical before this chapter, and decided to talk about her biography only upon returning to Germany in 2009, and as part of the process of raising her daughter, Ella, in the country. It is her wish that this chapter is dedicated to her daughter, as a way to honour the past, but to stand up – and fight – for the living, as her grandparents, and parents did in their own ways, because the children are our future.

Anthony Levin is a human rights lawyer and published writer. His occasional features have appeared in publications around the world including *Men's Style*, *Prospect Magazine* (UK) and *News.com.au*. Anthony is also a poet who published his first book of poetry, *House of the Collective Unconscious*, in 2012. As well as writing award-winning comedy for television, stage and film as part of the comedy troupe *The Nice Guys*, in 2010 Anthony received the Marten Bequest Traveling Scholarship for Prose – a prize awarded to candidates who show great promise in the arts and literature. He used the scholarship, in part, to complete his masters in modern and contemporary literature (University of York), where his research focused on post-Holocaust fiction. As a human rights lawyer, Anthony frequently speaks on social justice issues, drawing on his experience representing people with disabilities, prisoners and other vulnerable client groups. He has also worked with refugees, survivors of torture and asylum seekers for approximately ten years, both in Australia and England. Anthony is the junior vice-president of the Australian Association of Jewish Holocaust Survivors and Descendants and its first third-generation board member. He is also the grandson of beloved Holocaust survivors, Olga Horak and the late John Horak.

Michael David Lukas has been a Fulbright scholar in Turkey, a night-shift proofreader in Tel Aviv and an afterschool creative writing teacher in Oakland. Translated into more than a dozen languages, his first novel, *The Oracle of Stamboul*, was a finalist for the California Book Award, the NCIBA Book of the Year Award and the Harold U. Ribalow Prize. A graduate of Brown University and the University of Maryland, he is a recipient of scholarships from the National Endowment for the Arts, Santa Maddalena Foundation, Montalvo Arts Center, Bread Loaf Writers' Conference, New York State Summer Writers' Institute, Squaw Valley Community of Writers, and Elizabeth George Foundation. His writing has appeared in *The New York Times*, *Wall Street Journal*, *Slate*, *National Geographic Traveler* and *Georgia Review*. He lives in Oakland, California. Michael is the grandson of Abraham and Guta Brum, both of whom were Holocaust survivors.

Golan Moskowitz is a doctoral student in modern Jewish cultural studies at Brandeis University and a freelance visual artist and writer. He is the author and illustrator of an unpublished graphic novella about his own childhood experience of internalizing his family's Holocaust heritage. Golan holds a joint masters degree in Near Eastern and Judaic studies and women's and gender studies from Brandeis, as well as a bachelors degree in art from Vassar College. In addition to the Holocaust and its aftermath in the lives of individuals and families, Golan's interests include Jewish graphic novels, gender and queer studies, and American material culture. Born to an Israeli-American family in upstate New York, he is the grandson of Polish and Romanian survivors Esther and Moshe Signer.

Diana I. Popescu is a cultural historian of Romanian origin and an alumna of the University of Southampton, UK, having received both an MA (2008) and a PhD degree (2012) from this institution. Her research and publishing interests are situated within the interdisciplinary fields of Holocaust memory studies and Israel studies, contemporary visual art, Jewish art and representation of trauma in art and popular culture. She has contributed essays to a number of peer-reviewed journals including *Holocaust Studies: A Journal of Culture and History*; *PaRdeS: Journal of the Association of Jewish Studies*; *Jewish Culture and History*; and *Images: A Journal of Jewish Art and Visual Culture*.

Ben Silverstein is a lecturer in indigenous studies at the Nura Gili Centre for Indigenous Programs at the University of New South Wales. He has published a number of works on colonial and Indigenous histories, and is currently completing a monograph to be published by Manchester University Press titled *Governing Natives: Indirect Rule and Settler Colonialism in Australia's North*. Ben's family has lived in Melbourne, Australia, since his grandparents arrived from Poland, via Germany and France, as refugees in 1949.

Jordana Silverstein is a postdoctoral research fellow in the School of Historical and Philosophical Studies at the University of Melbourne, with the ARC Laureate Fellowship Project 'Child Refugees and Australian Internationalism: 1920 to the Present'. She has published widely on modern Jewish identity, sexuality, memory and history, including in her book *Anxious Histories: Narrating the Holocaust in Jewish Communities at the Beginning of the Twenty First Century* (Berghahn Books, 2015). Jordana's writing is influenced heavily by the memory of two of her grandparents, Zosia and Wolf, who came to Melbourne from southern Poland, and spent the war in an unknown range of ghettos and camps.

David Slucki is assistant professor in the Yaschik/Arnold Jewish Studies Program at the College of Charleston. Previously, he was an early career development fellow from 2011 to 2013 at Monash University, where he received his PhD in 2010. His book, *The International Jewish Labor Bund after 1945: Toward a Global History*, was published by Rutgers University Press in 2012, and looks at the attempts of Bundists to adapt their shattered movement in the wake of the Holocaust. His current research focuses on Holocaust survivor networks in the 1940s and 1950s; humour and Holocaust representation; and Yiddish travel writing in the twentieth century. All four of his grandparents were Polish Jews who survived the war after escaping to the Soviet Union in late 1939, and they migrated to Melbourne between 1950 and 1958.

Mitch Smolkin is a psychotherapist, performer and writer. He holds a master of arts in counselling psychology, is a certified emotionally focused therapist, and is currently completing his training as a Jungian psychoanalyst. Prior to becoming a therapist, he was the artistic director of the Ashkenaz Festival of Yiddish Culture and a curator at Harbourfront Centre, Canada's largest presenter of contemporary multidisciplinary art. He continues to perform as a singer and has toured extensively across North America as well as to South America and Israel. He is the cantorial soloist for Neshamah Congregation, a reform synagogue north of Toronto. His grandfather, Boris Gelgor, was the sole surviving member of his immediate family in the Holocaust. He survived in the Russian army and then by working in the mines before marrying Mitch's grandmother, Sonia Gelgor (née Diminshtein), who survived with her family, having been displaced from Vilnius to Alma Ata, Kazachstan (present-day Almaty). Mitch lives in Toronto with his wife, Holocaust scholar Sylwia Szymańska-Smolkin, and his son Gabriel.

Hadas Wiseman, PhD, is associate professor in the Department of Counseling and Human Development, Faculty of Education, University of Haifa, Israel. She is also a certified clinical psychologist in private practice in Tivon, Israel. She was recently the president of the Society for Psychotherapy Research (SPR), an international, multidisciplinary, scientific organization. Her major research interests are: client–therapist relationship processes and attachment in psychotherapy; the personal and professional development of psychotherapists and counsellors; and intergenerational communication of trauma and interpersonal relationships in families of Holocaust survivors. She co-authored, with Jacques Baber, *Echoes of the Trauma: Relationship Themes and Emotions in Children of Holocaust Survivors* (New York: Cambridge University Press, 2008). Among her other related publications are: H. Wiseman, E. Metzl and J.P. Barber, 'Anger, Guilt, and Intergenerational Communication of Trauma in the Interpersonal Narratives of Second Generation Holocaust Survivors', *American Journal of Orthopsychiatry*, 76, 2 (2006), pp.176–184; H. Wiseman, 'On Failed Intersubjectivity: Recollections of Loneliness Experiences of Offspring of Holocaust Survivors', *American Journal of Orthopsychiatry*, 73, 3, (2008), pp.350–8; H. Wiseman, 'Intergenerational echoes of the story of the Holocaust in families of survivors', in M. Rieck (ed.), *Social Interaction after Massive Traumatization: Was the Holocaust Survivors Encounter with the Post-War Society Conductive for Generating Private and Collective Memories?* (Berlin: Regener, 2009), pp.77–93.

Lea Wohl-von Haselberg is the daughter of Jewish-Gentile parents and granddaughter of Jewish grandparents who fled Poland and died before she was born. After studying film and media studies in Frankfurt am Main, she started her PhD thesis on the representation of Jewish characters in German feature films after 1945 at Hamburg University, and finished it in early 2014. She has been active in educational and cultural work and regularly writes for both academic and non-academic audiences. Her research focuses on Jewish life in Germany after 1945, the representation of contemporary Jewish topics in film and media, and questions of Jewish identity. Lea currently lives in Berlin and is the mother of two children.

Liv Zaslawski, MSc, lives and works in Vienna. For several years she has been working as a clinical psychologist and psychotherapist in the hospital sector as well as in her own private practice. In particular, she provides psychotherapeutic support to deaf people, assisting this cultural and linguistic minority in cases of crises and mental disorders. Her approach is based on a culturally sensible, humanistic and emancipatory concept of assistance. What is essential for her is being aware of her own power as a member of the majority society (hearing population) in dealing with minority groups. Her interest in working with people from a different cultural background is related to the story of her own family and life. She is a granddaughter of a survivor, who was saved by the Kindertransport. She is currently working on her doctoral thesis in psychology which explores transgenerational traumatization of grandchildren of Shoah survivors, comparing a sample from the United Kingdom with Austrian participants. The aim of this study is to show how the way society has dealt with the events of the Second World War has affected the psychological state of the third generation.

Foreword

SHIRLI GILBERT

The Holocaust was a quiet but constant presence in my childhood Johannesburg home. It hovered in the air, pervaded the bookshelves. It was evident in the kitchen especially, in the prohibition on throwing away any morsel of food, and in the ingenious economy with which every part of the chicken was used. My maternal grandparents managed to make it out of 'there' alive through a combination of initiative and sheer luck, yet to my childish imagination their story was curiously distant: bombs dropping over Warsaw, illicit border-crossings, Siberian labour camps.

My fierce attachment to my grandmother had somehow to do with the enormity of the burden she bore. The photographs on her wall evoked a vanished world in which I envisioned myself. The child she had lost I re-imagined as my own absent sibling, much to my mother's chagrin. In my mind I magically guarded my grandmother against inscrutable forces, acutely aware of a vulnerability that I did not understand. Not a word of this - or much else - was ever spoken between us, and by the time my flood of questions about 'over there' was released, she was no longer around to answer.

For a long time, I resisted the idea of belonging to a 'generation'. I objected to the idea of being labelled and categorized, even pathologized. Why did my personal chain of identity necessarily extend to a commonality with a larger collective? This question lies implicitly at the heart of this rich new collection, which explores the complex impact of the Holocaust on the grandchildren of survivors. That some of those grandchildren are profoundly affected by their grandparents' legacies is clear from many of the contributions in this volume. Not all experience the same intensity of connection, but many feel a link to the past and a compulsion to preserve its memory. Seventy years on they are also removed enough to challenge long-held taboos, and they are beginning to bear witness in fresh and provocative ways.

If the chapters in the volume have one unifying feature, it is their extraordinary diversity. Some offer intimate explorations of a grandparent's influence; others wrestle with intellectual questions of memory and positionality. Some are conversational; others experiment with the language of poetry or anthropology or psychoanalysis to articulate their thorny subject matter. The contributors bring to bear a remarkable range of perspectives - professional, religious, gender, national - that belie any attempt to reduce the third generation to a monolithic set of characteristics. Scattered across five continents, the survivors of the Nazi onslaught sought to rebuild their lives under vastly differing conditions in Melbourne and New York, Tel Aviv and Sao Paulo, Johannesburg and Berlin. Two generations later, those circumstances have also powerfully shaped the ways in which their descendants attempt to understand the past. In the land of the perpetrators, some grandchildren attest to a permanent feeling of displacement. In the land of the victims, they confront opposing but no less complex dilemmas of identity. In the United States, Australia, South Africa, and elsewhere, the encounter with the Holocaust has led variously towards social activism, Zionism, renewed religious practice, and myriad other life-views more and less informed by the residue of the past.

This book does not strive to be just an academic study, nor is it merely a compendium of personal narratives. It is a beautifully curated collection of pieces - eclectic, curious, incisive, and immensely moving - that attempt to untangle the intricate ways in which our 'back stories' shape who we are. The third generation clearly cannot be reduced to a set of definable features, but woven through the contributions are some shared connections that also cannot be ignored. I remain sceptical about categories and labels, but as my own children begin to grow up and ask about their history, the question of my family's past becomes increasingly persistent. Because my grandparents are still there, hovering in the air of my London home, on my bookshelves, in my writing. There are many layers to my identity, and yet - even though I know my grandfather only through photographs, and built a relationship with my grandmother through a barely shared language - they have formed a powerful and enduring part of who I am. My mother bears her own complex experience of their legacy. I have a little more distance: a desire to unravel stories, unearth emotions, open difficult conversations. This book opens precisely those kinds of conversations, and it poses penetrating and timely questions about the future of the Holocaust in a survivor-less world. The multiplicity of voices it represents is a potent indication of where the conversation is going, and it reflects the vitality and acuity with which this generation is carrying forward its inheritance.

Introduction: The Third Generation

ESTHER JILOVSKY, JORDANA SILVERSTEIN,
AND DAVID SLUCKI

What does it mean to be a descendant of Holocaust survivors? More particularly, what does it mean to be a member of the 'third generation', a person whose grandparents survived the horrors of the Holocaust? This is the central question explored in this book. We start from the idea of impossibility and openness: that there is no one way in which this sense is manifested in our memories, histories, identities and emotions; that there is no one way of being a survivor, or being a member of the third generation. It is clear, though, that the grandchildren of Holocaust survivors have a particular relationship to the Holocaust. Mediated through their interactions with grandparents and parents who discuss the topic to varying degrees, through different levels of engagement with Jewish communities and through global Holocaust discourse, the third generation is at once remote from, and at the same time intimately connected to, the Holocaust.

When we first discussed editing a volume that dealt specifically with the experiences of the third generation, we realized that for each of us the Holocaust had become a central part of how we understand the world, but also that the experience of each of our grandparents radically differed. For one of us, our Polish grandparents were in ghettos and camps in Poland and Germany from 1939 until 1945; for another, survival of all four grandparents involved escape from Poland to the Soviet Union in the early months of the war; and for the third, one grandparent survived using a false identity in Poland and Germany, while another spent the war in the Middle East, serving in the Jewish Brigade of the British Army.

These differences highlight that the complexity of third-generation experiences begins with the Holocaust narratives themselves. Yet our perspective is one of aftermath, belatedness or inherited memory. This book therefore explores both the diversity and belatedness of the narratives, memories, histories and experiences of the third generation, recognizing that they will play an important role in carrying the mantle of Holocaust memory to future generations.

From scholarly work that deals with questions of trauma and its transmission across generations, to literary and creative works that reflect the experiences of growing up carrying the burden of their grandparents' trauma, this book includes contributions from historians, literary and cultural studies scholars, psychologists and sociologists, amongst others. In addition, we have invited members of the third generation to reflect on how the Holocaust has been interwoven into their own life stories. These autobiographical narratives incorporate many of the concerns raised by scholars and illuminate the scholarly research presented here. Simultaneously, the scholarly research depends upon these personal narratives. The two tell overlapping stories, but in different forms.

In this book we are looking at the transfer of memory, trauma, history and identity across generations, while also examining the aspects of these things that members of the third generation make anew. In that sense, the third generation is both a group of descendants and also a peer group. But we would caution against any attempt to homogenize the generation. As becomes clear through even a cursory examination of the chapters in this book, the third generation is diverse. There are similarities in ideas and approaches, in emotions expressed and histories recounted, to be sure, but there are also substantial differences. One can note, for example, the different ways in which people from different national locations express their emotions; or the divergent family histories that are told depending on the relationship that was built between grandparents and grandchildren. As a result, at times there are lines of connection being built across and between the members of the generation.

Pondering this opens for us the problems of defining ancestry and descendants in terms of generations. On what are generations based? How do we reach a third generation? In this book, we, and the individual authors, have primarily relied upon hereditary notions of generation. These are, in most cases, the grandchildren of survivors of the Holocaust. But we must caution against this conception of generations being considered the only one: for some victim groups, the generational bonds come in the form of collective memory, rather than nuclear family ties. Erik Jensen has written of one example of this in his discussion of homosexual communities, noting that some have 'attributed their political consciousness as gay men and women, at least in part, to a particular collective memory of the Nazi persecution of homosexuals'.[1]

And yet we must also recognize that the boundaries around what constitutes a survivor of the Holocaust have at times been tightly drawn, depending, for instance, on mode or location of survival, or the victim group from which a survivor came. In this collection we have actively tried to work against the institution of these boundaries. We have not defined who a survivor was and we have attempted to include members of the third generation from different locations, with different histories, and from different victim groups. Unfortunately, despite our best efforts, we were not completely successful in this last aspect. You will note that we have one chapter by a descendant of survivors who were Romani, and we have chapters by descendants who are both Jewish and homosexual. We also have chapters by Jews who are leftists, who could perhaps locate their political ancestry to those who were, in that time and place, communists.

Despite these partial moves, however, the present collection is not able to include a thorough examination of the differing experiences of being a member of the third generation of all of the different victim groups. This is, perhaps, a major limitation in being one of the first books which takes on this task of examining the third generation. We hope then that this is a gap that future books, articles, and edited collections will fill.

An Emerging Field in Holocaust Studies

In 2003, S. Lillian Kremer's two-volume *Holocaust Literature: An Encyclopedia of Writers and their Work*, a comprehensive reference to writing about the Holocaust, was published.[2] This landmark work 'present[s] critical analyses and assessments of literary representation of the Holocaust and its consequences' and includes 'the writing of over 300 memoirists, poets, novelists, dramatists'.[3] Encompassing a broad definition of Holocaust literature, including articles on authors and works of fiction and non-fiction, survivors and the second and third generations, this ambitious work has become an impressive authority on writing about the Holocaust. However, if one was to look under 'F' for perhaps the most well-known third generation writer about the Holocaust, Jonathan Safran Foer, disappointment would ensue. This is because his bestselling novel *Everything is Illuminated*, which won a slew of awards and critical acclaim, was first published in 2002.[4] This unfortunate mismatch of timing illustrates the vast development in Holocaust literature and scholarship over the last decade or so. Ten years ago, the third generation was just beginning to make its voice heard; today there are a number of books by third-generation authors, as well as countless articles and many doctoral theses about the third generation. These scholarly works analyse the writing of the third generation, interview them and tell their stories – yet volumes dealing with the third generation are virtually absent from Holocaust historiography. It is this gap that we hope this current book begins to fill.

And thus this book is timely, coming at this moment when there has been a significant expanse of literature about the third generation. But there is another reason this book is important now. Nearly seventy years since the Holocaust, the number of survivors is fast dwindling, and, in the not too distant future, there will no longer be any living Holocaust survivors. The third generation will one day be the last to have known Holocaust survivors personally. They thus form a bridge between the past and the future: they will take their memories of their grandparents into a future when the Holocaust no longer exists in living memory. The perspective of the third generation, their memories, their stories and their experiences will therefore increase in importance in years to come, and thus it is important to capture their perspectives now.

This book stands alongside the vast literature on the second generation which has emerged since Helen Epstein's book *Children of the Holocaust: Conversations with Sons and Daughters of Survivors* was published in 1979, following her article in *The New York Times* in 1977.[5] In the three decades since, scholarship on the second generation has developed to the point where it has an entry in the *Encyclopedia of the Holocaust*, and is a recognized and accepted part of Holocaust studies discourse.[6] Renowned works such as Art Spiegelman's *Maus*, as well as numerous memoirs by members of the second generation, such as *The Fiftieth Gate* by Mark Raphael Baker, *The War After: Living with the Holocaust* by Anne Karpf, and *Jewels and Ashes* by Arnold Zable, as well as the fiction of Lily Brett, mean that the second generation's perspective is not only widely disseminated, but has entered the mainstream.[7] The third generation, on the other hand, is just beginning to be heard and we hope that this book becomes an important part of the conversation.

Indeed, for some, the distinction between the second and third generations is not always recognized. As we have written above, we do not prescribe a certain definition of the third generation or of a Holocaust survivor. We are interested in how people who identify as members of the third generation articulate this identity. Some scholars, on the other hand, such as Geoffrey Hartman, Efraim Sicher and Annelies Schulte Nordholt, deploy the term 'generation after' to encompass both the second and third generations, and therefore emphasize the commonalities of these generations born after the Holocaust rather than their different perspectives.[8] While this eliminates ambiguity about whether someone might belong more to one generation than to the other, it also obliterates the strong identification many members of the third generation feel, exemplified by the many grassroots third-generation groups which have emerged in recent years in places such as New York, Melbourne and London. Enabled and fuelled by social media platforms such as Facebook (the Facebook group 'Grandchildren of Holocaust Survivors' has over 3,500 members as of February 2015), members of the third generation have organized meetings, workshops and other activities as opportunities to interact with others who share a similar family history. The strong response to our initial Call for Papers further underlines a growing desire among the third generation to collectivize their experience.

Defining the Third Generation

While the field of literature on the third generation is small, it is steadily growing as the third generation comes of age. Some of what has been produced offers us guidance as to how to conceptualize a third generation of descendants of Holocaust survivors. We must first reiterate that there is no one homogenous definition. This is evident throughout this collection, and brought to attention through the explanations and explorations that others have provided. The third generation has been defined at times by age, rather than descent: variously, for instance, as 'authors born in the 1960s or later'[9] or those 'born between 1979 and 1989'.[10] For Gerd Bayer, the third generation is defined primarily as being a 'later generation' who 'will not have [a] direct, face-to-face confrontation with the past'.[11] Alan L. Berger and Asher Z. Milbauer have suggested that while Holocaust survivors have produced literary works that focus on the horrors and 'the realities of concentration camps', for example, these elements are avoided by the third generation, who instead write, for instance, of the 'archetypal events in the history of the Holocaust' such as Kristallnacht and the Warsaw Ghetto.[12] They highlight the ways that writers of the third generation feel a sense of absence, of a loss of connection to the world of their grandparents, as well as an 'urge to bear witness'.[13] There is, for them, an imperative to both pass on the 'inheritance' gained from the grandparents, and 'to ensure the existence of yet another generation'.[14] This procreational impulse and pressure is explored in some of the chapters contained in the present volume.

Jessica Lang similarly focuses on Krauss's works (indeed, Krauss and Foer have in some ways come to represent the American third generation par excellence) and argues that her books provide a unique moment of documenting 'a future of Holocaust literature where imagination and history ... are interpolated': in this writing 'the Holocaust can become a historical event in the writer's imagination, even if it is not part of her personal history'.[15] Lang distinguishes between first, second- and third-generation literary works, noting the ways they engage with different themes, styles and 'characterizations'.[16] Third-generation writers, more specifically, provide an 'indirect' 'representation of the Holocaust', which is caused by 'historical distance'; their texts lack the 'shock' produced by the texts of previous generations; and, finally, 'the third-generation writer views these events [of the Holocaust] as an indirect part of the narrative, one balanced by other, also important, histories'.[17]

For Nicole Fox, the third generation 'demonstrat[es] the ways that culture and memory can support recovery and resiliency'. They are both proximal to the survivors of the Holocaust and 'distant enough from the event that they did not experience a great deal of the everyday trauma that the children of Holocaust survivors experienced'. Moreover, the 'third generation has also grown up in an environment where there is a plethora of Holocaust literature and discourse', sharply contrasting with the experiences of the generations before.[18] Fox writes also of feeling a sense of connection to other members of the third generation as she engaged with them and learned of the similarity of their familial experiences and ideas about Jewishness.[19] She summarizes a key characteristic of the members of the third generation in America as being that they 'have disrupted their parents' fear and turned the trauma, memories and recollections of history into a sense of Jewish pride'.[20] But of course different national contexts have the capacity to produce different expressions of being a member of the third generation, and Daphne Seemann brings this fact to our attention through her exploration of Austrian members of the third generation. She explains that 'Jewish writers in Austria have been responding to a fundamental generational shift which deprives descendants of the opportunity to resort to their parents' testimonies and assigns to them a felt sense of responsibility for the difficult task of translating communicative memory narratives into cultural practices of remembrance, representation and commemoration.'[21] This is, moreover, a response to the specificities of Austria's 'memory culture': 'a transition from memory narratives rooted in the traumatic experiences of survivors to new generational narratives that are characterized by an increased mediation of Holocaust memory and a perceived need to move beyond post-traumatic models of identity'.[22]

All of these various elements, when taken together, can give us a sense of what is carried in the term 'third generation'. It is, in short, simultaneously broad and quite specific, connoting relationality and investment in Holocaust histories, a sense of 'bearing witness' to the aftermath of the Holocaust, a distance from the events, and a way of making use of these connections. The third generation is defined in relation to ancestors, to the Holocaust, and to each other. It is never only one thing.

Our Approach: Diversity and Inclusiveness

Taking an interdisciplinary approach, this book raises questions about what responsibility the third generation holds in maintaining and transmitting memories of the Holocaust, of both survival and destruction (and the various ways in which life after the Holocaust can involve both of these things, ambivalently). Drawing on literary, historical, psychological and gender studies methodologies, the contributors in this book are concerned with the different ways that members of the third generation conceive of themselves as inheritors of their grandparents' memories and how this has shaped their life trajectories.

Many of the contributions in this book are based on interviews with members of the third generation in various contexts. These interviews provide unique insights into how these grandchildren of Holocaust survivors imagine their own relationship to their grandparents and parents, and also to the past. The methodologies underpinning these scholarly contributions vary: a psychoanalyst talking to the third generation in Austria; a Romani musicologist interviewing third-generation Romani people in the United States; Israeli psychotherapists asking young Israelis how they relate to the memory books of their grandparents; a gender studies scholar interviewing grandsons of survivors; a sociologist interviewing granddaughters of survivors; and an anthropologist talking to German members of the third generation about notions of home and exile.

This book is not only *about* the third generation, but is very much written *from* third-generation perspectives. Many of the scholars and authors who have contributed do so having been raised asking many of the questions this book explores. Some take a hybrid approach, drawing on their life experiences to raise broader questions about the third generation and its relationship to the past. One literary scholar reflects on the nature of historical sources in light of the recent discovery of letters between family members in the early years of the war. A historian looks at her mother's memoir, and reflects on how memories are passed through generations.

This book draws on narratives and scholarship from four continents, highlighting not only the diversity of the third generation, but also the elements that bind its members. By its very nature, the study of the third generation demands a transnational approach. After the Holocaust, survivors emigrated from Europe to all corners of the world. The biggest proportion went to Israel, the next largest to North America, and then smaller groups found themselves in places throughout Latin America, Australia and South Africa. A smaller number remained in Europe, where they were confronted by national debates over memories of the Second World War. In other parts of the world, survivors joined thriving Jewish communities, as in the major centres in the United States, or breathed new life into small communities, such as in Melbourne. Two generations later then, grandchildren of survivors can be found around the globe.

Survivors' experiences in their new locations have also come to shape the diversity of the third generation. It is not only cultural and political differences that account for this diversity, but also how the Holocaust has been remembered, misremembered and debated in these specific contexts. So, for example, those contributors raised in Australia, which has a higher proportion of Holocaust survivors among its Jewish community than most other locations (Israel being the most obvious exception), have a very different relationship to the Holocaust from the one that their peers in the

United States have, where Holocaust survivors play a less prominent role in Jewish life. Grandchildren of survivors raised or residing in central Europe again face different challenges, living as they do among the ruins of pre-Holocaust European Jewry. These are societies that have vociferously debated the meaning of the Holocaust and their roles in its execution. Questions of collective guilt, responsibility and victimhood have been important in mediating how the Holocaust is remembered and discussed in countries such as Germany, Austria, Poland and France. In Israel, by contrast, where an idea of the Holocaust permeates the national psyche so profoundly, the third generation relates in a unique way to their grandparents' experiences, which have occupied a particular role in the public sphere. It is clear, then, that a range of cultural and historical factors shapes the third generation, which both the scholarly and autobiographical contributions in this volume reflect.

Overview of Chapters

This book is divided into four sections, each of which focuses on different aspects of the third-generation experience. It opens with a section entitled 'Intergenerational Encounters', in which authors map the interactions between survivor grandparents and their grandchildren. Julie Gottlieb explores the memories contained in a book written by her mother about her daughterhood, and thereby provides a negotiation of the relationships that are created between mother and daughter in the writing of family histories. In doing so, she also questions the notion of post-Holocaust generations. Jaye Houston explores the specificities of relationships between grandmothers and granddaughters, looking at the stories and memories that are inherited in this particular gendered configuration. Houston makes clear for us that there is something importantly particular in these histories of female members of the third generation. Golan Moskowitz provides an alternative tale, exploring the ways that being a male member of the third generation produces a particular form of masculinity. The legacy inherited through contact with grandparents who were survivors serves 'as a source of pride' for these men, and helps them to produce cultural artefacts which will enact these memories. Dalit Kaplan narrates her experiences of negotiating a personal investment in being the granddaughter of survivors, coupled with a desire to fully encounter, hear and learn from her grandparents who survived. Mitch Smolkin provides us with a similar exploration, focusing on his encounters and relationships with his grandfather, Boris, and the ways this has shaped his own ideas of family after the Holocaust. Finally, Michael Lukas gives an insight into his encounter with his grandmother Guta's memories of the Holocaust.

The following section focuses on the question of 'Inheriting Memories'. Like the second generation, the third generation has inherited memories of the Holocaust. Unlike the second generation, whose experience and therefore memory of the Holocaust comes predominantly from their parents, the third generation's sense of the Holocaust is based on their grandparents as Holocaust survivors, as well as their parents as members of the second generation. The third generation's mediated memory of the Holocaust therefore amalgamates both these connections, which is of course assimilated with their engagement with the collective and cultural memories around them.

Adi Duchin and Hadas Wiseman's chapter explores how the engagement of Israeli grandchildren of Holocaust survivors with their grandparents' published memoirs shapes their perspective on the Holocaust. They present their findings along a continuum, showing that these stories, with all their complexities, nevertheless share important characteristics. Liv Zaslawki's chapter moves the focus to Austria, where the third generation exists in a society shaped by both perpetrator and victim narratives of the Holocaust. Zaslawski's insights as a psychotherapist treating members of the third generation in the therapeutic context shed light on the complex difficulties experienced by Austrian members of the third generation. Esther Jilovsky's chapter explores another instance of inherited memory, in this case a tangible one: a collection of letters which belonged to her grandfather. She analyses how they function as 'points of memory', to use Marianne Hirsch's term, arguing that their specific importance is framed by her position as a third-generation scholar of the Holocaust.[23] Felice Cohen's and Anthony Levin's chapters both broach the topic of inherited memories of the Holocaust from a personal perspective. Cohen's chapter describes her experience of writing the book *What Papa Told Me*, about her grandfather's Holocaust experience.[24] The process of creating this work was a life-changing experience. Levin's chapter is a fictional piece, nevertheless based on fact, which draws on elements of astrology and Jewish mythology to tell his grandmother's story, interspersed with memories from his own childhood, along with his more recent experience of visiting Auschwitz. All of these pieces illustrate the great care and sensitivity with which the third generation approaches their grandparents' stories, as well as the difficulties faced in ensuring the preservation and transmission of these precious pasts to future generations.

The section 'Home, Belonging, and Exile' explores the idea that notions of home, homelessness and where we belong are, for members of the third generation, indelibly overwritten by postmemories of the Holocaust. Dani Kranz focuses on ideas of home and belonging amongst members of the third generation in Germany. She explains that notions of home, homelessness and belonging 'form a matrix of possibilities for Third Generations to put words to their identities', and describes how German members of the third generation have made homes in other national locations, simultaneously becoming exiles and finding themselves tentative new homes. Diana Popescu's chapter explores the ways that Israeli theatre productions can serve as a vehicle for the expression of third-generation identities. She shows how these identities can become rooted in the particularities of their national homes, demonstrating some of the complexities of making a third-generation collective memory which is at home. With Lea Wohl-von Haselberg's chapter we return to Germany, where she brings ideas of belonging to the fore. She illustrates for us the difficulties in locating oneself when one is in-between: feeling variously German or Jewish, or both at the same time. Ben Silverstein and Jordana Silverstein's chapter concludes this section, opening for us a discussion of the problematics of an inherited idea of exile. They use this idea to explore some of the ways that being a member of the third generation can inform a politics of making oneself at home, after the Holocaust.

The final section deals with varying aspects of how 'Representation' comes to shape memory for members of the third generation. Representation of the Holocaust, as is well known, has in many ways determined how the Holocaust is remembered in society more broadly. From public memorials to popular culture to the memoirs and testimonies of survivors, memories of the Holocaust have come to be mediated to a large degree by how they are collected, displayed, performed and interpreted. It is in this context, in which global memories of the Holocaust have become entrenched with the rise of a culture of public commemoration, that Petra Gelbart examines the question of Romani Holocaust remembrance. Her chapter, which looks at the ways that Romani memories of the Holocaust are preserved in song, examines the impact that the absence of representation of Romani suffering during the Holocaust has had on descendants of Romani survivors. Gelbart also challenges us to think about how we define the Holocaust and its survivors, calling for broader recognition of the suffering of groups that are more marginalized in Holocaust historiography, such as the Romani. Riva Godfried combines her personal narrative with a scholarly analysis of Holocaust literature and poetry in addressing questions around the limitations and possibilities of honestly representing and understanding traumatic pasts, particularly for generations who did not themselves experience the trauma. Two personal narratives punctuate these scholarly contributions. Danny Cohen's fictionalized autobiography reflects on the different ways that popular representations interact with family memories in creating a consciousness of the Holocaust. David Slucki also examines the question of representation by looking at the conventions and limitations of remembering the Holocaust. His narrative focuses particularly on the medium of commemoration and the boundaries that his local Jewish community in Melbourne established around what was considered acceptable in Holocaust memorial services.

Beginning the Conversation

This book is only a beginning. We hope that it will open up new discussions about what it means to be descended from Holocaust survivors, how the legacy of the Holocaust can be understood, and how it will be remembered into the future. We hope this book will create space for further studies on the third generation. Most importantly, we hope that it provides an opportunity for members of the third generation to continue the conversation about their grandparents, about the Holocaust and about their own lives. If it is true that the future of Holocaust memory rests, to an extent, with the third generation, then this volume raises pertinent and urgent questions for scholars and members of the third generation to grapple with as they consider how the Holocaust might be remembered in coming generations.

NOTES

1. E.N. Jensen, 'The Pink Triangle and Political Consciousness: Gays, Lesbians, and the Memory of Nazi Persecution', in 'Sexuality and German Fascism', special issue, *Journal of the History of Sexuality*, 11, 1–2 (January–April 2002), p.320.
2. S.L. Kremer (ed.), *Holocaust Literature: An Encyclopedia of Writers and their Work*, 2 vols (New York and London: Routledge, 2003).
3. S.L. Kremer, preface to ibid., p.xix.
4. J.S. Foer, *Everything is Illuminated* (London: Penguin Books, 2003).
5. H. Epstein, *Children of the Holocaust: Conversations with Sons and Daughters of Survivors* (New York: Penguin Books, 1988); H. Epstein, 'The Heirs of the Holocaust', *The New York Times*, 19 June 1977.
6. E. Fogelman, 'Survivors, Second Generation of', in Israel Gutman (ed.), *Encyclopedia of the Holocaust* (New York: Macmillan, 1990).
7. See, for example, M.R. Baker, *The Fiftieth Gate* (Sydney: Flamingo, 1997); A. Karpf, *The War After: Living with the Holocaust* (London: Minerva, 1997); A. Zable, *Jewels and Ashes* (Newham, Victoria: Scribe, 1991); L. Brett, *Too Many Men* (Sydney: Pan Macmillan, 1999).
8. G.H. Hartman, *The Longest Shadow: In the Aftermath of the Holocaust* (New York and Basingstoke: Palgrave Macmillan, 1996), p.111; E. Sicher, '"Tancred's Wound": From Repression to Symbolization of the Holocaust in Second-Generation Narratives', *Journal of Modern Jewish Studies*, 5, 2 (2006), p.192; A.S. Nordholt, 'Writing the Memory of the Shoah at the Turn of the Century: An Introduction', *Journal of Modern Jewish Studies*, 5, 2 (2006), p.184.
9. J. Lang, '*The History of Love*, the Contemporary Reader, and the Transmission of Holocaust Memory', *Journal of Modern Literature*, 33, 1 (Fall 2009), p.46.
10. N. Fox, ' "Their history is part of me": Third Generation American Jews and Intergenerational Transmission of Memory, Trauma and History', *Moreshet*, 8 (Winter 2010), p.7.

11. G. Bayer, 'After Postmemory: Holocaust Cinema and the Third Generation', *Shofar: An Interdisciplinary Journal of Jewish Studies*, 28, 4 (Summer 2010), p.131.
12. A.L. Berger and A.Z. Milbauer, 'The Burden of Inheritance', *Shofar* 31, 3 (2013), p.65.
13. Ibid., pp.66–7.
14. Ibid., p.67.
15. Lang, '*History of Love*', p.44.
16. Ibid., pp.44–6.
17. Ibid., p.46.
18. Fox, '"Their history is part of me"', p.7.
19. Ibid., pp.10–11.
20. Ibid., p.14.
21. D. Seemann, 'Moving beyond Post-Traumatic Memory Narratives: Generation, Memory and Identity in Doron Rabinovici, Robert Menasse and Eva Menasse', *Austrian Studies*, 19 (2011), pp.157–8.
22. Ibid., p.171.
23. M. Hirsch, *The Generation of Postmemory: Writing and Visual Culture After the Holocaust* (New York: Columbia University Press, 2012), p.61.
24. F. Cohen, *What Papa Told Me* (New York: Dividends Press, 2010).

Intergenerational Encounters

Memory, Mourning and Maternal Inheritances: A Daughter's Reading of her Mother's Holocaust Memoir

JULIE V. GOTTLIEB

Erika Gottlieb, the author of *Becoming My Mother's Daughter*, was a woman of many talents and endless artistic ambition, much of which was fulfilled, some of which was inevitably frustrated.[1] While she did not live to see her memoir published, she was working on the proofs in her last days and had the satisfaction of knowing it would appear, not only a memoir but her memorial, the memoir a more fitting one than any stone monument to be visited only on occasion by nearest and dearest and able to communicate nothing of the personal narrative, the emotion, the hope and the vision of the individual. It is more than somewhat ironic that this text appeared posthumously, especially as its central theme is mourning and a daughter's search for herself after the death of her own mother. Erika Gottlieb's mother was Elizabeth – lightly veiled as Eliza in the book – who died in her sixties, not an old woman in years but frail in health, while Erika – lightly veiled as Eva in the book – would also not survive to be 70, cancer taking her from us at 69 years of age, only four months after the birth of her second grandchild, the first girl, named Elizabeth. Nor is the book about these two women alone; it starts with an earlier link in this female ancestral chain. The first portrait in this family triptych is of Ethel, Eliza's mother, a girl from a Jewish working-class Budapest family, who started work at the tender age of 12 in an elegant furniture store and factory, fell in love with one of the owner's sons, Stephen, and bore him an illegitimate child in 1914, months before the outbreak of war. Ethel – who is one of the few in this book whose name has not been changed – also lived a tragically short life, dying of a stroke when she was in her mid-forties. On the one hand, this early death robbed Ethel of a life of bourgeois comfort and hard-won respectability that had come with her eventual marriage to Stephen when their daughter was already 17 years old, and the joy of seeing Eliza married well and settled with two small daughters, but perhaps, on the other hand, spared her even worse horrors. Ethel died before the Holocaust came to Hungary in the winter of 1944, and would never have to know of the murder of her husband, a veteran of the First World War, the near-death moments experienced and horrors witnessed by her daughter and two little granddaughters, and the loss of countless relations.

Life Writing and 'Memory-Scapes'

1. First, 2.5 and Third Generations: Erika Gottlieb, Julie Gottlieb, and Julie's son Benjamin, 2006. Copyright/permission granted by Julie Gottlieb.

This is a many-layered and multi-stranded story. The narrative itself has many threads, intertwining the stories of these three generations of women, and then bringing it up to the 1980s and thus weaving in a fourth generation which is born outside Europe in the comparatively peaceful and prosperous new world of Canada. It is a story that covers two continents, Europe and North America, and the clear contrasts between them in terms not only of landscape and built environment, but of mentality and response to the pressure imposed by the weight of history. It is a story set against the backdrop of two world wars and one revolution. It is a text in which much of the language describes images, both painterly and photographic, its generic hybridity evoking a synaesthesiac response in the reader. It is a narrative structured by the dynamics of memory rather than linear chronology, opening in Toronto, Canada, in the early 1980s, and switching backwards and forwards from one to another decade of the twentieth century.

It is important to point out that Erika originally wrote the book in the mid-1980s, as an immediate response to and as part of a therapeutic process following her mother's death, and thus when the narrator speaks in the present tense she is referring to the mid-1980s, not to be confused with the time of actual publication which was some twenty years later. Indeed, its final acceptance for publication as part of a life-writing series at Wilfred Laurier University Press came when Erika's 'death sentence' had been passed, the diagnosis of stage four colorectal cancer, a disease that had afflicted now at least the fourth generation of the women in her family. While Erika had worked vigorously to find a publisher since the completion of the manuscript, it would take the intervention of a dear close friend and fellow academic, Professor Eva Karpinski (York University, Canada), to secure a publication deal some twenty years after Erika had committed her memory, her story and her sorrow to paper. Eva was young enough to be Erika's child, but what they shared bridged the generational divide. Eva and her husband Daniel had immigrated to Toronto from Poland on the threshold of their respective brilliant careers, and Erika had nurtured Eva's academic ambitions and mentored her when they were colleagues in the English Department at Seneca College. Eva was intimately involved in the contract negotiations; she brought the text to the attention of another one of her mentors, Marlene Kadar, who was editor of the life-writing series, and who would come to write the preface; Eva and Daniel represented Erika's concerns when the press's copy-editor misappropriated the authorial voice and missed the poetry and pathos of her prose, much to Erika's distress; and they acted as midwives to the manuscript when in the very last months of her life the cancer was finally sapping Erika's seemingly endless supply of creative energy and defeating a most determined work ethic. Indeed, Eva was a long-standing champion of the manuscript, excerpting parts of the unpublished version for a reader on multiculturalism that she edited, and recognizing its importance, its literary merit and its representativeness in the overlapping genres of life writing, memoirs of immigration and cultural adjustment, and feminist confessional.[2] Indeed, these were the genres that were the focus of Eva's scholarship.[3] The story of its publication and its 'becoming' as a book is an integral part of its history.

And, of course, the narrative of the book is also many layered because of my relationship to the book and my place in its story, not to mention the next chapters that could be written to connect the organic links in the ancestral chain. From the start, then, I should state that this essay is very different from the ones I am accustomed to writing in a professional capacity. It is my first attempt, at least self-consciously, to write in the style of *ego-histoire*, 'a mainly methodological enterprise, aiming to establish a ground of meta-historical reflection'. *Ego-histoire* is to be situated 'half way between – and to connect – the practice of history with philosophical and existential systems of thinking held by historians'.[4] As the pre-postmodernist Edward Carr put it: 'before you study the history, study the historian'.[5] Therefore, writing about my mother's book forces me – or, more encouragingly, invites me – to reflect on my own personal and professional identity, as well as to consider how my gender, generational, ethnic and national profile inevitably conditions the choices I have made and the way I approach historical research and writing. It would not be possible, nor do I think it would be desirable, for me to come to this text as a detached analyst or an empiricist, as my relationship to the book could not be more personal and thus my reading of it unavoidably subjective. Had my mother lived I am certain she would have promoted the book and made sure it found its audiences. But in her absence I have felt that it falls to me to ensure that *Becoming My Mother's Daughter* has an afterlife, that is a living memorial, and that the story it relates is a continuous one, speaking to audiences that include the author's family and friends, children and grandchildren, the wider transnational community of survivors, as well as those who have and will appreciate it as a distinguished example of feminist life writing.

The question of generations is an interesting one too. As I see it, I would fit a category between second- and third-generation survivor. Three of my four grandparents were born at the very dawn of the twentieth century, while both my parents were in their mid-thirties when I was born (my brother is my senior by eight years). As was more typical of my generation of university-educated and professionally minded women, I started my own family in my mid-thirties. In short, in the course of 105 years my family managed to spawn only four generations. Both my parents were 'children of the Holocaust', and not in the sense of Helen Epstein's groundbreaking study that was published in the same decade as my birth[6] – my mother was 6 and my father 8 years old in 1944. They were instead 'child survivors', the 1.5 generation and, even more precisely, 'children "old enough to remember but too young to understand" (approximately age four to ten)', according to Susan Rubin Suleiman's taxonomies.[7] It follows, then, that I am part of not a third but a 2.5 generation of survivors. Reading Julie Orringer's *The Invisible Bridge* was a something of an epiphany, as it so evocatively fictionalized a family story that had so many parallels with my family history. But this novel was based on the story of Orringer's grandparents, even though the author is only one year younger than I am.[8] It is thus a slightly but significantly different position to be the child of children of the Holocaust. And yet, because of my parents' sadly shortened life spans, it remains to me to transmit their stories to my children, while at the same time imparting a sense of Jewishness that is more uplifting and hopeful than the one imparted to me by parents.

I appear in *Becoming My Mother's Daughter* as 'Judy', a precocious and restless 10-year-old who struggles with her mother's mourning her mother. Young Judy cannot possibly understand an adult's state of mind and her mother's retreat from the pursuit of happiness. The little girl misses her grandmother, it is true, but she does not understand why she is also losing a part of her mother. Yet Judy is a very minor character in the book; she is important as a plot device, and in her few appearances she is used to illustrate continuities in emotional ambivalences between mothers and their daughters and intergenerational alienation. And it is not only because of a misplaced sense of vanity that I regret my mother having written such a minor role for me – the role of merely a minor. The book has added resonance for me because it was published just as I was faced with mourning my own mother, her own book, perhaps deceptively, providing me with a guide to bereavement, a psychological and philosophical tract on how to mourn one's mother. It could well be seen as a guide to how the women in our family *should* mourn our mothers, what is expected of us in this regard, and the dilemmas faced by the previous generation in coming to terms with loss and trying to break free from the past in order to embrace the future. More intimately, being able to write about the text and transmit its story through my own mirrors the process of bereavement through artistic endeavour that created the book in the first place. Just as Erika had written the text to process her mother's passing, I am writing this to achieve an analogous personal catharsis.

But is all that illusory? Are these lessons that can be learned at all? Are emotional responses hereditary? As we will see, mothers and daughters can have a secret language, a subterranean means of communication – at the psychic level the umbilical cord is never cut. And yet they may also assume *too much* mutual understanding; mothers may also believe that the love they feel for their children is understood and they often cannot fathom why their little ones feel blistering hurt and injury from those who love them deepest of all. With this in mind I would be more cautious before I said that *Becoming My Mother's Daughter* has played a straightforward role in helping me come to terms with becoming motherless myself. Nonetheless, the poignancy of the posthumous publication of *Becoming My Mother's Daughter* is obvious. For Erika's family, and especially her children, it has extra special meaning of circularity.

On another level I feel well placed to speak about the book, to share it, to explicate and analyse it, because I am a historian. While my own research does not focus on Hungary or on Canada, this period in European history is the one I study, particularly the first part of the twentieth century. Further, I am a historian of women, familiar with feminist research methodologies, the importance of testimony and oral history for recording the experiences of that half of the population that has traditionally been under-represented in works of grand historical narrative, and celebrating the more subtle ways in which women have contributed to history. I have therefore studied family history in a more generic sense, giving me quite a different perspective from that of the curious and dedicated genealogist. Women's historians are also especially sensitive to the ways in which the recording of history is gendered, recognizing the validity of women's experience regardless of their powerlessness, and noting that women tend to take a more subjective and emotional approach in their own witness-of-history statements, and narrate their life stories in perceptibly different ways from men.

Furthermore, the specific study of women and the Holocaust has burgeoned in recent years, a result of both the gradual legitimization of women's and gender history in the academy, and the expansion of the study of the Holocaust itself and related controversies about its meaning in the public sphere. Writing in 1942, the Warsaw Ghetto historian Emmanuel Ringelblum recognized these gender differences: 'The historian of the future will have to devote a fitting chapter to the role of the Jewish woman during the war. It is thanks to the courage and endurance of our women that thousands of families have been able to endure these bitter times.'[9] Certainly we can bring to mind those iconic tragic-heroes of the Holocaust who, as it happens, were female, such as Anne Frank and Hannah Senesz, the former a few years older than the narrator of *Becoming My Mother's Daughter*, and the latter another Hungarian. But that is not where the study of women and the Holocaust begins and ends. Rather, gender historians of the Holocaust are interested in how men and women were treated differently by those who persecuted them; how sexism reinforced racism; the roles that Jewish women played in the family when they were separated from their menfolk; the sexual segregation of the ghetto, the concentration camps and the extermination camps; the changing status and experience of motherhood under persecution; and the choices that were open to women as women, such as easier emigration in the pre-war years when upwards of 10,000 German Jewish women came to Britain as housemaids as a means of escape, for example. On the other hand, families tended to encourage young men to leave if and when they had a chance, and thus on the eve of war the Jewish population of Germany was actually 60 per cent female, and it followed then that more German Jewish women died in the Final Solution than their male counterparts. In making sense of these sex-based differences, historians of gender and the Holocaust have been careful not to suggest a hierarchy of suffering, and do not wish to engage in a debate about who suffered more. Rather, historians have argued that

> no calculus of cruelty should be used to make the insidious wholesale judgment that what happened to one gender during the Holocaust was worse than what happened to the other, or that one gender's reflections and memories are clearer or more truthful and important than the other's. Similar experiences are not identical, however, and, in the Shoah, differences between men and women made a significant difference.[10]

As Myrna Goldenberg aptly sums up the situation, 'the hell may have been the same for women and men during the Holocaust, but the horrors were different'.[11]

And yet there are those who still take exception to a gender perspective on the Holocaust. For instance, some historians argue that focusing on the particularity of women's experiences involves two dangers: first, it may denigrate the Holocaust's significance by turning the Shoah merely into an example of sexism. Second, it may detract from the much more fundamental fact that the Holocaust happened to victims who were not seen as men, women or children but as Jews.[12]

As a historian, I can see, then, that many of these critical points help contextualize and explicate *Becoming My Mother's Daughter*, and the world Eliza and her young daughters are forced to inhabit and try to survive during the siege and those intense months of persecution is very much a female world, a world where women have only themselves to count on. First, the three women take refuge, for a hefty price, in a convent not far from the labour camp where Paul – Eva/Erika and Sandy's father – is incarcerated. When they are in hiding back in Budapest, they are without their father and grandfather again, and women dominate life in the ghetto, both in numbers – as all the young men are meant to be enlisted in the labour battalions – and in organization, as it is competing maternal instincts that create the bonds and feelings of sisterhood but also the tensions and conflicts in these extreme conditions. And of course it is under these conditions that the unyielding if problematic bond between mother and daughter is forged. Mother and daughter are welded together by fear, to be sure, but their bond is further cemented by their sense of triumph at their own courage and their ability make do, to provide and survive, in the absence of men. In this sense, then, coming to this text as a women's historian has given me a certain insight and critical distance.

However, while I am happy to describe myself as a women's historian, I am also a political and cultural historian, and, more significantly for our purposes, my work has focused on the perpetrators rather than the victims. My first book, *Feminine Fascism: Women in Britain's Fascist Movement 1923–1945*, published in 2000, examines the roles, representations and experiences of women in Oswald Mosley's British Union of Fascists in the 1930s.[13] It is somewhat ironic, given the topic of this chapter, that only a couple of years ago I was the consultant on and interviewed for BBC Radio 4's 'Mother was a Blackshirt' (2010), a programme about the children of British fascist women, concerned with how they had come to terms with their mothers' sinister histories. I have gradually moved away from exploring the perpetrators, with my current research looking at women's rising status and their deepening engagement with international affairs and foreign policy between the two world wars. In this work on women and foreign affairs I am coming into closer contact with many British women whose hearts were in the right place and who had the interests of the victims of fascism in mind. In any case, the proverbial apple does not fall far from the tree, and it is equally true for many historians that their research interests can be explained subjectively, grounded in their own family history, asking academic questions to illuminate personal and ancestral mysteries. Therefore, what I am trying to offer here is a reading of *Becoming My Mother's Daughter* as the historian-daughter of the author would interpret this text.

Reading and Re-reading *Becoming My Mother's Daughter*

2. Erika Gottlieb, 'Night Peril' [n.d.], in the private collection of Julie and Peter Gottlieb. Copyright/permission granted by Julie and Peter Gottlieb.

Erika was a writer, of both fiction and academic work, and the book reflects these gifts and insights. I would offer as a suitable genre classification that of 'literary memoir', something more than a piece of life writing or autobiography. It is never a blow-by-blow account or a tale of surviving the Holocaust. Its genre classification is not unique for those texts by child survivors among which 'there is a privileged place for the literary ... and generally for the artistic representation of their experience'.[14] This is not to deny the central place of the Second World War in the narrative, but the Hungarian Holocaust is merely one site of mourning, as life cycle and generational time do not always coalesce with historical time, and certainly never so in the interest of narrative neatness alone. Its complex structure adds to the text's transformative power and no reader could come away from it without reflecting on her or his own most intimate relationships and emotional conflicts.

Erika was also a painter, and her prose is that of a painter, imagistic and visually provocative, much of the language at the service of describing paintings, family photographs, landscapes and scenery. The book is generously illustrated with her own oil paintings and sketches, the pen-sketched life drawings inspired by family photographs, while the paintings are in the Expressionist style. If photographs are proof of life then surely sketches of these photographs are proof of transcendence.[15] It is thus quite unique in this genre, a Holocaust memoir that is both something more and something less than a Holocaust story. It is also something more than a text, in that it is illustrated by the author's own hand, a testament in the round.

The form is intrinsically related to one of the central themes, and that is the emphasis on renewal and recovery after loss and bereavement. Erika never denied her Jewishness, nor did she hide her past, but she did not want to dwell on either of these identities. Her relationship to the religion was a personal one based on a profound belief in God and spirituality rather than reverence for custom and observance, and her view of herself playing myriad roles, and never principally that of 'survivor' or 'victim'. When we meet Eva/Erika in the book she is a very young child, and however scarring her childhood trauma she wants to *live* life when finally given the chance, to move on, to move forward, to create a self, to discover a self. In the scenes that take place after the war the youthful Eva/Erika must come to terms with her mother's mourning for the dead of the family and the dead of their people, a foreshadowing of Eva/Erika's daughter Judy/Julie's frustration with how Eva/Erika deals with the loss of Eliza/Elizabeth under very different circumstances almost forty years later. Victims, even survivors, are never free, still shackled by their nightmares even after wakeful life has returned to a better state, a more normal and tolerable state. The conflict that has to be resolved is the one between the self-created self and the self created for us by our mothers, our families and the wider world, a fundamental conflict in the process of becoming. The central trope in the book is Eva/Erika's painting of portraits and self-portraits. Eva shows her mother a new self-portrait, annoyed by her response to it:

> Why does Mother always have to insist on a sentimental interpretation? And why is it that whatever I do in Mother's eyes it suddenly becomes appropriated by the family, it becomes part of the collective? As if I always have to justify every thought according to the consciousness to be shared by all. Always, always, the family, the tribe. Can I never be permitted to break way, to become nothing but myself?[16]

On the eve of Eliza/Elizabeth's death in 1982, Eva/Erika has an exhibition of self-portraits called *Faces* at the Koffler Gallery, part of the Jewish Community Center in Toronto. The very physically feeble Eliza/Elizabeth sees the pictures after they return from the framer and before they are hung, only to tell her daughter that in one way or another each of these self-portraits evokes the visage of another member of the family, as if Eva/Erika does not have her own face, her own identity or individuality, but is a composite figure of the entire clan. Eva/Erika bristles at this suggestion and cannot quite fathom why she is so irritated by her mother's remarks. Eliza/Elizabeth does not live to see the show itself, and Eva/Erika does not return to her own exhibit after the vernissage; in her mourning she cannot bring herself to face the faces, to see the accumulated heritage, to confront her guilty feelings for having dismissed her mother's interpretation of her work. This trope is carried on into the period after Eliza/Elizabeth's death when Eva/Erika is blocked in her creativity and ceases to paint, regretting that she has never painted her mother's portrait from life. It will be part of her recovery, her renewal, to find the means to paint her mother's portrait from memory, her way of coming to terms with her mother and with the Eliza/Elizabeth within her, her way of accepting the process and becoming her mother's daughter. We see, then, how intrinsically linked are style, format and content. The treatment of the Holocaust as one of several formative episodes in the narrative reinforces this theme of resisting living life as a victim. The inclusion of the sketches and paintings, meanwhile, are by no means merely illustrative or an attractive added feature, but the search for Eva's selfhood and self-understanding is through the visual which for her can ultimately speak that which cannot be expressed by language.

This temporally non-consecutive and imagistically rich text nonetheless tells a coherent and psychologically realist narrative. The author's voice is all her own, and even a daughter cannot hope nor should she want to ventriloquize it for the sake of brevity or summary. The style of its expression is fundamental to the story and to the dilemmas, personal and historical, that are being explored. The defining conflict in this family saga began with the love affair between Stephen, one of five sons from a prosperous Jewish family who originated from the country but moved to Budapest at the dawn of the new century and started a high-end furniture store and factory, and Ethel, a poor Jewish girl from a working-class family who went out to work at the age of 12, was seen to have promise, and was even promoted to the role of buyer in the same furniture store. Stephen's family was well off and acculturated, demonstrating the traits, attitudes and physique of the Hungarian peasantry more than that of urbanized Jews. Their love affair was not doomed because of religious difference but rather due to class stratification. Stephen's family vehemently objected to the match on the grounds of class miscegenation, fearful that the poor girl's family would become a burden on the rich one. But Ethel was pregnant, and the shame of this was deeply felt by her own family who banished her from the house. Thus, Ethel was sent to Vienna for her confinement, and Eliza/Elizabeth was born in the Austrian capital in February 1914. While Eliza/Elizabeth's parents remained devoted to each other, Stephen did not have the courage to stand up to his father or to his snobbish brothers who had each married more socially suitable woman. Eliza/Elizabeth's childhood was therefore quite miserable, and certain phases positively Dickensian, the little girl being farmed out to a childminder in the country when she was still a toddler, and grossly mistreated under this woman's care. Ethel tried her best to provide for the child, and Stephen was never out of their lives, nor did he fail to provide for their basic needs, but he served in the Great War – four years in the trenches – and after the war he was with them several times a week but lived separately. When Eliza/Elizabeth turned 16 she was sent to an elegant boarding school in Paris. This was the turning point in her life, a preparation for entering a new class as she approached maturity. The narrator speaks of the significance of Eliza/Elizabeth's (her mother's) time in Paris:

> This is the most exciting year in Eliza's young life. She has the opportunity to learn a new language, and in a few months she speaks it like a native ... Eliza enjoys the school, her classmates from all over the world, and her teachers. Her art teacher recommends that she try for admission to the Fine Arts Academy.
>
> There is no doubt that Eliza's parents are proud of her achievements, but they will not hear about higher education for her. What purpose would it serve? A girl has to get married; no profession

> is an alternative for marriage. And art school, of course, is completely out of the question. It is not practical, and what's more, it is not respectable ... Eva can still hear the bitterness in Eliza's voice, her lifetime's worth of disappointment and resentment.[17]

While their daughter was in Paris, Ethel offered Stephen an ultimatum: he must either marry her and thereby make Eliza/Elizabeth legitimate and give her a chance to make a respectable match, or Ethel would take her and go to South America where she had a sister. Stephen agreed, and they had a civil marriage. When Eliza/Elizabeth returned from Paris at 17 years of age she found her circumstances transformed, her status elevated all of a sudden, and a life of comfort and amusement in front of her.

Apart from the early death of Ethel, the years that followed were more than satisfactory. Eliza/Elizabeth married Paul Steinbach, an ambitious chemical engineer twelve years her senior; they were treated to a honeymoon visiting the fashionable sites of Europe only to have to return early and be bailed out because the groom got carried away in Monte Carlo. They had two daughters, and they enjoyed a life of culture, with a vibrant social life, freed from drudgery by the help of domestics and a governess for the children. Ethel's early death, of course, came as a real blow, but otherwise these were settled years with little foreboding of what was to come. Eliza and Paul had Sandy/Susan (born in 1935) and Eva (born in 1938). Despite the anxious times and political turmoil, the daughters enjoyed happy childhoods – raised by a German-speaking governess; going to see Hollywood's latest offerings for children, the much-loved Disney films; being treated to birthday parties where they had masks and costumes that allowed them to re-enact the whole story of *Snow White and the Seven Dwarfs* – and felt relatively safe and protected. This world disappeared overnight, or at least that is how it seemed to young Eva/Erika, who had been shielded from so much during the war years and before the Germans came in and the Arrow Cross, the Hungarian Nazis, came to power in 1944.

The Holocaust came late but with great alacrity to Hungary, almost like a lightning bolt. German forces occupied Hungary on 19 March 1944, to forestall the Horty regime's attempt to negotiate an armistice with the Allies when it became clear that the Germans were going to lose the war. Miklos Horty was kept in power as titular head for the short term, but the Arrow Cross seized power with German help after Horty announced that had he appealed for a ceasefire in mid-October 1944. The Arrow Cross leader, Ferenc Szalasi, then took command. There were 200,000 Hungarian Jews in Budapest at this time, and the Red Army would not liberate the Pest ghetto until 18 January 1945. In less than a year, out of 825,000 Hungarian Jews, 550,000 were killed, either in forced labour, in individual acts of murder or after being deported to the extermination camps, Auschwitz being the main destination. So this is the wider context of my mother's story; and the fact that she, her sister, her mother and her father all survived when so many perished was nothing short of a miracle. The odds were certainly against them. Indeed, my father's story was more typical. He too was born in Budapest in 1936 to comfortably-off middle-class Jewish parents, and while they were not deported, as they managed to find various places to hide, at a steep price, his father was murdered by German soldiers only weeks before the liberation.

We can never satisfactorily explain why one person survives and makes it, and another one does not. In Hungary in 1944 it was down to sheer luck; perhaps an element of survival instinct and intuition could play a part, but as my mother's stories illustrate, it was really down to chance. Certainly Eliza/Elizabeth and Paul exhibited tenacity, courage and the life instinct to a remarkable degree, trying to evade their persecutors, never giving in. But many others who shared this dedication to life, a deep desire to live, failed in their attempt and would not live to tell their stories. Yet perhaps tenacity and the spirit of resistance did play its part in tipping the scales towards survival. One passage illustrates this well. After taking refuge in the Matra Mountains in the spring of 1944, the Steinbach family was forced, with all other Jews in the surrounding area, into the closest ghetto in Gyongyos, a small provincial town. Eva/Erika tells the story:

> We're surrounded by our luggage. Although we have had to observe the restrictions in terms of weight, we have elegant, sturdy leather cases, and parcels wrapped in heavy woollen blankets. Mother looks around and cannot bring herself to unpack.
>
> To see Mother cry.
>
> All through these months she has been unshakable in her faith: we're going to make it, no matter what. Suddenly she breaks down in sobs. Father watches her shoulders quiver, then turns on his heel. He has changed his mind instantly. It is the very last day he can act, just a few hours before the gates slam shut, a few hours before – something no one expects – the ghetto is to be surrounded with barbed wire.
>
> Father rushes out of the ghetto, through the streets to the police station. We need a permit to leave the Gyongyos ghetto and return to our residence in Budapest. In an hour he is back with our papers. He has returned in a horse-driven carriage, with a moustachioed coachman. The two men quickly load our unopened baggage ... And now we are free to rush ahead with only a few pieces of hand luggage to catch the Budapest train. Had Mother not started to cry, she, who had been so anxious to put on a brave face, to spare us fear, and had

> Father not been so decisive to get us out before they shut the gate, there would be no one here to remember. Not one of the women or children with whom we spent that spring in Gyongyos returned from the concentration camps.[18]

We see the atrocities though a child's eyes, but throughout this tale of near-death moments and ultimate survival, the child's eyes are fixed on the mother Eliza/Elizabeth. Eva/Erika's greatest fear is to be separated from her mother, to be 'snipped off', to lose her lifeline.

When they enter the ghetto in Budapest, by which point the three women are alone, father in hiding elsewhere and grandfather already dead, Eva is struck by the changes in human nature occasioned by the inhuman conditions, and her separation anxiety is exacerbated by pangs of jealousy. She notes:

> The only strange thing I notice about the ghetto is that it's the most crowded place in the city I have ever seen. As we arrive, the street seems to be swarming with children, old people, and women carrying big bundles. Some of the children are wandering by themselves, in search of an adult they can attach themselves to. They're orphans, their mothers have been deported or marched away. What if Mother decides to adopt one of them? I see a girl about Sandy's age with long, dark hair and a grim, adult's face. What if Mother agrees to take her with us? After all the girl is alone and the three of us are together. I cling to Mother's skirt. As long as I hold on to her, I'm safe and no one can touch me. I'm so privileged. I don't dare to look back at the girl with the adult's face.[19]

From here on, the key players in the drama are the three women, Eliza and her two little daughters. Both Eliza and Sandy become ill, Sandy with a serious heart condition, Eliza with crippling diarrhoea. The six-year-old Eva/Erika is torn between her need to preserve and protect her mother and self-preservation. The narrator remembers:

> Sandy is unwell. Mother keeps reading to us, sometimes giving Sandy a tiny bit of chocolate from her handbag. I also get some, of course, but I still feel hungry. Dizzy and lightheaded with hunger.
>
> Before we are driven to the ghetto, Mother had given me a chunk of our chocolate. Hard, unsweetened baking chocolate. I'm to guard it in case someone from the family needs it. Probably she is also thinking that if we get separated, I should have something edible with me.

> Now Mother is also ill. She no longer sits with us on our cushion on the floor; she is lying on her back on a wooden box close to the cellar door. She has had diarrhoea for a long, long time. A day? Two? Three? I can't count the days. She's become too weak to walk or sit up. I watch her, helpless. Now she summons me with her hand to give her a piece of the precious chocolate. It could stop the diarrhoea if she had some food, something solid. Under her black silk kerchief, her broad forehead is damp and pale … I reach into the bag, search around, then reach into my pocket. But there is no chocolate. I want to see Mother's eyes bright and clearly focused again, her mouth solid and beautiful like before, I want her to get well again. I must find the chocolate, at least some of it.
>
> 'I've seen her eat it on the sly,' says one of the women, rising from her armchair. She points in my direction, gloating maliciously. She moved closer to Mother, not to help her but to tell on me. Trying to persuade her that I have betrayed her trust, that I've eaten the chocolate she has entrusted to me. And of course I must have. Not that I ever wanted to eat it. At least not the whole thing. Having a little, a very little bite every once in a while, yes maybe. But all the time I was telling myself that I was saving the big slab of chocolate for all of us nevertheless.[20]

Eliza's inability to be angry with her own child, her emotional clarity even in her own physical suffering, is exemplified by the way she stands up for her daughter.

> She does not want me to feel guilty, and she refuses to listen to the women in the armchair. 'If it's gone, it's gone,' she says. 'There's nothing to explain.' … After a long, long time – there's no means to count days when we never see the sun – Mother somehow begins to improve. It must be by sheer effort of her will. Finally, the three of us are sitting together again. She's reading to us the story of little Lord Fauntleroy, and encouraging Sandy and me to play with our cut-out dolls.[21]

There are other brushes with death for these vulnerable three on their own, but something keeps them alive. They eventually meet up with Eliza's cousin Agnes and her twin girls, the two mothers doing all in their power to provide and survive, to find food and shelter in the winter of 1945. Only on 13 February 1945 do they hear a knock on the door – it is already a month after the liberation of the ghetto. The joy of seeing father there, almost unrecognizable, is beyond description. To emphasize the miraculous element of this family reunion, Eliza's cousin's husband does not return, and this is the fate of so many other Jewish families. When life starts to get back to normal and the girls start school, they are very much in the minority for having two living parents. Eliza's response to this personal and collective tragedy is to have another child, and Ada/Andrea is born in 1946.

The next part of the book covers Eva/Erika's youth, her success in school and her joy at studying at Budapest's high school for the fine arts (something her mother had been prevented from doing by her puritanical parents), all against the backdrop of the still-threatening Soviet regime where many Jews find themselves again persecuted if they are deemed capitalists. Thus the revolution of 1956 is an opportunity for so many Hungarians, Jew and Gentile, to start again, and Eva/Erika and Sandy/Susan escape, coming to Canada as refugees in the winter of 1957, and working by day and studying by night so that they can have the $500 in the bank that is required by the Canadian government to sponsor their parents and youngest sister. The family is again reunited in 1958, in the promised land.

Nonetheless, Eva will be haunted by nightmares throughout her life, well after she and the family have reached safety in Canada. The nightmares come back with greater intensity after Eliza/Elizabeth dies and Eva/Erika is in mourning. As she explains most evocatively:

> To be a victim is like going through a nightmare. Your limbs are lead, you're paralysed, helpless, out of control. In my dreams I still become trapped by the faceless forces of enemy powers. In my dreams, almost every month, the Germans still march in to occupy the city. In my dreams I am still running with a child in my arms to find shelter, and when I approach I find that there is no shelter. In my dreams I am still lost among meandering byways and corridors. Looking, hopelessly, for my destination. I've become separated from Mother: I am snipped off her sheltering, protecting body. I am lost. She is lost to me. To be left without her is what being lost means.[22]

Becoming My Mother's Daughter: The Next Generation

Finally, I want to explore another layer of the story, one that is stimulated by the book but is not in the book because it couldn't be. How did I first encounter the story of my mother? While a completed draft of *Becoming My Mother's Daughter* has been available since the mid-1980s, I did not read the manuscript until some twenty years later. I read it again when it was published, and again since with a more critical eye when I decided I wanted to write about my mother's book. I have given talks about the book to the Manchester Jewish Historical Society and synagogue groups because, as already mentioned, I have wanted to give it the exposure it deserves, but also take the opportunity to refine my own sense of personal and professional selfhood through it, making this most personal of histories public history. But why had I not read it earlier? Why did I wait so long, and, with hindsight, too long, as there are questions I now have that my mother is not here to answer? Certainly my mother applied ample pressure and coaxing for me to read her manuscript, a way of reaching out and allowing me to contact her at a different level, to impart and communicate in a way unachievable by discussion alone. But I think I resisted for so long partly because I was not ready, and partly because I felt I knew the stories; I had heard them so many times, I felt I could already recite my mother's, and my father's, personal narratives. I had been hearing their stories since I could remember, and as a budding historian, I always asked to be told these stories in lieu of fairy tales and fantasy, preferring to live in the real world, inquisitive about what really happened. My earliest memories are about asking my parents to tell me about their childhoods at bedtime, developing a morbid fascination with these menacing tales that no doubt contributed to my inability to go to sleep alone and to an atavistic condition of separation anxiety. In retrospect, I wonder why they indulged my curiosity so much, especially at such a young age. My brother, on the other hand, was less inclined towards history and had a much more active life of the imagination, which was also an inheritance from our parents and happily nurtured by them: our father was a great and an inventive storyteller, funny and playful; our mother too was immersed in the world of the imagination, a literary critic and professor of English literature whose scholarship stemmed from the deepest passion for literature, poetry and the theatre.

I suppose that on some level I felt I knew what was in the book, I had figured it out for myself, filling out the wider context as I learnt more about history – the facts and figures of history, but also the methods and theoretical dimensions of the discipline. In other ways the stories already belonged to me without having to read them, and I did not need them to be channelled through a narrator. My mother's stories were part of an oral tradition of family storytelling. I had already illustrated each of them in my head, building up pictures in my mind from a combination of my mother's paintings which had always dominated the interior of our homes, family photos – some sepia toned, others taken in studios and touched up with colour, and still others the vibrant snapshots of later years – and, of course, my own imagination and that rolling movie camera that we all have in our inner eye. Therefore, to have read the book at an earlier stage would have shattered my own illusions in some way, divested me of stories that had become my own and from which I, in many ways, drew my own morals and my own lessons for life. An obvious analogy would be when one of our favourite books is made into a movie, and that inevitable disappointment felt when it does not live up to expectations and forces an interpretation that we do not share. These family stories, as I had come to relate them as part of *my* personal narrative, served to help me make sense of my own 'survivor guilt' neuroses. Marianne Hirsch's definition of postmemory is useful for understanding the ways I have processed my family's Holocaust texts and images: 'Postmemory characterises the experience of those who grow up dominated by narratives that preceded their birth, whose own belated stories are evacuated by the stories of the previous generation shaped by traumatic events that can be neither understood nor recreated.'[23] These stories had become my backstory, rather than merely my parents' experiences, and I was involved in a tussle for authorship and intellectual property.

My reluctance was also linked to my own desire, surely, not to dwell on the family past, not to be shackled by the iron cuffs of family tragedies. Erika was receptive to this, and in one scene at a family meal in Toronto after her mother's death, she wrote:

> But obviously, the family was not ready to follow her back to the past in pursuit of Eliza ...
>
> 'As for my own children,' Eva tells herself as she starts stacking dishes, 'they may feel they've already heard too much about the war, the persecution.' Judy and Rob are impatient with her stories of the family past. Is it because they really cannot discuss these things with their own friends, because this past makes them feel like outsiders, or is it just in this instance they've taken their cue from their father?[24]

Perhaps this was true of my 10-year-old self, but my memory is different, and I recall always being curious and receptive to the stories, but also somewhat impatient when I sensed repetition and rerun. Still, there is some truth to my mother's diagnosis here, and it was often more than a bit uncomfortable to be lumbered with this family history. Did we not get a new and fresh start as a clan when our parents emigrated, escaping the Soviet regime in 1956 which was in many ways a continuation of the terror of the wartime authoritarian regime? I was not born in Hungary; my connection with the old world was tenuous. My first trip to Budapest was in 1989, together with my mother, a momentous year in the history of the Eastern Bloc, and I cannot say it felt anything like a homecoming. It was both foreign and somehow inhospitable. I was born in the new world and into a new world, a safer place. When I went to Budapest again with my husband in 2004, my parents were already not well enough to accompany us but they were still able to furnish us with the most detailed map pinpointing the city's most significant sites in the family history, thereby acting as our vicarious guides. But even in 2004, this was not my home, this was not where I felt I belonged, my smattering of Hungarian not enough to make me feel that I was among friends. There is no denying that my reaction was conditioned by the very stories that form the core of my mother's book, and Budapest represented street after street of memory, maps of menace, and the city felt to me like the set for a thriller that was not fiction but my parents' respective childhoods. It was interesting that the street on which my mother lived with her family in that elegant apartment had since been renamed Wallenberg Utca, after the Swedish diplomat who saved the lives of so many Hungarian Jews. No, Budapest was never going to feel like home for me, even if both my parents experienced their own temporary homecomings in the 1990s, my mother returning on a teaching exchange; my father, too, returning to teach advertising and media to a nation in the process of de-Sovietization and hungry for the media of capitalism.

Why else was I not ready to read the manuscript earlier? I was also not ready because, like my mother before me, I wanted to become myself before I became my mother's daughter. So you see, my mother was right, there are distinct patterns in the relationships between mothers and daughters, in the desire to break away before we can possibly be ready to come home again. As too many daughters discover, and this has certainly been the pattern in my family and one that is so vividly portrayed in the *Becoming My Mother's Daughter*, by the time we daughters realize we want our mothers again, that we are ready to accept the maternal inheritance, it may too late, and we have to locate them in our memories.

NOTES

1. E. Gottlieb, *Becoming My Mother's Daughter: A Story of Survival and Renewal* (Waterloo, ON: Wilfrid Laurier University Press, 2008).
2. E. Simon [maiden name], 'Montreal Days', in E.C. Karpinski and M. Lecompte (eds), *The Language We Share: A Canadian Cross-Cultural Reader for Learning English* (Toronto, ON: Harcourt Brace, 1995), pp.195–204. Once published, *Becoming My Mother's Daughter* was also excerpted in V. Lopicic (ed.), *Migrating Memories: Central Europe in Canada, Vol. 1 – Literary Anthology* (Brno: Central European Association for Canadian Studies, 2010), pp.169–71.
3. See E. Karpinski, *Borrowed Tongues: Life Writing, Migration and Translation* (Waterloo, ON: Wilfred Laurier University Press, 2012).
4. L. Passerini and A.C.T. Geppert, 'Historians in Flux: The Concept, Task and Challenge of Ego-Histoire', in 'European Ego-Histoires: Historiography and the Self, 1970–2000', special issue, *Historein*, 3 (2001), pp.7–18.
5. E.H. Carr, *What is History? The George Macaulay Trevelyan Lectures Delivered in the University of Cambridge January–March 1961* (London: Macmillan, 1961), pp.34–8.
6. H. Epstein, *Children of the Holocaust: Conversations with Sons and Daughters of Survivors* (New York: Penguin, 1979).

7. S. Rubin Suleiman, 'The 1.5. Generation: Thinking About Child Survivors and the Holocaust', *American Imago*, 59, 3, (2002) pp.277–95.
8. J. Orringer, *The Invisible Bridge* (New York: Penguin, 2010).
9. Quoted in J. Tydor Baumel, *Double Jeopardy: Gender and the Holocaust* (London: Valentine Mitchell, 1998), p.3.
10. C. Rittner and J.K. Roth (eds), prologue to *Different Voices: Women and the Holocaust* (New York, 1993), p.3.
11. M. Goldenberg, 'Different Horrors, Same Hell: Women Remembering the Holocaust,' in R.S. Gottlieb and N.J. Mahwah (eds), *Thinking the Unthinkable: Meanings of the Holocaust* (Mahwah, NJ: Paulist Press, 1990), pp.150–66.
12. See Tydor Baumel, *Double Jeopardy*.
13. J.V. Gottlieb, *Feminine Fascism: Women in Britain's Fascist Movement 1923–1945* (London: I.B. Tauris, 2000).
14. Rubin Suleiman, '1.5. Generation', pp.277–95.
15. 'The Holocaust photograph is uniquely able to bring out this particular capacity of photographs to hover between life and death, to capture only that which no longer exists, to suggest both the desire and the necessity and, at the same time, the difficulty, the impossibility, of mourning.' M. Hirsch, *Family Frames: Photography, Narrative and Postmemory* (Cambridge, MA: Harvard University Press, 1997), p.22.
16. Gottlieb, *Becoming My Mother's Daughter*, p.22.
17. Ibid., p.44
18. Ibid., p. 58–9.
19. Ibid., p.101
20. Ibid., p.104–05.
21. Ibid.
22. Ibid., p.160.
23. Hirsch, *Family Frames*, p.22.
24. Gottlieb, *Becoming My Mother's Daughter*, p.16.

Thy Children's Children: Survivor-Grandmothers and Third-Generation Granddaughters

JAYE A. HOUSTON

> Yes, thou see thy children's children, and peace upon Israel.
> (Psalms 128:6)

> There are survivors who bemoan the fact that their parents were deprived of ever seeing their grandchildren ... One woman had trees planted in Israel in memory of her parents ... One day she was watching Claude Lanzmann's Shoah and as she began to cry, her granddaughter put her arms around her and said, 'Grandma, don't cry. We are your family now.'[1]

Seeing the birth of one's children's children is an invaluable experience. Despite the Third Reich's attempt to annihilate the Jewish population, as well as having experienced emotions of physical and spiritual barrenness, many female Holocaust survivors have greatly contributed to Judaism's ever-flowing stream of Jewish lineage. They gave birth to a generation that Jewish people throughout the world thought would never exist – that the Third Reich aimed to annihilate.

The celebration of generational prolongation is touched by the reality that the majority of both female and male survivors could never again encounter a personal relationship with their grandmothers because most died in the concentration or death camps. Thousands of family stories about grandmother–granddaughter relationships rose in plumes of ash in the death camps, or their rich heritage vanished in places such as ghettos and forests. As a result, while considering the accounts of the relationships between female Holocaust survivors and third-generation granddaughters, I assumed those stories of ash and rubble might be the foundation of survivor-grandmother and granddaughter relationships. However, the narratives focus not on the literal recounting of a survivor-grandmother telling about her experiences in a death or concentration camp, but more on a treasured relationship between grandmothers and granddaughters in an ever-changing society. Embedded in both generations' accounts are traditional values, family rituals, storytelling and generational tensions.

It could be argued that the grandmother–granddaughter relationship is unique whether we take the Holocaust into account or not. Notably, the value I place on the unique intergenerational relationship emerges out of my personal experience with my maternal grandmother. I always knew that our relationship greatly differed from the relationship I experienced with my mother. In part, a close relationship with my grandmother led me to consider female survivors' relationships with their granddaughters as a very distinct family bond. Additionally, having studied the topic of women and the Holocaust, my grasp of what it meant to be female in the midst of the Third Reich's evil provided greater awareness of female intergenerational relationships.

These insights are the framework of thirty-five one-on-one interviews I conducted with survivor-grandmothers and their granddaughters in the southern California region. The following five accounts of the granddaughters whom I interviewed give voice to the ways in which Jewish women's experiences in the death and concentration camps affect their granddaughters' understanding of the Holocaust as it shapes their contemporary Jewish identity. The granddaughters' accounts raise questions such as: what does it mean to be the granddaughter of a survivor-grandmother in a post-Holocaust world? What do these granddaughters really want to ask their survivor-grandmothers, that they have never asked? Such questions are clearly warranted because, over the years, survivors have expressed the difficulty of understanding what others might comprehend about their past. Overall, their accounts stem from survivors' attempts to recount the destruction of their homes, the loss of their belongings and horrendous death of family and friends.[2] A hermeneutical approach clarifies the ways that survivor-grandmothers' recounting of the Holocaust affects the unique survivor grandmother-granddaughter relationship. Ultimately, the greatest hope is that the survivor-grandmother–granddaughter relationship evidences forms of legacies that a post-Holocaust society might grasp.

Legacy

What are legacies? In the survivor context, legacies surface in the trauma surrounding each survivor as she recounts fragments of her stories. While legacies may seem to come only from the Holocaust experience, it is possible that they also emerge as survivors search for words to recount their stories. To put it another way, female survivors simultaneously refer to lives and family relationships before the Holocaust, experiences that occurred during the Holocaust, and the way they see life in the shadow of atrocity.

I claim that granddaughters of survivor-grandmothers seem to sift through their remnant accounts and identify distinctive complexities that create their unique generational relationship. Many granddaughters explain that they heard only fragmented stories from their survivor-grandmothers. This reveals only one of the ways in which survivor-grandmothers have become editors of their legacies and what they want the world and their granddaughters to know about their Holocaust experiences.[3] Their recounted fragmented 'clips' are simultaneously edited and shaped by what they have lived in the past, and what they recall in the present. The two worlds never completely converge.[4] It is a continual process, filled with compromise. Each survivor-grandmother is the editor of what she wants her granddaughter to know about her Holocaust experiences and the legacies she inherits.

Drawing on what we know about survivors' recounting and granddaughters' contemporary Jewish experiences I ask: what have survivor-grandmothers bestowed to the third generation? What do the granddaughters understand regarding their grandmothers' hopes for the third generation? What makes each granddaughter uncomfortable? In what ways do the granddaughters feel part of a hopeful and hindered generation? In an attempt to understand their contemporary Jewish experience, the following granddaughter voices try to answer those questions. In their own generational voices, the granddaughters are oral historians in their own right. They transmit intimate accounts woven with facts that might not coincide with our history books. Overall, the following five granddaughters' accounts illustrate how granddaughters make sense of their historically unique grandmother–granddaughter relationship.

Research concerning the third generation and legacy is in its beginning stages. Thus, these five voices are not necessarily representative of the entire third generation. Importantly, they do not follow in the footsteps of the second generation, who often report living in homes filled with sorrow, grief, loss or trauma.[5] The relationship between survivor-grandmothers and their granddaughters is distinctively based on their personal interactions and reflections. Notably, the granddaughters, aged from 17 to 27, are close to the wartime ages of their survivor-grandmothers. As long as their grandmothers are still alive, many of the granddaughters feel their current life choices are somewhat restricted. Why?

Third Generation Voices: Hopeful and Hindered

Jennifer, Rena, Anne, and cousins Claire and Beth exist in a double bind.[6] They live beyond the Holocaust, while also honouring their grandmothers' pasts. They make choices in their everyday lives because of the choices their grandmothers were never able to make. Their lives often feel hindered due to their choice of friends, whom they might marry, or how they view themselves as the third generation.[7] Because their grandmothers surpassed great odds by surviving the Holocaust, these five granddaughters have unknowingly inherited the role of conveying their grandmothers' life experiences. Therefore, aspects of the following might likely be what they transmit to the fourth generation.[8]

Beth, Age 17

Beth,[9] born in southern California, describes her life as affluent and rather protected. She categorizes herself as an American Jew, whose family celebrates a couple of Jewish High Holidays each year. She loved her grandmother speaking to her seventh-grade class about the Holocaust. Beth, along with her classmates, learned from the horrific accounts that her grandmother struggled to tell. Beth claims it seems impossible that a human being could live through such experiences. She states: 'I always rather knew about my grandmother living through the Holocaust, but I didn't know all the details.'[10]

When Beth was 13, the entire family made a pilgrimage to Israel. At that time, her cousin celebrated his bar mitzvah while Beth and her cousin Claire were honoured at their bat mitzvah. During their stay in Israel, the family toured Yad Vashem, the Holocaust museum in Jerusalem. After exiting the museum, her grandmother led the family to a nearby tree and told them her story. Beth comments: 'I had known for a long time, but I think that was the first time my grandmother and grandfather sat down and told their stories – all of us together.' She acknowledges that her grandparents never tried to hide their past, but neither had she experienced a moment like the one under the tree, with all the family gathered to hear accounts of their grandparents' past. Beth notes that she grew up hearing her grandmother's stories at home, in the classroom and in Israel, yet because of the pilgrimage to Israel and the whole family listening together, she believes that she now knows her grandmother's whole story.

According to Beth, her grandmother leads a dual life by simultaneously struggling with the past and present. Beth describes her as 'coming out of it and leading a normal life' and yet, with pangs of sorrow, she confides: 'My grandma has *this past*. I don't know how anyone can move on from that.' Yet she quickly defended her grandma, saying, 'But she is the most optimistic person I know!' When I asked Beth about stories regarding her grandmother's past, she replied:

> She carried her mother on the death march because her mother was sick and she thought the hospital was going to be bombed that her mother was in. She was forced to carry her in the march and the day after the

> Holocaust ended, her mother died. She didn't know what was best for her mother and tried to make the best decision, however, she had to walk across death. To walk with that alone, by yourself is something I can't imagine just walking. But, for her to carry another human being, who is her mother and her mother was dying. It was more important to her than anything in the world that her mother would make it. And, she told me that her mother really was what got her through the Holocaust. She wouldn't have been able to survive without her. They were a support system for each other. And, that her mother died the day after the war shows, I think, that her mother held on for her, just to make sure she made it through the war alive. And, if her mother hadn't been there, who knows? Her liberation was bittersweet ... She buried her mother in the ground where they were liberated.

Beth's powerful phrase 'she had to walk across death' emphasizes her grandmother's strength and accentuates loyal family relationships. Beth's insight regarding her grandmother, 'holding on for her, just to make sure she made it through the war alive', points to Beth's interpretation of her grandmother's bittersweet liberation and courageous acts.

Because of her grandmother's experiences, Beth sees life more in the context of caring for others. For Beth, 'everything in life should be valued'. She explains that 'It's so unfair. Some have amazing families, while others have no one.' And adds 'I definitely think that it has affected my personality and my growing up in life.' According to Beth, their relationship is 'an emotional experience ... it is ingrained in my personality and images, which of course will reflect everything I do'. She believes, therefore, that her grandmother's past affects what she does in life. Believing her life is ingrained with images of walking across death is not viewed as a hindrance, but instead it shapes a hopefulness that influences Beth's value of their close relationship. Reflecting on what makes their relationship meaningful, Beth comments that her grandmother tells her more about what happened than she does her cousins. She attributes this to her listening more intently.

Claire, Age 17

Claire,[11] Beth's cousin, presents a different account. From Claire's perspective, their grandmother has shared only a few of her stories of what happened. Claire reasons that 'it is hard for my grandma to talk about. It's very emotional for her. Maybe that is the reason I don't know the whole story.'[12] These words reveal a complexity in these survivor-grandmother–granddaughter relationships because Claire heard the same stories as the family gathered under the tree after touring Yad Vashem.

Reflecting on her relationship with her maternal grandmother and grandfather, Claire feels the emotions, secrecy and respect surrounding her grandfather's Holocaust survival. The secrecy emerges from her grandfather's governmental ties in Romania.[13] Claire perceives that her grandmother's emotions and her grandfather's past determine what they discuss about the war. Her relationship with her grandparents involves talking about the past when they want to share an experience; otherwise they remain silent to protect themselves.

A shift takes place when Claire refers to her paternal survivor-grandmother, who was in the resistance movement. Claire sees their relationship as rather turbulent. She describes her paternal grandmother as 'very worried and almost high-strung. She's a little more difficult – but it isn't that I love her less ... She is not as open about it.' Trying to unravel her frustrated feelings, Claire explains that her paternal grandmother constantly calls her from the east coast, demanding that she marry someone Jewish. Claire complains: 'It happens every two weeks; she is almost obsessive about things ... It is very important to her to be around Jewish people and to be around Hungarian people. She is almost racist, which is kind of ironic. You'd think where she comes from, she'd be a little more accepting and understanding.' She clearly finds it upsetting that someone, especially someone who survived the Holocaust, categorizes people according to their race.

Claire confronts her grandmother, asking 'Why are you so racist?' She reports having yet to hear a satisfying answer. As much as she would like to convince her grandmother that society is changing, Claire concludes: 'At seventy-something, she's not moving. She's set in her ways.' She perceives the relationship with her paternal grandmother as a power struggle that revolves around her grandmother's fear that Claire might marry outside of Judaism, someone of a specific race or religion that the grandmother would judge harshly.

When asked about the details of both grandmothers' stories, Claire comments: 'The Holocaust is a big picture and slowly you work through it. You'll never know everything and I guess that knowing that you won't know everything about it – that is important.' Undoubtedly she sees the immensity of the topic and she has compassion for herself by acknowledging that she will never know its entirety.

Thinking about what she knows, Claire shifts back to her relationship with her maternal grandmother. She wants to believe that their relationship is not solely based on Holocaust stories. What is most striking about Claire's account – and it differs from her cousin Beth's - is that Claire plans to hear her grandmother's entire story someday. She could view her grandma recounting her stories on the Survivors of the Shoah Visual History

Foundation videotape; however, Claire has yet to watch the video. When asked about viewing the video, Claire comments that being aware that she has not watched the Shoah video makes her feel 'weird'.

> I should have watched the video, but just because I don't know the whole story doesn't mean I don't *respect* the story. But I almost feel that I don't have to know it all to understand her experience and in order to appreciate it and to just be influenced by what happened ... The details would almost make the picture a little more clear, but I don't feel that it really changes that much. It's more what I've grown up with that is the result of the Holocaust and what they went through. It's almost that it's not the actual story. It's hard to explain.

Claire's insight that 'It's more what I've grown up with that is the result of the Holocaust' conveys a respect for her grandmother, and the foundation of their relationship.

Claire's interpretation of her relationships with her maternal and paternal grandmothers is like two sides of the same coin. Her maternal grandmother presents an optimistic view of life filled with helping others, while her paternal grandmother focuses on the detriments of intermarriage and racial issues. She loves her paternal grandmother, yet feels hindered, obligated, to go along with her grandmother's insistence on marriage within the tradition. These issues illustrate the complexities woven through their relationships of balanced emotions and honouring the past.

Beth and Claire are making choices and facing issues embedded in hope and hindrance. These granddaughters value family loyalty. The Holocaust is always in the background of how these granddaughters view their grandmothers and it affects how they interact in everyday life. At times, they feel hindrances, such as the haunting images, trauma and prejudices that their grandmothers carry today. Yet they find hope through the belief that someday they will know the *whole story*.[14]

Anne, Age 16

Anne[15] is a high school student who believes that being categorized as part of the third generation is 'not that big of a deal', nor does she think that her grandparents being Holocaust survivors affects her life 'all that much'. Anne avoids being labelled with a Holocaust-related identity because she believes that people who are not Jewish are not that interested in what happened. She equates these concerns with what it feels like to be in high school because 'it is the hardest time where you are judged by everybody, like I am going to sit here and go, like I am Jewish ... I am not like my mom, who went to a Jewish school.' She says: 'My mom will stand up to skinheads; I am not for that, I am not on that level of standing up for being Jewish.' And yet, when it comes to her grandmother, Anne emphasizes that she wouldn't exist if her grandmother had not survived.

Instead of focusing on what happened to her grandmother during the war, Anne refers more to her relationship with her grandmother. She describes her grandmother as funny. For instance, during her overnight stays with her grandparents in her childhood, Anne recalls hearing her grandmother's made-up stories about cats and monsters, and how some of the phrases were Hungarian, while the rest of the story was told in English.[16] She reminisced about looking forward to her grandmother telling the funny stories every Sunday. For Anne, their relationship is based on sharing good times and hearing her grandmother tell stories in foreign languages.

When asked about her grandmother's accounts, Anne explains: 'My grandma really couldn't explain what the Holocaust was. She told me she had to wear a big gold star and how she was in concentration camps and how she had to get on her knees and hold a book in her hand for an hour or two. If she dropped the book, I don't know what would happen. She would tell me, but not really what it was and where it was.' Given Anne's sketchy remarks, it seems that her grandmother recounted only fragments of what happened. Anne thinks she was in a concentration camp, Auschwitz, but she is not sure.[17]

Anne remembers that her grandmother obtained a false Christian identification card and that she worked for a doctor or dentist but, again, she is not sure:

> Most of all, she made it. She was not like her brothers and sisters, who were too proud. They were Jewish and died because they were so proud. Grandma lived because she wasn't too proud and basically she made it through because she learned to cook all sorts of stuff ... I am glad that she showed them a fake ID ... My mom would have probably been like my grandma's brothers. I would be like my grandma.

Recounting this experience is important on two counts. She remarks that her grandmother learned to cook, but Anne does not develop that part of the story. Anne's grandmother passing as a Christian was a significant factor, yet she survived because of her cooking skills. From a religious identity standpoint, it is interesting that Anne relates more to her passing as a Christian.

Anne sees being Jewish as a private matter. She also fears discrimination. She exclaims: 'I am not ashamed, I'm not proud. If I don't have a giant

Jewish star like my mom's that hangs from her neck, like she's all proud, but things are different today. She doesn't understand.' Again, Anne is unwilling to publicly identify herself as Jewish, unlike her mom who proudly wears a large Star of David. Although her father is a Lutheran, Anne clings to her Jewish roots. She explains that she 'was probably more proud of being Jewish when I was around ten, because I wasn't really affected by people around me. Nobody even knew what religion I was, but now it's like people say really harsh things and I don't like to get involved.' Anne's words reveal how religion can become a distinguishing factor as one matures. Clearly, she feels the impact of others' viewpoints and although she would like to avoid confrontation, she finds herself sometimes taking a stand:

> My view on religion is that people shouldn't be separate ... I don't think anyone should hate anyone for something so stupid as what they believe in ... If everyone could just believe what they believe and just get along, that would be great ... If I were to stand up and say, 'Well, I am Jewish. I have a problem with what you said,' but I do sometimes step in and say some things that are harsh.

When I asked Anne what question she would like to ask her grandmother that she had never asked, Anne contradicts her earlier claim that she didn't want to know the whole story while her grandmother was alive. She wants to ask about it, but feels hindered: 'Just what happened? I vaguely remember that her sister, my great-aunt, was raped, but I just feel uncomfortable, I just don't ask.' Protecting her grandmother, Anne reasons that she learned about the Holocaust in religious school and she doesn't ask because 'it would be too sad hearing it from your loved one. She doesn't deserve to be sad ... I love her to death. I want her to be happy.' Wanting her grandmother to be happy, in contrast to hearing her grandmother's actual account of a troop of Russian soldiers raping her would bring about sadness for both of them. Unconsciously, this survivor-grandmother and granddaughter relationship exists in protective silence. The survivor-grandmother withholds her horrific experiences, while the granddaughter does not ask.

Turning again to her childhood experiences, Anne is inclined to focus on the relationship they formed when she was younger. She recalls times when her parents were away; she stayed the week with her grandmother. She recounts: 'My mom has no patience for making food. My grandma has the patience. She taught me to make matzo ball soup. I used to cook chicken and dumplings ... cauliflower bread. I learned it and we wrote it down. I have the recipes in my room in a box, you know, for when she dies so I can pass them on to my children.'

As for asking for more information about her grandmother's past, Anne explains: 'When I decide to hear her story, I'll view her Shoah Foundation videotape. It will tell me the whole story.' Her comment, like Beth's and Claire's raises more questions: what is the reluctance to view the video before their grandmother's death? Do they fear hearing new horrific accounts and then not knowing what to do with their emotions? Or would they want to hear more and feel the need to silence their questions?

Rena, Age 25

Rena[18] blames the Nazis for her grandmother not reaching her educational goals. However, the education that her grandmother completed before the Holocaust did aid her survival. While in Auschwitz, each night before going to sleep, her grandmother recited her favourite poems in four different languages. Focusing on something other than the cold, lice-infested straw she slept on kept her alive day after day.

When her grandparents shared stories about their experiences during her childhood, Rena always felt a heaviness and intensity in their accounts. She understood that the horrific event that they discussed was 'The War' or 'The Nazis'; never was it referred to as 'The Holocaust'. The use of the phrase 'The War' occurred when Rena was 12 years old. Her school previewed Holocaust films. She said: 'I watched the people getting on the trains, and the people in the ghettos and the people in the concentration camps … I was wondering if I was going to see my grandmother walk by. I was petrified. I was completely traumatised.' Her fears grew even more during her Jewish educational classes:

> They had these weekends, one was the Holocaust – it was torture. They didn't let us eat. When we did eat, it was potatoes all day. They were re-enacting, you know – I felt lumped in. It would have been nice if they had taken us grandchildren of survivors aside. By the time I got home, I was sick. Two weeks later, I burst into tears. My mom said, 'You seem depressed' … I felt hurt, I felt hated, I felt like I understood what it meant to be hated. I was shocked at how awful, how awful, and it happened to Grandma and Grandpa. It's beyond – for me, it was beyond my worst nightmare.

Years later, as a college student, Rena's recounting of the weekend experience brought tears to her eyes and her voice trembled. She commented that being forced to recreate concentration camp starvation experiences and eating only raw potatoes was overwhelmingly traumatic for her as a pre-teen. Rena had difficulties in processing the terrifying weekend as she thought about her grandparents' past. She describes not being able to talk about it, to verbalize her depressed feelings or emotional reactions. Today, she realizes that this experience hindered how she reacted to her grandparents. Trying to come to grips with the issues, she asks 'How do you digest that, even as an adult?'

When asked about her grandmother's experiences, Rena replies: 'Her missing out on a college education, her not being able to attain her goals, and marrying someone less interested in intellectual ideas were central.' She also comments: 'She never got to be the person she wanted to be, go to college, or marry someone more into poetry. She is in her Garden of Eden right now in her life and in her home in Beverly Hills ... But, she's so sad about everything she lost.'

Rena refrains from discussing their relationship without including her grandfather. She comments that initially her grandmother, more than her grandfather, shaped her understanding of the Holocaust, but, when it comes to recounting her grandmother's stories, she says that 'grandmother leaves things out; she leaves the gruesome parts out'. When asked how she knew that parts were omitted, Rena exclaims: 'Because Grandpa is the one who tells the truth!' For example:

> I know the story of my great-grandmother escaping Auschwitz towards the end of the war. The Germans were panicking, so she hid. She walks back to Chmielnic, a three-hour drive. She went to the Polish people hiding her son and his wife. The man says, 'They ran off, the Germans came.' My grandfather's mother goes around the town asking people what happened. I'm talking chutzpah! I don't know where she got them after six years in a camp! Finally, some townspeople told her what happened and where they were buried. She insisted that they be dug up, so they could have a proper burial. If you want to know strength? No wonder I want to start a business. It's nothing. Talk about integrity and strength! So, here's the part my grandmother leaves out in her memoirs. She just says, 'They were shot.' My grandpa's the one who says, 'No, I helped dig them up. They were decapitated.'

Rena respects her grandfather's ability to tell the truth and his courage to face the horrific events.

In college, Rena enrolled in an arts course in metalwork and explains that her first class project was to cut three pieces of metal. The first was a peace sign, the second a heart, and the third piece was a Jewish star trimmed with barbed wire. Struggling to verbalize what they symbolized, Rena sees the connection. For the first time, she publicly uttered: 'My grandparents are Holocaust survivors.' Those words echoed through her head. She had grasped that the art class and her two other courses, on the Holocaust and Genocide and on Women's Studies, were linked with her survivor-grandparents' experiences.

The professor urged Rena to dig even deeper into her feelings. The encouragement led to her cutting a die for three mezuzahs.[19] She probed deeply into her feelings about her grandparents' experiences as persecuted Jews. As she cut the first piece the thoughts came, 'If I am going to make mezuzahs, it is not going to be this proud love of God.'[20] These words expose her anger toward God's action or lack thereof during the Holocaust. Rena confesses, 'For me at that time, being Jewish, it was not something that I could ever see why anyone would want to be Jewish.' Even though she resisted being Jewish – 'it felt like jail' – she created art pieces symbolizing Judaism and God. Her second mezuzah was designed in the shape of a *shin*. Shin is a Hebrew letter also used as a symbol for God. Rena describes how this model symbolized decay because flames burst out of it, and because Holocaust literally means 'burnt offering'. Finally, her third mezuzah was again a Jewish star wrapped with barbed wire. Importantly for Rena, the mezuzahs exposed a complexity of feelings about what it meant to be Jewish:

> There is a level of self-hate, there is a level of, you know, internalising. Who wants to be Jewish? ... I identify with people who know what it's like to be hated. It's very interesting to be a white person who knows what it is to be hated ... white skin, so you have white privilege. I feel like I have a deep sense of hatred, hate crimes, and racism ... I know it is coming out in my work now.

Today, Rena sees being Jewish more as an honour than the self-hatred she previously felt.

Thrilled with her talent in working with metals, which she inherited from her great-grandfather and grandfather, Rena also appreciates the way her grandmother created a home filled with love, strength and hope. She describes it as 'a way of merging with you that is so close it fills you up, it makes you feel not alone ... I don't know if it's the sheets she puts on or the sleep clothes I wear when I am there. She creates a safety on a soul level – she knows how I feel. She will always be my inspiration.'

The atmosphere in her grandmother's home fills her with something that other homes do not. Even as an adult, she prefers going to her grandmother's home instead of her parents' house when she feels depressed. She explains: '*Nachis* – it's a Yiddish word for a specific type of joy, which is the joy that comes from your grandchildren and children.' To

Rena, her grandmother somehow filled the home with joy, love and *nachis*, instead of the horrors she carried inside.

When asked, 'What would you like to say to your grandmother that you haven't said?', Rena exclaims: 'to find a way for her not to die in all that hell, in all that pain! So, I would ask her how to help empower her to let go, so that she can make a peaceful transfer ... My grandfather is filled with peace.' Rena fears that her grandmother might die before releasing the hell she carries from the past:

> I have very intense dreams around her death having to do with when she dies, when she's in the process of dying ... She was on her couch, she was going crazy and the paramedics were out front, my grandpa was sitting in the car, you know people were everywhere, she is awake, but dreaming, she's not at peace ... I went over, went down on my knees, picked up her face [held her face in my hands], I looked at her ... I saw it, I felt for one instant, I felt like I could cry every day for the rest of my life. I saw the horrors! I woke up and cried for three hours. I called her and said, 'How did you sleep last night?' She said, 'Fine.' I said, 'I had nightmares.' She said, 'Well, yes, I have those every night.'

The dreams accentuate Rena's acute sensitivity to her grandmother's haunting past and eventual death. She wrestles with who will be present at her grandmother's death; what it will entail. Rena seems to adopt a memorial candle role.[21] She accepts the responsibility of liberating her grandmother from hell by becoming a storyteller. She believes that telling others what happened to her grandparents frees them.

Regarding her religion, Rena responds with her grandmother in mind:

> It's always confused me how she can be so strong; she seems to find her strength away from a belief in God. Like, believing in God is the thing that is going to make her somehow weak. It deeply affects my spirituality. For a long time I decided that there must not be one and that people who believe in God are somehow weak. And, that is not going to be me! But, I don't agree with her anymore. In Judaism they are always asking you the questions. It's not enough that you just consider God – you don't even have to believe.

For Rena, believing in God is part of her Jewish spiritual identity. She breaks from her grandmother's conviction that a belief in God makes individuals weak. On the other hand, she connects with her grandmother's way of creating warmth in the home. Installing her art pieces in public locations, Rena hopes the world will understand what happened. She explains each piece's symbolism, how they represent her family's history, religion and the Holocaust. Overall, genocide overwhelmingly has affected this grandmother–granddaughter relationship.

Jennifer, Age 21

It was only at the age of 13 that Jennifer[22] met her survivor-grandmother. When she was three months old, Jennifer's mother abducted her, taking her to live in the Midwest with her maternal Christian grandmother. Her mother rarely spoke about Jennifer's father or her paternal grandparents. At about the age of 10, she started asking questions about her father and her paternal grandparents. She was told they were Jewish and survived the Holocaust. At the age of 13, the same age as when her paternal grandmother entered Auschwitz, Jennifer's family moved back to southern California.

After their arrival in California, she courageously asked, for the first time ever, to meet her father. Within days of that conversation, an event occurred that changed the entire family dynamic forever. Chance led Jennifer to select a restaurant that her father frequented. That evening, while at the same restaurant, he looked across the dining room and saw a woman with two teenage children. Within seconds, he recognized his former wife and felt sure that the young girl must be his daughter. Fearing that he might never make contact with them, her father secretly followed them home. His former wife had fled with his children once, and he did not want that to occur again.

Jennifer describes the incident as fate. For some time she had believed that her deceased grandfather was her guardian angel, and she thought he was responsible for their being in that particular restaurant on that specific night. She explains the hurt she felt knowing that her father was living somewhere close by: 'I really prayed that the day would come that I could meet him and my grandmother.' Within a few days, Jennifer's father found the courage to walk to her front door and introduce himself. That happy encounter was the answer to her prayer of building a relationship with her father and her grandmother.

The interrupted life that Jennifer experienced is fraught with questions. She explained how confusing it was to understand why her father allowed all ties to be cut off. She rationalizes that if her grandfather had been well and had not died, he would have forced her father to find her and her brother. She tries to understand her childhood feelings that something in her life was missing, and is still confused as to how to articulate these feelings: 'I was just never completely fulfilled; I wanted to know my father, grandfather, and grandmother.' She had questions about herself, but they were unarticulated. Even when Jennifer met her grandmother, she was afraid to ask why she had never tried to find her. She commented that the situation, from all sides, was not fair or right. It greatly hindered her ability to share meaningful relationships with the entire family.

Asked what she knows about her grandmother's experiences, she comments: 'Things come up: I love to hear stories about how it was while she was in the camp ... Unfortunately, we talk more about life after the Holocaust. I know she was in the hospital for a long time, but how did she get there? I don't know! ... We don't want to start crying and crying about her Holocaust stories.' She comments that the more her grandmother shares what happened after the Holocaust, the happier she seems, because she recounts stories about Jennifer's deceased grandfather. Keenly sensitive to her grandmother's feelings, Jennifer remarks that 'She has to let it out, she has to let us know what happened. I get pieces of where she was. It was as though she closed everything inside and bottled it up, like ... or she went into a cave. She unconsciously begins talking about her brother and how they used to play. Then she recalls that he died and she stops talking.' Such fragmented stories are not enough information for Jennifer. She hopes that watching her grandmother's video testimony will fill in the gaps: 'When she did make the video for Survivors of the Shoah Foundation, she started to let it out, telling more of her story.' Jennifer plans to watch it, but not until her grandmother passes.

Attempting to create close bonds, she explains that she 'always felt that I had this strong thing inside me. Today, I know it was the fact that I was Jewish. It will always be with me. I always knew something was missing. I never felt completely fulfilled. I see so much of my grandmother in me physically and mentally, and we have the same thoughts.'[23] Perhaps Jennifer recognizes a few similarities between her grandmother's loss of identity in the camps and the loss of her singing voice, with her own loss of her Jewish identity and the loss of her family during her childhood. Her grandmother remarks, 'I grieved twice. I lost my family in the Holocaust and I lost my grandchildren to an abductor. Today, I am complete and so is Jennifer.' In this case, both the grandmother and granddaughter suffer from loss and interrupted lives.

The bond in their relationship is twofold. Jennifer wants an open relationship that allows them to talk freely, but both are affected by the past and neither finds words to articulate it. Their relationship fluctuates between hindrances from the past and hopes that they will continue to bond.

Conclusion

I observed that survivor-grandmothers' lives have affected the ways in which their granddaughters relate to them. Through hearing their grandmothers' life experiences, which include the strong bonds that they shared with lost relatives, these granddaughters internalize the images of their grandmothers' identities as survivor-grandmothers. Their granddaughters reported hearing stories about what happened, yet nearly all believe there is more to hear.

Regarding growing up in a survivor-family, the granddaughters, in various ways, remarked how they sort of always knew, and how they do not remember ever becoming explicitly aware of their grandmother being a survivor. It was always there. From these granddaughters' perspectives, there was no *first moment* experience. The Holocaust and their beloved grandmothers were always present in their lives – it was normal.[24] Therefore, the Holocaust was normative.

Each granddaughter confessed that she has not viewed her grandmother's Survivors of the Shoah Foundation testimonial video. For the most part, they feel guilty that they have not heard the whole story, but they all plan on viewing it after their grandmothers pass on. The postponement suggests that the granddaughters believe that their grandmothers' stories are immortal – their experiences during the Holocaust will never die. Their delay also implies a reluctance to confront the trauma that accompanies their grandmothers' recollections of the Holocaust. In some ways, it is perhaps easier to watch a video and have the grandmothers' testimonies distanced and removed.

What arises after these granddaughters view their grandmothers' videos remains to be seen. Their delay in viewing the video suggests that the granddaughters assume that the whole story has been told to the Survivors of the Shoah Foundation, but as Holocaust literature reveals, survivors recount only fragments – whether it is in a testimonial video or in a one-on-one setting. In other words, with salvaged words, survivors recount remnants of their Holocaust experiences.[25] Ironically, most survivors know that there is no recounting of the whole traumatic horrors of what they endured.[26]

Given the granddaughters' comments after our interviews, it is likely that they will ask themselves 'Why didn't I ask her more questions?' I recall granddaughters sometimes commenting, 'I need to talk with my grandmother.' They seemed more aware of the significance of the survivor-grandmother–granddaughter relationship after the interviews. Most of all, the granddaughters were attentive to how little they knew of their survivor-grandmothers' pasts.

In the context of legacy, Anne inherits cooking skills and treasured recipes preserved in a little box. This illustrates a legacy of moments when the survivor-grandmother is not a survivor hindered by the past. She is just cooking old family recipes; however, she survived the Holocaust by utilizing her cooking skills. Claire's remark about loving her grandmother despite her insistence that she marry someone Jewish suggests that she has moments when the Holocaust is not central. Perhaps, for a few minutes, Claire sees her as a Jewish grandmother wanting a traditional Jewish marriage. Additionally, Claire's remark, that just because she does not know her grandmother's story does not mean that she does not love her, illustrates her attempts to relate to her grandmother in ways that are not related to the Holocaust. These granddaughters' voices illustrate their ability to separate the Holocaust from their grandmothers at certain times. Granted, the Holocaust is central in the lives of these survivor-grandmothers; however, there are times when that identity does not hinder this relationship.

And yet, there are also hindered moments when the second generation mediates how granddaughters respond to their grandmothers. Notably, the second generation's mediating role appears in Anne's family situation. She refers to her mother wearing a gold star, when she herself does not. Anne creates a relationship between a survivor-grandmother and her granddaughter that is not totally based on the past or Judaism. These dynamics are relevant in understanding the impetus behind granddaughters' interactions with their grandmothers.

The accounts of Beth, Claire, Rena, Anne and Jennifer are indications of how their survivor-grandmothers affect their contemporary Jewish identities. Their grandmothers' concentration and death camp survival influences many of the choices that the granddaughters make today: who they marry, their religious beliefs, who they socialize with. Is the background of these choices an effort to counter the Third Reich's intent to destroy the Jewish lineage? At times they feel hindered, and perhaps feel guilty for wanting to move on. At other times they are hopeful, because they want the world to know what happened. Most of all, their survivor-grandmother–granddaughter relationships contain an element that is absent from other grandmother–granddaughter relationships. The unique distinction – the Holocaust – is the foundation of this intergenerational relationship. Whether one sees it as a religious or cultural identity, these relationships are part of a historical Jewish lineage that reaches back to the biblical days of Sarah.

NOTES

1. D.B. Whiteman, *The Uprooted: A Hitler Legacy: Voices of Those Who Escaped before the 'Final Solution'* (New York: Plenum Press, 1993), p.384.
2. C. Rittner and J.K. Roth (eds), *Different Voices: Women and the Holocaust* (New York: Paragon House, 1993), p.2.
3. This was the first time that survivors had recounted their stories within the framework of grandmother-survivors. All were interviewed by Survivors of the Shoah Visual History

Foundation. I viewed those testimonials and discovered that while some of the basic facts on their videotapes were consistent with what they told me, survivors were sometimes vague about geographical locations or not exact with dates. During our one-on-one private interviews, the women seemed more emotional and recounted a few different personal experiences.

4. H. Greenspan, *On Listening to Holocaust Survivors: Recounting and Life History* (Westport, CT: Praeger, 1998), pp.9–10.
5. D. Wardi, *Memorial Candles: Children of the Holocaust* (New York: Routledge, 1992); A. Berger, *Children of Job: American Second Generation Witnesses* (Albany, NY: SUNY Press, 1997).
6. Names of survivors and granddaughters are pseudonyms.
7. A Hillel organization on college campuses provides opportunities for college students to travel to Israel. See www.birthrightisrael.com.
8. The cousins each presented differing perspectives about their maternal or paternal grandparents. On a few occasions, granddaughters also discuss their grandfathers.
9. Private interview, Beverly Hills, California, February 2001.
10. Private interview, Beverly Hills, California, February 2001.
11. Private interview, Beverly Hills, California, March 2001.
12. Private interview, Beverly Hills, California, March 2001.
13. Claire mentioned that the family fears visiting Romania. Additionally, Claire never mentioned the family's trip to Israel and the experience that Beth mentioned after leaving Yad Vashem, while Beth never mentioned her grandfather's political involvement.
14. Their accounts raise the question: from where did the idea emerge that there is a possibility of hearing a whole story of what happened? Greenspan, *On Listening to Holocaust Survivors.*
15. Private interview, Huntington Beach, California. February, 2001.
16. Although she could not retell them, Anne attempted to tell one of the stories, including a few Hungarian phrases. During those moments in the interview, she dropped her protective shield as she laughed at herself trying to speak a few Hungarian words.
17. As recounted by Anne's grandmother in a private interview, she was never in Auschwitz. She survived as a cook near the Danube River, was kidnapped, and then raped by a troop of Russian soldiers. She never told her daughter or granddaughter for fear that they would see her in a different way, perhaps feeling extraordinarily ashamed for her.
18. Private interview, Bel Air, California, April 2001.
19. Mezuzah means 'doorpost'. It is usually a narrow wood or metal container with a scroll inside. By custom, the mezuzah is placed on the interior or exterior of the front door. The practice of affixing a mezuzah is based on the biblical passage from Deuteronomy 6:1–4. M.A. Fishbane, *Judaism* (New York: HarperCollins, 1987), p.144.
20. Private interview, Bel Air, California, April 2001.
21. D. Wardi, *Memorial Candles*, pp.26–47.
22. Private interview, Rancho Cucamonga, California, August 2001.
23. J. Rodriguez, examined the idea 'Sangre llama a sangre', which means blood cries out to blood. As a Roman Catholic, Rodriguez wrestled with religion and meaning in the twentieth century; the Holocaust was a catastrophic event that haunted her thoughts. As a result of her probing questions, Rodriguez's father finally told her that she had Jewish roots. See A.M. Isasi-Diaz and F.F. Segovia (eds), *Hispanic/Latino Theology: Challenge and Promise* (Minneapolis, MN: Fortress Press, 1996), p.117.
24. The second generation could make the same claim. A. Reading, *The Social Inheritance of the Holocaust: Gender, Culture and Memory* (New York: Palgrave Macmillan, 2002), pp.143–7.
25. See Greenspan, *On Listening*, p.5.
26. See ibid., p.xvi.

Grandsons of the Holocaust: Contemporary Maleness and Post-Traumatic Meaning

GOLAN MOSKOWITZ

Introduction

> Trauma cannot be transmitted to others. 3Gs are not experiencing Nazi racism or genocide. What is transmitted to 3Gs are values, worldview, family interaction and love – not trauma. It is time for this hackneyed phrase to be retired. 3Gs are not suffering from 'silent scars.'
>
> (Eva Fogelman[1])

> So many of us just have this … emptiness, and this feeling that things aren't quite right in the way that we grew up, and this underlying pain or anxiety, despite the fact that we're basically functional people … I think it's an unspoken identity … through my life, I have met people who … are third generation and just got them instantly. (Josh, aged 30, HSG interviewee)

What is third-generation Holocaust identity? And do its various manifestations and tropes, often contradictory, coalesce as a tangible category? Sociologically speaking, the 'third-generation' grandchildren of Holocaust survivors (HSG) are by no means a distinctive group.[2] They are demographically dispersed, maintain diverse religious and professional identities, and subscribe to a host of different value systems. Not only do their grandparents' survival stories encompass a broad spectrum (from those in hiding to others in death camps, and many other kinds of experiences), but the tone of the narration within individual families varies from empowering to debilitating. In Israel and the United States, HSG grew up sharing their claim to the Holocaust with a surrounding culture that commemorated, taught and commercialized narratives of survival in the mainstream;[3] '3G' organizations are increasingly visible, offering opportunities for educational outreach, community and philanthropy. This kind of collective HSG voice is a recent and still-evolving presence; it was only in 2005 that 3GNY, one of the largest and most active HSG organizations, with a membership of over 1,500, convened its first interest meeting.

Generational distance and normalization of their histories within American and Israeli life have led many to conclude that HSG are not affected by their grandparents' traumas and that they represent a graduation from survivors' crippling shame and *tikkun atsmi* (self-repair) to pride and *tikkun olam* (world repair, or social justice). Therapist Eva Fogelman writes, for example, of 'a transformation from shame to pride in the third generation'.[4] Though they do benefit from cultural resources and generational distance and achieve impressive professional feats in fields as diverse as law and popular entertainment, many HSG privately undertake quests to affirm their positioning and make sense of the weight of internalized responsibility, guilt or anxiety toward traumatic family narratives that defy comprehension. They seek to fulfil grandparents' unmet dreams, chart and preserve family history, and produce art that offers greater psychological coherence to conflicted positions and inassimilable feelings.

Based on interviews which explored interactions between contemporary American male positioning and family Holocaust legacies,[5] this study examines personal self-narrations of survivors' adult American grandsons. More specifically, it asks how family trauma and its afterlife interact with the particular expectations and pressures involved in positioning oneself as a twenty-first-century Jewish American man. It demonstrates how such pressures and expectations negotiate with post-traumatic positioning. Depending on how one understands and internalizes family heritage, post-Holocaust positioning might complicate or reinforce one's masculine self-image or one's sense of being American. Conversely, the relationship one has to American or male identity might influence how one understands or internalizes a family Holocaust heritage. Sometimes these negotiations operate on emotional, even embodied levels and sometimes on dispassionate, intellectual levels.

These interviews challenge the conventional wisdom about the experiences of HSG on several levels. For instance, in his recent article for *The Jewish Daily Forward*, Josh Nathan-Kazis highlights several contemporary studies on HSG and concludes that grandchildren of survivors are doing just fine.[6] Studies suggesting otherwise are often criticized for highlighting clinical cases that do not reflect the population as a whole. Offering reassurances about the larger group of HSG, articles like Nathan-Kazis', however, miss the individual negotiations and conflicts, often highly important to – but below the surface of – functional American grandchildren. Contemplating a transmission of overt post-traumatic symptoms, these approaches overlook the subtle inner representations and personal-emotional mentalities of a traumatic afterlife in the production of subjectivities. As the following interviews illustrate, the experience of internalizing post-Holocaust identifications is not typically one of clinical debilitation, but of meaningful internal tensions and negotiation.

Some of the most nuanced social scientific studies addressing elements of subjectivity in HSO (Holocaust Survivors' Offspring) and HSG come from the Israeli context. Julia Chaitin's 2002 study[7] of 20 Israeli families suggests that what passes from survivor to HSO to HSG is not trauma per se, but a double-edged value of intense family cohesion and conflict – a need for tight emotional unity accompanied by feelings of claustrophobia, darkness or fragility. Her concept of 'paradoxical relevance' suggests that some HSG internalize elements of post-traumatic family relations, which clash with their own secure, contemporary lives. Their experiences of Holocaust legacies are not direct traumas but disarming effects of enduring post-traumatic family chemistry – residues of the seriousness, ambivalence, emotional volatility, numbness, protective worry, boundary-violation and interdependency that have coloured their parents' childhoods and influenced their own upbringings.

A 2011 study by Miri Scharf and Ofra Mayseless of 142 Israeli HSG and their families argues that HSG, like their parents, are functional individuals with subclinical sensitivities.[8] These sensitivities correspond to the experience of having overprotective parents who focused on survival issues, coerced their children to satisfy their overwhelming needs, and lacked emotional resources. Post-traumatic parenting may violate children's needs for autonomy, competence and emotional relatedness to parents, producing feelings of helplessness, fear, loneliness or desertion, and anger. Parental manifestations of these trends, in both survivors and HSO, included overprotectiveness, mentalities bent on saving resources and abstaining from pleasure, obsessive preoccupations with eating and high scholastic achievement, and mutual parent–child separation anxiety. Though less intense for HSG than HSO in this study, these trends were most psychologically disorganizing when they were chronic, related to potent issues in children's development, characterized by pre- or non-verbal communication, and when children felt helpless to counter or contest them.[9]

In order to address these multidimensional, subsurface and nuanced ways in which HSG self-conceptions integrate or even spotlight their survivor grandparents' legacies, this study employs the theoretical framework of gender (in this case, masculinity) to conceptualize post-Holocaust legacies along the complex individual lines of subjectivity and embodiment.

Theoretical Framework

Cathy Caruth calls trauma an 'unclaimed experience', a glimpse of one's own death that is by definition illegible and overwhelming to the human brain, inducing a kind of psychological disjunction and paralysis.[10] It is anti-reason, a fissure, an internalized threat, a dislodging of emotion beyond social norms. Conversations about who may claim experiences of trauma are sensitive, controversial and not always productive. I operate on the assumption that 'reality' is a context-specific social construct that may be disrupted and that all Holocaust survivors have experienced some degree of this disruption, or trauma, via proximity to threats of death and life-altering losses.

This study does not deal with trauma per se, but with post-traumatic legacy, positioning and subjectivity. Traumatic legacies are not equal in substance, weight or duration across post-Holocaust families. Yet common tropes reflect the experience of growing up in families marked and often defined by internalized threats of death, immense personal losses (i.e. of family and home), and by a serious disruption in psychological reality. Individual identification with these tropes interacts with contemporary realities and available social positioning, based both on environmental context and on salient physical markers, such as race or sex. Complacent American masculinity, for example, the male majority position of compliance with the norms of hegemonic masculinity for the male complacent with those ideals, invites and requires men to operate as rational, independent and emotionally restrained people, thus clashing with the emotional, family-embedded and sometimes anti-rational qualities of a traumatized parent.[11] This same American male positioning, however, corresponds seamlessly with a survivor's heroic tales of endurance and individual resourcefulness.

To explore what influences and is implied by a post-Holocaust positioning, my study avoids clinical language and generalizations about the experience of entire generations. Instead, I focus on individual lines of subjectivity, the dynamic experience of self-in-negotiation. Rather than discuss 'identity' in its traditional constraints, I use 'positioning' to account for the contemporary individual's negotiation of multiple affiliations, personal drives, values, narratives and environmental influences. Similarly, I use 'subjectivity' to refer to the self-in-negotiation, its fluid interaction with these internal and external factors.

The study of subjectivity is especially important as contemporary individuals in the western world increasingly resist fixed identity categories, opting instead for multiple (even contradictory) identifications along lines of race, ethnicity, religion, nationality, peoplehood, sexual orientation, age, occupation, political affiliation, geographic region, and other spheres of imagined community.[12] A mix of liberated potential and paralysing anxiety accompanies the larger contemporary erosion of traditional identity categories.[13] Identity is increasingly fluid and a matter of individual negotiation, declaration and performance, as Judith Butler, Raewyn Connell and others stress in terms of gender, and as Herbert Gans[14] stresses in terms of ethnicity, which he describes as increasingly superficial and flexible for the American post-war generations. As the concept of identity within the western world continues to become predominantly individualistic rather than collective, symbolic rather than directly experienced in the life of a group, the influence of family heritage, especially of narratives that do not merge easily with the larger social ethos, becomes a matter of inner negotiation on the individual level.

Taking parent–child closeness as a precondition, Marianne Hirsch's theory of 'postmemory' provides a model of a subjectivity pervaded by post-traumatic family effects.[15] The post-memorial child experiences his or her forming self as dispossessed by the dictates of the parent's larger-than-life traumatic past, which the child comes to crave and despise simultaneously. This past often frames the terms of the parent's love for the child as reparation for the parent's loss, and it gives the parent licence to violate boundaries, whether by invading the child's subjectivity or by overly withdrawing. Hirsch colours HSO experience in terms of psychological impregnation, dispossession and passivity, illustrating a post-traumatic dynamic in which the child is emotionally bound to the parent and barred from the instrumentality and independence that comprise traditional masculinity, at least in the context of this dynamic within the nuclear family. The survivor parents' weighty, haunting memories are

> transmitted to [their children] so deeply and affectively as to *seem* to constitute memories in their own right ... To grow up with such overwhelming inherited memories, to be dominated by narratives that preceded one's birth or one's consciousness, is to risk having one's own stories and experiences displaced, even evacuated, by those of a previous generation ... to be shaped by traumatic events that still defy narrative reconstruction and exceed comprehension.[16]

Hirsch and others additionally stress the survivor parents' overprotection of their children. This ambivalent relationship, which leaves the child as both a negated, insignificant receptacle and a privileged, cherished prize of a threatened legacy, persists in its emotional influence, even as the child achieves greatness in the outside world. This kind of subjectivity is weighted by the seriousness of its genesis, as well as shrouded in a profound inner anxiety about its own right to exist, express, enjoy and protest, even as it draws strength from the proud history on which it stands. In some post-traumatic families, this is the stuff of transmitted 'values, worldview, family interaction and love', which Fogelman takes pains to contrast with the Holocaust trauma itself. While it is an essential distinction that she makes between trauma and post-traumatic subjectivity, it is also important not to gloss over what are for some HSG significant legacies of the latter.

Gender is a useful lens for studying post-traumatic subjectivity, because it directly addresses the process, even if unconscious, of weighing personal and familial vulnerabilities against socialized identity and its utility in the here-and-now. Like postmemory, it is an inner component of experience with profound influences on self-understanding. Hegemonic masculinity holds the individual male-bodied person responsible for rejecting 'feminine' vulnerability and emotional connectedness.[17] Stephen Ducat's model of 'anxious masculinity' suggests that, for most men, the culturally enforced male repudiation of the feminine requires a drastic separation of boys' emotional identification away from their mothers; this binds the boy's entrance into masculinity with anxiety about losing connection to the warmth, sensitivity and support with which all human infants initially identify and depend on through their mothers.[18]

American boys and girls usually incorporate mothers or other nurturing women into their initial sense of self, because mothers and female adults predominate as caretakers of American infants. Before the age of 4, children understand gender as mutable, not fixed, and boys more often report wanting to grow up to be like their nurturing parent than like their breadwinning parent. When unbridled, the initial fluidity of non-verbal identification preceding socialization fosters the boy's connection to the maternal into his conscious sense of self. Julia Kristeva's theory of reaching an ability to live with threatening 'others' through consciousness of the unconscious, the repressed 'other' within one's psyche directly relates to the need for masculinities in a masculinist culture to access repressed and repudiated identifications with basic nurture and vulnerability (the feminine maternal), as experienced through boys' identification with mothers. Hegemonic masculinity upholds strength, control, independence and emotional repression, and it equates compassion, emotional sensitivity, interpersonal need and vulnerability with a man's failure. While the majority of men do not meet the ideals posed by such a model, Connell argues, the majority avoid the threat of subordination via complicity with the social benefits that hegemonic masculinity provides for the male complacent with those ideals.[19]

Jewish American maleness has its own genealogy separate from – but also influenced by – the ideals of disembodied, Protestant, western masculinities. In *Unheroic Conduct*, Daniel Boyarin assembles a history of embodied Jewish masculinity rooted in ideals of domesticated gentleness, intellect, spirituality and expressiveness. Lawrence Fuchs credits this Jewish male difference to Torah study, the involvement and pressure of rabbis, and internalized religious responsibility. According to Fuchs, Jewish masculinity has impacted American family norms by promoting fatherly involvement in childrearing.[20] Yet I add that Jewish masculinities were not influential until Jews became American insiders, a process which in itself required its own forms of male refashioning into clean-shaven, rational breadwinners of the secular American public. To varying degrees, Jewish American men of European origins have successfully achieved white male statuses, adjusting to the dominant fiction of their accompanying gender expectations, even if sometimes working to widen those boundaries.[21] To become the doctors, lawyers and businessmen that can finance their children's education and support their development, Jewish American fathers have also needed to devote much energy to work and American socialization, decreasing their involvement in the emotional life of the home.

Holocaust heritage, however, places one further away from comfortable American privilege and closer to Jewish-based fragility, intensity-infused family relationships, foreign otherness, and the emotional disorientation of severe losses. To actively identify with a grandparent's Holocaust history is often to negotiate a conflict between the vulnerability of this recent family experience and the self-sufficient, invulnerable traits offered and expected by the privilege of normative American masculinities. As Connell articulates, gender interacts with 'position in the world order', leading individuals to base conceptions of 'masculine', in part, on their own position in history and larger society.[22] Positioning oneself in direct relation to Jewish and family victimization interacts with one's identification with vulnerability and a sense of unrest within widespread masculine complicity. Within contemporary hegemonies that work to enforce a disembodied male subject ideal, Jewish male identifications with personal or embodied Holocaust heritage cause individual negotiations between identifying with vulnerable roots and orienting as complicit men benefiting in social systems that oppress and exploit the vulnerable.

Hegemonic masculinity, which by definition impacts most other masculinities, defines itself against the child's emotional attachment to his or her parents, as well as against outward emotional vulnerability and expressiveness in general. It privileges instrumentality and social power above individual sensitivities and empathy. Mid-twentieth-century stereotypes of the overbearing Jewish mother and accompanying anxiety and hostility towards this figure in the American cultural imagination speak directly to the Jewish American man's struggle to overcome Jewish tropes of emotional family embeddedness to resituate himself within normative American masculinities.[23] Emotional family embeddedness does not, however, clash with American norms for women. Thus, while more Jewish women than men have been able to maintain roles of managing and responding to family emotions, they are also potentially in a more vulnerable position than men with regard to traumatic family legacies; this is because social norms keep them closer to the emotional weight that sets survivor and immigrant families apart from their comfortably Jewish American counterparts. Vogel argues that female development's emphasis on emotional involvement and identification with parents, contrasting the starker differentiation from parents required of male development, accounts for why studies show HSO females to be more vulnerable than HSO males to distressing effects of parents' trauma (as well as for why control studies show females to be more anxious and emotionally distressed than males in the general population).[24]

Though it has been little examined, there is something strikingly gendered in Hirsch's postmemory about the submission to parents' emotional worlds at the expense of one's own inner drives and concrete needs. This kind of submission complicates the ability to experience oneself as independent, cohesive and instrumental (and thus, as 'masculine'). Even Art Spiegelman, in his graphic novel *Maus*(completed 1991), depicts himself as literally shrinking beneath his father Vladek's monumental Auschwitz survival, his manhood and success so quickly usurped by Vladek's protective and controlling impulses, as well as by the imprint they leave on Spiegelman even after his father's passing. Mastery over his post-traumatic subjectivity is not easily achieved – even within the pages of Spiegelman's own self-making do we find his parents' binding legacy in Art's self-depictions in prison, crying, in therapy, shrinking to child-size, and ultimately mistaken for his deceased brother on the last page. The neatly organized boxes and panels of his comic form cannot contain the sense of indebtedness, anger, guilt, intense love, and sadness with which he regards his parents.

Connell notes that, at least in the western world, gender identity functions on the level of the individual in interaction with larger social structures, meaning that a subject is masculine inasmuch as he or she fashions his or her self along the lines of his or her society's form of hegemonic masculinity.[25] Personal narratives are one vehicle of such attempts at gendered self-fashioning. Whereas a personal story of heroism or endurance positions one as masculine by virtue of instrumentality and a successful denial of personal sensitivities (as does silence in place of a story), an emotionally exposing story without empowering conclusions is a threat to masculinity, which is by definition a secure and controlled positioning.

Methodology and Participants

Through in-depth, loosely structured interviews with twenty-four HSG, I sought to delve deeper into the nuances of personal experiences of negotiation in self-identified grandsons of Holocaust survivors. I found my interviewees by posting public announcements in 'third generation' Facebook groups, sending individual electronic messages to their members, using word of mouth, and posting a message on the Bronfman Youth Fellowships listserv.[26] While some responded to my public postings, I obtained the majority of participants by individual message replies. As an interviewer, I sought to create a safe space for subjects to openly explore aspects of what it means to them to be HSG, American and male. I did this by providing extensive written information about my project before speaking, and shared my own position as an HSG graduate student researching gender and post-Holocaust positioning. With the exception of one interview conducted in person and six conducted in typed real-time Internet correspondence, I conducted all interviews through Skype. Real names are used only where permission was explicitly granted. What follows is a discussion of several interviews that illuminate tensions and negotiations of particular interest.

Findings and Discussion

Most subjects reported generally secure, happy and healthy positions. Those who did exhibit or report psychological distress in their upbringings and current personalities usually indicated anxiety, nervousness, aggressive impulses, frustration, grief or early developmental struggles.[27] The distinctions I found were not along the lines of 'normal' versus 'pathological', but rather along the lines of different narratives about how a lived experience of post-Holocaust legacy enhanced or troubled personal positioning in the here-and-now as a Jewish American man. Responses ranged from feeling that the Holocaust had no effect on identity to experiencing it as the central most important factor for positioning oneself. Jonathan, for example, calls his Holocaust heritage 'probably the most important part of my life' and insists that 'it wasn't something engrained in me; it's something that I wanted, that I brought out of myself, and that I sought after'. The majority considered Holocaust heritage a significant part of who they feel themselves to be. Most interviewees related to the

Holocaust on an embodied, emotional level, while five described an exclusively intellectual relationship with their heritage. Often the former correlated with lifelong conscious identification with the Holocaust, the latter with interest beginning in adulthood, coinciding with mature values and interests, and quests for meaning in the world. Regardless of these differences, most grandsons were firm about the pride, strength and benefits derived from their Holocaust heritage. Several attributed feelings of personal gratitude and values of persistence, ambition, family closeness, Jewish communal responsibility, and cautiousness to their heritage. A number of them, however, articulated ambivalence or mixed feelings about their heritage as both important and distressing. And a minority experienced their Holocaust heritage as primarily an obstacle or a debilitating force in their lives.

Important factors related to differences across HSG experience included: the manner in which the Holocaust was conveyed to the grandson, the psychological security and emotional sensitivity of the grandson, the grandson's sense of sociocultural belonging, and the grandson's comfort level with his own definition of masculinity. Those who related to their heritage more dispassionately or intellectually often recall a calmly articulated Holocaust education with less emotional salience or sensitivity. Conversely, most of those grandsons who related to the Holocaust more emotionally remembered feeling sensitive to childhood internalization of the Holocaust and articulated a relationship to their heritage that spotlighted anxiety, defensive aggression, or sometimes a sustained emotional salience or personal resonance, creativity or expressiveness.

A minority who struggled with masculinity and/or felt rootless or marginal in their sociocultural context identified with the uprootedness, alienation and psychological crisis of their grandparents' traumas. Necessitating a process of working-through, these feelings ranged from those of overwhelming grief to feelings of personal endangerment. Danny Ghitis, a 29-year-old freelance photographer and HSG who grew up with immigrant parents who frequently relocated, recalls that he grew up feeling like 'an endangered species' and almost as if he were himself a survivor:

> I've always felt like I've had an identity crisis, not feeling like I belong in one place or another, sort of, you know, floating along, which is kind of what has led to my career with constant exploration of culture and my own identity through other people's identities, always ... moving around, curious, asking questions, unsatisfied, and that definitely comes from moving around a lot while I was developing ... I was moving every few years ... this constant transition ... I got used

> to that momentum. And when I was finally in one place, I never really felt completely grounded in that spot … having immigrant parents, speaking a different language at home, and also having half my family in Israel.

Identity crises or not, many interviewees perceived their third-generation position as a kind of rank or marking, and they responded to that marking with mixed reactions. Some clung to the privilege, difference or exceptional quality of this identity. Jonathan admits feeling part of 'an elite group, a special group, as opposed to the other [Jewish] kids who didn't have grandparents who were survivors'. Joseph uses the terms of badge markings to express how he feels especially unique as a gay HSG:

> if you're gay, you had a pink triangle. And if you were a – a gay Jew, you had … two pink triangles making a Star of David. And I remember that – seeing that as the ultimate … for a Nazi, I feel like they got points, in regards to killing Jews and things like this … getting a gay Jew was, like, a high point … So I feel like I'm a – sort of like a rare breed … that adds to the 'one in a million' – the special feeling that I feel.

A considerable number of HSG differentiated themselves from American Jewish mentalities. Gary admits having a more 'cynical' and ambitious outlook than most of his friends due to family stories of losing everything. These distinctions between HSG and non-HSG American Jews appeared often around clashes with romantic partners. Gary relays that his non-HSG fiancée's ideas about their future children's discipline and education are too lax for his taste which is 'much more serious' than hers. Similarly, Evan Kleinman, whose minority status as an HSG makes him not 'feel white', explains:

> even my fiancée, who's … Jewish, but not of Holocaust survivors … I – I notice a difference in her family and I notice a difference, culturally, in manner. Like it's a different mentality … I've observed this in my father, my uncle, my aunt … You're careful … you don't ever want to complain about something, because what right do you have to complain … to not be wasteful … and you have to watch your back.

Historically, traits of self-consciousness, guilt, anxiety and seriousness are certainly not exclusive to families of Holocaust survivors. In the popular imagination of late twentieth-century America, these traits, personified by Woody Allen and other famous Jewish icons, may have seemed quintessentially Jewish-American. Considering that most twenty-first-century Jewish representations, however, are normalized and even fashionable by American standards, I would suggest that these anxious and destabilizing traits do not characterize Jewishness per se, but proximity to experiences of discrimination and displacement. While Gary and Evan feel those experiences from living grandparents and the marks left on their own parents, their Jewish fiancées stand presumably far from persecution and immigration, let alone the Holocaust.

Because of this kind of historical distance within the larger Jewish American atmosphere, as well as the distance of two generations from the Holocaust, Eva Fogelman and others have claimed that American HSG grow up without internalizing antisemitism in the ways their parents did as HSO. Yet several of my interviewees do feel sensitive to threats against them as Jews. Evan Kleinman describes an incident of being called a 'dirty Jew' by a middle-school bully. Josh shares a similar position: 'I have perceived people to have little bits of antisemitism. You know, the way they talked about Israel, the way that they question me about things, and it was a hot topic for me.' Isaac, a modern Orthodox HSG, takes cues from his European HSO father:

> he's the kind of guy that every single movie he goes out and sees is antisemitic. He'll find a way to make it antisemitic ... and it's rubbed off on me, big-time ... I can see most things as antisemitic. And then I – I, uh, I see anything that is antisemitic and I freak out. I – I mean, I'm ready to run away into a woods and hide, you know. Because that's what I – I learned growing up.

One theme in some HSO testimonies has been a feeling of being cheated of healthy parental guidance, of lacking a strong basis for cultivating their own identities. In Helen Epstein's pioneer study, HSO interviewee Al thinks only in terms of 'my mother', not 'my parents', as his traumatized father was for him a passive and absent source of shame. Al says: 'He was completely out of it and I felt myself becoming the same way. I didn't know how to act as a man. It was almost impossible for me to make friends with boys and, later on, with men. I had no concept of how men behaved together.'[28] For some HSG, post-traumatic legacy continues to revolve around what parents were unable to provide in early development, such as an enduring sense of emotional security or tools for mediating sensations of threat, anxiety and emotional intensity. Josh, a 30-year-old graduate student whose maternal grandparents spent the Second World War in camps and hiding, shares the following experience of feeling lost under his HSO mother's parenting, which emphasized monolithic ideals of Jewish identity and academic achievement but did not fully address more nuanced emotional skills:

> I was just so confused growing up about my emotional experience, and what I needed to do and what I didn't need to do. I knew that I needed to be smart, but that was about it, you know. I needed to be smart and Jewish, but how does that fulfill you in any way, you know. It doesn't mean anything, unless there's more to it ... being smart doesn't tell me anything about your values, your politics, your sexuality, or ... temperament, your personality ... something like 'You are smart and a Jew because of the Holocaust' doesn't give you any sort of deeper understanding of who you are.

Josh describes his mother as physically and emotionally abusive and starkly intolerant of his energies and life decisions: '[She] could be incredibly loving, and protective, and really there, but at the drop of a dime, she would just yell, and slap, and just – something would trigger her ... growing up was ... it was ... it was ... yeah. It was very, very hard with my mother.' Josh's identification with the Holocaust legacy, as filtered through his troubling relationship with his mother, produced ambivalence and guilt, and culminated in a major personal contribution to the legacy – for Josh, a psychology dissertation on relationships and attachment in HSG. However, for Josh, the Holocaust legacy remains stifling to his identity, associated with his mother's 'superficial' takeaway messages, which, as discussed above, he perceived as obstacles, rather than reinforcement, for self-actualization: 'You will be a Jew because your grandparents survived the Holocaust. You will not marry a *goy*. You will ... go to Hebrew school and have your Bar Mitzvah and do all the Jewish stuff because your grandmother ... was in the Holocaust.' Josh confesses, 'I don't think I derive any pride from being a Holocaust survivor anymore, or from a family of Holocaust survivors. I see it as more of a burden than anything else.'

This degree of emotional bereavement by the parent seems less common in HSG testimonies, however, than in preceding HSO accounts. But what does appear more often in my interviews, is the struggle to negotiate family pain and its associated rigidity, mystification and stereotypes with positions of mature, nuanced and 'masculine' (instrumental, decisive, confident, resilient) positioning. HSG Kevin effectively articulates how masculine performance conflicts with the sensitive proclivities of his HSO mother, who raised him to walk on eggshells:

> my mom always told us to be really nice and, like, overly apologetic at times. And I think, like, over time, I learned that I have to toughen

> up a little bit and just make a decision ... she always wanted me to please her, and I think more recently, I've been like, 'I've just got to do what's best, you know, in my own life. I've got to do what's best for me'. Sometimes I've got to make my mom unhappy, but you know. That's what being a man is.

If successful masculine performance, even for non-HSG, involves emotional differentiation from caregivers and suppression of the vulnerable traits that elicit or require such care, an emotional investment in the Holocaust legacy or in the unfinished processing of family trauma may, like any family burden, pose a frustrating obstacle for the stark emotional separation demanded in masculine development. When imparting a traumatic heritage has the effect of threatening the masculine claim to emotional reservation, autonomy and power (which becomes especially salient in early adolescence), reactions of frustration, anger and even violence may ensue. Many HSG learn most extensively about the horrors of the Holocaust around the ages of 11 to 13, a time accompanied by boys' initiation into early manhood. Danny Ghitis, who had a 'heavy Holocaust education', recalls his Hebrew school teacher's approach: 'she told us ... the horrors of the Holocaust without any sugarcoating ... making us feel like ... we are responsible ... for carrying on the memory of the Holocaust and almost carrying on the burden of surviving'. Isaac, who learned his grandfather's traumas as frightening bedtime stories, recounts his own process of violent deflection beginning at the age of 11:

> When I started physically growing, that's when I started getting angry ... originally it was anger at the Holocaust ... probably a six- or eight-month period I remember I was just angry that the Holocaust *happened*, and I would lash out at most people about it ... but I would disguise it in 'No, I don't like this food, Mom! I hate you!' and all this stuff ... it was always in the back of my mind – how could they let them do this? How could they let the Nazis come in and kill their wives and children? How could this happen?

Isaac remembers that his male cousin who did not have Holocaust ties 'never really understood my violence ... I would snap, and I would start beating a kid up, and he wouldn't get it. He would not understand. Not many kids did, looking back on it ... none of my friends really understood what that was.' Gary, who learned his grandparents' stories as a younger boy, internalized them as accounts of fantastic might:

> My grandfather fought with the partisans. And my grandmother, even though she was a woman back in those days she still played a part in fighting the Nazis. Just hearing stories about how she would create train bombs to blow up the tracks so the Nazis couldn't transport Jews, you know my grandfather had white dots on his body from where he was shot, running away ... sounds kind of like heroes to me. So when all these stories were handed down to me as a young boy I immediately grabbed interest, because I was like 'oh my God, this is like a superhero story'.

Gary's process of integrating these treasured 'superhero' stories into his own life as a Jewish American man and corporate lawyer involved demystifying those stories but maintaining their impact on his performance of strength and endurance:

> today it's a lot more realistic than something like superheroes ... As I got older I appreciated more exactly what was involved with being a Holocaust survivor and what my grandparents had to endure. This is going to sound crazy, but sometimes when I'm having really trying times in my life, or when I'm really stressed out, I always think back like 'this is nothing; this is nothing compared to what my grandparents went through,' and that just calms me down. It gives me strength.

Jonathan links his desire to serve in the Israel Defense Forces with his grandfather's story of losing seven younger siblings and both parents to the Nazis:

> The problem was that there was no state of Israel, no country with a strong Jewish identity ... with an army ... If you could have told him at that time that 'in sixty, seventy years from now, your grandson is going to be on the front lines as an infantryman in the modern Jewish army,' you know, I think that's an unbelievable thing. And I definitely want to take a part in it.

His identification with his grandfather's narrative over that of his grandmother, to whose stories he had closer access, perhaps reflects the kind of masculine identification Jonathan seeks from his family history.

As these accounts demonstrate, a framework of masculinity norms and ideals may both ground HSG in feelings of pride and empowerment, as well as generate defensiveness or aggression. It also may obscure or limit those personally meaningful narratives that do not contribute to ideals of masculine empowerment. A great-nephew of the famed Bielski partisan brothers shares with me that he distances himself from his family's heroic narrative specifically because of the macho revenge fantasies it invites and because of the way it overshadows the experience of his grandmother, the Bielski partisans' sister, who spent the war hiding in various locations. He explains that, while the Bielski partisans' story is 'a beautiful, powerful, and incredibly inspiring story',

> [it] isn't actually my grandma's story, and I've always had a little bit of a grudge that my grandma's story was obscured (by no one's fault ... by no means the fault of the brothers) ... it was downplayed ... everyone wanted to talk about the heroism ... [My grandmother] went off on her own. She was 16 years old and found a way, hiding in various places ... she lived out the war essentially on her own, not with the partisans ... As I was maturing and becoming more self-aware, young adult, I became much closer with [her] ... We would do Sunday brunches, and she would do borscht and cook all these Eastern European foods, and she lived very close to us, so I saw [her] all the time ... She died [in] my senior year of high school.

Testifying to the power of family mythology, he says that his relatives repeatedly tell the stories of his great-uncle Zus Bielski's violence against Nazis, and 'it gets more elaborate at each retelling'. For this great-nephew, 'the heroism becomes too much of a lurid fascination, that people want to know [about] Jews killing Nazis, you know, *Inglorious Basterds*,[29] that type of mentality. But I don't think that's the proper reaction to the Bielski story.' Rather, what he values is the moral strength modelled by Tuvia Bielski, whose character, played by Daniel Craig in the feature film *Defiance* (2008), says 'I'd rather save one old Jewish woman than kill ten German soldiers.'

When Holocaust legacy is experienced as a call to masculine positioning and resilience, it may also increase inner tensions for those males already struggling with masculinity pressures on a personal level. Unlike Isaac, whose initial feeling of powerlessness led him to aggression, Simon, a gentle HSG who grew up averse to sports and valuing emotional openness, felt that his grandparents' survival was an added pressure on him to embody those unwanted parts of masculine positioning. He states that although the legacy sometimes 'helps me to feel proud of my identity and to see that I have – or that I *should* have – the capacity to be resilient', it is sometimes 'a burdensome weight that goes against my inner voice, so that can make it difficult to live as my individual self and identify as myself'. Simon reflects on the stereotypically masculine behaviour required to survive, even after the war. His maternal grandparents 'had more of a need to be 'masculine' ... to hunt out [a] living'. He shares that his grandparents' and HSO mother's 'emotion-hiding' and 'stiff mouth' to ward off tears sent him a message about taming emotion with strength. He describes the dissonance of being a gentle, creative person under a tough survivor grandfather:

> When I think of my Papa ... I think of his demeanor and persona being pretty integral to his survival ... a tough village boy who can be secretive and fend for himself very independently and fight his way through ... I don't feel like him ... It's a problem in a certain way. I don't want it to be a problem. It's a problem on an *internal* level, because since he valued that toughness ('When I was a kid, you needed to know how to *fight*') ... Part of me wants to say, 'Yeah, but Papa, I don't *need* to know how to fight.' And I want to believe that, but there's part of me that doesn't, because I respect him, and I respect what that attitude and that toughness did for him. [He] had to fight his way over to America. And he had to fight his way when living in Israel, because he was in the army. And he had to struggle for making a living for his family in America when they came here. And my – my father did not grow up with a – such a privileged life either ... So, for me to grow up with this kind of stability and, like ... the kind of love that I was given – at least the amount of love ... It gives me ... Like, I don't have that sense of need to be that classic male, I guess ... There's – there's the pressure for it, but, like, it's almost more like in theory. Like in theory, you're a young man ... These are the examples in your family that you have to go from, but they are coming from a very different place. ... I have, sort of ongoing resentment ... having to do with what my grandfather and father did. Which is to ... work hard and build a family ... Yeah, I'm trying to figure that out ... I think it's because ... like, despite the pride that they ... seem ... to ... carry around ... their – their masculinity ... that there is – that they're, like, missing something. That they're, like, missing the sensitivity and ... have blinders on to, like, a way of living and thinking that I see as, like, inherent to myself.

The model Simon feels pressured to inherit feels anachronistic to him – a masculine resolution at odds with his own values yet intertwined with his understanding of who he is and where he comes from.

Among other interviewees who experience their Holocaust heritage as more emotional than intellectual, Simon feels it on a bodily level: 'I think it translates into fear for me in some ways that I can't even explain ... That ... you know, just, like, kind of a bodily level sometimes.' He perceives related anxieties, especially in the area of his mouth and jaw:

> There are times when I see that come out in my mother and I will see her mouth tighten up in similar ways [to my grandmother]. Sometimes I wonder if my mother knows that that's happening. Just, you know, even little instances … I've experienced a lot of anxiety in the past few years. And I'll find that I'm – I – I'll have – I'll, like, lose control of my jaw in a sense and start shaking. And I think of my mother and Nana when I have that feeling. You know, I associate it with … with some, like – there's a feeling of insecurity that I think I didn't know about my grandmother having.

Physical embodiment of post-Holocaust anxieties appeared also in issues related to food and fitness. Gary and Evan both credit their grandparents' stories of physical suffering and endurance as motivating factors for their own bodily fitness and athletic persistence. The pressure to eat much and waste little was also associated with inherited mentalities. Brian's grandmother 'always got angry when there was food left on the plate'. Simon tells of his grandparents, who wanted to avoid heavy psychological burdens: 'they just want to give me cookies and have things be nice for me … I was given a lot of … cookies. [Laughs] And really, like, a lot of desserts and food. Like, being given lots of food.' He lists the pressure to eat enough as one of the effects of his Holocaust heritage. According to Gary's grandparents,

> if you don't have something in your mouth there's something wrong with you … everything was based around food in my family … so if you weren't like ten pounds overweight, there was something wrong with you. Like the way my dad used food and eating … at a young age, I realized, this is so *silly*. I'm not *hungry*. Why am I eating just because Grandma's telling me to eat? Like I can only eat so much.

Chaim, aged 27, recounts a similar dynamic in his family:

> my father, growing up in a family of – of survivors, they were forced – almost forced to eat. My – my grandfather was a butcher, and his wife just cooked and cooked and she was a Hungarian cook. And everyone had to eat incredible amounts, just because maybe tomorrow, there wouldn't be food. Obviously, that was absurd, but that's how they grew up. And subsequently, that's kind of how I grew up … needless to say, all of my aunts and uncles and my father were all … overweight … Maybe my uncle is even obese, I don't know. But … this is clearly connected. Like, there's no, you know, coincidence … The third generation – some of them are overweight. Not all of them.

Isaac also tells me that his HSO father 'eats very, very quickly. And whenever you ask him, "yo, Abba, why do you eat so fast?", he says, he looks you right in the eye, and says, "I wanna finish before the pogroms come." And yeah, he's probably kidding, but not all the way kidding, you know what I mean?'

The trope of physical embodiment merges with an earlier-discussed trope of being marked, and reaches new extremes in a provocative, recent phenomenon in Israel. An article by Jodi Rudoren in *The New York Times* presents HSO and HSG who obtain tattoos of the number worn on the arms of their survivor (grand)parents from the camps. Reactions of the survivors within these families are mixed, but the point seems to be an expression of embodied memory, which intimately ties the HSO or HSG to the survivor. Ayal Gelles, who wears his grandfather's number, explains that the tattoo is a constant reminder to call his grandfather. Oded Rebak, an HSO, who obtained his mother's tattoo for himself and his adult son, tells how his mother cried with him when she saw the tattoo, and he told her, 'you're always with me'.[30] For these HSG, personal closeness with and investment in their grandparents necessitates keeping the Holocaust's felt legacy of endangerment, loss and pain salient and remembered.

American HSG ward off feelings of vulnerability by identifying more with American liberators than with Jewish victims, by focusing on family strength or heroism, or by what Dominick LaCapra calls 'working-through',[31] the process of integrating contradictory past and present meanings through therapeutic narration or artistic creation. HSG working-through continues to employ creative investments in the traumas and losses, but, as Gerd Bayer argues, it departs from the original generation of postmemory in its future-oriented attempt to integrate the horrors of the past into a comprehensive approach to contemporary reality as nuanced, subjective and in perpetual motion.[32] In other words, HSG working-through incorporates new levels of individualism and wariness toward definitive or knowable truths.

Narrative, documentary or artistic outlets may channel inner conflicts and anxieties into feelings of instrumentality, authorial confidence, and cohesion. Chaim takes on the role of family historian, doing archival research to assemble a family website with photographs and histories. Evan Kleinman's documentary *We Are Still Here* (2011, wearestillheremovie.com) returns to the sites of his grandparents' losses to reaffirm his place within his family and fill the instrumental role of laying a gravestone for his great uncle. The takeaway message of Kleinman's film, as he narrates it, maintains the grief and rupture of his family past while proposing a drive for future-oriented creativity in its memory:

> I have learned that it's okay to cry about what they went through, but tears are not enough. We have to take power from these stories. If the phrase 'never again' holds any bearing, then it's up to us here today to take all the pain and all the suffering and use it as motivation to do something great. How else do you let the world know that you are still here?

In his interview with me, Kleinman offers that 'living happy' is 'the best revenge'.

Danny Ghitis tackles a somewhat related inner conflict in his photography project *Land of Os*,[33] comprised of thirty images of contemporary life in Oświęcim, the Polish town in which the remains of Auschwitz stand. Ghitis approached this project, in part, to demystify the horrors of Auschwitz hanging over him. Learning about the atrocities in an emotionally charged childhood context, he had

> developed assumptions about Germany, about Poland, about Eastern Europe, about the places where my ancestors came from, and what people are like now … I remember my mother saying, you know, some things are just black and white. You just can't – those people just don't deserve our respect. And … at the time, I was like, yeah … Who are these people to, you know, to live in – in such a place, and continue living normally. It should be … preserved only as a memorial. And after having gone, I realized that she was very much wrong.

With titles like 'Parking Lot at Birkenau', 'Watching Friends Play', 'Fence between Museum and Apartments' and 'Punk Rocker at Auschwitz', he offers a vision in which post-traumatic identification with the site of loss can coexist and negotiate with alternative perspectives, evolutions and shades of grey. Ghitis describes his point of entry as follows in his artist's statement: 'Most travelers are unaware Auschwitz is in an old Polish town called Oświęcim. Those who do notice – a nearby shopping mall, high school sweethearts holding hands, nicely-dressed families headed to church – are faced with an impossible question: how can life exist in the aftermath of such overwhelming evil?'[34] Highly saturated clothing, fire, balloons and flowers negotiate with the greys and browns of camp remains and barren landscape in Ghitis's photos. Visual symbols of danger and antisemitism evaporate as quickly as they suggest themselves. In 'Controlled Burn near Birkenau', the first photograph of the series, a line of blazing orange flames parallels the winter horizon of wooden barracks and bare trees. A man stands in the centre of the frame, his head bent, face in hand; he seems in despair, his agonized gesture fitting expectations of what it means to visit a concentration camp. Yet one quickly notices a figure bent in shadow on the periphery of the frame, purposefully patting a rake against the controlled flames. The central figure is no longer a pained witness but a neutral agricultural labourer, perhaps shielding his eyes from the smoke or wiping sweat from a tired brow. The vibrant flames now refuse to connote the destruction we seek in images of the concentration camp; they are flames of productivity, of present vitality. Like an optical illusion, the image hums, wavering between the traumatic reality we expect to find in an Auschwitz photograph and the living, sometimes unremarkable, human reality that the camera finds there.

Conclusion

Though HSG may, as a group, be 'more American' than their parents and grandparents, have more resources and more confidently pursue causes of social justice, attention to subjectivity reveals that many of these grandchildren continue to harbour strong identifications with their grandparents' Holocaust survival and feel personally defined, to varying extents, by those identifications. Those interviewees who described this subtle inner force did so with adjectives such as 'cynical', 'different', 'intense', 'serious', 'special' and 'nervous', differentiating themselves from non-HSG peers, even while simultaneously describing their external optimism, popularity, success and confidence. The 'values, worldview, family interaction and love' received by HSG from their parents and grandparents are not without the arresting complexities of post-traumatic family dynamics, as implied by the rosy pictures that Fogelman and others paint of the third generation. To be sure, post-traumatic dynamics in a twice-removed generation depend on personal disposition and environmental factors. Yet it remains evident that embodied post-traumatic trends and fierce identifications with family traumas persist as defining personal characteristics in some survivors' descendants.

Interviewees expressed greater security in their HSG identities when they were able to accomplish a sense of perceived coherence, to imagine and articulate themselves as cohesive subjects in a tangible and empowering history, rather than a paradoxical, disarming legacy.[35] Sometimes this was accomplished by an artistic project – Danny Ghitis made the present less rigid and threatening for himself; Evan Kleinman made room for his own active place in relation to his grandparents and their traumas. Others found coherence in fashioning themselves as strong protectors, family men, fighters, Jewish community activists and Zionists. Sociocultural marginality, which sustains greater feelings of difference or endangerment, as well as personal sensitivity leave some HSG vulnerable to internalizing the larger-than-life story defining their family legacy in ways comparable to Hirsch's postmemory. Most, however, experience their legacy as a source of pride with accompanying pressures or contradictions to be worked through below the surface, variably beneficial and challenging to contemporary life.

This fall, I happened to meet with an undergraduate who, tears welling in his eyes, recounted the centrality of his grandfather's survival to his own sense of self. His grandfather had fought with the Bielski partisans and had been forced to stop learning Torah at the age of 13, the very age at which this student began studying for his Bar Mitzvah. He expressed a fear shared by many: that the Holocaust will become like the disembodied massacres of which we read in history textbooks, no longer personally or emotionally meaningful to contemporaries. As HSG, the last generation to know survivors at first-hand, come of age, this fear remains pressing and valid. But the devotion that these young adults feel toward their family Holocaust legacies, as well as the creativity and energy with which HSG respond to them, are generating meaningful and undeniable legacies of their own.

NOTES

1. E. Fogelman, 'Third Generation Descendents of Holocaust Survivors and the Future of Remembering', *Jewcy.com*, 1 May 2008, http://www.jewcy.com/religion-and-beliefs/third_generation_descendents_holocaust_survivors_and_future_remembering.
2. I take this acronym, which emphasizes the individual rather than his or her collective generation, from M. Scharf, 'Long-Term Effects of Trauma: Psychosocial Functioning of the Second Generation of Holocaust Survivors', *Development and Psychopathology*, 19 (2007), pp. 603–22. I also use her acronym HSO (Holocaust survivors' offspring) for children of survivors.
3. One of my interviewees in this chapter, a great-nephew of the Bielski brother partisans, even saw his family history become a Hollywood production starring Daniel Craig in 2008 (*Defiance*).
4. J. Nathan-Kazis, 'Can Holocaust Trauma Affect "Third Generation"? Studies Debate Impact on Grandchildren of Survivors', *Jewish Daily Forward*, 5 September 2012, http://forward.com/articles/162030/can-holocaust-trauma-affect-third-generation/?p=all.
5. Portions of this article appear in earlier versions within Golan Moskowitz, 'Grandsons Who Remember: Intersections of Holocaust Heritage and Contemporary Male Positioning' (unpublished MA Thesis, Brandeis University, Waltham, MA 2012). Research was funded by the Tauber Institute for the Study of European Jewry and the Rena Olshanksy Grant for Research on Jewish Family Life.
6. Nathan-Kazis, 'Can Holocaust Trauma Affect "Third Generation"?'
7. J. Chaitin, 'Issues and Interpersonal Values among Three Generations in Families of Holocaust Survivors', *Journal of Social and Personal Relationships*, 19, 3 (2002), pp. 379–402.
8. M. Scharf and O. Mayseless, 'Disorganizing Experiences in Second- and Third-Generation Holocaust Survivors', *Qualitative Health Research*, 21, 11 (2011), pp.1539–53.
9. Ibid.
10. C. Caruth, *Unclaimed Experience: Trauma, Narrative, and History* (Baltimore, MD: Johns Hopkins University Press, 1996), p.62.
11. R.W. Connell, *Masculinities* (Berkeley, CA: University of California Press, 2005).

12. B. Anderson, *Imagined Communities: Reflections on the Origin and Spread of Nationalism* (New York: Verso, 1991). Anderson's term 'imagined communities' refers to those personal and cultural elements that create feelings of specifically national belonging.
13. J. J. Arnett, *Emerging Adulthood: The Winding Road from the Late Teens through the Twenties* (Oxford and New York: Oxford University Press, 2004). Arnett argues for the recognition of a new life stage called 'emerging adulthood', reflected in the flux and indecision of Americans between ages 18 and 29.
14. J. Butler, *Bodies That Matter* (London and New York: Taylor & Francis, 2011); J. Herbert Gans, 'Symbolic Ethnicity: The Future of Ethnic Groups and Cultures in America', *Ethnic and Racial Studies*, 2, 1 (1979), pp.1–20.
15. M. Hirsch, *Family Frames: Photography, Narrative, and Postmemory* (Cambridge, MA: Harvard University Press, 1997).
16. M. Hirsch, 'The Generation of Postmemory', *Poetics Today* 29, 1 (2008), p.107.
17. Connell, *Masculinities*, pp.71–6.
18. S. J. Ducat, *The Wimp Factor* (Boston, MA: Beacon Press Books, 2004).
19. Connell, *Masculinities*, p.79.
20. L. Fuchs, *Beyond Patriarchy: Jewish Fathers and Families* (Hanover, NH: Brandeis University Press, 2000).
21. See M. F. Jacobson, *Whiteness of a Different Color: European Immigrants and the Alchemy of Race* (Cambridge, MA: Harvard University Press, 1999); K. Brodkin, *How Jews Became White Folks and What that Says About Race in America* (New Brunswick, NJ: Rutgers University Press, 1998); and S. B. Fishman and D. Parmer, *Matrilineal Ascent/ Patrilineal Descent: The Gender Imbalance in American Jewish Life* (Waltham, MA: Cohen Center for Modern Jewish Studies at Brandeis University and Hadassah-Brandeis Institute, 2008).
22. Connell, *Masculinities*, p.75.
23. J. Antler, *You Never Call! You Never Write! A History of the Jewish Mother* (Oxford: Oxford University Press, 2007).
24. J. Lurie-Beck, 'The Differential Impact of Holocaust Trauma Across Three Generations' (unpublished PhD dissertation, School of Psychology and Counseling, Queensland University of Technology, 2007).
25. Connell, *Masculinities*, p.81.
26. The Bronfman Youth Fellowships (BYFI), founded in 1987, is a network offering fellowships for leadership development and advanced Jewish education for about 1,000 Jewish Israeli and American high-school juniors, who become part of a lifelong alumni community emphasizing Jewish text study, pluralistic discourse, and social responsibility. http://www.bronfman.org
27. These reports cannot be generalized or attributed to post-Holocaust experience, but are worth noting. Brian, aged 18, was diagnosed in elementary school with generalized anxiety disorder and Tourette's after suffering from enduring fears of robbers and outside danger. Josh, aged 30, struggled with anxiety and an abusive HSO mother. Greg, aged 34, who grew up with a single HSO mother, could not speak until he reached the age of 5, with the help of therapy. Danny Ghitis, aged 29, suffered nightmares and anxiety. Evan Kleinman, aged 29, felt an enduring 'black cloud' of grief and powerlessness after what he describes as a traumatizing exposure to graphic Holocaust history. Simon, aged 27, lists anxiety and difficulty with his family's emotional repression. Seth, aged 26, and Isaac, aged 21, describe violent outbursts in relation to their Jewish identities in the face of perceived antisemitism.
28. H. Epstein, *Children of the Holocaust* (New York: Penguin Books, 1979), p.225.
29. A 2009 feature film by Quentin Tarantino in which a group of Jewish American soldiers, under the command of a lieutenant played by Brad Pitt, commit brutality against Nazis during the Second World War in occupied France in order to spread fear among the Third Reich.
30. J. Rudoren, 'Proudly Bearing Elders' Scars, Their Skin Says "Never Forget"', *The New York Times*, 30 September 2012, http://www.nytimes.com/2012/10/01/world/middleeast/with-tattoos-young-israelis-bear-holocaust-scars-of-relatives.html.
31. D. LaCapra, ' "Acting-Out" and "Working-Through" Trauma', interview excerpt, 9 June 1998, *YadVashem.org*, http://www1.yadvashem.org/odot_pdf/Microsoft%20Word%20-%203646.pdf.

32. G. Bayer, 'After Postmemory: Holocaust Cinema and the Third Generation', *Shofar*, 28, 4 (2010), pp.116–32.
33. D. Ghitis, 'Land of Os', *DannyGhitis.com*.
34. Ibid.
35. For the theoretical relationship between discursive positioning and cohesive subjectivity, see B. Davies and R. Harre, 'Positioning: The Discursive Production of Selves', *Social Behaviour*, 20, 1 (1990), pp.43–63.

'But what about our Persian rugs?' Inventing a Family History

DALIT KAPLAN

Trying to Forget

One summer evening, Bronia's father came home with an announcement. 'I have tickets and visas for us all to go to America.'

'But what about our Persian rugs?' Bronia's mother exclaimed. 'I'm not leaving the rugs behind!'

So they forfeited their tickets and visas, and stayed in their elegant upper-middle-class home in Kraków, with their servants, their fine china, their crystal glass sets, their gilded Louis XIV furniture and their Persian rugs. The year was 1939.

* * *

My maternal and paternal grandparents were part of a wave of Jewish refugees who resettled in Melbourne immediately after the Second World War. All of my childhood friends were, like me, grandchildren of Holocaust survivors. Until my late teens, I assumed that every Jew over the age of 60 had a thick Yiddish accent, numbers tattooed on their forearms, and had survived a genocide. I often joke that my community was comprised almost exclusively of people who grew up in the same shtetl in Poland, were deported to the same barracks in Auschwitz and finally settled in the same suburb in Melbourne.

My maternal grandmother, 'Nana', and grandfather, 'Nana-Zeyde', were born in Kraków and Lodz respectively. They were proud to come from large, developed cities boasting factories, theatres, universities and a flourishing middle class. As young people, their worlds bustled with the creativity of Yiddish theatre, the revolutionary spirit of Jewish youth movements and the excitement of new possibilities as Jews in big cities had begun to enjoy greater acceptance in wider Polish society. My paternal grandfather, 'Bube-Zeyde', and grandmother, 'Bube', were from Volomin and Chelm respectively – two predominantly Jewish towns, or *shtetlekh*. Theirs was a world with less freedom and opportunity. Anti-Semitic attacks and discrimination were part of daily life, as were poverty and hunger. But their lives were rich with family and community, and their coming of age was also marked by the tension between tradition and modernity that characterized Eastern European Jewry during the early twentieth century.

In the eyes of Australians, the similarities between these two couples far outnumbered their differences. They spoke the same strange languages, ate the same heavy Eastern European foods and had all left behind a ravaged continent with nothing but the clothes on their backs. But the two couples perceived each other to be from fundamentally different worlds, which led to much friction. My Nana, in particular, ridiculed my paternal grandparents for being unsophisticated 'small town Jews', while my Bube-Zeyde derided my maternal grandparents' snobbery and affectedness. Though all the Jewish

3. Moshe Kaplan (born 1920 in Volomin, Poland; died 2015 in Melbourne, Australia), Dalit Kaplan's paternal grandfather, together with his son, the author's father, Albert Kaplan at her wedding in 2010. Copyright/ permission granted by Kaplan family.

communities of their big cities and small towns had been utterly decimated, their contempt for one another's pedigree endured for decades.

* * *

Shortly after Bronia's family forfeited the tickets and visas, the Germans invaded Poland. Bronia was forced to discontinue her studies at an elite private girls' school and engage in slave labour for the occupying German army. Soon after that, her family was ordered to move into a single room in a cramped apartment in Kraków's Jewish ghetto, leaving behind their elegant upper-middle-class home, their servants, their fine china, their crystal glass sets, their gilded Louis XIV furniture and their Persian rugs.

Life was insufferable in the ghetto. Bronia's younger sister died of typhus. As rumours of what awaited Jews in the concentration camps began to circulate, Bronia's parents desperately pursued all their connections in Polish high society to find a way out. They eventually secured fake papers which would enable them to flee to Hungary. However, they obtained papers only for themselves – not for Bronia. In 1940 they fled, leaving behind their 18-year-old daughter. Bronia was soon sent to the concentration camps, alone, among the other deportees.

* * *

Sitting at her kitchen table with me, her granddaughter and my Nana-Zeyde, Heniek, Bronia laid out the details of her parents' escape from the Nazis during the Second World War over tea and biscuits.[1] Her eyes were glazed over and vacant, and she barked out short, staccato sentences between shallow breaths. She was at the terrifying early stages of dementia, and – a smoker for sixty years – had severe emphysema.

'Do you know why they left you behind, Nana?' I prodded.

She said nothing.

Nana-Zeyde pushed her further. A survivor himself, he was no stranger to the desperate and cowardly measures people took to save their own lives. However, Nana-Zeyde had selflessly given his own hiding place to his brother, sister-in-law and nephew, so that they might have a better chance of survival. He and his first wife were deported to Auschwitz. He survived; his wife did not. Now, decades later in Melbourne, he was deeply troubled by his parents-in-laws' decision to abandon their child while saving their own skins.

'I cannot understand why a parent would leave their child in the ghetto and escape to Hungary to save their own lives. You don't know why they left you?'

4. Hanina Glasman (born 1914 in Lodz, Poland; died in Melbourne, Australia 2013) and Bronia Glasman (born 1921 in Krakow, Poland; died 2012 in Melbourne, Australia), in Germany just before they married, 1946. Copyright/permission granted by Kaplan family.

5. Hanina and Bronia at a Mother's Day lunch in Australia in the early 1990s. Copyright/permission granted by Kaplan family.

'I don't know!' Bronia was visibly flustered. 'Please. I don't want to think about it.'

So we changed the topic, and sipped our tea.

* * *

The destruction of European Jewry and the later Antipodean exile pervaded every aspect of Jewish communal life as I grew up. While many survivors, such as my grandparents, spoke rarely about their war experiences with their own children, once those children – my parents' generation – were old enough to read history books, many began to ask questions. Where were all their uncles and aunts? Why didn't they have cousins? Why did their parents leave Poland? Today, communal publications are filled with editorials, news items and letters to the editor dealing with the subject of the Holocaust and Jewish survival. Jewish schools designate disproportionately large amounts of their curricula for Holocaust education. One of my earliest memories is seeing photographs of pits filled with corpses in concentration camps on display in a makeshift Holocaust exhibition at my school's library. I was six years old.

No community debate takes place without someone invoking the Holocaust. The Holocaust serves as the justification for everything: why we should only marry Jews, why we should become doctors or lawyers, why we should never throw away food, why we must never criticize Israel ...

As a teenager and young adult, I found this communal obsession suffocating. I assiduously avoided any courses at high school and university that dealt with the Holocaust. I did not read the canonical Holocaust literature of Eli Wiesel or Primo Levi, or see Holocaust film classics, such as *Schindler's List*. I deliberately tuned out when Holocaust survivors were invited to speak about their experiences at school assemblies, and on the rare occasion that one of my grandparents mentioned the war years, I would quickly change the subject. As I grew older and developed a stronger political consciousness, I would claim that my community's preoccupation with the Holocaust was narcissistic, and argued that our time and energies would be better spent focusing on preventing the persecution of others. Chinese sweatshop workers. Tibetan monks. Indigenous Australians. Palestinians.

Naturally, I made many enemies in the community. Eventually, I took my leave altogether, and sought to make a new home among the secular Australian left. To my new gentile friends, I would coolly describe myself as 'an Australian with Jewish background', downplaying the centrality of my ethnic and cultural heritage and pretending that I had a 'normal' Australian upbringing replete with Vegemite, lamingtons (a traditional Australian dessert cake), beach holidays and no genocide. But this charade was short-lived. After a few failed romances with Anglo-Australians, around whom I always felt that I was too neurotic and overbearing, I decided to seek out other Jewish communities for whom the Holocaust was not so central.

This led me to the United States, home to over six million Jews, myriad Jewish identities, political allegiances and customs. Most were as American as apple pie and could trace their roots in the United States back for several generations. I was eager to meet young Jews who came from 'normal' families, free of Holocaust-induced neuroses about food, or showering with the door open, and the obsessive preoccupation with survival.

I found myself mixing in circles of young Jews, largely from assimilated families, who were attempting to return to tradition themselves. Strangely, they appeared to envy the fact that I had strong ties to the Old World, as embodied by my European grandparents. They themselves were only vaguely aware of their own family's origins before coming to the United States. They were impressed by my descriptions of my own community, which more closely resembled the uncorrupted *shtetlekh* of Eastern Europe that they had so romanticized. Beyond buried anecdotes about a distant relative who had arrived at Ellis Island early in the twentieth century, their family stories had been accidentally or deliberately forgotten, and replaced with accounts that conformed to the grand narrative of the American immigrant: the migrant who arrived with nothing, discarded the trappings of dead Europe, and found fortune in the New World.

Some of my new friends would remark that my experience of Jewish culture in Melbourne seemed much more 'authentic' than theirs; they seemed to believe that the wounds from the tragedy that marks every aspect of Jewish communal life in Melbourne had produced a richness and intensity absent from the diluted and detached cultural life in the United States.

'I'll take your tenuous connection to your heritage over my family's history of genocide and the resultant paranoia any day', I would think to myself. But to some extent, I could not help but agree. Jewish communal events in the United States, while well organized and innovative, often felt inorganic and clichéd. Where Jewish life in Australia was dominated by the past, Jewish life in the United States felt severed from the previous generations, the earlier custodians of our culture. There was no past. No sense of continuity.

What I witnessed in the United States provided me with a glimpse into the possible consequences of my own wilful disinterest in my family and community's past. It roused a desire to capture everything from that past – not only the years of the war, but information about the world that existed before the Holocaust.

Digging up the Graves

And so I joined the ranks of those who had been the subjects of my derision for so many years. I became preoccupied with my family's past and tried desperately to mine my grandparents for stories from Poland. Initially, I avoided the Holocaust, focusing my questions on life before the war. I wanted to learn about the communities before they were destroyed. But all roads lead to the Holocaust, and it was virtually impossible to avoid the events around the unravelling of my ancestors' lives.

Unfortunately, my eagerness to listen was not met with an eagerness to share. When I asked my Nana-Zeyde about his past, he responded, 'Well, I was born in Lodz, the war happened, we were liberated, we came to Australia and you know the rest!'

My Nana was more forceful in her efforts to erect walls around her past. When I announced that I was researching survival in the concentration camps, she exclaimed, 'Why do you need to write about the Holocaust? You don't need to give our enemies any ideas. Just write about racism.' She wanted the whole world to forget the Holocaust.

My Bube-Zeyde was actually eager to share stories about his past – in theory. But within two minutes of speaking, he would digress into a tirade about Israel's enemies, the rise of antisemitism and the dangers of my progressive politics. This degenerated into a heated argument and it was impossible to bring him back to the subject at hand.

There have been a few precious occasions when a fragment or an aside would unfold into an elaborate personal narrative about the Holocaust. I devoured these rare outpourings, cancelling engagements so that I could spend the rest of the afternoon with my grandparents, absorbing their history. I would scramble for my phone or other electronic device on which I could record these stories that so rarely see the light of day. In between spreadsheets, university essays and research memos, my hard drives are peppered with sound files titled 'Heniek talks about the bunker he never used, June 2009' or 'Moshe talks about the labour camps, December 2010'. I felt sneaky doing this, but justified my actions as being for the greater good: saving the soul of Jewish culture in Australia.

Eventually, the words would stop flowing. The silences between sentences would grow longer. My questions would become more verbose, but the answers would become briefer. We would reach the point at which we both knew that the day's session was over. Silence followed. I would always honour that silence, either changing the topic or leaving. It seemed cruel to force my grandparents to speak about their painful past. How can I demand that they relive the terror of the Holocaust, or that they dwell on memories of the happy communities that were destroyed?

Making Sense of the Gaping Holes

To fill these holes, I have constructed elaborate narratives in my head based on their quirks and idiosyncrasies. I have 'reverse engineered' the broad contours of my family members' lives, their relationships, their experiences and the circumstances around their survival, based on snippets of fact I have garnered and observations of their behaviour.

Based on my impressions of my Nana's insufferable vanity, I have woven a tale of betrayal and heartbreak, in which a beautiful and charismatic 18-year-old had to charm her aggressors into letting her live after being abandoned by her parents. Her father was rumoured to have been unfaithful and emotionally abusive. Her mother, desperately attempting to recapture his attention, ignored my Nana completely. I have imagined my Nana observing her father's philandering, while her mother tried to charm him into falling in love with her again. In my mind, my Nana repeated this dance with her own captors during the Holocaust, attempting to charm them so they would let her be. I imagine her hating herself for this, but drawing the lesson that in beauty lies power.

My father recently learnt that his late mother, my Bube, had another husband and child who both perished in the Holocaust, a fact that had been hidden from the family until now. Her widower, my Bube-Zeyde, is now in the early stages of dementia. He has an explosive and somewhat paranoid personality, and despite my newfound interest in the topic, I was hesitant to press him for details for fear that it may trigger an outburst. I am left with nothing but my imagination to fabricate the details of this family secret. Applying my method of reverse engineering, I have imagined the moment when this new widow, having escaped the Nazis alone, first encountered my Bube-Zeyde in a labour camp on the Russian border. He was younger and less mature than my Bube. Aching from the loss of the love of her life and the death of her only child, did she see my impulsive and energetic grandfather as a new child to care for? His larger-than-life personality always overshadowed her gentle demeanour. Did she wish to be engulfed by the whirlwind of his passion and intensity, in the hope that it would drown out the heartbreak of her loss? I imagine her first impressions of this fiery young man; the calculation she made in her head when he proposed to her. *He will protect me. He will distract me.* Ultimately, my family's story is nothing but an elaborate web of fantasy, theories and hypotheticals, hanging off tiny pegs of fact that I have managed to piece together over the years.

Today, I work as a lawyer with refugees from Africa. Most are women who have fled genocide, famine, forced marriage and persecution. Many are HIV-positive, and a return to Africa, where HIV stigma is high and treatment is inadequate, would mean certain death. Most have been subjected to genital mutilation to mark their entry into a new stage of womanhood, and continue to suffer from debilitating pain or disability as a result. Almost all have been embroiled in a situation of domestic violence, either at the hands of a tyrannical husband to whom they were forcibly married, or at the hands of a relative who objects to choices they may have made. These could be seeking an education, protesting the circumcision of a daughter or marrying someone from the wrong tribe. Some escaped their countries as hordes of soldiers and militias were rampaging, raping and hacking up members of their tribe. As their lawyer, I help them navigate the web of legal bureaucracy that is supposed to deliver some relief: asylum, welfare payments, a restraining order or work authorization. Since the law demands that applicants substantiate an appeal with a detailed outline of their experiences, I must elicit from my clients all of the painful details of their stories.

Suddenly, I am given carte blanche to uncover the memories and stories of those who have lost everything. In the name of zealous advocacy, I can ask all the personal and invasive questions I want so that I can faithfully describe every detail of the journey that brought them to my desk. The more personal, the more pain-inducing, the more I can pry. Some clients find the retelling cathartic, even empowering, because it is the first time that their stories matter. Other clients pepper their narrative with darkly humorous side-comments. A few attempt to detach themselves emotionally, as though they are speaking about a stranger. This veneer of detachment invariably dissolves at some point, often in response to a seemingly banal question, and floods of grief surface.

As I learn my clients' stories I feel that I gain a greater insight into the lives of my own grandparents and their families. The cultures, languages and political realities are worlds apart. But the raw human emotions that emerge are the same. Mourning the loss of a child, a sibling, a parent or a whole village is universal. In my mind, this glimpse into the lives of people who have had to survive such extreme circumstances gives flesh to the skeleton that is my family history.

As I put together the puzzle of their lives, my burning curiosity about my own family's puzzle recedes. I begin to feel that I can appreciate the profundity of my grandparents' suffering without needing them to relive it. I can be at peace with the limitations of my own knowledge.

How does one commemorate grief that has no shape? Jewish tradition offers models for the expression of personal and collective trauma. These models are not contingent on specific facts or a detailed narrative, but rather they create a space to acknowledge absence and loss. It is a custom to leave a wall unpainted in a new house in memory of the destruction of the Temple and the ongoing imperfection of *golus*, 'Exile'. Similarly, breaking a glass at the conclusion of a wedding ceremony reminds the participants that even at the greatest moment of joy, grief is present: grief for the absence of loved ones, grief for a broken world, grief for the grief of others. These symbolic acts both localize and focus the pain of loss.

By confronting my sadness or bewilderment at life's cruelty in those moments, I am freed to fully experience joy in all other moments. Rather than submitting to an obsession with tragedy, or effacing its presence entirely, I can make space for it through ritual and custom, and then live in the present moment with hope and wonder.

NOTES

1. After he died, my mother informed me that my grandfather actually preferred to be addressed as Hanina, the name his parents gave him. My grandmother Bronia, though, who insisted on speaking Polish rather than Yiddish in the home, always addressed my grandfather by his Polish name, Heniek.

Strength in the Shadows: Shifting Perspectives on the Integrity of Intergenerational Healing

MITCH SMOLKIN

> The essence of that which has to be realized and assimilated has been expressed so trenchantly and so plastically in poetic language by the word 'shadow' that it would be almost presumptuous not to avail oneself of this linguistic heritage.
>
> (Carl Gustav Jung[1])

> Unter dayne vayse shtern
> Shtrek tsu mir dayn vayse hant
> Mayne verter zaynen trern
> Viln ruen in dayn hant
> [Under your white starry heaven
> Offer me your pale white hand
> All my words are flowing teardrops
> I would place them in your hand]
> (Avrom Sutzkever[2])

I sang these words of the great Yiddish poet Avrom Sutzkever into the darkness of an auditorium where my late maternal grandfather, Boris Gelgor, was sitting among 400 other patrons. In my memory, I have the faint outlines of his face, although not enough to see or remember how he reacted. Before singing, I looked at him and said: 'Because you cannot tell me what you went through, I am forced to imagine.' The words of Sutzkever were a balm to my wounds, a rich narrative to fill the void that consisted of fragments and fantasies. Sutzkever wrote the piece in the Vilna Ghetto, and in my imagination it echoed what my grandfather must have felt when he learned of the deaths of his mother, Sore, his father, Chaim, his sister Reyzl and his brother Monye, and of the destruction and decimation of his community at the hands of the Germans.

The words of Sutzkever also describe the way words and teardrops meld into one when it comes to describing such horrors. For me, they also painted the picture of the intimacy required to convey such pain, and, while confronting my grandfather with my need to know, I also learned to respect that he could not tell me. As I attempt to paint a picture of the ways the shadows of the Holocaust have been cast in my life, I in no way, shape or form stand in judgment of how previous generations in my family have been able to deal with the psychological ramifications of such utter destruction. I merely offer my own assessment of what my struggle has entailed, and the rich meaning such a confrontation has enabled me to find.

The very fact that, in my case, the narratives, images and actual experiences remain mostly in the shadows betrays a limitation on the accuracy with which I can discuss the subject matter. At the same time, the degree to which we now understand unintegrated traumatic experience to remain in an almost static recurring form allows me, perhaps, to come to some conclusions about the nature and authenticity of what is being transmitted. Psychiatrist and psychoanalyst Shamai Davidson proposes that when there is silence and an aura of secretiveness around Holocaust experiences, it has the effect of prompting subsequent generations to create horrifying fantasies.[3] He suggests that the cumulative effect of psychotherapy may allow some degree of 'release from feelings of guilt, shame, blocked aggression and inhibited mourning, making it possible for parents to communicate their traumatic experiences more appropriately to their children'.[4] Without this appropriate form of communication, we are perhaps left in subsequent generations to build our own sanctuary where the tremors can be housed and understood. This is the story of my own such building, and what I have come to believe about the shadows in my midst.

Where Do You Begin, and Where Do I End?

My grandfather, Boris Gelgor, was born in Vilnius in 1918. Approximately ten years before the outbreak of the Second World War, his family moved to Molodechno, which at the time was in Poland and now is in Belarus. In 1939, the town was occupied by the Red Army, to which Boris was conscripted in 1940.[5] My grandmother, Sonia Gelgor, told me that for a time the Jewish soldiers were housed in Molodechno. The only memory that has been relayed of this period is that Boris' mother, Sore, would bring food for him to the barracks. Between 1941 and 1943, the majority of the Jews in Molodechno were murdered by the Germans in a number of killing *Aktionen*, culminating in a sign erected at the railway station that read: 'No Jews here – clean'.[6]

Boris was transferred from the army[7] and sent to work in the mines, although the location of where he was sent is unknown. I know that he ended up in the Russian city of Molotov, now called Perm, near the Ural Mountains. It was from there, after the end of the war, that he returned to Molodechno to learn that there was no one left.

I remember the moment I really confronted Boris about learning something more than the fact that he had lost everyone. We were sitting at the dining-room table at his home. I had brought maps of Eastern Europe, particularly a map showing Poland, Lithuania, Belarus and parts of Russia. He started sitting with me, uncomfortably, but at some point he got up. My grandmother noticed that he had left the table and yelled from the kitchen to tell him to go back, sit down and talk to me. He did. As we both stared at the map on the table, he started to slowly move his hand over it, back and forth. I asked him how he got to Russia: did he take a train? A bus? A smile slowly began to form on his lips, a smile that unmistakably let me know I had it all wrong. He slapped his knee. 'You walked?' I asked. And he just nodded his head as the smile slowly melted away.

He had a hard time making eye contact with me. I asked him about his family, the names of his siblings. I was sitting down, facing him. He paused; he seemed to want to tell me, but his mouth would not let him. He began to form a word on his lips and, as he did, I felt an overwhelming sensation come over me. As he struggled harder, the sensation grew until something rose in both of us. My field of vision began to fade, and then it snapped. I almost fell back with my chair from the force of whatever was happening. As I regained my composure, a voice inside let me know that I could go no further; this was the edge. He too had stopped, his arms now by his side, as he seemed to look in no direction at all.

Leading up to this watershed moment, I began to ask what right I had to keep pushing to know. I began to feel in a way that my own integrity of being was somehow connected to knowing, and yet I began to see that Boris's integrity of being was intimately tied up with his right to remain silent. There is a photo of him and me sitting together on the evening when I confronted him in public as I sang Sutzkever's words. I do not know if it was after the concert or before; time seems to have taken a backseat to that particular pilgrimage. What I do remember, and what I do see in my eyes, is anguish around my role. How far should I push? What am I doing? Is it not my right to know? What does this mean to him? Regardless of not having clarity on these issues, a form of communion was taking place. By virtue of my blind faith of wanting to know, something was happening.

Social psychologist Julia Chaitin, alluding to a study that looked at survivor families in Germany and Israel, describes protective 'bonds of silence' that are created between the second and third generations.[8] She argues that this protects the manifest content from a kind of betrayal, yet perpetuates the latent trauma. Psychologist Diana Fosha describes trauma as being related to the overwhelming experience of an event that the usual systems responsible for emotional integration cannot handle.[9] She explains that 'psychopathology is the result of an individual's response to overwhelming experience from a place of aloneness'.[10] These various phenomena related to trauma, especially in the context of the family system, create quite a paradoxical dilemma.

I found myself trying to breach this place of aloneness, and came in contact with the very bewildering landscape that may have kept Boris from ever being able to share what he went through with others, let alone experience it safely himself. Psychiatrist and psychoanalyst Dori Laub, in his essay 'Traumatic Shutdown of Narrative and Symbolization: A Death Instinct Derivative?', posits that one's ability to tell one's own story requires an internal 'thou' that can empathically listen, a relationship that is severely assaulted at the hands of massive psychic trauma.[11] He describes the internal landscape as 'utterly desolate ... totally void of life and humanity, permeated by the terror of the state of objectlessness'.[12] I was trying to relate to a part of Boris that he himself had severe difficulty locating. Being in the shadow of his experience, with the myriad ways in which it may have shaped our family dynamic, I was in no position to be able to help overcome this emptiness. On the other hand, there was a clearly felt imperative to know and understand this rupture and its legacy.

The night of that incident, I dreamt that I saw Boris naked. My analyst and I hypothesized that indeed I had seen him, that although he could not put words to his pain, the struggle to connect with him had resulted in me touching an aspect of his masculinity that he could otherwise not consciously share. It was immensely relieving to come in contact with him on this symbolic level. It felt as if it relieved me from having to pursue and fill this void through external means, particularly around needing to hear the factual history from him. Ultimately, we are immensely limited in our pursuit of satisfying internal symbolic needs through our projections onto others. These projections most often betray a need to dig deep and develop a sophisticated and ongoing internal relationship with the symbols that we so often wrestle with and play out unconsciously in our environment.

My grandfather was an extremely formal man, who would never leave the house without a tie. In fact, I learned the Yiddish word for tie before I ever learned Yiddish because of how often it was mentioned. Of course this formality would have been a product of his Eastern European milieu, but it may have also been a way to create a state of proper appearances, a dressing for the wounds that lay beneath the surface. Perhaps the dream was a reflection of our encounter and him revealing this deeply disabled part of his soul. Boris and I were to never speak together about any of these details together.

Holocaust historian Michael Marrus notes:

> any people, any society that has experienced victimization whether it is black slavery or whether it is aboriginal people in this country [Canada], to deal with this kind of victimization is very very difficult and it is a difficulty that is communicated from one generation to the next. We are really dealing with a transgenerational issue of overcoming humiliation. We shouldn't assume that these great burdens can be lightly cast off. We have to be very careful and attentive when we choose the means by which we deal with these great burdens.[13]

I was about to find out how Boris had dealt with these great burdens all these years. After trying to utter the names of his family, he told me that he can only open himself up to their memory once a year, at *Yizkor* on Yom Kippur. For a while, this remained a footnote for me. It made some implicit sense, and perhaps I understood it as a way of him organizing his world and the terrible feelings that the memory of their deaths provoked. It was not until much later, though, that I began to consider the mechanism by which *Yizkor* would help to make it possible for him to bear this experience.

Out From the Shadows

My wife and I travelled to Molodechno in 2003. We were studying at the time at the University of Vilnius in their Yiddish diploma programme. That summer, my wife discovered that the National Yiddish Book Centre in Amherst, Massachusetts, had a copy of a book that was written by Boris' uncle, Lazar Engelstern. I had traces of memory about this book being written, and I believe I had asked to see it at some point, but I was met with silence. We ordered the book and arranged to have it sent from Amherst to our apartment in Vilnius. I remember the day it arrived. I was heading to a lecture by the now deceased Yiddish poet Avrom Karpinovitch. The package had arrived just in time for me to take it with me. I sat in the classroom waiting for the lecture to start, holding the package in my hands, and I began to open it, tearing through the thick manila packaging. It was written entirely in Yiddish, yet I had just recently become proficient enough to read it on my own, without an intermediary.

Astoundingly, the book, an autobiography entitled *On the Way with the Holocaust Survivors*, turned out to be a 200-year history of our family in Vilnius, the very city in which I was sitting, with pictures of my ancestors going back five generations.[14] Lazar had worked at the *Vilner Tog* (The Vilna Day) newspaper and began writing during the Holocaust when Jews were compelled to record their experiences of persecution. The editorial committee consisted of, among others, Avrom Sutzkever, and Avrom Karpinovitch who was standing at the front of the room. I was completely overwhelmed. I quickly scanned through the book and found the chapter devoted to Boris's mother and her sisters, Lazar's siblings. There, in black and white, Lazar communicated the following: 'A torrential downpour of blood came and everyone burned. Only one son escaped, Berl Gelgor, who fled with the Russian Army to Russia, where he studied for a number of years to become a dentist. Until today, he lives with his wife and two daughters in Toronto, Canada, where he practices as a dentist.'[15]

In describing their fate, he used the same adjective for the blood that rained down as the one used in the Bible for the rains of Noah. It was so utterly surreal to have a text, however brief, that in black and white memorialized their fate, never mind the extensive history of our ancestry. I would come to know that my grandfather never showed us this book because of how ashamed he was that more had not been written about him and his life – or at least that was what I was told.

That afternoon the phone rang in our apartment in Vilnius. It was my grandmother, Sonia, calling from Toronto. She had not called us all summer, so I was a bit shocked at her timing. I told her that we had found Lazar's book and that I wanted to read to her the words about Boris's family perishing. She grew silent. I read them out loud, in Yiddish, and then, from the silence, she began to wail. Her crying felt like an ocean washing over me, and through her tears she began to say how badly he had wanted to tell me. To this day, my grandmother does not remember this conversation, or the tears. It has, in some way, joined the silence, where it had always lived.

A year earlier, when Boris was hospitalized in the last two weeks of his life, I received an urgent call that he had had some kind of episode at night and was in crisis. I was the closest of the family to the hospital and I arrived to find him holding his intravenous pole, huddled in the hallway, speaking exclusively in Yiddish to the nurses. He said to me that I had to help him escape, that we could go out of the window, and he rushed me to a room at the end of the hallway. My grandmother later told me that he asked her on the way home why she had put him in jail. Supposedly, he had tried to leave in the middle of the night and their holding him back triggered a powerful flashback that continued to dominate his present reality, what we might refer to as a psychosis.

Psychiatrist and Jungian analyst Angela Connolly, in the context of considering how massive psychic trauma can affect the individual, introduces Jung's notion that in such circumstances entire aspects of one's being can plunge into the unconscious.[16] It is striking to me, the degree to which language has played a role in my ability to connect with these aspects of the unconscious that emerged in such varying ways. Connolly articulates the tensions in memory that are a repository for dead facts without meaning.[17] Is it possible, though, that as generations unfold, the transmitted experience becomes more and more elusive to interpret? That transmitted experiences, divorced from place, time and language, become frustratingly foreign to us, unless there is enough to anchor us in their meaning?

There was an overwhelming sense of the importance of place as these aspects of my ancestral history were revealed to me. As I followed the trail, it was as if I was restoring a kind of cultural memory required to receive these gifts. Psychotherapist Malgorzata Kalinowska considers the cultural ramifications, describing how

> for the most part, in a group sense, trauma damages the texture of a community – its ability to serve as a cushion for pain, a context for intimacy, and a repository for binding traditions. The tissues of the social organism can be damaged in much the same way as the tissues of mind and body since collective trauma is a blow to the basic underlying structures of social life.[18]

It is in this sense that I understand the slow rebuilding of a sense of place, deeply connected to that which previously felt outside of my awareness, or even my ability to know. Laub writes about the need in the analytic context to establish an object that 'introduces new and illuminating historical information'.[19] Can we consider place in the same way? Laub presents a clinical vignette where a patient's healing occurs when the analyst suggests that he take up an opportunity to live in a country more closely related to that of his cultural heritage.[20] There the patient is finally able to develop a relationship of significance and father a child, things which he was previously entirely incapable of doing.

When we visited Molodechno later in the summer of 2003, we were joined by a historian, the president of the Jewish community, and our friend who would translate for us from Russian and Belarusian into Yiddish. It was pouring rain outside as the five of us travelled, surveying what was once the Jewish landscape of this town. We saw the market, the area where my grandfather most likely had lived, and then we were taken to one of the two places where the Jews were rounded up and shot. I ran my hands through the earth. I could finally touch what had previously been unmentionable. I spoke to my ancestors and told them they were not forgotten and I marvelled that I could finally be in a place where I could properly grieve for their memory.

When I returned to Canada, I discussed the possibility of putting up a monument or helping the historical community in this town. My mother said that to her it did not make sense to invest in a monument in Molodechno where no one would see it. I felt otherwise, though. It was not about optics or the ability to visit; it was about knowing that this place had not been abandoned, had not been divorced from our awareness. Quite literally, intergenerational attempts to deal with this massive psychic trauma had been to focus on what we could see, which was limiting, rather than also looking to see what was in the shadows. And yet, true wholeness only comes when an investment is made into what one cannot see, what is covered in darkness, and what requires a true leap of faith to uncover.

Leaving Only to Return

The leitmotif in our family was that we were small in number. This was a common phrase I heard growing up, especially when my mother was trying to express her disagreement with the choices we made. Being reminded of this was how I was most likely introduced to Boris's loss. When there was a felt sense that the unity of our family was threatened, there was an inappropriately high response of fear, sadness and ultimately rage. This was around meeting new friends, falling in love and ultimately moving away. Rites of passage, especially those that involved leaving the family nest, were met with extreme anxiety; the threat of loss was too overwhelming, too reminiscent of past losses. Laub proposes that customary defences no longer work in situations that are reminiscent of a personal-historical context, pointing specifically to cases of familial exposure to Holocaust violence.[21] The end result, unexamined, could have ended up in a perpetual kind of fusion, a cyclical process of threat, distancing, rage and guilt, a cycle that existed for quite some time. The only option was to step out of this cycle.

The more I began to create meaning around the anguish, the more I began to experience my own relief from feelings of anxiety, anger and utter confusion. Psychoanalyst M. Gerard Fromm argues that 'the experience of trauma must be communicated, or at least communicable, if the traumatized person is to carry on as a whole person'.[22] Otherwise, the transmission of feeling states such as anxiety can be passed on through generations. Davidson considers the ability to communicate these experiences as closely tied to the parent's degree of working through 'blocked aggression, guilt, shame and self-hatred'.[23] The rage and pain that before had been bewildering to me became much clearer. In fact, I developed empathy towards the shame and helplessness and it was an antidote for the misunderstanding and rage that I had fought against and that consumed previous generations before me.

I remember that after the tsunami in Asia in 2004, I saw a picture of a man sitting on the ground, crying, his arms spread wide. The caption explained that he had lost his entire family, and the rubble in the picture was once his home. It hit me that that was the same loss endured by my own family; that at some point an entire family had been wiped out. And yet, growing up, there were barely murmurs of this pain, at least in language I could understand.

Years later, I found myself able to be close to my parents in ways I could have never imagined. I particularly felt able to be close to my mother, and this was brought home to me when I was able to be there when she was overwhelmed with grief. The old confusion had vanished, and in its stead, with the knowledge of its origin, was a deep empathy for the disarray and the insatiable need for comfort. At its extreme, in considering research on psychosis resulting from trauma in previous generations, Fromm suggests that the patient is endlessly searching to give mind to that which has been ruptured from the surrounding social fabric.[24] In a sense, the more I was able to offer a container to the rupture, the more the rupture disappeared.

6. Gravenhurst, Ontario, Canada, 1986. Mitch Smolkin seated next to his grandfather Boris Gelgor on summer vacation at Pinedale Inn. Copyright/permission granted by Mitch Smolkin.

Yizkor (Remember)

I grew up singing liturgical music. It was something that I innately gravitated towards, conducting the Hebrew school choir when I was not yet 10 years old. This inevitably led to my working as a cantor in various capacities, particularly for the High Holy Days in various communities. I was always extremely ambivalent about this role. My own personal religious ambivalence was for me an obstacle to feeling completely at home as a conduit for the congregation's prayers, and I eventually stopped. I know that for a time following the war, Boris was also deeply ambivalent about his religious convictions, having had them shaken by the tragedies in his life.

A few years after Boris' death, I was in the kitchen of my parents' house, over for a family dinner. I overheard my grandmother saying that she would take Wheel-Trans, a public transportation service for elderly and disabled people in shared vans, to Yom Kippur services. I immediately felt compelled to say I would drive her; I could not imagine her going to such sacred services alone. She quickly turned away from me, and when she turned around again, tears were streaming down her face. Through her tears, she told me that Boris' family was killed during the High Holy Days; this was why *Yizkor* was so important to him. I remember having the feeling that this confirmed certain instincts I had; now everything made sense.

I remember that when we were in shul together, I looked over and she had fallen asleep. An overwhelming sense of responsibility came over me, and I knew that a part of her had already left this world; she was a vessel, and I was to pick up where she could no longer be. I remember having thought of this notion of *Yizkor* somewhat flippantly - that it was a vestige of a previous time - and having felt a resistance to wanting to take ownership of it myself. And yet I could begin to feel how it could act as a container for my own memory, the memories of those that preceded me.

Upon further investigation, it is not clear if it is factually correct that Boris' family perished during the High Holy Days, although I discovered this only in 2012 with the publication of *The Encyclopedia of Camps and Ghettos 1933–1945*.[25] The city of Molodechno had a relatively small Jewish population, swelling to around 1,000 people in 1941 with the influx of Jewish refugees from Poland.[26] Between 1941 and 1943 there are records of three *Aktionen* in the town, with no indication that they occurred during the High Holy Days.[27] The historian and leader of the Jewish community also told a similar tale recalling two particular instances and locations where the majority of the Jewish population was murdered. Supposedly, my grandfather was told of their fate and the timing when he returned to Molodechno to find them. Of course, we may never know the truth, and this phenomenon of the introduction of anti-Jewish measures by the Germans during Jewish holidays is well known. Nonetheless, this discrepancy points to perhaps a different phenomenon taking hold.

Kalinowska draws a distinction between factual knowledge and the emotional relatedness to the content. She addresses the common feeling of being 'lost in history' and suggests that without a created narrative that integrates its wider social and cultural context, we are apt only to experience a sense of meaning for a short while, which is easily lost.[28] The circumstances around Boris discovering this information are vague, simply returning to a barren landscape and not even wanting to see the remnants of his family's belongings. Is it possible that this narrative, which was perpetuated to the day he died, and fittingly aligned with the timing of his ability to mourn, created a symmetry that allowed for their memories to be held in a more sacred view? That in a way it invested their deaths with a meaning that would have otherwise been difficult to achieve. Laub points out that this phenomenon of remembering traumatic experience in such an aesthetically pleasing way can actually be a defence against experiencing and mining one's personal trauma.[29]

Yizkor, as a container, provides a formality of experience, a collective moment of mourning that may surpass the ability of the single individual to hold deeply affective experiences. The psychic energy required to process such an experience gets bolstered by the collective. So much of the current literature on the reparation of trauma focuses on the dyadic experience. And yet, as Kalinowska points out, trauma also has the potential to destroy the 'binding traditions' of the community.[30] It is no wonder, then, that I finally found my most profound understanding of the traditions I inherited through the interweaving of my own struggles with those of the past.

After a six-year hiatus of working as a cantor, I received a call from a local rabbi who was leaving one of the largest congregations in the city to start her own community. She asked if I would join her and be the cantor for the High Holy Days. I had routinely said no to these opportunities over the past six years, but I felt an energy run up and down my spine as she asked. I knew I had to listen to this, even though I did not understand what it meant. I had the instinct that it would eventually become clear to me.

My ambivalence was ever-present throughout our preparations, even though my love for the music returned in full force. She asked me if I would like to include other music in the *Yizkor* service, perhaps something in Yiddish, and after thinking about appropriate pieces, I chose Sutzkever's 'Under Your White Starry Heaven'. There was no conscious link to my grandfather, simply an intellectual decision concerning the subject matter and the appropriateness of the text. Sitting on the *bimah* (altar), as the *Yizkor* service began, the rabbi read:

> At this hour of memorial we recall with grief all Your children who have perished through the cruelty of the oppressor, victims of demonic

> hate: the aged and the young, the learned and unlettered – all driven in multitudes along the road of pain and pitiless death. Their very presence on earth was begrudged them, for they brought Your covenant of mercy and justice to the recollection of Your enemies; they perished because they were a symbol of Your eternal law; their death has brought darkness to the human soul.
>
> They lie in nameless graves, in far-off forests and lonely fields. And the substance of many was scattered by the winds to the earth's four corners. Yet they shall not be forgotten. We take them into our hearth and give them a place beside the cherished memories of our own loved ones. They now are ours.[31]

By the time the rabbi was finished, I was weeping in a way I had never wept before. Here I was, not only at the heart of the *Yizkor* service, this symbolic container that years earlier had been a footnote in my mind, but I was about to stand up and hold the prayers of the community, the very community that had once allowed my grandfather to go on living. I literally sang the words of Sutzkever through my tears, and wondered how the winds had brought me to the very nucleus of my family's grief. I marvelled at how ten years earlier I sang into a dark auditorium, barely making out Boris's face, publicly admonishing him for not telling me about his woes. How much more meaning these words contained that day. They were not a replacement for unknown memory, they were not a fantasy intended to cajole; they were a bridge for a community to mourn. Underneath the sorrow, I knew that there could be no more fitting place for me to arrive, that it was my calling to connect the strength Boris derived from the community and to give it back. I remember a man who approached me after the service, tears streaming down his face. He shared with me how moved he was; that although he did not understand Yiddish he had the sense that something very powerful was being communicated.

I have no idea when Boris' family perished. I don't know that it matters. He found a container steeped in tradition that fortified the walls of his heart enough to remember. At his *shiva* (mourning service), I finally felt that I understood or at least respected his motive to protect us; I chose to see it as a form of immense strength and not of weakness. I stood up at the *shiva* in my parents' backyard, and spoke about how all along, all he wanted was to create a new life and leave the old one behind. This was for me an act of courage.

The Work Goes On

I began this chapter with a quote from the pioneering Swiss psychiatrist Carl Jung about the degree to which 'shadow' corresponds to our work of assimilating that which has to be realized. Preceding this thought, he discusses the practical nature of our psychological work, particularly 'the realization of the shadow, the growing awareness of the inferior part of the personality, which should not be twisted into an intellectual activity, for it has far more the meaning of a suffering and a passion that implicate the whole man'.[32] Insofar as this applies to intergenerational transmission, I would argue that regardless of their origin, the shadows that are cast become our own. My assimilation has often involved dancing around the boundaries of integrity, trying to determine which feelings are my own, and which have been inherited. I may never really know, and perhaps this is what Jung refers to when he suggests abandoning the idea that somehow this is an intellectual pursuit. That course of action was not possible with Boris, and I was lead to the only route available to us, that which implicates the whole person.

Boris used to play a game. He would slowly move his hand over his face from top to bottom, and underneath his hand, as it passed, he would change the expression on his lips, revealing something new every time. I used to adore it – the comical smiles, the circus-like gestures. And yet as I struggle to understand this man, to now look back and hold the myriad ways that his trauma was kept in the shadows, this is the image that keeps coming back. It is as if every time I touch something new, his hand moves across the image, only to reveal something else.

After his death, when I performed in concerts around the city, I would often mention him and his work as a denturist. I would do so in the context of singing Yiddish songs that referenced teeth, such as 'Sheyn Vi Di Levone' (Beautiful as the Moon). Audience members began to point to their mouths, or come up to me after the concert and flash wide grins showing off the dentures he had made for them. I thought what a fitting legacy, to have my Zeydie's teeth spread out across the city. Symbolically, teeth can be understood as that which allows us to chew through life, to properly digest our experiences; where people's original teeth had failed, Boris was able to build them new ones.

NOTES

1. C.G. Jung, *Collected Works of C.G. Jung, Vol. 8: Structure & Dynamics of the Psyche* (Princeton, NJ: Princeton University Press, 1969), p.208.
2. Avrom Sutzkever (1913–2010) wrote this poem while in the Vilna Ghetto in 1943. It was set to music by the composer Avrom Brudno.
3. S. Davidson, 'The Clinical Effects of Massive Psychic Trauma in Families of Holocaust Survivors', *Journal of Marital and Family Therapy*, 6, 1 (January 1980), p.14.
4. See ibid., p.19.
5. Molodechno is a city sixty-nine kilometres north-west of Minsk.
6. G.P. Megargee (ed.), *Encyclopedia of Camps and Ghettos 1933–1945*, vol. 2, part B, (Bloomington, IN: Indiana University Press, 2012), p.1244.
7. My grandmother relays that he was at the front, although this is unverifiable. It is unlikely, if he were on the front lines, that he would have been able to leave.

8. J. Chaitin, 'Issues and Interpersonal Values Among Three Generations in Families of Holocaust Survivors', *Journal of Social and Personal Relationships*, 19, 3 (June 2002), p.383.
9. D. Fosha, 'Affective Receptive Capacity', paper presented at the Third International EFT Summit, New York, 12–14 July 2012.
10. Ibid.
11. D. Laub, 'Traumatic Shutdown of Narrative and Symbolization: A Death Instinct Derivative?', in M.G. Fromm (ed.), *Lost In Transmission: Studies of Trauma Across Generations* (London: Karnac Books, 2012), p.41.
12. Ibid.
13. 'Numbered: Auschwitz Tattoos', a programme in the series *The Current*, Canadian Broadcasting Corporation, Toronto, ON tx. 6 November 2012.
14. L. Engelstern, *On the Way with the Holocaust Survivors* (Givatayim, Israel: Organization of Vilna and Neighbourhoods in Israel, 1976). Engelstern wrote a second book published four years earlier, entitled *In Ghettos and Woods* (Tel Aviv: Hakibbutz Hameuchad, 1982), which is a memoir chronicling his survival in the ghettos and as a partisan in the forest with the Bielski brothers.
15. See Engelstern, *On the Way*, pp.55–6 (author's translation).
16. A. Connolly, 'Healing the Wounds of our Fathers: Intergenerational Trauma, Memory, Symbolization and Narrative', *Journal of Analytical Psychology*, 56, 5 (November 2011), p.609.
17. Ibid., p.612.
18. M. Kalinowska, 'Monuments of Memory: Defensive Mechanisms of the Collective Psyche and their Manifestations in the Memorialization Process', *Journal of Analytical Psychology*, 57, 4 (September 2012), p.427.
19. See Laub, 'Traumatic Shutdown', p.52.
20. Ibid., p.45.
21. Ibid., p.35.
22. M.G. Fromm, 'Treatment Resistance and the Transmission of Trauma', in Fromm (ed.), *Lost In Transmission*, p.104.
23. See Davidson, 'Clinical Effects', p.19.
24. See Fromm, 'Treatment Resistance', p.104.
25. See Megargee, *Encyclopedia of Camps and Ghettos.*
26. Ibid., pp.1243–4.
27. The *Aktionen* occurred on 13 July, 18 July and 25 October 1941. At the end of June 1942, 700 Jews from the ghetto were shot outside the town: see ibid.
28. See Kalinowska, 'Monuments of Memory', p.431.
29. See Laub, 'Traumatic Shutdown', pp.50-51.
30. See Kalinowska, 'Monuments of Memory', p.427.
31. C. Stern (ed.), *Gates of Repentance: The New Union Prayerbook for the Days of Awe* (New York: Central Conference of American Rabbis, 1996), pp.489–90.
32. See Jung, 'Structure & Dynamics', p.208.

Of Blessed Memory

MICHAEL DAVID LUKAS

The summer before my senior year of college, Grandma Guta packed up her life and flew across the country to California. Her health had been failing for some time – a broken hip, heart problems, chronic obstructive pulmonary disorder – and eventually my mom decided it would be best if Grandma Guta moved into the recently vacated house next door. I remember being struck by the idea that she bought a one-way ticket. This was her last move, her last flight. After forty-eight years in New Orleans, seven before that in Paris and twenty-nine before that in the wilds of Eastern Europe, her final stop in life would be Berkeley, California.

Although she was a tiny woman herself, Grandma Guta had an enormous amount of stuff. Over the years, she had accrued a house full of white-and-gold Rococo furniture, many sets of crystal, china, and boxes upon boxes of bedding, linens, clothes and kitchen appliances, all of which she insisted on bringing with her to California. My mom tried to convince her to leave some of these things in New Orleans. Maybe it didn't make sense to ship that old toaster oven across the country. But Grandma Guta was adamant and, in the end, she got her way. In our family, surviving the Holocaust entitles one to a certain amount of stubborn irrationality.

A few weeks after Grandma Guta arrived in California, a moving truck pulled up to her new house and left a dozen or so huge cardboard boxes in the middle of the driveway. My mom and I spent the better part of the day ripping packing tape with kitchen knives and pawing through the seemingly endless dessert bowls, little ceramic animals and crystal brandy glasses, trying to figure out what went where. If Grandma Guta had been able to look through the boxes with us, surely she could have explained each object's meaning and history – the lamp my mom almost knocked over once when she was a little girl, the nutcracker from Jerusalem, the apron that inexplicably brought to mind the smell of Lake Ponchatrain – and I imagine some of these objects held significance for my mom as well. But to me they were just things, boxes upon boxes of stuff in need of sorting.

The kitchen appliances, a set of everyday dishes, and the gilt-framed photographs of me, my brother and my sister at various stages of development – these things all went to Grandma's new house. The bedroom set was carried upstairs to my sister's room and the toaster oven turned out to be broken. Everything else was destined for the garage. After going through it all once, we repacked the boxes and labelled them according to their contents – 'Grandma bedding'; 'Grandma clothes'; 'Grandma pots and pans' – such that possession was removed and 'Grandma' became nothing more than an adjective. By the end of the day, the boxes were all labelled and stored neatly at the back of the garage. I thought our work was done. But we were only getting started. Organizing Grandma Guta's stuff was the easy part. Her stories and her memories would take another decade to sort through.

That evening after dinner, my mom brought out an old photograph she had found among the boxes. It was black and white, from the old country, a portrait of sixteen children and two teenage girls posed in front of an exotic-looking backdrop. Grandma Guta was in the back row, second from the left, unmistakable with her short fringes and broad forehead.

'My youth group', she said when my mom showed her the photograph.

'Your youth group?'

7. Guta Brum (nee Wexler) and her HaShomer HaTzair youth group in Staszow (120 km north-east of Krakow). Copyright/permission granted by Michael David Lukas.

For most of high school and college I was involved with a Labor Zionist youth group called Habonim Dror. I had been to Israel twice and worked for a number of years at an affiliated summer camp. In all that time, Grandma Guta had never mentioned her youth group.

'Was it Dror?' I asked, excited by the possibility that she might have been involved with a group similar to mine. 'Hashomer Hatzair?'

She looked deep into the photograph, as if the answer to my question was hidden somewhere beneath its glossy surface.

'It was so long ago.'

Over the next couple of weeks I tried a number of times to nail down exactly which youth group she had been involved with. But as much as I pressed, I never got a clear answer. Instead, she would shift the conversation, asking questions about the summer camp where I had worked, or writing what Hebrew she remembered on a piece of scrap paper. Eventually I gave up, worried that my questions might jostle other, more painful memories. For I knew that everything before the war was filtered through the war itself, and everything after fell in its shadow. There was always that dark mass of memory hovering over her and Grandpa Abe, like a great murky planet bending the light around it.

When it came up, Grandma Guta was always the one to talk about the Holocaust. Over Grandpa Abe's mumbled attempts to nudge the conversation towards happier topics, she would describe the horror of watching her town's synagogue go up in flames. It wasn't a story really, so much as the distillation of a particular moment, standing on top of a hill outside town with her family, watching the Nazis incinerate their synagogue and all the holy books inside. It was in this moment that she understood what was happening. The past cleaved off from the present. The life she had left at the bottom of the hill was gone forever.

At this point, I always imagined Grandma Guta running off into the woods with her friends from the youth group. But the truth is, I don't know what happened next, whether or not she went home to collect her things, whether her family objected to the idea of her leaving. The story ends there. That horrible image of the burning synagogue was tempered only by our knowledge that she made it through the war somehow and emerged on the other side.

Those years between were left mostly to our imaginations. Grandma Guta often said she spent the war 'on the run through Europe', without specifying what exactly that meant. Over time, my mom was able to determine that she was in Lvov at the beginning of the war, and that she spent a few years working at a sanatorium in the Ukraine. How she got to Lvov, whether she was there during the Allied bombardment of the city, where the sanatorium was located, how she secured employment – all these questions were left unanswered. The only details we had were gleaned from the story that Grandma Guta would tell sometimes if pressed for more information.

She was on a train, presumably somewhere in occupied Europe. Halfway through the journey, the train stopped and a high-ranking SS officer got on. He went down the car, checking to make sure everyone's identification papers were in order. She wouldn't have had any papers, most likely. If she did, they would have been forgeries. What she did have were blue eyes and blonde hair. When the officer came to her, she put on her best German accent, turned up her charm and told a story about leaving her papers at home. Again the story ends at the climax, leaving us with the emotional truth, this moment of fear, but no concrete details.

At least a half dozen times, my mom resolved to ask all the questions she had built up over the years, to sit down with Grandma Guta and pin down exactly where she was during the war, to figure out exactly what she was doing. But it was never the right time. When she was finished talking, the conversation was over. The topic was closed. Any questions were like needles in a wound. And so, all we had were her stories.

* * *

About a month after Grandma Guta arrived in Berkeley, my girlfriend, Aviva, came to visit. We had been together for four or five years at that point, depending on how you counted. Except for the first year, living on a kibbutz in Israel, we spent most of our relationship apart, flying back and forth between Providence and Washington DC, taking the bus to New York City, and meeting up for shared vacations. We decided early on that it made the most sense to have an open relationship. And since we thought ourselves to be mature adults, unencumbered by jealousy and willing to face the truth head-on, the ground rules for our open relationship included a radical honesty policy we called 'Do Ask, Do Tell.' In other words, we were free to see other people, but had to inform each other of any liaisons, past, present or future. This radical honesty was, in a way, the opposite of the spirit that guided my conversations with Grandma Guta.

After four or five years of this, we were facing a truth more difficult than any random hook-up. Aviva had been accepted into the Peace Corps, which placed her in Uzbekistan. I still had another year of college ahead of me, but was already starting to research fellowships that would allow me to continue studying Arabic. Unless one of us shifted course, we were looking at another three years of flights and phone calls, love letters, long-distance pining and visits squashed full of significance. Despite our radical honesty policy, neither of us wanted to admit this painful truth.

Considering the context, we had a good time, enjoying that particular, guiltless brand of leisure known only to college students on summer vacation. We stayed out late, went to brunch, took hikes along the beach and made elaborate dinners in the kitchens of parents who had gone out of town. Every so often, we stopped over to visit Grandma Guta, watched a little *Jeopardy* and drank a cup of tea.

'She's a smart girl', Grandma Guta told me. 'The kind of person you can talk to.'

Halfway through Aviva's visit, my mom and step-dad went out of town for the weekend and we were put in charge of looking after Grandma Guta. She had a home health aide who spent most mornings with her, took her to physical therapy and made sure her oxygen was working. Our role was to hang out in the evenings and be around in case something happened.

That first night, we went over to her house for an early dinner, followed by a *Jeopardy* double-header. Unlike most fans of the show, Grandma Guta didn't try to play along. She didn't shout out answers and didn't seem to root for any particular contestants. She would just sit there and watch, satisfied that someone knew the fourth most populous country in the world or the continent Columbus discovered on his third voyage. She was particularly happy when Aviva or I would chime in with the correct answer. Her own knowledge of capitals and composers was unimportant, so long as we knew, so long as every clue had its answer, phrased in the form of a question.

On Saturday night we took her to a neighbourhood Italian restaurant, hung with clothes lines and old movie posters to evoke the ambiance of a Venetian square. Outside the thick air of her living room, away from the chatter of Alex Trebek and Larry King (the hosts of *Jeopardy* and CNN's *Larry King Live*), Grandma Guta was more animated than I had seen her in years. She asked questions about our day and reminisced about Paris, describing their corner store and imitating the little French kids who would call out to my mom from the street. When the main course arrived, the conversation turned to Aviva's Peace Corps placement.

I had assumed Grandma Guta would have positive associations with Uzbekistan, where Grandpa Abe had lived for a number of years after escaping from a Russian work camp in Siberia. As it turns out, I was wrong.

'Uzbekistan', she said, with a disgust she usually reserved for Germany and Poland. 'It is not a good place.'

Aviva tried to reframe the comment as a lamentation on the poverty in which the Uzbek people were forced to live.

'It's a hard place', she said. 'But that's why I'm going, to help out.'

'It's dirty place', Grandma Guta replied, and made as if to spit on the floor. 'Animals in the street. Camels, elephants. And the people, they're worse than animals. It is not the place for a nice girl. You're a smart girl. Go somewhere else.'

Not sure how to respond, I tried to change the subject.

'Do you like the fish, Grandma?'

She shook her head and grimaced, as if recalling some distant memory. We moved on to a different topic and the question was closed. Or so I thought.

In retrospect, it wasn't particularly shocking that Grandma Guta would have a hard time understanding Aviva's desire to spend two-and-a-half years in an underdeveloped Muslim country halfway around the world from her grandson. Maybe, I reasoned, Grandpa Abe had told her stories about camels and elephants in the street. Maybe he had been treated poorly there and she felt compelled to shoulder his memories as her own. Whatever the source of her vehemence, we didn't talk about Uzbekistan again. Eventually, Aviva went home. Summer vacation ended and I went back to school. I forgot about the conversation until a few months later when my mom called to tell me that Grandma Guta had passed away.

She was buried in New Orleans, in a plot next to Grandpa Abe. A few months later, there was an estate sale. Most of her furniture was sold and the house was rented. Later that spring, Aviva went off to Uzbekistan and I started packing for a year in Tunisia. A few months later, we broke up. My mom and stepdad went on vacation to France. My brother started college and my sister thought about joining her high school soccer team. Life carries on. The concerns of the living trump those of the dead. Or so we would like to believe.

* * *

The story might have ended there, riddled with holes and unanswered questions, had my mom not decided, a few years ago, to start researching her parents' experiences during the war. She knew the basic outlines – Grandpa Abe's arc from Poland to Siberia to Uzbekistan; Grandma Guta's years on the run through Europe – but she wanted to go deeper, to answer the questions she wished that she had asked when they were alive. The idea was to look through their letters, contact a few librarians, poke around Facebook and get in touch with anyone who might be able to fill in the holes.

On those rare occasions when Grandpa Abe talked about the war, he kept to the facts. After his home town of Vielun was captured by the Russian Army, he and his mother were sent to a work camp in Siberia. Towards the end of the war his mother died and he escaped into Uzbekistan. He stayed there until the German surrender, at which point he started making his way back towards Europe. As circuitous as his route may sound, hundreds of thousands of Polish Jews survived the Holocaust in precisely the same manner. A few months into her research, my mom came across a documentary called 'Saved by Deportation', which confirmed the details of Grandpa Abe's story while answering a number of lingering questions.

Grandma Guta's trajectory was much more difficult to pin down. Her stories obscured as much as they revealed, allowing a glimpse into the terror of particular moments without providing any context or verifiable facts. Without the architecture of narrative, we were forced to dwell in the emotional truth of those moments that she recalled again and again: the fear and helplessness of watching her childhood synagogue burnt to the ground, the cold brick of dread in her gut as she talked with the SS officer on the train. To me, this uncertainty seemed appropriate. Having been shielded from the sharp edge of my grandparents' trauma, I was drawn into her stories, these memories spiralling ever closer to a pitch-black hole I would never be able to fully understand.

My mom viewed Grandma Guta's stories in a different manner. She had heard them nearly her entire life, starting at the age of 5. The Holocaust hung over her childhood like a thick fog, seeping into the upholstery and shorting out the appliances. It was a constant presence. For her, the question was not how to connect to her parents' trauma. The question was how to step back, how to make sense of these stories, how to separate trauma from fact. To her, the holes were meant to be filled, the questions meant to be answered. In order to break the gravitational pull of Grandma Guta's stories, my mom had to create stories of her own.

She hired a professor to translate her parents' letters from Yiddish and, using these translated letters, was able to track down a number of her parents' friends from before the war. Eventually, she got in touch with the daughter of a woman from Grandma Guta's youth group. As it turned out, this woman had also escaped to Lvov and spent a few years working at a sanatorium in the Crimea. Whether they escaped together, whether it was the same sanatorium, the daughter didn't know. But it was certainly something to go on.

Focusing her attentions on Lvov and the Crimean sanatorium, my mom continued her research for years with little success. With the determination of an investigative journalist pursuing a huge scoop, she combed through archives, tracked down self-published memoirs, cold-called octogenarian survivors whose numbers she found on the Internet, and sent dozens of emails to librarians at various Holocaust memorials. No stone was left unturned. At one point, she dug up a family history my sister had written when she was in the fourth grade. More than once she asked me to recall what exactly Grandma Guta said about Uzbekistan that night at the restaurant. Not wanting to send her down another rabbit hole of unanswered questions, I tried to downplay the vehemence of Grandma Guta's reaction, suggesting that perhaps she was repeating things she had heard from Grandpa Abe.

In the course of her research, my mom uncovered reams of information about Stasow – Grandma Guta's hometown – and learned nearly everything there is to know about the Lvov Ghetto. She joined a Stasow Facebook group, connected with former residents and swapped sources with other second-generation survivors. The Facebook group yielded a number of tantalizing leads. The elderly friend of one source confirmed a story Grandma Guta often told about her brother, who was shot by Nazi guards as he handed money through a fence to his partisan brother-in-law. Still the questions loomed louder than the answers. Emotional truths outweighed the facts. Feeling stuck, my mom put her research aside for a few months and started to reckon with the possibility that she would never find answers to her questions.

Then one day, clicking around on Facebook, she came upon the missing link. Someone had posted an old directory of the Toronto Stasower Society. And there, buried amidst dozens of addresses and phone numbers, was a listing for Bill Wittenberg, Grandma Guta's childhood boyfriend. Bill had passed away a number of years earlier, but my mom was pretty sure that his wife, Ann, was still alive. She called the number and left a message on the machine. The next day Ann Wittenberg called back.

'I hear you've been looking for me', she said.

After years of searching, my mom had finally found someone who might be able to tell her how Grandma Guta survived the war, when she left Lvov, where exactly the sanatorium was located, who she was with and where she went next. Here was one of the only people in the world who could answer her questions definitively. And still, they were difficult questions to ask. Even though they were talking about Grandma Guta's experience, Ann was a survivor too. And my mom didn't want to push too hard, didn't want to bring up painful memories. But in the end, she found a way.

In the course of their conversation, Ann confirmed that Grandma Guta had escaped from Stasow to Lvov and then from Lvov to a sanatorium in the Crimea. Then she continued on the Samarkand, Ann said, as if telling my mom more information she already knew.

'Where?'

'Samarkand', Ann said. 'In Mittel Asia.'

According to Ann, Grandma Guta spent the final years of the war in Uzbekistan, working in a factory less than 200 miles from Grandpa Abe. Surprising as this was, it made geographic sense and certainly explained her reaction to Aviva's Peace Corps placement. But Ann's answers only brought up more questions. Was Grandma Guta with anyone in Samarkand? How was she treated? Where did she live? What kind of factory was she working in? Was it possible that she and Grandma Abe met on their way back to Europe? When pressed, Ann admitted that it was possible Grandma Guta was actually in Bukhara. Or maybe it was Bukhara and Samarkand. When my mom asked how she knew that Grandma Guta worked in a factory there, Ann demurred.

'That was what most people did.'

And so, we are left with stories, some letters and that photograph of Grandma Guta's youth group. She's in the corner of the picture, with her short fringes and wide forehead. Her boyfriend, Bill, is in the middle, a dapper young boy with a new haircut and the beginnings of a smile. I don't know much about their relationship – whether they ran off together into the woods, what kinds of promises they made to each other, whether those promises were kept – but it's a handhold, the one aspect of her story I can grab onto. I don't think I'll ever be able to fully understand the Holocaust. I hope I'll never know the pain of losing my entire family, the horror of watching my synagogue burnt to the ground or the anger of knowing that my brother was shot down in cold blood. But I do know what it means to be 21 and in love. I know the gnawing pain of young love crumbling under forces greater than itself. And through that tiny window, I think I can begin to understand. Or at least I can try.

When my mom told me about finding Ann's number, about Uzbekistan and the question of whether or not Grandma Guta worked in a factory there, I wasn't thinking about Lvov or the Crimea. I wasn't thinking about Samarkand or Bukhara or any further questions that might arise. I was thinking about that moment on the hill, about the tinge of heartbreak Grandma Guta must have felt, on top of everything else, when she realized that she would most likely never see her childhood boyfriend again.

I would love to know more about her experience during the war. But the truth is, I'm satisfied with the story as it stands. I'm content to lurch through that messy pit of the conditional, to imagine what might have been, what it might have been like. As I learned from Grandma Guta, there are some truths better left uncovered, some stories better unfinished.

Inheriting Memories

The Third Generation's Encounter with their Survivor Grandparents' Holocaust Memoirs

ADI DUCHIN AND HADAS WISEMAN

Rachel, Assaf's grandmother, is a survivor who wrote her Holocaust story around forty years ago.[1] In her book, Rachel describes her Holocaust experiences as an adolescent, first living under the false identity of a Christian girl working as a servant for a Nazi family, and then, after she was exposed as a Jew, her experiences at the Auschwitz death camp. After surviving the death march, Rachel arrived in Palestine as part of the illegal *Aliyah Bet* immigration. Her first years in Israel were not easy, but after recovering from a serious illness she began to make a life for herself. She acquired an education, married and started a family. Rachel began writing her story when her eldest daughter turned 17, around the age she herself had been when she was deported to Auschwitz. Her book was published twenty years after it was written, and can still be found in libraries and bookstores. Assaf, her grandchild (Rachel's eldest daughter's son) and thus a member of the third generation, describes his first encounter with his grandmother's book: 'The book put me in the role of the grandson of someone who survived the Holocaust ... The book is a statement of sorts, that's how it was ... it shows how difficult it was.' For Assaf, the encounter with the Holocaust memoir that his grandmother wrote positions him first and foremost as a member of the third generation.

Noga's experience differs from Assaf's. Her grandfather, Shmuel, did not write his story until just a few years ago. Shmuel was a young boy during the Holocaust, and after being separated from his parents he spent more than two years alone in hiding. Noga was presented with her grandfather's memoir right after it was published, around the time of her bat mitzvah (aged 12): 'I was given the book with a personal inscription that he wrote for me, and since then it's been with me, on my bookshelf. I've read it many times to refresh my memory and remember.' She clearly feels attached to the book and to her grandfather's Holocaust story, and has reread it often.

In recent years there has been a significant increase in the number of memoirs written by Holocaust survivors and published in Israel, as well as in Europe, the United States, Australia and other countries. In their old age, Holocaust survivors seem to want to tell their stories.[2] The Yad Vashem International Institute for Holocaust Research has supported the publication of many of these books, while others have been published by private publishers or within limited family circles.[3] This recent increase in the number of published Holocaust memoirs can be explained in a number of ways. First, it is related to the survivors' growing understanding that their time is running out and that their stories will never be told if they do not write them down. Second, it can be viewed in light of the general shift in attitudes toward the Holocaust and the survivors during the past two decades.[4] In Israel, this shift finds expression in the inclusion of the history of the Holocaust in the school curriculum and in the change in attitudes of Israeli society toward Holocaust survivors.[5] Worldwide, it can be seen in the United Nations resolution, which established 27 January (the day the Red Army liberated Auschwitz in 1945) as International Holocaust Remembrance Day, as well as in the establishment of Holocaust museums in Washington and many other locations around the globe. In this context, the marked rise in the number of published Holocaust memoirs written by survivors constitutes an intriguing point of departure for this chapter.

This chapter focuses on narratives of members of the third generation whose grandparents wrote and published their Holocaust memoirs. We examine the role that the family's Holocaust story plays in the lives of members of the third generation, particularly in the context of their encounters with the book written by their grandparents. Our focus is on personal memoirs written by survivors themselves that have been published by recognized publishing houses and that are available in libraries in Israel.

In studying the personal experiences of this encounter of grandchildren with the memoirs written by their grandparents, we aim to reveal the impact and meanings they attribute to their family's Holocaust story on their own lives, their family's life and the societal-collective memory. The literature on intergenerational transmission and relational patterns in families of Holocaust survivors serves as the theoretical and research background for this chapter and we employ the narrative-qualitative research methodology to listen to and analyse the narratives of members of the third generation.

Intergenerational Transmission and Holocaust-Related Communication in Families of Survivors

While the literature generally agrees that the trauma of the Holocaust left its mark on the survivors, this is not the case when it comes to members of the third generation.[6] The literature examining Holocaust survivors referred to a 'survivor syndrome' characterized by chronic depression, anxiety, guilt, sleep disturbances and ongoing nightmares, among other things.[7] Moreover, the age of the survivors during the Holocaust and the nature of their Holocaust experience (such as concentration camps, hiding, fighting with the partisans) appear to impact significantly upon their symptoms or characteristics.[8] For example, the term 'child survivor syndrome' was attributed to survivors who were children during the Holocaust.[9] Child survivors were commonly thought to have adopted unique defence mechanisms such as emotional apathy and split personalities and to suffer from depression more frequently than other survivors.[10] The nature of the Holocaust experience can also cause symptoms that may develop later. For example, survivors who spent the war with foster parents were found to be more likely to develop post-traumatic distress in old age than survivors who hid in the woods or with the partisans.[11] Nevertheless, there is evidence that the survivors demonstrated surprising resilience and after the war most managed to start families and lead full and productive lives.[12]

Studies on the second generation and, more recently, the third generation reveal mixed evidence with respect to the question of whether the trauma of the Holocaust has left its mark on these generations, and whether they are distinguished as groups with unique characteristics. Clinical studies, in particular with respect to the second generation, point to the psychological effects of trauma among the survivors' children, including guilt feelings, aggression, marital problems, problems of identity, separation conflicts and feelings of obligation to compensate their survivor parents for their suffering.[13] In contrast, empirical studies including recent meta-analytic reviews have found no evidence for transmission of the trauma to the second and third generations.[14] Researchers have explained this discrepancy between the clinical and the empirical studies as the result of using different methodologies, especially subject selection (clinical versus non-clinical samples) and measurement tools.[15] For example, the measurement tools generally used in empirical studies were not sensitive enough to assess the complexity of the relevant phenomena under study, and the research questions they posed were not necessarily the most relevant to the experiences of the second generation.[16]

In regard to the question of whether the members of the second and third generations constitute groups with their own defining characteristics, studies point to common relationship patterns among families of Holocaust survivors. However, these studies have found no evidence for psychopathology but rather point to common modes of familial communication about the Holocaust.[17] This refers mainly to how the family relates to the story of the survivor and the impact of patterns of parental communication on the interpersonal relations among children of survivors.[18] Many survivors were unable to find the words to tell their children and other family members what they experienced during the war. The difficulty of narrating a story out of events that are impossible to communicate caused them to entrench themselves in their silence. When they did attempt, in spite of everything, to tell their stories, the stories were fragmented and lacked chronological coherence, like many other narratives concerned with various types of trauma.[19] This lack of a coherent and sequential narrative left its mark on many of the families of the survivors and became a central component in their patterns of communication. The untold story had a significant silent presence in the life of the family and often involved gaps in the communication between the survivor and the rest of the family, who, despite their frequent expressions of interest in the survivor's story, had only partial knowledge of what their loved one suffered during the war.[20]

In many cases the second generation's silence regarding their parents' Holocaust stories resulted from feelings of guilt, fear and helplessness toward their survivor parents. The children of survivors often felt incapable of doing anything to lessen their parents' suffering and therefore preferred not to initiate discussion on the topic so as not to further burden their parents. Moreover, they often feared that their questions about the Holocaust would upset their parents and therefore chose to meet their parents' silence with silence on their own part.[21] This dynamic created what Dan Bar-On referred to as a 'double wall' of silence which is mutually supported by both generations – 'Parents do not tell, and children do not ask.'[22] In many survivor families the children tended to fill in the gaps in information through imagined and fantasy-based scenarios, which often led them to consider situations that were even more threatening and unbearable than what their parents experienced in reality, difficult though it was.[23]

In other families, however, survivors did talk readily and openly about the Holocaust, both out of a desire for their children to know about their past, and also a need to testify about their experiences. This talk was often met with awkward and uneasy responses.[24] Family members felt that the survivors' stories were too difficult for them, and they refused to believe that what was described had actually happened, thus deeply injuring those they loved. Such responses often led the survivors to again retreat into silence, and resulted in familial communication patterns that ranged from incessant obsessive speech to outright silence.[25]

In their study of trauma-related styles of communication and interpersonal patterns in the second generation, Hadas Wiseman and Jacques Barber identified a communication style that was characterized by non-verbal knowledge of the parents' Holocaust experiences ('knowing') coupled with little or no informative verbal knowledge of parents' Holocaust stories ('not knowing').[26] To capture this dialectical relationship between knowing and not knowing, they termed this communication pattern 'knowing-not knowing'.[27] In families in which intergenerational communication was characterized by the knowing-not knowing pattern, the sons and daughters experienced the non-spoken presence of the parents' trauma 'without words' and their relationship with their survivor parents often involved 'mutual overprotection'.[28]

It should be noted that the above communication modalities are concepts used to map the communication patterns in the families of Holocaust survivors and are not meant to encompass all the variant ways Holocaust-related intergenerational communication plays out in different families.

Research on intergenerational communication and how the Holocaust story is passed on to the third generation is still limited. The rise in the number of memoirs written and published by Holocaust survivors offers us a unique means of examining the place of the survivors' written Holocaust stories in the narratives of the second and third generations.[29] In this chapter we focus on the encounter of members of the third generation with their grandparents' memoirs by in-depth examination of the narratives of five grandchildren of survivors. Qualitative-narrative analysis served as the methodology for this study of the subjective perceptions and the meanings the grandchildren attribute to the place of the Holocaust story in their lives. This kind of context-sensitive analysis takes into consideration the specific family context of each interviewee, as well as the socio-historical context of the third generation in Israel more than sixty-five years after the end of the Second World War.

Method

The narratives of members of the third generation were collected by means of semi-structured interviews conducted by the first author in the interviewees' homes. All interviews were conducted in Hebrew, the interviewer's mother tongue, and were translated into English by a professional translator, without additional editing.

Interviewees

Of the five interviewees, two are university-educated young men, one in his twenties and the other in his early thirties and married, and three interviewees are adolescent girls in high-school ranging in age from 15 to 18. All are Israeli-born grandchildren of survivors whose grandparents were either children or adolescents during the Holocaust. Three grandparents were in concentration camps, and two were in hiding for long periods of time. All were separated from their parents. At the time of the interviews, all of the grandparents of the interviewees were alive, with the exception of one interviewee, whose grandfather passed away one year prior to the interview. Three of the interviews were conducted in 2006 (Assaf, Galia and Hodaya), and the rest in 2012 (Roey and Noga). On both occasions the age range of the interviewees was similar.

Narrative Analysis

The principles of narrative methodology were applied in listening to and studying the narratives of members from the third generation. Narrative research is based upon the assumption that people are natural storytellers and are interested in telling their stories. According to the narrative approach, personal stories define the identity of individuals. The focus is not on the historical truth, but rather on the narrative truth. Personal narratives are viewed as representing individuals' inner representations of their outer reality while at the same time shaping their identity and personality.[30]

In-depth interviews were used to examine the encounter of the grandchildren with their grandparents' Holocaust memories as they appear in the written accounts in the grandparents' published books. The purpose of these interviews was to trace the experiences of the members of the third generation in their encounter with the books that their grandparents wrote, as well as to examine the general and broader role of the Holocaust story in their own lives. The in-depth interviews enabled us to examine more closely the meanings that family members assign to the written Holocaust stories of the survivor in their family, as well as to identify and characterize the intergenerational communication patterns with respect to the Holocaust and the concomitant family dynamics. The narrative-qualitative analysis consisted of two stages. Firstly, we analysed each transcribed interview as an independent unit and identified core categories and themes. Secondly, we used comparative analysis across the five interviewees to formulate group attributes, enabling us to identify common themes among the five third-generation narratives. We used an iterative process in our narrative analysis of the five interviews until we were able to arrive at a depiction of the themes in the five narratives presented below.

The Narratives of the Third Generation

The narratives of the five third-generation interviewees are presented along a continuum. We begin with the narratives of Assaf, Galia and Hodaya, who have not read their grandparents' books in their entirety; after that we present Roey, who identifies intensely with his grandfather's story; and finally Noga, who identifies with her grandfather's book and whose narrative illustrates the complex place of the Holocaust story in the lives of members of the third generation.

Assaf's Story: Distancing from the Survivor's Written Story

Assaf is a university student in his twenties. His grandmother, Rachel, was a young girl during the Holocaust who hid under a false identity and after being exposed to the Nazis was sent to Auschwitz. As described earlier, Rachel wrote her book and gave it to her eldest daughter Shosh (Assaf's mother) when her daughter was 17. Shosh, who was interviewed separately, had not known her mother's story until then and encountered it for the first time through her mother's written narrative.[31] In the interview with Shosh, she stated that her mother gave her the book:

> Because she couldn't think of any other way to suddenly start telling me what she endured during the Holocaust. Until then, in her desire to protect me as a child she hadn't told me anything. Suddenly when I was seventeen she felt the time had come to tell me, but she didn't know how, so this way seemed more comfortable for her ... the book was 'a substitute' ... When I turned fifty my mother told me that when she realized she *did not know how to tell me*, she began writing her story and gave it to me to read, so in this way she could know that I would now know. That's it! Nothing more. Everything she didn't allow herself – to deal with her feelings, to work it through – she didn't allow us either.

While the responses of the second generation to their survivor parents' written book are not the focus of this chapter, it is of interest to note that Shosh, as a daughter of a survivor, encountered her mother's story for the first time as an adolescent through reading her mother's book. For Shosh, this sudden encounter was an overwhelming experience that was never discussed openly and directly with her mother.

In referring to her son's experience with his grandmother's book, Shosh states: 'I don't even know whether or not he read it.' Assaf describes his encounter with his grandmother's book differently: 'The book itself didn't tell me much. I more or less knew the story, with different nuances here and there.' He states that he never spontaneously read the book all the way through, thus partially corroborating his mother's notion of doubting whether he read the book. Assaf was already familiar with his grandmother's story before reading the book and thus he felt that reading the book itself was not essential. He recalled:

> The book mentions nothing about emotions ... nothing about how difficult it was, how it was to be alone ... and that's how she talks to me now as well. People who read the book think of my grandmother as a hero ... for me, well she's simply my grandmother who's fun to be with. I can talk to her, I like hearing her stories ... just Grandma ... for me the story is irrelevant. What matters to me is how my grandmother is today.

It appears that for Assaf, the protagonist in the book who underwent horrifying experiences in the Holocaust is not his grandmother as he knows her, and he seems to differentiate between the 'literary character' and the real person. At the same time, Assaf perceives the unemotional nature of the book as associated with the way he experiences his grandmother in real life. In this sense he actually does link the literary character in the book with the real person.

How are we to understand the grandson not reading or only partially reading his grandmother's written memoir? This 'non-reading' enables Assaf to maintain some distance between himself and the book, and between himself and his grandmother's wartime experience. This type of distance is not possible for his mother, the daughter of the survivor. Thus, the family dynamics surrounding the Holocaust story emerge, representing the process whereby as generational distance increases, intensity in identification with the story diminishes. In other words, the distance between Shosh and the story in general, and the book in particular, is small, and to a great extent because of her identification with her mother's Holocaust story she experienced reading her book as if reading her own personal story. In contrast, Assaf does not feel this way, and he experiences more distance between himself and his grandmother's story, as he states that the story told in the book is not his story but rather hers.

Assaf makes an additional attempt to distance himself from the story when he observes what he views as his mother's difficulties with the book and with his grandmother. 'Somewhere in my parents' house there's some sort of halo of emotional and psychological difficulties when it comes to my grandmother.' By distancing himself from the book, Assaf declares that it is not his story. Thus, he remains outside of the complex family dynamics. For him, 'my grandmother is simply Grandma'. For third-generation Assaf, the role of his grandmother's Holocaust story in his life has to a large extent been shaped by the mediation of his second-generation mother and the way she related the impact of the past on her life and her relationship with her mother (his grandmother). This point regarding the significance of the second generation in mediating and processing how the members of the third generation shape their stories was evident to a certain extent in the narratives of all the third-generation interviewees.

Galia's Story: One Generation Removed – Knowing the Story from Her Mother

Galia is a 16-year-old high school student. Her grandfather experienced the Holocaust as a young boy in Auschwitz. He wrote his book about twenty years before the interview, after he retired and was able, in his daughter's words, to do what he had dreamed of for a long time. The interview with Galia took place around a year after her grandfather's death. Galia did not receive the book directly from her grandfather but rather from her parents. Galia, who like Assaf stated that she never read the book from beginning to end, explains her partial reading as follows: 'Reading it automatically brings back my longings for him, so if I can avoid this ... it's a bit of a childish response.' Reading her deceased grandfather's book Galia is overwhelmed by feelings of longing for him. She prefers to avoid this and 'to remember Grandpa the way he was', and perhaps not in the context of him being a Holocaust survivor but rather, like Assaf, as 'simply my grandfather'. In her narrative Galia seeks to differentiate her grandfather's story and his definition as a 'Holocaust survivor' from her grandfather–grandchild relationship with him, and perhaps also to distinguish between the way she perceives herself and her identification as a member of the third generation.

Galia adds that 'even if I wasn't familiar with the specific details of the story or with the nature of the story in all its sharpness and clarity as it emerges in the book, these are things I knew. The book didn't tell me anything I didn't know ... but I never heard my grandfather tell his story.' Essentially, Galia was familiar with her grandfather's story, however, interestingly she never heard it directly from him, in his own words.

As opposed to the lack of direct communication with her survivor grandfather about his experiences during the Holocaust, Galia states that she knows her grandfather's story 'from my parents'. Thus Galia, similar to Assaf, sheds light on the important role the second-generation parents play in mediating the survivor's story and its impact and meaning on the lives and identity of members of the third generation. The third generation seems to position themselves as 'one generation removed', while they view their second-generation parents as being closer to the impact of the Holocaust – hence, being 'too close for comfort'. She wrote:

> There is, after all, the fact that he's her father, for better and for worse, a father she was with during different periods, closer to that time, some farther away. It has to be different, because Mom was also with him through the time he wrote the book. Because she's his daughter, and she helped him a lot with all this ... obviously she also knows him better. It's just a different feeling.

In Galia's experience, the book and the entire story first and foremost belong to the second-generation parents and are connected to the relationship between them and their parents, the survivors. The way in which the second generation told the survivors' stories to their own children or kept the stories from them affects how these stories impact the lives of the third-generation children. This seems to impact the space in which members of the third generation contemplate their own identity as third generation.

It should be noted that Galia is the only member of the third generation we interviewed whose grandparent was no longer alive at the time of the interview. Since he died, rather than the book serving as a link to her absent grandparent by providing an opportunity to 'hear' him again in his own words, the possibility of reading the book actually had the opposite effect due to the sadness and longing it evokes in her, leading Galia to avoid fully reading the book. She appears hesitant to adopt the legacy of the story and while she knows this legacy and considers it important, she does not perceive the book as a way to feel connected to her deceased grandfather. This suggests the complexity of members of the third generation's discourse around the interface between the Holocaust family legacy and their own identity as grandchildren of survivors.

Hodaya's Story: Public-Collective versus Familial-Personal Story

Hodaya is 15 years old, attends a religious school and lives in a rural community. Her grandmother was a young child during the Holocaust, who was kept in hiding, separated from her parents. After the war she drifted from one orphanage to another, until she eventually immigrated to Israel. She wrote her book only recently in old age and, as she indicates in the book's foreword, writing the book was part of the psychotherapy she received at Amcha, a non-profit organization whose mission is to meet the needs of survivors and their families.[32]

Hodaya describes her first encounter with her grandmother's book and story, which occurred when her grandmother gave a talk at her school (two years prior to the interview):

> When I was in eighth grade my grandmother came to my school to talk about the book and everything, and that opened up something.

> And I had *not* heard her story before that. So it was like I heard it for the first time actually together with my girlfriends. To hear it like I'm only somebody hearing a story from someone else, but it's not the same thing. And you're not just somebody. It's important to hear it from her, but really it should be just the two of us alone.

Hodaya discloses that she was not familiar with her grandmother's history and story before this event, together with the experiences of hearing her grandmother's story for the first time at a public event. It appears that Hodaya would have preferred hearing her grandmother's story with only the two of them present, where being the granddaughter was important, as opposed to with all her girlfriends, where she was just one of many, where she had no privacy or sense of intimacy. Hodaya adds: 'If she [grandmother] had wanted the book to be something personal she would have printed only five copies of the book and would have brought them and distributed them to her family only. But that's why she had the book published publicly. I think she wanted everyone to know what happened, for everyone to know how she feels and how everyone feels.'

In referring to what the publication of the book means to her personally, Hodaya suggests that publishing the book in some sense also 'published' the fact that she is a member of the third generation. This point is relevant to the meaning attributed to publishing memoirs, compared to providing testimony that is not disseminated and advertised. It appears that Hodaya may have felt more comfortable with what her grandmother had to say if the book had been distributed only to the immediate family. The public nature of the book revealed a part of Hodaya's identity that perhaps she would have preferred to keep to herself, or within her immediate family circle. She is forced to cope with parts of her family's story that until then she had preferred not to make public. Especially considering her relatively young age, Hodaya may be expressing discomfort regarding this part of her family's history. This complex response implies that Hodaya does not feel comfortable with the place of her family's Holocaust story in her life, instead feeling somewhat hesitant and embarrassed about it. Until her grandmother spoke at her school and told the story to her and her friends, Hodaya had not yet dealt with the personal meaning of the story.

Hodaya views the place of her grandmother's Holocaust story in general, and the written book in particular, rather differently for her second-generation father. Like the other interviewees, Hodaya made a spontaneous reference to the meaning of the book for him:

> I think it was very emotional for my father ... yes. Like, my father is a very strong person. I don't think I've ever seen him cry, cry. Um ... like ... my father said that he didn't have an easy childhood. Because

> she [his mother] was a Holocaust survivor. It was sort of difficult. Me, I don't know. I can't go into details because I'm tired. But I think it was very emotional for my father. The book was to tell my father why, like, why his childhood was so much harder, I'm sorry it was so hard for him.

It seems that Hodaya, similar to Assaf and Galia, attributes the Holocaust-related emotional complexity and difficulty in her father's relationship with her grandmother to being the son of a survivor. She wants to cleanse her relationship with her grandmother of the heavy emotional burdens she attributes to the difficult relationship between her father and his mother, so that her relationship with her grandmother can remain as simple as possible. At this point, perhaps as a consequence of her young age, Hodaya seems to be attempting to avoid the overwhelming task of emotionally coping with and coming to terms with the story.

Roey's Story: Breaking the Silence and Connecting to the Survivor and His Story

Roey is a young married man in his early thirties. He was an adolescent when he first encountered his grandfather's book, at the time of its publication (fifteen years prior to the interview). Roey's grandfather was a child during the Holocaust and was in a number of concentration camps together with his younger brother. Roey read the entire book when his grandfather had published it and since then has reread it on a number of occasions. Roey has a warm and close relationship with his grandfather, though they have had little open communication about the book. According to Roey, the book significantly changed what he knew about his grandfather's experiences during the Holocaust. 'It's a book that he wrote after many years of silence and of blocking out his memories and what he had experienced, that I know he didn't really talk about things, he spoke very little, and this was his way of *getting it all out*.' In contrast, to Assaf, Roey refers to how the book caused a change in family communication about the survivor's experiences and helped break the silence surrounding it.

Roey describes his experience of reading his grandfather's book:

> I knew a few things, a number of details, but I discovered the more colorful and in-depth details from the book ... I think it affected me emotionally, both as a book on a moving and difficult topic and as a book that my grandfather wrote that made me proud. It still makes me proud, and I enjoyed reading it, I found it moving and interesting.

> I also think that in fact it was a way to connect to him because he's not really talkative. Even after the book it's not always easy for me to get close to him, and for this reason, and surely for other reasons, for me it was a way to get into his head and connect to him in a deeper way than I could have. It was simply a large part that was missing and I am completing my picture of things, because without that, well I think it would be easy to describe who he is in his work, a grandfather, a father, but it would be a picture of him in which *something major is missing!* (Emphasis added)

By means of his grandfather's book expanding his knowledge of the family's Holocaust story, Roey was able to get to know his grandfather better and become closer to him. The book and the story it tells are to a great extent the missing pieces in the puzzle that links Roey to his grandfather, and perhaps even to Roey's own identity. The book is 'to a large extent part of my own story, part of who I am'. For Roey, the book serves as a 'reference, and it's really like crossing part of the way, most of the way ... like some desert separated between the things we wanted to talk about and the questions and the answers, and now this book is like crossing almost the entire desert and all you have to do is take only a few more steps'. The book, then, by representing the grandfather's story, becomes a meaningful and unique bridge between the survivor grandfather and the third generation grandchild.

Roey's view of himself as a member of the third generation is evident in his emotional ties to his grandfather's story. He identifies with his grandfather and imagines himself in his grandfather's shoes, but at the same time he recognizes the distinction between himself and his grandfather: 'On the one hand it all seems very far from me, like I don't see myself as some sort of heroic resourceful kid, like he was during the Holocaust, and on the other hand I do innocently see myself in certain situations as someone who is daring and knows what has to be done.' Roey seems to identify with the story and, at the same time, to distance himself from it. These two poles do not cancel each other out, but rather coexist in his narrative, running in parallel to one another.

Because Roey has read his grandfather's book over and over again throughout his life, he compares reading it as a teenager to reading it later as a young adult. He notes that 'it was very different, a much more developed vision, more critical and definitely different on many levels'. Thus, when considering the appropriate distance from the book, as a young adult, Roey is able to distance himself from the story and to read it from a critical viewpoint that does not negate his identification with the story but rather adds to it and reveals the greater space he allows himself when confronting the book. He has sufficient space to be able to move toward the story and adopt it as his own, but also to move away from it, and be capable of seeing it with greater perspective. This points to an approach-avoidance theme with respect to the survivor grandfather's story, and the perception of having space that is typical of the narratives of members of the third generation.

Roey shared that his family decided to publish a new edition of the book that includes questions that he, representing the family's third generation, and his aunt, representing the second generation, pose to his grandfather, who answers them in writing as part of the new edition of the book. Roey states that 'our decision to include questions asked by family members really provided another opportunity to reach him'. Thus he stresses that the intergenerational communication surrounding the survivor's story is a process that involves ongoing working-through, rather than something static. Roey's involvement with the book does not come to an end simply by reading it, as over the years he has become an active partner in the writing and has thus become even more deeply connected to his grandfather's story.

Noga's Story: Unique Openness with the Responsibility to Carry On the Memory

Noga is an 18-year-old young woman. Her grandfather was a young child during the Holocaust and was in hiding for a long period of time. He wrote his story a number of years ago, after long years of silence and in response to repeated requests by his family and friends that he put it in writing. He gave the book to Noga immediately after it was published; she read it at the time and has reread it several times since. She is the oldest grandchild in the family and the first of the third generation to be exposed to the grandfather's story after he broke his silence. In this sense, Noga's narrative represents the recent revelations of survivors who were children during the Holocaust who, after years of not talking about what they experienced, finally broke their silence.[33]

Noga, similar to Roey, feels a deep and special connection to her grandfather, and she refers to this again and again during her interview. When she mentions her grandfather's book, she describes the process her grandfather underwent while writing the book and the channel of communication that opened up between them. In her view, this form of open communication was impossible between her grandfather and her second-generation father. Showing an awareness that is surprising for her age, Noga describes the special nature of the dialogue between her grandfather and herself, as well as her special position in the generational chain:

> Looking back I think that my grandfather underwent some sort of change. And that change began slowly ... I think that I got even more, because over the years something really happened, something moved. Grandpa himself says that he also sees that when he talks to me it's easier for him to tell us than to tell my father, you know, than to tell his own kids ... that's great, it gives me a place, but it's also weird that he's more open with me, because they are his children and what can be closer than that. Maybe because it's so close, they're so close to him that it's even harder. I dared more, because I come from a different place, you know, of course I thought about it all the time and even I knew when to stop myself and not ask more. Because there are those places, right now I can't give you an example, but when you start talking with someone, in any conversation, you know when to stop. The point where it just gets too personal. Maybe my father is more cautious. Although that's not characteristic of him, but I think he is. Like, in order not to harm this shell.

In her narrative Noga attempts to understand her special position in her relationship with her grandfather. On the one hand she indicates how strange it is that her grandfather is more open with her than with his own son (her father). On the other hand, she is also aware that the close father–son relationship makes things more difficult, and that she is freer to ask questions and that it is easier for her grandfather to speak with her openly. Thus, to a great extent, Noga expresses the unique place of the third generation in the family that affords different levels of grandfather–grandchild open communication that were not possible in the survivor father–son relationship.[34] This greater space enables Noga to dare to ask her grandfather questions about his traumatic experiences in a way that was not possible for her father, whose communication with his survivor father was more cautious and wary.

Nevertheless, Noga also speaks about other emotions that go along with her open communication with her grandfather, especially her sense of responsibility:

> But also, it bothered me, this matter of 'okay' so you can tell me more of your story, so now does that mean that I even need to ask you more, see more? ... that's a role, that's responsibility ... so I have this responsibility to know and to pass it on and to make sure that happens, because if I feel that if I won't succeed in passing it on also to my children, it's as if I've failed. It's a lot to bear, as you get older the responsibility gets heavier, and all of a sudden you realize that maybe, if I forget something then I can ask Dad, and then I realize that maybe

> I won't have anyone to ask, because maybe now I will be the one that needs to, or should, or can know the most. And that's even a greater responsibility ... and that's what so frightens me, I'm scared that I will just go on, that I won't be able to withstand it.

Being a member of the third generation appears to create a heavy burden of responsibility for Noga – the responsibility to ask, to observe, to pass on her grandfather's story to the coming generations. Her sense of obligation is accompanied by her fear of forgetting the story, as part of the sense of responsibility that she heavily stresses – 'to remember and not to forget'. As a third-generation member, she is painfully aware that perhaps she is among the last who will know her grandfather personally. Alongside her feelings of privilege at experiencing something with her survivor grandfather that her father was unable to, she expresses the accompanying heavy burden of responsibility and obligation. In this sense, the book serves as an additional and meaningful link in the intergenerational chain of communication, because for the fourth and subsequent generations it will offer the only mode of knowing the survivor's story in his own words.

Noga states that she has 'a thirst to hear her grandfather's story'. She describes her grandfather as someone 'who is afraid to tell' and herself (and perhaps her father as well) as 'very much interested in hearing'. Thus she alludes to an opening in the double wall of silence that characterized the communication between the survivors and the second generation. This seems to have been facilitated by her unique third-generation position. 'It's precisely the age and the time. Like I'm in the right place at the right time. I think that's what makes the difference. I am privileged to have come to know my grandfather in a special way through his story, precisely at the most difficult and most painful place.'

Breaking the Silence, Space to Speak Openly and Processes of Working Through

In this chapter we have presented and analysed the themes that emerge from five narratives of members of the third generation. Our analysis of the narratives encompasses these grandchildren of survivors' experience of encountering the book written by their grandparents and the place of the survivor's story in their own identity and life. The experiences they shared with us are complex, touching and at times difficult. Across these different narratives we have found that while the family Holocaust story has many meanings, it has a place in the grandchildren's experiences, and to a certain extent plays a role in the third generation's own identity and personal story.

In contrast to the vast research literature that examined the second generation, there is still not much research focusing on the third generation.[35] The intergenerational transmission to the third generation remains unclear.[36] The members of the second generation were born only a few years after the war ended and grew up in the shadow of the Holocaust.[37] The picture, however, is different for members of the third generation. Their second-generation parents stand between them and the survivors, coupled by the distance of time and of personal sociocultural processes. This is particularly apparent in relation to the nature and processes of intergenerational communication about the Holocaust.

In discussing the identity of the second generation with respect to the family Holocaust story, Bar-On coined the term 'working through' to describe the process by which an individual learns to cope with inner conflicts and attempts to resolve them.[38] This term was expanded for the descendants of survivors by adding the concept of 'partial relevance'.[39] Partial relevance refers to a process in which the descendants of survivors assign to the Holocaust some sort of relevance and meaning in their lives, positioned between 'over-generalization' (i.e. the individual believes that everything happening in the present can be attributed to the Holocaust) and 'under-generalization' (i.e. the individual believes the Holocaust has no connection whatsoever with the present). Julia Chaitin adds the concept of 'paradoxical relevance' to Bar-On's notion of partial relevance. Paradoxical relevance describes a situation in which the descendants of survivors recognize that the Holocaust is meaningful and relevant in their lives, but cannot explain how.[40] The third-generation narratives in this study typify Chaitin's notion of paradoxical relevance, but in addition to the participants' difficulty in explaining how the story is relevant to them, they sometimes distance the story from themselves, avoid it and even openly declare that it is not their own story. The third-generation narratives are marked by movement: movement toward the story and at the same time movement away from it. The five narratives in this chapter can be positioned within this dialectical space. They are not limited to over-generalization or to the sense that the family story tells their story, yet they do not declare that the Holocaust story is unrelated to them (under-generalization).

This freedom of movement that emerged as a central theme in the third-generation narratives appears to have been made possible first and foremost by their relative generational distance from the trauma and the concomitant diminished intensity of the associated emotions. While their second-generation parents identify intensely with the traumatic experiences of their survivor parents and consequently with the books their parents have written, members of the third generation have room for more open dialogue.[41] In contrast to their parents, their lives are less in the shadow of the Holocaust, but at the same time they continually examine and so more than others struggle with the issue of their own position with respect to it. This appears to describe both the experience of the adolescent interviewees and the young adults. In the context of the 'echoes of the trauma', it appears that the pitch and loudness of the echoes that members of the third generation hear are less powerful, more openly voiced and discussed, and therefore perhaps underwent more working through and, as a result, are less threatening.[42]

Many members of the second generation were found to experience throughout their lives a commitment to their survivor parents that posed 'an unsolvable task' that they could never completely carry out.[43] In contrast, the narratives of the third-generation grandchildren do not contain this same sense of obligation, but rather a different type. When members of the third generation refer to their obligation to their grandparents and their story, they see themselves as responsible for telling the story and passing it on to the next generations. This is not only a different type of task, but they also seem to have more freedom to take this task upon themselves. Not all our interviewees related to this obligation to the same degree.

The task of members of the third generation is not necessarily an easy one. They are uncertain about their ability to pass on the story; they do not necessarily express their acceptance of this role, and it seems to weigh heavily on them. For this reason, they at times distance the story from themselves, saying 'It's not my story.' The freedom they allow themselves in relation to the grandparents' past is greater and more tolerant, and although the story is meaningful and dominant, they do not feel the burden that the second generation experienced in light of the 'double wall' and 'of the mutual overprotection' that characterized their relationship with their survivor parents.[44] In this sense, for members of the third generation, there is an opening in the lines of communication (i.e. in the 'wall') with the survivors that was not possible in the relationship between the second generation and the survivors. In her book *The Silence: How Tragedy Shapes Talk*, Rutj Wajnryb writes about her young daughter's 'freedom to talk about dead grandparents in an open conversation that she as a daughter of survivors could not have had as a child'.[45]

The notion of 'memorial candles' is another conceptualization used to refer to the second generation that is worth examining in relation to the third generation. According to Dina Wardi, in many survivor families one child is chosen to be the memorial candle for family members who perished in the Holocaust and to serve as a link in the chain joining the past, the present and the future.[46] Wardi describes the memorial candle child as the one who carries the heavy burden of taking part in the emotional world of the survivor parents. In the third-generation narratives, the interviewees seem to identify their parents as those who to some extent carry this burden. Four out of the five interviewees referred to this explicitly. It is possible that identifying this burden and its difficulties experienced by their parents causes members of the third generation to avoid and distance themselves from the survivor's story, perhaps out of fear that they too will find themselves living in the shadow of the Holocaust.[47] This brings us back to the ambivalence expressed by members of the third generation with respect to being given the story for safekeeping and taking on the demanding role of passing on the legacy. The more the members of the third generation experienced their parents as carrying a heavier burden, the more they seem to distance themselves and attempt to create a different role for themselves. In other words, the survivors' grandchildren are not evading the role that might be passed on to them. In fact, identifying this role and taking the time to explore whether or not it is appropriate for them enables them to reshape it and to choose how to fulfil it in a manner that suits them. In this sense, living in the shadow of the memory of the Holocaust is not experienced so much as something that is forced on the grandchildren, rather, they have more freedom in choosing where to position themselves in relation to the past or to what extent to listen to the echoes of the trauma.

It should be noted that our third-generation interviewees were born and raised in Israel. All interviewees had studied in the past, or were currently studying, in the Israeli education system, in which the Holocaust is part of the compulsory curriculum. Most of them participated in a family roots seminar (Israeli school projects of exploring family roots), and some joined the school-organized journeys to Poland and the concentration camps.[48] These experiences had an impact on the interviewees' narratives, and it seems that in some cases these experiences have drawn them closer to the family story, while in others they have distanced them from it. The specific impact seems to depend on the general family atmosphere around the story. It is important to note that in Israel the journey to Poland is highly valued by the local community and the society in general and it has even become an integrative event in young Israelis' transition to maturity, and a rite of passage.[49] The impact of these experiences is beyond the scope of this chapter; however, it needs to be considered as part of the context in which our narratives were collected and analysed.

The unique place of the members of the third generation in relation to the survivors' legacy is summed up in Noga's moving words reflecting her awareness that the survivors are an increasingly 'vanishing generation':

> I think that they've really raised awareness by all this talk about how Holocaust survivors are a vanishing generation. I don't want my grandfather to vanish, look what he's been through! I don't know. That's it, I try, I know ... I have a sister who is ten years younger than me. No one can promise that when she's my age and she will have to do a school assignment on Poland and on Holocaust survivors there will be someone around to tell her. But I think this is something I see my father taking upon himself. Because I remember, and see how he tells me, and I know that it's important to him too. So it will always be important to me because there are lots of things that disappear with the generations. And it's really really important that these stories don't vanish, so we have to tell.

NOTES

1. All the names in this chapter are pseudonyms.
2. D. Porat, *Israeli Society, the Holocaust and its Survivors* (London: Vallentine Mitchell, 2008).
3. D. Porat, 'The Story Has Not Been Told', *Haaretz*, 21 January 2007 (in Hebrew).
4. Porat, *Israeli Society*.
5. H. Yablonka, *Foreign Brothers: The Holocaust Survivors in Israel, 1948–1952* (Jerusalem: Ben-Zvi, 1994).
6 E. Barel, M.H. Van Ijzendoorn, A. Sagi-Schwartz and M. Bakermans-Kranenburg, 'Surviving the Holocaust: A Meta-Analysis of the Long-Term Sequelae of a Genocide', *Psychological Bulletin*, 136 (2010), pp.677–98.
7. W.G. Niederland, 'Clinical Observations of the "Survivor Syndrome" ', *International Journal of Psychoanalysis*, 49 (1968), pp.313–15; I. Felsen, 'Transgenerational Transmission of Effects of the Holocaust: The North American Research Perspective', in Y. Danieli (ed.), *International Handbook of Multigenerational Legacies of Trauma* (New York: Plenum, 1998), pp.43–69.
8. Y. Danieli, 'Families of Survivors of the Nazi Holocaust: Some Short and Long Term Effects', *Stress and Anxiety*, 8 (1982), pp.405–21.
9. R. Krell, 'Child Survivors of the Holocaust: Strategies of Adaption', *Canadian Journal of Psychiatry*, 38, 6 (1993), pp.384–9.
10. O.F. Kernberg, *Psychodynamic Psychotherapy of Borderline Patients* (New York: Basic Books, 1989).
11. R. Lev-Wiesel and M. Amir, 'Posttraumatic Stress Disorder Symptoms, Psychological Distress, Personal Resources, and Quality of Life in Four Groups of Holocaust Child Survivors', *Family Process*, 39, 4 (2000), pp.445–59.
12. D. Bar-On, J. Eland, R.J. Kleber, R. Krell, Y. Moore, A. Sagi, E. Soriano, P. Suedfeld, P.G. van der Valden and M.H. Van IJzendoorn, 'Multigenerational Perspectives on Coping with the Holocaust Experience: An Attachment Perspective for Understanding the Development Sequel of Trauma Across Generations', *International Journal of Behavioral Development*, 22 (1998), pp.315–38.
13. Felsen, 'Transgenerational Transmission', pp.43–69.
14. Z. Solomon and J. Chaitin (eds), *Childhood in the Shadow of the Holocaust* (Tel Aviv: Hakibbutz Hameuchad, 2007) (in Hebrew); M.H. Van IJzendoorn, M. Bakermans-Kranenburg and A. Sagi-Schwartz, 'Are Children of Holocaust Survivors Less Well Adapted? A Meta Analytic Investigation of Secondary Traumatization', *Journal of Traumatic Stress*, 16 (2003), pp.459–69; A. Sagi-Schwartz, M.H. Van IJzendoorn and M. Bakermans-Kranenburg, 'Does Intergenerational Transmission of Trauma Skip a Generation? No Meta-analytic Evidence for Tertiary Traumatization with Third Generation of Holocaust Survivors', *Attachment & Human Development*, 10 (2008), pp.105–20.

15. Bar-On et al., 'Multigenerational Perspectives', pp.43–69; Solomon and Chaitin, *Childhood*, pp.304–36.
16. G. Rosenthal (ed.), *The Holocaust in Three Generations: Families of Victims and Perpetrators of the Nazi Regime* (London: Kassel, 1998); H. Wiseman, J.P. Barber, A. Raz, I. Yam, C. Foltz and S. Snir, 'Parental Communication of Holocaust Experiences and Interpersonal Patterns of Offspring of Holocaust Survivors', *International Journal of Behavioral Development*, 26 (2002), pp.371–81.
17. Van IJzendoorn et al., 'Are Children of Holocaust Survivors Less Well Adapted?'; H. Wiseman and J.P. Barber, *Echoes of the Trauma: Relationship Themes and Emotions in Children of Holocaust Survivors* (New York: Cambridge University Press, 2008); Sagi-Schwartz et al., 'Does Intergenerational Transmission of Trauma Skip a Generation?'; D. Shomotkin, A. Shrira, S.C. Goldberg and Y. Palgi, 'Resilience and Vulnerability Among Aging Holocaust Survivors and Their Families: An Intergenerational Overview', *Journal of Intergenerational Relationships*, 9 (2011), pp.7–21.
18. Wiseman and Barber, *Echoes of the Trauma.*
19. L.L. Langer, *Holocaust Testimonies: The Ruins of Memory* (New Haven, CT: Yale University Press, 1991); J.L. Herman, *Trauma and Recovery* (New York: Basic Books, 1992).
20. M. E. Jucovy, 'Telling the Holocaust Story: A Link Between the Generations', *Psychoanalytic Inquiry*, 5 (1985), pp.31–50; R. Krell, 'Holocaust Families: The Survivors and Their Children', *Comprehensive Psychiatry*, 20 (1979), pp.560–8.
21. Krell, 'Holocaust Families'.
22. D. Bar-On, *Fear and Hope: Three Generations of the Holocaust* (Cambridge, MA, and London: Harvard University Press, 1995).
23. J. Chaitin, 'Facing the Holocaust in Generations of Families of Survivors: The Case of Partial Relevance and Interpersonal Values', *Contemporary Family Therapy*, 22 (2000), pp.289–213.
24. Bar-On, *Fear and Hope.*
25. Ibid.; Z. Solomon, 'Transgenerational Effects of the Holocaust: The Israeli Research Perspective', in Y. Danieli (ed.), *International Handbook of Multigenerational Legacies of Trauma* (New York: Plenum Press, 1998), pp.69–85.
26. Wiseman and Barber, *Echoes of the Trauma.*
27. Ibid.; H. Wiseman, 'Intergenerational Echoes of the Story of the Holocaust in Families of Survivors', in M. Rieck (ed.), *Social Interaction After Massive Traumatization: Was the Holocaust Survivors' Encounter with the Post-War Society Conductive for Generating Private and Collective Memories?* (Berlin: Regener, 2009), pp.77–93.
28. H. Wiseman, E. Metzl and J.P. Barber, 'Anger, Guilt, and Intergenerational Communication of Trauma in the Interpersonal Narratives of Second Generation Holocaust Survivors', *American Journal of Orthopsychiatry*, 76, 2 (2006), pp.176–84.
29. A. Duchin, 'The Experience of Encounter between Written Stories of Holocaust Survivors and their Children and Grandchildren' (MA thesis, University of Haifa, 2007).
30. R. Josselson, A. Lieblich and D.P. McAdams (eds), *The Meaning of Others. The Narrative Inquiry of Relationships* (Washington, DC: American Psychological Association, 2007); A. Lieblich, R. Tuval-Mashiach and T. Zilber, *Narrative Research: Reading, Analysis and Interpretation* (London: Sage, 1998); R. Tuval-Mashiach and G. Spector-Mersel (eds), *Narrative Research: Theory, Formation and Explanation* (Jerusalem: Magnes, 2010) (in Hebrew).
31. In previous research we also interviewed the second generation: see Duchin, 'Experience of Encounter'
32. For more details, please see http://www.amcha.org/.
33. R. Krell and P. Suedfeld, 'Child Holocaust Survivors as Parents: A Transgenerational Prespective', *American Journal of Orthopsychiatry*, 74 (2004), pp.502–08.
34. G. Rosenthal (ed.), *The Holocaust in Three Generations: Families of Victims and perpetrators of the Nazi regime* (London: Kassel, 1998).
35. Sagi-Schwartz et al., 'Intergenerational Transmission', pp.105–20.
36. M. Scharf, 'Long-Term Effects of Trauma: Psychosocial Functioning of the Second and Third Generation of Holocaust Survivors', *Development and Psychopathology*, 19 (2007), pp.603–22.
37. A. Hass, *In the Shadow of the Holocaust: The Second Generation* (Ithaca, NY: Cornell University, 1990).

38. Bar-On, *Fear and Hope*.
39. D. Bar-On and O. Selah, 'The Vicious Cycle Between Current Social and Political Attitudes and Attitudes Toward the Holocaust Among Israeli Youngsters', *Psychologia*, 2, 2 (1991), pp. 126–38 (in Hebrew).
40. Chaitin, 'Facing the Holocaust', pp.213–89.
41. Y. Gampel, 'Thoughts about the Transmission of Conscious and Unconscious Knowledge to the Generation Born after the Shoah', *Journal of Social Work and Policy in Israel*, 5, 6 (1992), pp.43–50 (in Hebrew).
42. Wiseman and Barber, *Echoes of the Trauma*.
43. R. Shefat, 'Commitment to Parents as Unsolvable Problem in Children of Holocaust Survivors', *Sihot/Dialogue: Israel Journal of Psychotherapy*, 9, 1 (1994), pp.23–7 (in Hebrew).
44. Bar-On, *Fear and Hope*; Wiseman et al., 'Anger', pp.176–84.
45. R. Wajnryb, *Silence: How Tragedy Shapes Talk* (Crows Nest, NSW: Allen & Unwin, 2001).
46. D. Wardi, *Memorial Candles: Children of the Holocaust* (London: Routledge, 1992).
47. Hass, *In the Shadows*.
48. M. Lev, 'Knowledge, Feelings and Attitudes of Third-Generation Israeli and Canadian Adolescents Toward the Holocaust: Changes Following the Journey to Poland' (unpublished doctoral dissertation, Bar Ilan University, Ramat Gan, Israel, 2009). (in Hebrew)
49. J. Feldman, *Above the Death Pits, Beneath the Flag:ý Youth Voyages to Poland and the Performance of Israeli National Identity* (New York: Berghahn, 2008).

Grandpa's Letters: Encountering Tangible Memories of the Holocaust

ESTHER JILOVSKY

On Sunday, I found Grandpa's letters. Thin paper, yellow with age, neatly typed in a classic typewriter script. It was the dates that first grabbed me. 1939. May, June, October. The summer days before the war. Before everything changed. And the address – sent to Grandpa in Nicosia, Cyprus. Where he went after he farewelled his parents in Prague. In 1939, Grandpa was in his mid-thirties, a grown-up, a bachelor, living in Eindhoven, the Netherlands, where he worked for Philips Electronics. What he always told us was that at some point in late 1938 or early 1939, perhaps after seeing coverage of Kristallnacht, he decided to get out of Europe. He saw what was happening with the Nazis in Germany and Austria and he wanted out. He chose to leave, and managed to do so. In March 1939 he caught the train from Eindhoven back to Prague. He saw his parents. He said goodbye. He never saw them again.

As an elderly man, in his nineties, he became increasingly frail and his mind focussed more and more on this decision he had made more than sixty years earlier. He could not forgive himself for having left his mother. He wished he had taken her with him. His pain, regret and guilt were palpable. Living with this decision was perhaps harder than living with the fact that he had lost his parents in the Holocaust. It was the sense of responsibility that he felt. Guilt at being somehow responsible for the death of someone he loved, who gave him life and nurtured him into adulthood.

Glancing over the folder of letters, I am incredulous that I have never seen them before. That they were written in 1939, 1940 and 1941 means that Grandpa must have had them in his possession ever since he received them – but why had he never shown them to us? What's more, they are nearly all in German. Despite Grandpa's strong identity as Czech, these letters prove that he came from a German-speaking family. Moreover, it's a language I can both speak and read. Who would have thought – to find such shreds of the past, offering a window into the lives of Gabriel and Elsa Jilovsky, who surely in 1939 cannot have known that within three to four years they would both be dead, and whose correspondence appears simply to be exchanges of news between parents and their adult son. I want to bury myself in these letters, breath in their musty scent, transport myself to this time and place, a world of European grandeur, of technological simplicity, of communication by the written word which took days if not weeks to reach its destination. I want to inhale the words, the feelings, the life of my great-grandparents. I want to hold in my hands this sign of life from them, that they once lived, that they are not just unsmiling stern faces in black-and-white photographs. But people, people related to me, whose surname I share, who as middle-class Jews in 1939 Prague cannot possibly have imagined that all their great-grandchildren would be Australian.

* * *

I wrote the above words in 2012, after I found a folder of letters, in a box, in an attic. Leafing through them, I was astonished to find that they had belonged to my grandfather, Kurt Jilovsky (1905–2002), a Czech Jew who had survived the Holocaust by enlisting with the Jewish Brigade of the British Army and fighting in the Middle East. These letters were some of the last he ever received from his parents, who were killed in Theresienstadt and Auschwitz.[1] They are, therefore, newly discovered primary sources on the Holocaust, as well as priceless family heirlooms. They are particularly valuable to me, a scholar of the Holocaust who can read German, the language in which most of the letters are written. In this chapter, I will attempt to unpack the significance of these letters, drawing on Marianne Hirsch's idea of 'points of memory' to analyse them as objects whose significance arises from their context and interpretation.[2] Therefore, this chapter will explore the significance of these letters, as cultural objects, historical sources and objects of memory, showing how they enable members of the third generation, such as myself, to construct a tangible link to the Holocaust. I will suggest that my position as third generation uniquely shapes the way that I engage with these letters – something that will not be possible for future generations, those born into a time when there are no longer any living survivors of the Holocaust.

In making explicit my connection to the subject at hand, I am both responding to Pascale Bos's call for Holocaust studies scholars to be more explicit in discussing or at least acknowledging their personal investment in their work, and building on the large body of literature about the second generation (the children of Holocaust survivors) which explicitly connects the author to the subject and theories that they are writing about.[3] Indeed, although there is an established practice of both Holocaust survivors and the second generation producing scholarly work on the Holocaust, little such hybrid scholarship on the third generation has emerged.[4] Thus this essay not only builds on this established practice but extends it to a new generation.

As we approach seventy years since the end of the Second World War and the Holocaust, a significant shift in memory of the Holocaust is underway. With fewer and fewer survivors around to tell their stories, we are increasingly reliant on archives of testimony (video and written), museums and other sources such as film, websites and social media to relay what happened during the Holocaust. For those of us descended from Holocaust survivors, our interaction with such representations confronts what we know and do not know about the Holocaust from our parents and grandparents. Moreover, our engagement with the Holocaust is the product of both these types of knowledge: what we glean from representations, and what we glean from our grandparents. Hirsch's theory of 'postmemory' describes this perspective of those born after the Holocaust, stressing how our representations encapsulate our unique perspective.[5] Hirsch explains:

> Postmemory is a powerful and very particular form of memory precisely because its connection to its object or source is mediated not through recollection but through an imaginative investment and creation ... Postmemory characterizes the experience of those who grow up dominated by narratives that preceded their birth, whose own belated stories are evacuated by the stories of the previous generation shaped by traumatic events that can be neither understood nor recreated.[6]

Although not without criticism (particularly when it comes to extending its remit beyond those directly descended from survivors of atrocity), postmemory usefully captures the very particular perspective of people born into a family who have survived a traumatic event.[7] Interaction with parents or grandparents who survived is a key component of postmemory; Hirsch notes that 'postmemory is distinguished from memory by generational distance and from history by deep personal connection'.[8] But when there are no longer survivors living to interact with and engage with, postmemory becomes even more mediated.

One of the aspects that characterizes the homes of Holocaust survivors is the dearth of objects from the past. Leaving Europe as refugees, few had the opportunity to bring much with them – or indeed had anything at all to bring – to the countries where they created their new, post-war lives. The few objects that may exist from their pre-war lives therefore assume even more significance than they would otherwise. The discovery of old letters between family members who have long since passed away is no doubt normally cause for celebration for anyone who is interested in their own heritage. But the discovery of letters from, to or about relatives who were murdered in the Holocaust is especially and poignantly significant.

These letters not only provide valuable historical information through their content, but also function as objects of Holocaust memory. It is the fact that they are authentic relics, created by and touched by people murdered in the Holocaust, which makes them so. Like Holocaust photographs which decorate exhibitions at the Imperial War Museum in London or the United States Holocaust Memorial Museum in Washington, it is these letters' symbolic pedigree as objects which is all the more significant because of what we consider them to represent: they mediate between our time and the past to which they testify. In other words, it is the fact that we know that these people were murdered in the Holocaust which makes these photographs meaningful as Holocaust objects. Similarly, Hirsch writes about what she calls 'Holocaust photographs':[9]

> We ... know ... that they will *all* die (have all died), that their world will be (has been) destroyed, and that the future's (our) only access to it will be (is) through those pictures and through the stories they have left behind. The Holocaust photograph is uniquely able to bring out this particular capacity of photographs to hover between life and death, to capture only that which no longer exists, to suggest both the desire and the necessity and, at the same time, the difficulty, the impossibility, of mourning.[10]

Thus the significance of Holocaust letters as memorial objects functions in the same way: it is the fact that we know that these people were murdered in the Holocaust which makes the letters assume far more significance than they would otherwise. As points of memory, these letters connect me to my great-grandparents, Elsa and Gabriel Jilovsky, who died nearly forty years before I was born. Yet it is precisely the circumstances of their deaths, in Theresienstadt and Auschwitz respectively, that gives these letters their particular meaning, and makes them particularly important to me as a third-generation descendant of the Holocaust, and as a scholar of Holocaust studies.

* * *

A few days later, I start reading the letters. Returning to the attic I am confronted by an orderly pile of boxes. How will I ever find them? I open the first box labelled 'H & K Papers and Photos'. There it is, resting on the top, as if it is waiting for me: a pale cream Manila folder decorated in Grandpa's curly script with three simple, heart-wrenching words: 'Meine goldene Mama.' My golden mother. My wonderful mum. However you translate it, it evokes nothing short of absolute adoration.

Later, I sit on the couch. It is just dark, and a quiet wintry evening. It is silent. I sit on my new grey couch, in 2012 Melbourne, and prepare to be transported back to 1939 Prague. I start by sorting the letters into chronological order. Strangely enough, the letters between Grandpa and his parents mostly span the entire year of 1939 – the first is from January and they are pretty regular until December of that year, around seventy in total; in contrast there are only three from 1940 and eight from 1941. The last letter is dated 24 May 1941.

As I place each brittle, yellowing letter into its rightful month, I notice that while the early letters from 1939 are handwritten, the ones from March onwards are typed. The later ones from November and December that year are also written in a scrawly cursive. The letters from 1940 and 1941 are written on increasingly thinner paper, accompanied by envelopes stamped with 'Opened by censor' and often missing considerable chunks that have been cut out.

Toward the bottom of the pile lie two handwritten letters – dated 10 November and 27 November 1945. Frustrated at the difficultly of reading old-fashioned German cursive, I nevertheless manage to make out a sentence which makes my heart skip a beat:

> Nun mein lieber Junge kommt der traurige Teil, die liebe Mama ist am 8/11 42 in Terezín gestorben. Papa ist mit Tante Adele im Jahre 43 nach Polen gekommen und bis heute ist gar keine Nachricht von jemandem hier.
>
> [Now my dear boy comes the sad part, dear Mama died on 8/11 42 in Terezín. Papa went with Aunt Adele to Poland in 43 and there has been no news from anyone since.]

This is it. This proves the date of Elsa's death. This proves that she died in Terezín. I knew this, but I do not know how I knew. But this proves that I didn't imagine it. She died in Terezín, in 1942. Born on 24 October 1884 (this I know from Grandpa's memoir), this means that she died at fifty-eight. A middle-aged grandmother, an insulin-dependent diabetic, who doted on her children and granddaughter. What more of her there was, I do not know. In the letters from 1939, which until now I have only skimmed, she comes across as exuberant, happy, living her life. Not to know that it would all soon be over in an unimaginable way.

But who on earth wrote these news-bearing letters to Grandpa in November 1945? Written in Brno, addressed to 'Mein lieber Kurt', speaking of 'Mama' and 'Papa' and 'Tante Adele' suggests someone within the same close family – a cousin perhaps. I cannot make out the signature. The letter closes with the standard German 'Deine', 'yours',

8. Gabriel, Elsa, Kurt and Grete Jilovsky, Prague, early 1920s. Copyright/permission granted by Jilovsky family.

and then suddenly I see it – 'Deine Tante', 'your aunty' – yes, the curly scrawl of 'Tante' matches the same word above. And the name starts with an F and ends with a y … it crystallizes into 'Fanny'. I check the family tree in Grandpa's memoir. Indeed, Grandpa had a Tante Fanny, who was married to his father's brother Alfred. We do not know the names of their children. So Fanny survived the war. But what happened to her? And to the rest of her family?

* * *

To historians, letters are primary sources. When it comes to letters from the Holocaust, historians seem predominantly interested in these letters for their content, for the historical snapshot that they provide, and are perhaps less interested in the letter as medium for communication, and as historical relic. When it comes to Grandpa's letters, the content is more along the lines of a micro-level social history rather than providing information on contemporary events. The news contained in these letters is very much about family members, friends and acquaintances; about who has visited for lunch or who his mother has run into in the street; about who is applying for visas to America, to Australia, to Cyprus, to South America.

Many people are mentioned by name; it is assumed that the recipient knows who the writer means, but it is of course not necessarily obvious to those of us reading the letters outside of their intended time and place. The letters contain very little, if anything, about the war or the political situation. Whether this is for fear of censorship or whether it is because it was simply deemed less important or superfluous is unclear. They are micro-history, family history, the historical details of members of one family which occurred as part of the great historical event we call the Holocaust.

Thus one aspect of letters as historical objects is the information conveyed linguistically: the content. And it is this aspect which renders them useful to historians, no matter how parochial the information contained therein. Nevertheless, it is the role of these letters as points of memory which is most significant for my relationship to them. As Hirsch explains, points of memory are 'points of intersection between past and present, memory and postmemory, personal remembrance and cultural recall'.[11] Thus as physical objects which act as a conduit between incompatible times and places, it is the information about these letters not contained within them which amplifies their significance.

But how and why does this significance come about? Perhaps these letters not only represent my lost relatives, but stand in for them in some way. Because they are explicitly linked to their deaths, which occurred as part of mass murder based on racism, they become a substitute for the rituals of death, such as graves, funerals and death rites, which were not observed. Perhaps they even exist as a substitute for even knowing what happened to these people who simply disappeared. In her study of letters from First World War soldiers collected by the Australian War Memorial, Tanja Luckins observes that '[s]mall items such as wallets, photographs, coins, postcards, and diaries and letters were, in many instances, the only material things left for bereaved relatives and, as such, became substitutes for the absent body'.[12] Thus, the lack of rituals normally associated with death, such as burial of a body, a funeral and a grave, meant that other items take on the significance normally accorded to such rituals. As a result, Luckins explains, 'personal effects became treasured, even sacred objects of memory, kept in a suitcase, "Drawer of Remembrance" or placed on display on a mantelpiece [sic], dresser or bedside table inside the home, traditionally places of personal memory'.[13] So the unexplained deaths and absent graves of my great-grandparents means their letters also come to represent them. In the absence of a grave, these letters are perhaps the only tangible proof that these people once existed.

For victims of the Holocaust, most of whom were, like the soldiers killed in the First World War, not accorded individual or marked graves, objects potentially take on similar significance, with the added complication that the entire community of these victims was also destroyed. It follows that any objects directly relating to individual victims of the Holocaust therefore would likely become particularly valuable to their descendants. In their book *Death, Memory and Material Culture*, Elizabeth Hallam and Jenny Hockey explain that 'images, text and objects might stand as painfully isolated vestiges of those persons with whom they were once surrounded or associated. Surviving the people and places we love, these materials might highlight the passage of time.'[14]

When it comes to the Holocaust, the incidence of objects as 'painfully isolated vestiges' is evident in second-generation Holocaust writing. The importance of memorial objects as a link to Holocaust victims suggests that such objects which once belonged to their murdered relatives come to stand in for these relatives. Family heirlooms connected to relatives who were murdered in the Holocaust are particularly important to children of survivors, because they form a concrete representation of the no longer existing world of their parents. For instance, in the semi-autobiographical novel *Too Many Men*, Lily Brett writes about Ruth's (the protagonist's) grandmother's tea set and silver bowl. 'She wanted to touch them. To hug them. To hold them to her. She knew they were only inert objects, but they had been held and touched by all the people that she would never be able to hold and touch.'[15] These inert objects are a tangible link with people that she would never meet, who were murdered before she was even born. Their significance lies in the people who they belonged to, and as points of memory, the pieces of china and silver mediate between the past and present. In his memoir *The Fiftieth Gate*, Mark Raphael Baker writes about a shoe which once belonged to his grandmother: 'Sometimes I touch the shoe, wondering what it would have been like to have a grandmother to embrace me.'[16] Once again the object assumes, to a certain extent, the value of the actual person; the shoe emphasizes Baker's loss while simultaneously serving as a tangible reminder of the grandmother he never knew.

So do Grandpa's letters stand in for my great-grandparents? Perhaps. The tactile sensation of handling something not only touched by my great-grandparents but created by them is certainly uniquely valuable. This is because, as Hallam and Hockey claim, '[v]estiges of the past acquire resonance through their relation to something forgotten'.[17] Thus it is my relationship to what these letters represent – my great-grandparents who were murdered in the Holocaust; my grandfather who never stopped mourning his parents – which makes them hugely significant to me.

* * *

I have pored over Tante Fanny's letters, patiently deciphering the rust-coloured gentle swirls into recognizable German words. The language is brief, non-descriptive, factual. It is heartbreaking in its simplicity. Tante Fanny writes of her joy at hearing from her nephew, my Grandpa – 'Mein lieber Kurt!' – *My dear Kurt* – and her deep sorrow at what has happened: 'dies alles war grausam', *it was all horrible*. Yet she is scant on details. The second letter, clearly a response to a letter from Grandpa, expands a little on what happened to his parents, but does not give any more detail. I can almost imagine the response he wrote. I do not know where he lived when he received these letters – but as it was in late 1945, I assume it must have been Palestine (which to my grandparents was the Jewish homeland, the country which became the State of Israel in 1948), as my grandparents married in Ramat Gan, Tel Aviv, in 1946 – but I can imagine him, receiving this priceless piece of paper, a link from the past. The joy at hearing from a relative in Czechoslovakia, the heartbreak at the devastating news it contained. Knowing Grandpa, he would have written straight back. He would have wanted to know more, to know exactly what happened, was she sure, was there a funeral, where was his mother buried? And what happened to his father? I can only imagine that in the early days of receiving such news, just months after the war had ended, he had barely begun to grasp the enormity of it. Or maybe not. Maybe he, who chose to leave Europe in 1939, who knew he had to get out, had more than an inkling of what was coming. But I don't think any of them could have ever known. No one could have imagined what was to come.

I don't know when the last time he heard from his parents was. Of the letters I found, the latest was from 24 May 1941. That's a whole four-and-a-half years until Tante Fanny's letters. What happened in the meantime? When were they sent to Theresienstadt?

I google 'Prague transport to Terezín'. I find nothing. Well, not nothing. General information on the fortress of Terezín, on how to get there on a day trip from Prague. Not exactly the type of transport I was searching for. I decide to try jewishgen.org. This is what spurred Daniel Mendelsohn's search in *The Lost: A Search for Six of Six Million* – this is how he found the last of the Bolechowers.[18] It can be done! I click on 'Holocaust Databases'. I type in 'Jilovsky'. I get 1,500 matches! Upon closer inspection, this is a very clever search engine which incorporates possible variations in spelling as well as misspellings. Most of the entries I click on are 'Zewlowski?' and 'Sewlovski?' or similar. I click back. This time, I select 'Phonetically like'. This time, only seventy-two responses. I knew I had an unusual name! Most of the entries hold no joy, though; these are not names I recognize. But then I stumble upon entries from a 'List of Jewish Survivors found in Theresienstadt on 10.5.1945'. There are seven which match my search criteria. One of them is named as Fanny Jilowski.

It has to be her, has to be. It would make sense – she survived the war, she was in Theresienstadt, her surname was Jilovsky. This feels like a very small but significant step. I have started to place these letters in a larger context, to unravel the mysteries between their creation and their existence in 2012 Melbourne. I have proof that Fanny Jilovsky/Jilowski was in Theresienstadt, and that she survived. I have letters from Tante Fanny in late 1945 explaining that she was in Terezín. It is her.

* * *

These letters are a time capsule. Like photographs, they capture a moment. But unlike photographs, this moment lasts more than mere seconds, and is controlled by the person writing the letter, rather than the photographer who is the one who captures subjects whether or not they consent to being photographed. A letter writer, on the other hand, is the active agent who creates a letter. Thus, although Holocaust letters share similarities with Holocaust photographs, they differ in that they preserve the writer's choice of whether to write at all.

It is clear that Grandpa's letters take on a different significance in my possession than they did in his possession. To him, they were the last sign of life from his parents, people whom he knew and loved, whom he last saw in 1939. To me, they are from strangers, my great-grandparents whom I have never met and never will meet, yet the genealogical connection means that despite this disjunction, and perhaps because of it, I count them among my most treasured possessions. They provide snapshot of my great-grandparents as living, breathing, writing people – qualities of them which I have not come across in any other context. They thus mediate between memory and postmemory: Grandpa's memory and my postmemory.

When it comes to historical artefacts meaningful to an individual or a group, they are, according to Alan Radley, often objects 'not so intentionally created, but only later come to be marked in a way which designates them as special possessions, as part of the cultural heritage or of one's memorabilia'.[19] That is to say, memorial objects do not necessarily start out that way, but it is the displacement from their original context which makes them significant. Therefore, as Radley argues, 'the question of what or how objects evoke memories cannot be separated from the issue of the ways they have been displaced over time, and the forms of order to which they have been subject in marking them out as significant'.[20] So it is not only the context in which the objects are found which makes them meaningful, but how they have arrived in that context.

Radley differentiates between such differences in terms of intended and unintended features. He continues: 'it is the enduring nature of objects that allows them to proceed, often relatively unchanged, through the various periods of people's lives so that they can "re-invoke" the contexts of which they were once a part ... it is clear that the use of objects for remembering is both intended and has unintended features'.[21] The intended feature is, of course, communication from Grandpa's parents to him, and his decision to keep the letters is also intended, no doubt as precious mementos. However, that these letters should come into my possession, and that I should write about them, is an unintended feature. There is nothing in the original function of these letters as a tool of communication between parents and their son that they should end up with another descendant after the death of the recipient, although this is surely pretty common. But what is important is the connection that the recipient – in other words, me – has to these objects. And in this case it seems almost as if they were meant to come to me – of Gabriel and Elsa's nine great-grandchildren, I am the only one who speaks German.

However unintended this feature, it is dependent on the unique position of the third generation. As I have written elsewhere, the third generation comprises the 'last living link' to the Holocaust.[22] By this I mean that we are the last generation to know Holocaust survivors personally. Within our lifetimes, this will change. It is my personal connection to Grandpa which constructs my relationship to the letters. It is the fact that I knew him personally which makes these letters special to me.

According to generational theory, the average length of a generation is thirty years.[23] Due to average life expectancies in developed western countries, it is generally three living generations who overlap at any one time. It is this form and restrictions of generations which underlies Jan and Aleida Assmann's theories of 'communicative memory' and 'cultural memory'. As Jan Assmann explains about the former, to which he also refers as 'everyday memory', '[i]ts most important characteristic is its limited temporal horizon. As all oral history studies suggest, this horizon does not extend more than eighty to (at the very most) one hundred years into the past, which equals three or four generations.' [24] Thus, the grandchildren of Holocaust survivors are generally the last generation to know them personally, to hear their stories from a person rather than watch them on a video or read them in an archive, to know their grandparents as people rather than statistics. So the unintentional memorial function of Grandpa's letters to me is intrinsically bound up with my position as third generation. For subsequent generations who will never meet him, these letters will not have the same meaning. It is not that they will have no meaning, but it will be different, based on the Assmanns' idea of cultural memory: '[j]ust as the communicative memory is characterized by its proximity to the everyday, cultural memory is characterized by its distance from the everyday'.[25] This distance from the everyday means that '[c]ultural memory has its fixed point; its horizon does not change the passing of time'.[26] Once the living link is lost, these archival objects become just that: objects invested with the desires of people who find them meaningful, no matter how distant they are from the people who created them.

* * *

I turn, once again, to Google. To the Yad Vashem website. To what was once called the Information Superhighway. The World Wide Web. The gateway to so much of our lives these days, from banking, to job applications, to bills, to real estate – the core foundations of a modern western existence. Yet how ironic is it that the Internet is also the gateway to the past. That more and more documents are being digitized every day; that more and more databases related to the Holocaust are searchable; that search engines are becoming more and more sophisticated so that if you type in a name with a certain spelling, it will also search variant spellings of the name. So perhaps it is no wonder that in 2012 one can find so much more information about the Holocaust online than one could in 2002, the year Grandpa died. It is ironic that the further we get from this past, the more accessible it is. The flipside is that there is potentially so much information online that wading through it becomes a task in itself. Sorting the reliable sources from the unreliable ones, judging whether the misspelt names are the same person or not, trusting translations from unfamiliar scripts.

Even though I already have copies of the 'Pages of Testimonies' of my great-grandparents, which Grandpa submitted to Yad Vashem, I type in their names. Gabriel Jilovsky. Elsa Jilovska. After a few seconds not only does the search engine retrieve these documents, but it creates a narrative of their Holocaust experiences by plugging in information from several databases. I read: 'Gabriel Jilovsky was born in 1878. During the war was deported with Transport AAt from Praha, Praha Hlavni Mesto, Bohemia, Czechoslovakia to Theresienstadt Ghetto, Czechoslovakia on 23/07/1942.' Elsa, too was deported to Terezín on this date. So from the date of the last letter from them – 24 May 1941 – a whole year and two months passed before they were forcibly removed (one can only assume forcibly, except that if by then it was so obvious and so expected, perhaps it was a matter of quiet resignation, of acceptance, that this was happening) from their comfortable home in Prague and taken to the town by the fortress of Terezín, a mere sixty kilometres away, at that time a squalid, teeming ghetto for the Jews of Czechoslovakia.

How were they taken? How did it happen? Did the Nazis knock on their door and drag them to a train? Did they receive a letter, asking them to report to a certain place on a certain date? Did they have warning? At least they were together, I think. At least.

NOTES

1. This chapter uses the German term *Theresienstadt* interchangeably with the Czech *Terezín* to refer to the Nazi Ghetto and concentration camp located in north-west Bohemia in today's Czech Republic.
2. M. Hirsch, *The Generation of Postmemory: Writing and Visual Culture After the Holocaust* (New York: Columbia University Press, 2012), p.61.
3. P. Bos, 'Positionality and Postmemory in Scholarship on the Holocaust', *Women in German Yearbook*, 19 (2003), pp.50–74. Children of Holocaust survivors who have published research on the second generation explicitly linked to their own experience include Helen Epstein, author of the first book on the topic, *Children of the Holocaust: Conversations with Sons and Daughters of Survivors* (New York: Penguin Books, 1988); Aaron Hass, whose works include *In the Shadow of the Holocaust: The Second Generation* (London: I.B. Tauris, 1991); and of course Hirsch, author of *Family Frames: Photography, Narrative, and Postmemory* (Cambridge, MA, and London: Harvard University Press, 1997), as well as *The Generation of Postmemory*, among others.
4. Holocaust survivors who are also scholars of the Holocaust include Saul Friedländer, whose works include *Memory, History, and the Extermination of the Jews of Europe* (Bloomington: Indiana University Press, 1993); Geoffrey H. Hartman, who wrote, among others, *The Longest Shadow: In the Aftermath of the Holocaust* (New York and Basingstoke: Palgrave Macmillan, 1996); and Susan Rubin Suleiman, whose personal experience particularly shaped the articles 'Monuments in a Foreign Tongue: On Reading Holocaust Memoirs by Emigrants', *Poetics Today*, 17, 4 (1996), pp.639–57; and 'The 1.5 Generation: Thinking About Child Survivors and the Holocaust', *American Imago*, 59, 3 (2002), pp.277–95.
5. Hirsch, *Family Frames*, p.22.
6. Ibid.
7. See, for instance, G. Weissman, *Fantasies of Witnessing: Postwar Efforts to Experience the Holocaust* (Ithaca, NY, and London: Cornell University Press, 2004), pp.16–18; and R. Crownshaw, 'Photography and Memory in Holocaust Museums', *Mortality*, 12, 2 (2007), pp.176–92.
8. Hirsch, *Family Frames*, p.22.
9. Ibid., p.19.
10. Ibid., p.20.
11. Hirsch, *Generation of Postmemory*, p.61.
12. T. Luckins, 'Collecting Women's Memories: The Australian War Memorial, the Next of Kin and Great War Soldiers' Diaries and Letters as Objects of Memory in the 1920s and 1930s', *Women's History Review*, 19, 1 (2010), p.23.
13. Ibid.
14. E. Hallam and J. Hockey, *Death, Memory and Material Culture* (Oxford and New York: Berg, 2001), p.104.
15. L. Brett, *Too Many Men* (Sydney: Pan Macmillan, 1999), p.272.
16. M.R. Baker, *The Fiftieth Gate* (Sydney: Flamingo, 1997), p.248.
17. Hallam and Hockey, *Death, Memory and Material Culture*, p.104.
18. Daniel Mendelsohn's memoir was one of the first Holocaust memoirs to detail the role of the Internet in tracing family history. Mendelsohn details his global search for Jews from the town of Bolechow, propelled by genealogy websites, newly digitized archives and email contact with Holocaust survivors. See D. Mendelsohn, *The Lost: A Search for Six of Six Million* (New York: Harper Perennial, 2007).
19. A. Radley, 'Artefacts, Memory and a Sense of the Past', in D. Middleton and D. Edwards (eds), *Collective Remembering* (London; Newbury Park, CA; and New Delhi: Sage, 1990), p.48.

20. Ibid., p.52.
21. Ibid., p.54.
22. See, for example, E. Jilovsky, *Remembering the Holocaust: Generations, Witnessing and Place* (London and New York: Bloomsbury Academic, 2015).
23. B.M. Berger, 'How Long is a Generation?', *British Journal of Sociology*, 11, 1 (1960), pp. 10–23.
24. J. Assmann, 'Collective Memory and Cultural Identity', *New German Critique*, 65 (1995), pp.126 -7.
25. Ibid., p.127–8.
26. Ibid., p.129.

A Speechless Country: The Taboo Subject of the Shoah in Austrian Society and Psychotherapeutic Treatment

LIV ZASLAWSKI

After the Shoah, many survivors found new homes in various countries. Relatively few returned to their country of birth, particularly to those countries involved in the crimes against the Jewish population, such as Austria and Germany. As a member of the third generation and practising psychotherapist, I asked myself the following questions. How are Austrian psychotherapists dealing with the topic of the Shoah and the third generation in their daily work? In which aspects does the treatment of Jews affected by the Shoah differ from others? And in which parts are those psychotherapeutic processes similar to therapies with other client groups? To what extent do members of the third generation find both understanding for their situation and the necessary psychotherapeutic support in this country? It is only through consideration and recognition of the historical background and a collective consciousness that a psychological integration can become possible.

1. The Austrian Context

An essential element in this context is the fact that many people in Germany and Austria think that enough time has passed and that one should not have to speak about the Shoah anymore, and that the subsequent perpetrator generation is not at fault and therefore not party to any guilt. However, the Shoah remain a focal point of many therapies (for people on the perpetrator side who are in therapy).[1] It is often noted in families that the Shoah topic is avoided, and frequently the generation to follow takes on these behavioural traits without thinking about them. This further clarifies that the crimes committed during the Third Reich lie like a shadow over the families of the victims as well as their perpetrators.[2]

Although all Austrian citizens are affected by the Shoah in different ways, in my view even in the twenty-first century the crimes committed during the Shoah are still a taboo subject among psychotherapists in Austria. This is suggested by the fact that hardly any talks, speeches or workshops about the implications of the events during the Third Reich are ever offered. Because of Austria's victim-status and the decades-long denial of shared responsibility for the crimes, it has not been possible to approach this topic in a political, psychological and systemic way, nor to speak with one another, or to walk in the shoes of the perpetrators, victims, followers and members of the resistance.

In the psychotherapeutic community as well as in Austrian society there is still fear and anxiety over the events which took place during the Shoah. The mere existence of – or confrontation with – Shoah-affected families triggers shame. Obviously psychotherapists also have to deal with their own shame when treating these clients.

It can further be observed that psychotherapists often forget the political and historical context in which they work. Although the majority of psychotherapy schools in Austria and Germany were established by Jews (for example, Sigmund Freud, Lore Perls, Fritz Perls, Viktor Frankl) and are treasured and revered, they are rarely the subject of discussion nor seen in connection with the founders' consternation over the Nazi regime and the psychotherapy of today. Although many therapists have read Viktor Frankl's works (for example, his memoir *Man's Search for Meaning*[3]) and others, we have no evidence that they have actively dealt with the topic of Shoah in a self-reflecting way.

To date, there is no free discourse in relation to Nazism and its effects. The shame among many psychotherapists in vocalizing ambivalent feelings and thoughts is immense. In the first instance these are carefully examined and sorted, chosen according to appropriate societal norms. The paramount fear is to utter a wrong word and not only to be criticized for it, but also not to belong to 'the goodies' anymore.[4]

On the one hand, there are people in this profession whose relatives were active in the armed forces of the Third Reich, the SS or other Nazi groups and who feel the need to make things right on the basis of the actions of their families. On the other hand, there are many psychotherapists from families of Shoah survivors who still experience the effects of this event right up to the present day.

As previously described, the general method of many Austrians for coping with the crimes committed during the Shoah is with fear, denial and feelings of guilt. Despite the intensive preoccupation with intra- and interpersonal psychological processes, even psychotherapists are not immune to the emotions relating to this topic.

Therefore, as a psychotherapist, it is of particular importance to acquaint oneself with the historical background and relevant psychological ramifications of the entire societal context, not only as a whole, but also for every single individual with the use of intensive methods. The self-reflection of one's own family history and one's own opinion of the Shoah are necessary requirements to be able to offer and administer helpful treatment for survivors, their children and grandchildren.

Questions in relation to the familial circumstances in which this connection might be pursued include: which experiences did my own family have during the Nazi period? Were there perpetrators, victims, followers or people in resistance movements in my family? How did my relatives deal with the Shoah situation? Were there open discussions about the Second World War? Which stance or fundamental attitude did my family take in relation to the Nazi period?

It is not only one's own family history which plays a significant role in the challenges of psychological treatment of families who were affected by the Shoah. One's own prejudices and experiences with Jewish Austrians also come into play and have particular bearing: are there particular prejudices or resentments against Jewish people? What was imparted to me from my family in early years? Do I perceive definite antisemitic thought patterns in Austria, which influence me in particular ways and means?

What is crucial for a healing psychotherapeutic process, next to the aforementioned aspects observed, is without a doubt the reflection of one's own emotions, perceptions and reactions in reference to the crimes committed during the Shoah. Which feelings surface when I am confronted with events of the Third Reich? Are feelings such as fear, shame or emotional paralysis triggered? Is it possible for me to distance myself?

Further to this, one's personal process of coping and the consciousness of how one is affected are of central importance: have I been able to process my own injuries in connection to the Shoah? Am I insecure about feelings of mourning, death and guilt in association with these emotions? Which steps would help me to work my way through, and to psychologically integrate these feelings and emotions?

For psychotherapists, dealing with the consequences of the crimes committed during the Shoah is a special challenge in psychotherapeutic treatments. Due to this it is inevitable that one must reflect on one's own conduct, feelings and life experiences, as a balance between distance and empathy in therapeutic conduct is not always easy to achieve. Self-protection from overwhelming feelings such as fear, loathing, rage, sorrow, guilt and shame can often lead to defence of these emotions. This form of coping can cause complications in contact and empathy in a therapeutic relationship.[5]

The general assumption from a psychotherapeutic perspective is that Shoah survivors and their offspring suffer from heavy pathologies, and their abilities to cope with their lives present crude generalizations. However, one must also take into account the individual differences in relation to the biographical backgrounds, the resilience, personality and emotional strengths for coping with life. The majority of survivors and their families overcame the demands of life with aplomb. All things considered, one must determine that many suffer from a deep pain, which occasionally influences their interpersonal relationships.[6]

2. Helpful Attitudes in Dealing with the Third Generation

Which attitudes and values should psychotherapists have when dealing with members of the third generation? Understandably, even grandchildren of Shoah survivors need psychotherapeutic help and support to better overcome life crises or psychological illness. Alongside topics which are important to all human beings – things like love, appreciation and sacrifice – many psychotherapists ask themselves the question of whether or not special challenges in the treatment of Shoah victims should be taken into consideration.

At specific points in the therapy process it could perhaps become necessary for the healing process to address the experiences of the grandparents under the Nazi regime, thereby supporting the psychological integration of the family's history. An extensive emotional and cognitive knowledge about working with traumatized people and with minorities is especially helpful when working with relatives of Shoah survivors. In addition to this it is necessary to have a thorough understanding of the historical and cultural background of those affected. This enables the therapist to effectively deal with and understand the client's reference framework without too much explanation.[7]

However, it must be emphasized that every family has collected its own experiences during the Nazi regime, and therefore one must see every person as an individual and not as a generalization. To this end, working with resources on hand is of particular importance as many Shoah survivors and their families are happy and living a fulfilled life.

Just as in all psychotherapeutic situations, there are some fundamental human attitudes which have been found to be especially helpful, and thus just as valid, in the psychotherapy of grandchildren of Shoah survivors. However, there are certain topics which appear with more frequency in the foreground of the third generation, and therefore present special significance to the psychotherapeutic process.

2.1 Death and the Subconscious

At a certain point in the psychotherapy of the grandchildren, the experiences of the family during the Shoah become an important topic. Potential fantasies and images seen in dreams or in everyday life are influenced by the feelings of the persecuted or murdered relatives, in particular the omnipresent existential threat.

This begs the question, for the client as well as the psychotherapist, of whether these traumatic contents can be endured by the psychotherapist. The psychological health of the therapist plays a deciding role. Am I strong and stable enough to offer a room which has enough protection and safety?

Will I be capable of enduring that which may come and to accompany the person during their process?[8]

Essential in this connection is also the conduct of the client towards the therapist. Is he/she in a position to understand me? Or is my family history so shocking for everyone that I would prefer to just keep it to myself? At this juncture it is very important that a canvas is prepared in the therapeutic process, onto which the fears, rage and subconscious in connection with the crimes committed during the Nazi regime can be shown. Therapists should, therefore, dependent on client conduct, be defined as supportive and empathetic, in the sense of: I am listening to you, I support you and I am here for you!

However, the third generation is searching for a comparison to adopt which will take on all their existential fears, inundating sorrows and bubbling angers and support them in their coping and integration process: a comparison which can undertake the entire trauma of emotional burden and the forever resurfacing emotions and give them the feeling of being taken care of.

Psychotherapists must maintain modest expectations as the reality of the family in those days is not modifiable. However, for the grandchildren, the pain and the feeling of being alone can be alleviated. Mourning is an emotional expression for a relationship with a lost person and remains for one's entire life, reflecting the feeling of being alone.[9]

2.2 Jewish Identity and Growing Up in Austria

Of special note for the psychological process involving the third generation is the matter of one's own identity, which, due to the experience of living in Austria, presents the possibility that a certain ambiguity exists over which group one belongs to.

With Austrian Jews of the third generation, the 'stigmatization' factors, followed by 'historical/political aspects', are directly important for their own sense of identity. Based on this result, one can perceive that for grandchildren of Shoah survivors it is of particular importance that they are not seen only as Jews, but that they appear as, and are perceived as, an entire person with all his or her characteristics. Nevertheless, it is apparently very important for the process of identity development.[10] The characteristics of Jewish identity have been illuminated in diverse studies.[11] For some, the cultural affiliation to Judaism is characterized due to the religious way of life and traditional Jewish values. While in theory there are a multitude of interpretations, for the majority, the experiences of their families during the Shoah are considered to be the defining factor in their Jewish identity.[12]

To this end it appears extremely difficult for the children and grandchildren of Shoah survivors to unite the apparent un-unitable Jewish and Austrian/German[13] identities with one another. For children or grandchildren who have an Austrian or German parent, this integration of Jewish and Austrian/German parts of their identity seems to be a bit easier, as both sides are inherited.[14]

Third generation members frequently asked themselves 'Am I Jewish or Austrian?' The exploration of one's own identity and the consequences for one's own way of life is of central importance during the therapeutic process. The expression of doubt in relation to one's own affiliation is a deciding factor. Questions in important relation to this matter are, for example: do I want to make known the fact that I am Jewish? Am I afraid of encountering antisemitic reactions? Does the decision to include my Jewish roots mean the exclusion of my Austrian roots? Am I permitted to feel and define myself as Austrian at all? Is being Austrian the same as being a Nazi?

2.2.1 A case vignette: where do I belong?[15]

Iris, 32 years old, participates in a group therapy session offered during her self-awareness process. During the process within the group she suddenly feels a strong discomfort and unease, and the feeling of being different. This is first expressed through a sudden and heavy fit of crying upon recounting her experiences in a pair-exercise. Ever since her earliest childhood, Iris has had the impression that she is different, due to her family history, and even now in the group she feels extremely lonely. She often does not know where she belongs: does she feel Austrian or Jewish? Isn't it contradictory?

On a therapeutic level it is particularly important at this point to take a supportive position towards Iris. As her crying and shaking do not lessen it is crucial for me to offer physical support (to sit next to her and to place my hand on her back). In order to help her to express her feelings in spite of her shame, fear and horrendous grief, I show her she is not alone. While I remain sitting next to her she begins to tell, somewhat hesitantly, her family history.

The Shoah affected her family on her mother's side in numerous ways: many of her relatives were murdered in concentration camps and one part of the family was able to escape to America with the aid of different relief organizations. A large number of her relatives settled in the USA, and her grandmother and great-grandmother on her mother's side returned to Austria. The feeling of not being accepted as an Austrian resurfaces in her repeatedly, and she frequently hears antisemitic expressions.

The weight and shock of the other members of the group is tremendously palpable. However, they are currently not the centre of attention and as a therapist it is nonetheless necessary, regardless of the strong resonance of the group, to stand emotionally by Iris, and to spend time with her on her feelings. The expression of her enormous helplessness, rage and grief is supported through encouragement ('Let it out! Express yourself! Which images and feelings arise in you?').

Iris remarks, under heavy duress, crying and sobbing, that she repeatedly has the feeling that she is standing in a queue to the gas chamber and waiting for her death. Then the feeling of being dead overwhelms her and she doesn't feel anything anymore ... she becomes calm, the crying and sobbing subside. Silence ...

In a therapeutic context it is clearly obvious that when Iris says 'silence' she does not mean silence in the sense of being calm and quiet; rather, the silence of being dead. This is an important step for Iris and yet it is necessary to guide the activation of an intervention. Physically it is obvious that the client is bracing her shoulders and she expresses this verbally: 'I feel such a weight on my shoulders.' As soon as Iris says this it becomes obvious that a physical therapeutic intervention has become necessary, in order to support her expressing her emotions through physical impressions.

Therefore, with her consent I apply pressure to Iris's shoulders to illustrate the heaviness of the topic. At this point her breathing becomes laboured and she says that it is uncomfortable. It is, however, important, in spite of the physical pressure on her body, to continue and to encourage her to say something ('Try to make a noise! Or to say something!'). With each intake of breath it becomes easier for Iris to allow the making of noises and to scream. At the same time, she fights against the pressure with every ounce of her strength. At this juncture it is important for the therapist not to appear shocked, but to welcome every sound, scream and physical show of strength as an expression of strong feelings.

After some time Iris becomes visibly calmer. Her face is considerably more relaxed in spite of the many tears and previous display of rage. Even the physical tenseness has subsided. Following this exhausting physical work it is important that the client lies down and rests. In response to my question: 'Would you like to establish contact with somebody from the group?' Iris says that she feels alone and is almost ashamed. At this point it is important to give the client support and not to overwhelm her with the rest of the group. Therefore, the question must be changed somewhat: 'With whom do you feel safe?' Iris knows immediately which three people in the group she trusts and asks for one of those trusted persons to be with her.

Only through the group experience did it become possible for Iris to undergo and experience her strong feelings in the context of the events that happened during the Shoah, in their entirety and to their full extent. The supportive countenance of the therapist enabled her to express these feelings for the first time in front of so many people. This experience enabled the group to deal with the topic of the Shoah itself. For Iris it was the first time she had expressed herself in a group of non-Jewish people.

2.3 Hate, Mistrust and a Sense of Home

In one study regarding the attitude towards life of Jewish young people who live in Austria or Germany, a certain discrepancy could be observed in relation to their feelings of safety.[16] Although these young people lead materially safe lives in their native countries, there is still a feeling of subjective existential unsafety living as a Jew in Germany. Both these aspects lead on the one hand to an increased sensibility and fear in relation to current antisemitic occurrences and, on the other hand, to feelings of guilt towards older generations. In addition to this, confrontation with antisemitism means that sensitive wounds are reopened. This feeling of being vulnerable and threatened often leads to feelings of rage and hate.[17] To be able to continue living in this country at all it is necessary to be able to control and suppress such feelings of hate and revenge. This in turn can lead to restraining the spontaneity and also to a feeling of incompleteness – as certain emotions are phased out.

During the therapeutic process it is therefore of particular importance to give space to the feelings of hate towards Austria as a country, as well as its inhabitants, in terms of the way human beings were treated during the Shoah. Due to the psychological processes of transference and countertransference, clients have been known to view their therapists as perpetrators and even Nazis, and to confront them with all of their aggressions and feelings of rage. The sheer force of these feelings can sometimes evoke similarly strong reactions from the therapist. As well as feelings of guilt, fears are also an expression of these emotional answers to the transference and can often become a hindrance to the therapeutic process. Nothing is more difficult than opening yourself up with the feeling of overwhelming and upsetting the person sitting opposite you.[18]

Consequently, it is necessary for the therapist to have experienced the phenomenon of transference and countertransference in everyday life, in order to be able to deal adequately with this relationship dynamic. This means especially appreciating the grandchildren of survivors with all of their aggressive feelings and lack of understanding, and to help them express these very necessary feelings (through screaming, crying, ranting and raving). During the process it is good to constantly emphasize that they are doing well and that these feelings are a normal reaction to this family history, as only after exercising and expressing the rage and aggression will the feeling of impotence and helplessness subside, and the perception of one's own capacity be implemented. Only through conscious perception can it become possible to integrate these aggressive impulses and establish a balance in order to properly cope.

It was a lot easier for survivors in America and Israel to develop a sense of belonging, due to exactly these societal attitudes, than it was for those in Germany and Austria. This feeling again promoted the integration into society and further down the line, for their children and grandchildren to be able to develop a sustainable, national feeling of identity. Of observational note is that the generations who, for pragmatic reasons, settled in Germany after the Shoah, as far as the survivors wanted to emigrate, passed on this feeling of rootlessness and delegation to leave the country to their children and grandchildren.[19]

Because of these aggravated conditions in developing a certain affiliation and sense of home as a grandchild of a Shoah survivor, it is necessary for the therapist to support the process of a psychological approach between Austria as a country and its inhabitants. Here too it becomes necessary that the client perceives, recounts and better allocates all the uncomfortable experiences they have had with this state and its associated denizens. Even the guilt-and-shame feelings of the victims of the Shoah, that the 'place of subsistence' is in the 'perpetrator country', can play an important role in processing. With which prejudices against non-Jewish Austrians and Austria will I be continually confronted? Which prejudices of my own do I have? Do I see myself as a member of society or do I see myself according to my family history as an outsider? Does the desire to belong reside within me? Should such desires exist?

A further essential aspect in this context is the interpersonal relationships with non-Jewish Austrians. Presumably, the feeling of flawed inner psychological and societal integration with Jews living in Germany and Austria lead to a withdrawal from the non-Jewish majority and a preference for Jewish groups.[20]

Certainly the way a family copes is a deciding influential factor. Only when the grandchild experiences that there is no differentiation between parents and grandparents in dealing with Jewish and non-Jewish persons does openness to all human beings seem possible. Obviously, at different points in life it becomes necessary to have more or less contact with other relatives of the third generation, to be able to support one's own analysis of one's identity. However, it is undoubtedly a healing experience to discover that non-Jewish people are understanding, empathetic and can deal with one's family history reflectively.

During the therapeutic process this topic can be discussed and integrated in completely different ways. However, for the psychotherapist, some aspects should be noted. Even if the psychotherapist is not Jewish, is it possible to make our therapeutic relationship a disposable one, and to deal with possible prejudices and projections against Austria as a country? Only through the free, uncensored expression of all resentments does it become possible to see the other side, which has perhaps been shaped from the joy of living in that country.

Also of significance is the topic of contact with non-Jewish Austrians. Have feelings of mistrust and hate sometimes been experienced? Which images and thoughts are in my head in certain situations? Can someone speak freely about their family history or should one expect incomprehension and animosity? Are there also positive experiences? If so, what is the positive? Are there also moments in which I feel I belong, or feel I can belong? Is there also the possibility for me to face non-Jewish Austrians of the third generation?

2.3.1 A case vignette: friend or foe?[21]

Brian (35 years old) would like to undergo psychotherapy due to incidences of reoccurring, overwhelming feelings of emotion whilst travelling on the underground metro and in the company of large groups of people. During these situations Brian experiences extreme heart palpitations, perspiration and anxiety attacks. He has been suffering from fear of social interaction and mistrust of others for many years, and is very hesitant at making new friends. The young man has no close friendships or relationships to speak of, and intermittently suffers greatly because of it. During the therapy session Brian appears unsure of himself and gives only very hesitant accounts. He finds it very difficult to open up to strangers (in this case me, his therapist).

In two years of psychotherapy the central aspect during Brian's treatment was the therapeutic relationship. The therapist represents a stable counterpart and perceives her client with all his or her needs and fears. In the first session, Brian already speaks of having the feeling of infinite helplessness and impotence in his fear-related situations. To this, he adds how difficult it is for him to confide in me during his session. It was important here to work with Brian on identifying at which points during the conversation he had feelings of mistrust towards the therapeutic relationship: 'How do you feel with me?' 'In which moments is it difficult to open up?' In addition to the psychotherapeutic situation it becomes necessary to incorporate family history, which the client also considers a big influence on his current life.

Brian's grandfather on his father's side was, due to his Jewish background, forced to spend many years in hiding during the Second World War. The parents and the sister of the grandfather were murdered in the concentration camps. Brian was directly and indirectly told, by both his grandfather and his father, to exercise particular vigilance during the day, and that in order to prevent incidences such as the Shoah in the future, one must be politically active. The isolation of the family from the Austrian community is clearly evident to Brian. He describes his nearest relatives as warm-hearted and fierce. During the description Brian seems nervous and explains how the fear symptoms are getting stronger.

At this point in his rehabilitation it is a healing factor for grandchildren of Shoah survivors to experience that the therapist remains in contact even though the topic triggers particular difficulties for everyone involved. Only an internal therapeutic mindset of 'I can endure this! I will stay with you! We will work through this topic together!' makes it possible for the client to develop feelings of safety and security.

In spite of all the difficult experiences held in conjunction with the Shoah, it is of huge importance to keep the resources and needs of the client in the foreground. This means on the one hand creating and allowing space for the entire topic of the Shoah, but, on the other, underlining the client's positive experiences: 'You have accomplished much in your life, you have a satisfying job and close contact to your family. You have reported that your family is very close-knit. Do you feel this is a support for you?'

It is important at this point, as the therapist, not to appear entranced and be made to feel helpless in the shadow of the Shoah, and, as a result, avoid the topic. This often necessitates a reflection of one's feelings of countertransference: to what extent do I, as a therapist, feel overwhelmed and helpless in this situation? Are these my own emotions or are these uncertainties an expression of the spiritual state of my client? Only through the awareness of the relationship between therapist and client will it become possible to abet or bring about a changing process. Psychotherapy offers a field in which new and positive experiences can be had.

In addition to this it appears helpful as the therapist to discuss the client's views with him in a supportive and helpful way, and to make him aware of this. For example: 'The fear and grief your family had to undergo is undoubtedly a heavy burden for you to bear on some days! And it is therefore completely understandable that the reaction towards this terrible ordeal manifests itself in mistrust towards others.' At this point it becomes possible for Brian to approach the contents of his (in his own opinion, frequently irrational) fears, and to express them without censorship, so that he begins to have the feeling that he is understood and tolerated in all facets of himself. Of particular importance are the descriptions of his fears of persecution and his fear of death, which, at this juncture, form the two existential aspects important for the advancement of the formation of his well-being.

After about ten sessions Brian indicates that his nervousness during therapy has receded considerably. He feels that he is, here, in good hands confiding his family history and that he feels supported and secure. However, the client also remarks upon his mistrustful and insecure attitude towards others: 'here in therapy I feel secure but how will it be if I have to talk about my family history with others?'

It was important during treatment to highlight his fears in relation to the 'real world' together with him: 'In which situations do you have the impression that you are overcome with mistrust? How would people behave if you told them about your family history?' After some time spent upon the topic of his mistrust and uncertainty in contact with other people, the development of possible perspectives in experiencing other people arose, in particular the differentiated perception of here and now ('there are people I can trust and those who unfortunately, do not react as I would like them to. But due to the positive experiences I have had, it is possible for me to put up with non-reflective, upsetting behaviour') and the prospect of the future plays a deciding role ('I wish to have sustainable friendships and a partnership in which I will be accepted in all my complexities!').

The contact between Brian and the therapist made it possible for him to be more open and trustworthy towards meeting new people, and for him to be able to more accurately perceive himself and others. Only through the observance of his family history and the benevolent, appreciative demeanour of the therapist did it become possible for Brian to experience for himself that he could be tolerated, loved and accepted with all his emotionally draining yet also positive experiences.

3. Conclusion

Alongside the most commonly occurring topics such as relationships, sorrow, and fear from rejection in psychotherapy with the third generation, the following are often in the foreground: one's own identity, insofar as the Jewish and Austrian parts unite with one another, together with one's own mourning and impotence in relation to the crimes committed during the Shoah and the feelings of hate towards Austria and its population. Of essential importance in connection with the psychotherapeutic treatment of different client groups is the inclusion of knowledge about historical conditions and load factors in the historical process. The Austrian history of the Nazi period and the associated crimes against humanity especially still hold repercussions for the generations of today and thus the psychotherapeutic processes.

Psychotherapists are confronted daily with victims, perpetrators and followers of the Nazi period, as well as their relatives. But only a few members of this profession know that the crimes committed during the Shoah, the mourning for the victims, and the endorsement of this regime represent much more than just historical circumstances, and are instead to be understood as reoccurring, collective, current and subconscious conflicts that have far-reaching consequences.[22] To date, one can observe a certain shame in the psychotherapeutic scene in regard to the Third Reich. A certain type of shame, guilty feelings and fear is perceptible as soon as this topic is spoken about and noticed.

The fundamental issue is that psychotherapists are only in the position of being a suitable counterpart for grandchildren of Shoah survivors when they have grappled with their own and familial affectedness, their own antisemitic mindset and therefore stigmatized prejudice in reference to the third generation. Only through the reflection of their own role in the system, as well as their own values and conceptions of the world, will it become possible to recognize which points in the processes of transference and countertransference happen when, and which method of coping is helpful for the client.

For the psychotherapist, without this intensive preoccupation, he or she can become involved in the sense of a helper-syndrome, due to feelings of guilt or through his or her own family having been affected, and a strong identification with the help-seeker can develop. Both can have difficult consequences as the essential point, the emotions of the client, is lost from view. Only through the perception of a person in all his or her facets and characteristics is it possible to supportively accompany the client on his or her way to healing.[23]

Also, when at different points during the psychotherapeutic process the grandchildren become preoccupied with the family history and the crimes committed during the Shoah, it is extremely important to know and understand that every family has their own experiences and therefore the individual coping process is of central importance. Of course, according to all other psychotherapies as well as in the treatment of the grandchildren of Shoah survivors, the fundamental therapeutic behaviour of a resource-orientated, emphatic, authentic approach is of central importance.

For the therapeutic process it is necessary that psychotherapists welcome and can tolerate all emotions, including those of particularly distinct severity, including those of particularly distinct severity, as only then is it possible for the clients to feel that they can express themselves and do not have to suppress their emotions. To this end it is possible that at times they can transfer their aggressive feelings toward the psychotherapist. Understandably, it can happen that these feelings are very uncomfortable for the therapist. However, it is necessary for the integration of these impulses that the therapist tolerates this, and always reflects upon his/her own transference feelings.[24]

It is important to understand psychotherapy with the third generation not only as psychotherapeutic treatment of a minority group, but moreover to observe the consequences for the context of society as a whole. Therefore, it must not be overlooked that according to the perpetrators and followers, huge consequences of the Nazi period are as perceptible today as they were then. Only through the process of raising awareness and preoccupation with corresponding emotions is it possible for the future generation to be able to further integrate another piece of the trauma of the Shoah.

NOTES

1. U. Benz, 'Die Wiederkehr des Verdrängten in der Praxis. Kindertherapeutin im Spannungsfeld zwischen Psychoanalyse und Geschichte', [The Return of the Repressed in Practice: A Child Therapist in the Area of Conflict between Psychoanalysis and History], in R. Ludewig-Kedmi, M.V. Spiegel and S. Tyrangiel (eds), *Das Trauma des Holocaust zwischen Psychologie und Geschichte* [The Trauma of the Holocaust between Psychology and History.] (Zurich: Chronos Verlag, 2002), p.97.
2. K. Brendler, 'Die NS-Geschichte als Sozialisationsfaktor und Identitätsballast' [Nazi History as Socialization Factor and Identity Burden], in D. Bar-On, K. Brendler and A.P. Hare (eds), *'Da ist etwas kaputtgegangen an den Wurzeln...': Identitätsformation deutscher und israelischer Jugendlicher im Schatten des Holocaust* [Something Broke at the Roots...Identity Formation of German and Israeli Teenagers in the Shadow of the Holocaust] (Frankfurt am Main: Campus Verlag, 1997), p.79.
3. V. Frankl, *Man's Search for Meaning* (London: Rider, 2004).
4. See Brendler, 'Die NS-Geschichte', p.79.
5. J. Herman Lewis, *Die Narben der Gewalt: Traumatische Erfahrungen verstehen und überwinden* [Scars of Violence: Understanding and Overcoming Traumatic Experiences] (Munich: Kindler, 1993), p.311.
6. S. Uri, *Enkelkinder von Shoah-Überlebenden* [Grandchildren of Shoah Survivors] (unpublished masters thesis, University of Vienna, 2004), p.165.
7. S. Konrad, *'Jeder hat seinen eigenen Holocaust': Die Auswirkungen des Holocaust auf jüdische Frauen dreier Generationen* ['Everyone has their own Holocaust': The Effects of the Holocaust on Jewish women over three generations] (Giessen: Halland & Wirth, 2007), pp.424–7.
8. Ibid., p.424.
9. Ibid., pp.427–8.
10. E. Branik, 'Identitätsprobleme jüdischer Jugendlicher in Deutschland' [Identity Problems for Jewish Teenagers living in Germany] , in Gertrude Hardtmann (ed.), *Spuren der Verfolgung: Seelische Auswirkungen des Holocaust auf die Opfer und ihre Kinder* [Traces of Persecution: Psychological Consequences of the Holocaust for the Victims and their Children] (Gerlingen: Bleicher Verlag, 1992), pp.143–6.
11. See Branik, 'Identitätsprobleme jüdischer Jugendlicher', pp.143–6; and Uri, *Enkelkinder von Shoah-Überlebenden.*
12. See Branik, 'Identitätsprobleme jüdischer Jugendlicher', pp.143–6.
13. Austrian/German: the results of the study are valid for Austrian and German citizens.
14. See Konrad, *Jeder hat seinen eigenen Holocaust*, pp. 424–7.
15. The case vignette illustrates a psychotherapeutic treatment in German in my own practice. The name and age have been changed and I have translated the shown process into English.
16. N. Durst, 'Eine Herausforderung für Therapeuten: Psychotherapie mit Überlebenden der Shoah'[A Challenge for Therapists: Psychotherapy with Shoah Survivors], in R. Ludewig-Kedmi, M.V. Spiegel and S. Tyrangiel (eds), *Das Trauma des Holocaust zwischen Psychologie und Geschichte* [The Trauma of the Holocaust between Psychology and History.] (Zurich: Chronos Verlag, 2002), pp.94–5.
17. See Konrad, *Jeder hat seinen eigenen Holocaust*, pp.424–7.
18. Ibid., 427–8.
19. R. Ludewig-Kedmi and S. Tyrangiel, 'Zwischen Trauer, Schuldgefühlen und Opferneid' [Between Sadness, Feelings of Guilt and Victim Jealousy], in R. Ludewig-Kedmi, M.V. Spiegel and S. Tyrangiel (eds), *Das Trauma des Holocaust zwischen Psychologie und Geschichte* [The Trauma of the Holocaust between Psychology and History.] (Zurich: Chronos Verlag, 2002), pp.37–40.
20. See Konrad, *Jeder hat seinen eigenen Holocaust*, pp.424–7.
21. The case vignette illustrates a psychotherapeutic treatment in German in my own practice. The name and age have been changed and I have translated the shown process into English.
22. See Benz, 'Die Wiederkehr des Verdrängten in der Praxis', p.97.
23. See Ludewig-Kedmi and Tyrangiel, 'Zwischen Trauer, Schuldgefühlen und Opferneid', pp.37–40.
24. See Durst, 'Eine Herausforderung für Therapeuten', p.95.

JAP: Jewish American Preppy

FELICE COHEN

I am a grandchild of Holocaust survivors, but growing up on Cape Cod, Massachusetts, I had no idea what that meant. Despite my parents' earnest efforts to acculturate me into their Jewish heritage, my actual heritage was the sea, sand dunes, playing sports, watching cranberries being harvested, and polo shirts. Without question I was Jewish, but aside from Hebrew lessons, being Jewish was only one of many after-school activities to which my mother took me, along with tennis, basketball, piano and drama club.

When the Jewish holidays came around each December, I was one of only a few students who had a menorah at home instead of a Christmas tree. Even some of the other Jewish kids had a Christmas tree substitute, a 'Hanukkah bush'. I was aware of being somewhat different from my friends whose parents had cocktails before dinner. These differences were never really significant, as they were distinctive only during the Jewish holidays, after which they were quickly forgotten, like a passing shower.

That was until the summer my grandparents came for a visit when I was 10. To say that their personalities and their entire way of living were different from the lives of other Cape Cod adults I knew would be a huge understatement. They lived in Brooklyn, but their accents were not 'New York'; they were European, which sounded like a whole other world. To make this difference official, furthermore, they also spoke another language, Yiddish, which they would use when wanting to say something that my sisters and I wouldn't understand. I loved them like crazy, but they had lots of mystery and complexities.

Then there was the issue of food. They arrived with their car's trunk filled with kosher meats, breads and cakes. The markets on Cape Cod did not sell the foods they could eat. And when they ate, nothing was wasted. Nothing. Ever.

Their brand of Judaism was also quite different from our 'Cape' version. Theirs was tangible, practised in the home, and not just in synagogue once a year during the High Holy days in September. In my grandparents' home were two sets of daily dishes, one for meat and one for dairy. In our house we had two sets of dishes too, but one was for everyday and the other for 'company'. While my family went to temple – albeit a Reform temple, where the rabbi was an avid sailor and drove a sports car – my grandparents went 'religiously' to a Conservative shul every Saturday and my grandfather davened and 'laid on' tefillin every morning. Though my sisters and I went to Hebrew school and Sunday school, had bat mitzvahs and were confirmed, there was something peripheral about our Judaism. It was as though we were Jewish only on certain occasions and not on others, when we were just plain 'us'.

Despite the different approaches between our religious practices, I was always very close to my grandfather, whom I called Papa and whom I adored. Whenever he saw me, he would take me aside. 'Feigela', he'd say, putting a twenty-dollar bill into my hand. 'Go put this somewhere you shouldn't lose it.' Then he'd smile, though his eyes always contained a certain sadness. I knew he had been in something called the 'Holocaust' years before, but I thought the Holocaust was a place in Germany – a place, the message came through, that I never wanted to visit.

In seventh grade, during a lesson on the Holocaust, I finally learned that the Holocaust wasn't a town in Europe but a location of Hell. One day my mother was invited to speak to my class about being a child of Holocaust Survivors. I knew little about my grandparents' earlier lives and even less about what they'd suffered. As my mother spoke about their actual lives (and deaths) in Europe's concentration camps and hearing these facts for the very first time, I sat frozen, flooded with a special, terrible responsibility associated with being Jewish. And somehow, from that moment on, all the pink and green Lacoste shirts in the world weren't going to change that new layer of my identity.

Years later, in college, I accidentally discovered that my maternal grandmother, Fela, Papa's first wife, the woman I am named after, did not die from cancer as I'd been told when I was growing up. Driving in the car one evening with my father, crossing the Sagamore Bridge onto Cape Cod, the sun melting into its normal fringes of pink and orange, we got to talking about how my parents grew up. 'After all', he said, 'your mother had to care for her brothers after her mom committed suicide.'

'What?' I said. He thought I had known. I felt a wave of sympathy. Once home I found my mother reading in bed to my younger sister Jackie. I wasn't angry but apologized. 'I'm so sorry!' I said, falling onto her, tears spilling out. All those years of feeling that sometimes I did not understand my mother or being annoyed with her seemingly continuous concern, she had actually been shielding us from this information. In her eyes she was preserving our innocence and giving us an opportunity to grow up without fear.

Now, with the floodgates opened, I had questions. What made my grandmother do it? After all, hadn't she survived the Holocaust? To supplement my mother's knowledge, she suggested I also go to 'the source', her father.

'Papa, why did Nana commit suicide?' I asked him over the phone. He was silent. Papa had never spoken of her suicide before. In fact, he, my mother and two uncles had avoided discussing the event so central in their own lives for years, even among themselves. Even to other relatives and friends, they said something else. But it was always there, a shadow over my two uncles' bar mitzvahs and my mother's wedding. The four of them, bound together, protecting each other against this terrible truth, dealt with her suicide silently and separately.

Now there I was, twenty-five years after her death, asking Papa about a topic he had never wanted to unearth again. Perhaps it was that enough time had passed or because we, he and myself, his first grandchild, had always shared a special bond. Whatever the reason, Papa began to tell his story. But in order for him to put my question into perspective, he first had to explain another subject of which he never spoke: the absolute terror and near-crippling fear that had been his education about the world: the Holocaust.

My grandmother was the youngest of eleven children, all of them together in Poland. When the Second World War started they were trapped inside the Lodz Ghetto. The SS eventually murdered almost everyone in her family, leaving only my grandmother, one of her older sisters and that sister's 3-year-old twin boys. On one terrible day, as the four of them hid in their apartment, the SS stormed in and simply took away the older sister. As they dragged her out, she screamed to my grandmother, 'Take care of my boys! Promise me nothing should harm them!' Of course my grandmother, panicked and terrified also, promised. But that same afternoon, the SS returned for the twin boys who were wailing with fright. Though she struggled, hanging onto their coats to keep the twins, my grandmother, an emaciated young girl, was no match for the SS. In moments, she was left alone, with only a permanent stab-wound of guilt that she should have done more to save them from disappearing forever.

The next day, the SS returned, again like an implacable wave, and took my grandmother. She was brought to Auschwitz, where she realized what had happened to her nephews. She saw other babies whose bodies were broken in tugs-of-war, their remains tossed into fires, discarded like waste. Realizing this could have been the same fate her sister's children suffered, the guilt grew. It eventually accompanied her to Bergen Belsen, from which she was liberated and where she met Papa. But even free, this guilt followed her to America, where it remained like a shadow.

Over the next 20 years, while living in Brooklyn, physically far from the war, with her three children, and helping to run a small neighbourhood supermarket with her husband, the shadow would occasionally darken her vision to the point of immobility. There were attempts to 're-electrify' her personality with shock therapy at Bellevue Hospital in Manhattan, but none lasted. Ultimately the guilt bored so deep that the only relief she would find was to end her life, which she did by hanging herself in their apartment, where her youngest son, aged 6, and her daughter, aged 18, found her one afternoon after school.

'My God', I thought, after hearing Papa tell me the truth. 'How could this happen?' At the time I was a weekly columnist for *The Daily Collegian* at the University of Massachusetts Amherst. After talking with Papa, I wanted to break the cycle of silence in our family's history and attempt to ease the pain. I wrote an op-ed about my grandmother and was astonished at the size and intensity of the feedback from students and faculty. Apparently there were others – many others – who had been touched by this same history. But the most significant response was from Papa himself, who finally felt relief having been released from that secret.

'Feigela', he said, speaking my Yiddish name,

> I want you should write my story so that no one should ever forget. I want my children and grandchildren to know what I went through. How I survived, by working hard and being lucky, but also why I survived. Because every day in the camps I believed one day I would have a wife and children and more family to replace all those who were murdered.

Papa had never asked me for anything before. I said 'Yes, of course', figuring that he would tell me stories; I would type them and hand out copies to the family. I had no idea this request would take eighteen years to complete or that it would change the course of my life.

The two of us began this project on my visits to Brooklyn, New York, during the spring and to Boca Raton, Florida, during the winter. We would sit together, and as my grandfather would begin to speak, this man who was once silent on the subject found he had much to say.

But it wasn't always easy. By actually speaking these stories aloud, Papa was forced to relive his time in the camps. He spoke of the death marches, hunger, illness, the smells of human waste, and death. For many survivors, revisiting the past was not easy, as was the fatal case with my grandmother. But Papa was as determined to get his story out as he was to have survived it the first time. He wanted his family to know. And despite the moments when he'd pause when his emotions simply took over, he managed to survive the second experiencing.

I, on the other hand, tried to be 'professional', at a distance. 'So you woke up next to a corpse, then what did you do?' Or 'They shot your father because he stepped out of line to get a sweater? Then what happened?' It was not until

I was home assembling these stories, that it dawned on me that what I was writing were not facts from a text book, they were my grandfather's own personal experience, my family's history. That's when my own tears arrived. And as I wrote I began to see through a new set of eyes – Papa's eyes – that looked at the world through constant fear and pain and hope.

Finally, after hundreds of questions and hours of tapes, when Papa had nothing more to add or hide, and I had nothing left to ask, he told me I was ready to write 'The Book', as he had begun to call it over the years of interviews. During those years, though I moved from Massachusetts to Manhattan, changed careers, wrote another book and started new relationships, still there was one constant left on every To Do list: write The Book. I'd work on it regularly, yet for some reason I couldn't put a 'whole' concept to The Book – a concept that would express its meaning for me. And just in case Papa thought I had forgotten my assignment, he would remind me.

'Feigela, how's The Book?' he would say whenever we spoke on the phone. 'You know I'm not getting any younger. I want I should be here to read it.' Papa was right. He wasn't getting any younger. And neither was I. But even with all this information, something was keeping me from finishing The Book and I couldn't figure out what.

The 'what' arrived in 2008.

I was part of a tour group whose members were from - or who once had relatives in - Szczekociny, Poland, the town where Papa spent his adolescence. I travelled there with twelve others who lived in New York or Israel, to see where our parents and grandparents lived before their lives were interrupted (or terminated) by the Nazis.

We arrived in Szczekociny on a cloudy morning. Getting off the bus, we were welcomed by a silent group of thirty townspeople who stared at us as if they had never seen Jews before. Turns out most hadn't. Before the war, 1,500 Jews lived in this small town. That day in 2008? Not a single one.

The tour of Szczekociny was given in Polish and translated into English and Hebrew. It led us to an expansive green lawn that looked perfect for picnics. Seconds after wondering if Papa had picnicked there with his family, I learned it had been the location where the town's Jews had been forced at gunpoint to gather for 'selection' before being sent either to labour camps or to death camps. It was on that spot where I stood that Papa had also stood when he was considered healthy and taken away to the first of four labour camps and then four concentration camps. It was on that spot that Papa saw his family for the last time.

The grim tour eventually ended in front of public rest rooms. Rest rooms? I thought as I waited for the tour guide's speech to be interpreted. Why would we stop there?

'The rest rooms had been deliberately erected in 2002 on the site of the town's ancient Jewish cemetery', said the guide as it started to rain. Where my ancestors had been buried. 'The graves were excavated, their remains tossed, the headstones turned into people's backyard patios.'

My hands balled into fists, rage built inside me and I cried. That's it, I realized. That's what had been keeping me from finishing Papa's book. All during our interviews I had not experienced what Papa's journey had to do with me. Witnessing the immediate antisemitism, and in the exact same place where Papa first experienced it, made me realize that The Book was not just for Papa, but his story was for me, my sisters, nieces, nephews, cousins and perhaps many others. His recollections were universal enough that it justified the effort to tell his story publicly. We could not forget. I went home and finished The Book.

One day there will be no survivors left to tell their stories as Papa did for me. It will be up to us – the third generation – to understand and preserve these conversations. For the most part, survivors did not talk to their children about their lives during the Holocaust, as it was too difficult, and they needed to forget. It may be easier for them to rest the burden of their stories on the shoulders of their grandchildren, who didn't have such great reliance on the parenting responsibilities of survivors. Also, perhaps because they know we're probably the last generation to hear their stories first-hand and we have enough of the American experience to serve as a buffer to our grandparents' lives in hell.

After *What Papa Told Me*[1] was published, Papa and I appeared together at schools and temples. At one school in Florida we spoke to more than 100 fifth-graders. When Papa was done telling his story, the students ran up to him as though he were a rock star, wanting to shake his hand, hug him, touch this living piece of history. Papa's eyes, which during his talk had been misty, beamed with pride. Those five unbelievable years, during which my grandfather witnessed what no human being should, remain fresh in his nightmares, but by sharing his story it has lessened its burden. Papa now feels he survived for a reason, that his life now has a purpose.

As do I.

Writing this book with my grandfather at first felt like a burden, the pressure to get his story told. Now, after thousands of copies of The Book have been sold and distributed to schools, museums, libraries and individuals all over the world, and having spoken to thousands of people about The Book, I realize that as fortunate as I am to have been given this gift from Papa, I am just as fortunate to have been able to give the gift right back to him. Papa, at 92, has finally discovered how to relate to the world in a way he could not for years.

Today, when I say I am a grandchild of survivors, I know exactly what it means, and it has become a title I am more comfortable wearing than I do a shirt with an alligator on it. The process, the understanding and the acceptance of my grandparents' history have strengthened the connection to my Judaism, and have helped me to recognize that my grandparents' differences are honourable marks of survival.

9. Felice Cohen & Murray Schwartzbaum at the bar mitzvah of one of his eleven great-grandchildren, April 2012. Copyright/permission granted by Felice Cohen.

NOTE

1. F. Cohen, *What Papa Told Me* (New York: Dividends Press, 2010).

In-between

ANTHONY LEVIN

2 February 1982, 11.14 p.m.

I am about to be born. In a moment, the doorway will open and I will float across the bridge between realms. Above my head is a candle that for nine months has lit the path from this world to the World to Come. *But which is which?* My guardian, Lailah, Angel of Conception – though she goes by many names – has taught me well: all the books of the Torah, the meaning of purity and goodness, the history of my soul. Until now, in accordance with Jewish tradition, her task has been to teach and to keep watch. She has led me to the Garden of Eden to show me the righteous ones with crowns on their heads; and she has dragged me kicking to the underworld to show me the punishments of Gehenna, land of apostates.

Yet still I am disoriented. I can see her now, beginning to enter the womb, carrying planetary movements in her wake. She is stroking my mass of black hair, smiling beatifically. My cluster of fingers tightens slightly; waves of liquid warmth tremble and cool around still-webbed parts. I know what is coming. I have heard the rumours. I should be prepared, but I am not. I want to go; but not like this. There is too much I don't yet know. *I need more time*. They say that just before the moment of departure, Lailah taps her fingers above the lips, gently, and just like that, as if memory were an image inside a bubble of foam, she erases everything.

If knowledge is something acquired through space and over time, then I must tell this story from in-between cracks.

I am on my way to Auschwitz-Birkenau. It is a name I have known for too long. The ghost-house of my childhood where my grandmother's stories were staged. *Auschwitz* – that anteroom of sense that so darkly precedes the place. I am *going* to Auschwitz. *An* Auschwitz, not *the* Auschwitz – merely a version. And what apostasy is it that drives me to go, to think that in going I might fill the cracks, or even be capable of uttering that word and have it mean anything, anything near to what my grandmother means when her mouth opens and the painful onomatopoeia begins to take shape in her throat?

After Auschwitz, I will be born again, I tell myself. But I do not believe it. I am filled with pre-cathartic tension. Although I am travelling with a group of Jews and a survivor-guide named Arek, I know already that the journey will be solitary, interior. And that it began long ago.

Mid-September 1944

After being discovered in hiding, my grandmother and her immediate family were arrested and pushed into a cattle car in Sered, Czechoslovakia, along with 120 others, bound for Auschwitz. In her memoir, *Auschwitz to Australia*, she writes: 'The word "Auschwitz" was heard, but it meant very little to us at the time.'[1] When the dark carriage finally came to a halt, she heard music: 'An orchestra was playing light operatic tunes to "welcome" us. It hit me that the music belonged not to the world of the living, but of the dead. The merry tunes were really the songs of unbelievable heartache and immeasurable sorrow.'[2] I have never asked if she knew the opera being played as prisoners in striped clothing known as *Kanadakommando* came to take away her bags. Was it Bach? Or could it have been Schumann's *Träumerei*, which means 'daydream'?

2 February 1982, 11.15 p.m.

From womb to world, I draw in to my spirit a confluence of astrological events: Jupiter in nine degrees Scorpio, my ascendant in Libra; Mars and Saturn in the twelfth House of my astrological chart, the House of the Collective Unconscious. This is the place of dreams and the past; sorrow and loss. It is the House of events formed before conscious remembrance, the House of inherited family life. The chief planetary watchman, Saturn, governs sorrow, regret and things connected with the past. His accomplice, Mars, is the cosmic engine of growth. Mars, the colour of blood.

Lailah, *you bitch*. I *see* you now, donning your final appellation as the Angel of Forgetting, poised to issue the fillip that will awaken my voice from aqueous slumber. The rumours are true. Here you are with a bent spoon ready to snuff out my light. A bent spoon! Where did you get such a crooked implement, singed by infinite acts of forgetting? And my lips – I shall cover my mouth so you cannot touch them. Find another child to issue your empty tears. I will not bear the philtrum of babes as some unspoken testament to all that has come before, or to remind the world of our complicity in infinitude. I will do more than bear loss silently under my nose. I *will* cry out, but not from the shock of being struck by you, No, but from the wells filled with unfinished life and the wails that scramble towards the light.[3]

In the Harmony of the Spheres, what is the sound of Saturn? Is it the silent heaving sob? The Mourner's Kaddish? What raw songs rise from the taught strings of the saturnine?

15 April 1945

When she was liberated from Bergen-Belsen by British troops, my grandmother was just 18 years old. Soldiers emerged from tanks to hand out biscuits and baked beans. The first offering – powdered milk – caused an outbreak of vomiting and diarrhoea. She tongued the ulcers in her mouth and ate nothing. Other than this image, I can recall only the barest details of her story. Like what her body was like then: twenty-nine kilograms. The facts are part of my programmatic forgetting. I have only fuzzy mental lists: dysentery, lice, Mengele, typhus – words which have become a coda for loss too large to bear. To remember what they stand in for, I must consult her testimony again and again:

> We arrived at the tent and walked in facing the officer behind the table. My mother went first ... Each of us was then issued with a small white Displaced Persons card which we had to sign. My mother was so weak she could not hold the card firmly in her hands. I had to hold the card for her. We then made our way out of the tent. Then what I dreaded most happened. My mother collapsed ...
>
> She lay there ashen coloured and made no response to me. I placed my hands over her short dark stubs of hair and tried to speak to her, softly, but she did not respond. I begged her to say something to me, and kept saying over and over: 'Mama, please do not leave me now. We are free. We are going home. Please do not leave me alone!'[4]

January 1988

As a child, at night, I went to bed with the fear that if I left my arms outside the covers, they would be cut off. My solution was to lie extremely still, with arms pinned to my sides, the covers tucked tightly up around my neck. In the dark, I lay wide-eyed, searching the shadows for murder. This phobia proved interminable during the Sydney summer, when I would sweat through humidity until at last I fell asleep, capitulating to unconscious needs. In the morning I found my arms were on top of the quilt – attached.

The next night, not knowing why, I would repeat the ritual.

It is well known in trauma theory that survivors relive their experiences, haunted by images never fully assimilated into consciousness.[5] As the grandchild of two survivors who openly and frequently returned to such images during weekend visits, I have rarely needed to ask for stories. If the death camps are the locus classicus of the Holocaust, then the large white house on the corner is the font of testimony. There, my sister and I spent weekends watching my grandmother – a study in trauma.

The kitchen was the first site of initiation. Over frankfurters, sauerkraut, salted tomatoes, preserved cucumbers and fresh bread smothered in butter, I heard the story of how my grandmother's mother collapsed a hundred times. But when she tells it in person, across the table, there is a detail not contained in her book. I can mouth the words for you:

The day we were liberated, my mother died in my arms.

With our stomachs full of Bratislava and our minds reeling, initiation continued in the television room. On Saturday evenings, my sister and I endured Holocaust documentaries like Chinese dissidents in re-education camps. Almost always in black and white with grave male narrators, they featured footage of Hitler shouting maniacally at Nuremberg or photographs of mass graves. I realized much later that these nightly viewings – often the last activity before bed – were repetitions. As I watched, less learning facts than acquiring images of horror, my grandmother sat *reliving*. With every emaciated figure, her relatives materialized and amassed. Swimming in the air above us were clouds of melancholia, precipitating loss in waves, washing the pristine walls, leaving forensic residues. In our blue-lit *Träumerei*, I sensed the nightmare being entered through a wedged door. I sensed the illness driving the Return, its destructive bent. I could not give it words, but I knew after years of these sessions that I no longer wanted to watch. I stored that sense, for I did not know how to translate it.

> That phrase, *my arms*, *my arms*,
> her arms which held her mother, dead. This
> forged in mind – I cannot erase;
> it is there, a past that is not past.
> Immemorial, un-done.
> Did I fear to lose my arms – or hers?

Perhaps it was the psychic projection of my deeper fear that if I lost them I could not carry all the dead.

The effect of repetitive history lessons is amnesiac rather than edifying. A saturation of facts eventually leads to bastard knowledge. In spite of, or due to, being 'homeschooled' in Holocaust studies from an early age, I cannot tell you exactly where anecdote ends and archive begins. Perhaps it is where my grandmother's breath dives across space and condenses on my cheek, rich with homeopathic memory, craving to enter the pores of new purpose. I do not know if 'transmission' is the right word for this, or if it is, what exactly is transmitted. I prefer to think of it as *living in the aura of trauma*, since it conveys a sense in which something personal is shared without necessarily existing physically in space-time as we know it. If only because it makes sense of what is senseless, I must make room for such mysteries – for the host of mirror-effects hidden deep within the cells, which call to one another as relatives call to each other separated in a crowd, issuing songs from the heartfelt regions of sound that penetrate darkness and trial, each note inscribed with the distinctive timbre of a family's survival. Calls that connect mother to child, the very lineaments of love rendered in supernatural filigree.

From image to image and to image again, we descend, into the cruel light of things we do not understand and can never know.

How could I – a child – possibly understand? My grandmother's words themselves were all individually inoculated from shock by my own jejune ignorance and the failures of my imagination. In Auschwitz, I imagine myself a little Jewish Saint Jerome, walking the catacombs of the dead, Torah in one hand, Latin books in the other, searching for shafts of light – only this time, above ground, a figure in whom horror and silence are equally terrifying foes and equally gifted dissemblers. Perhaps I have always known that any peace I may make with that place and its significance in my life will come through the silences that accumulate like deposits of lime, slowly calcifying in-between all these words.

My favourite phrase as a little boy: *I don't remember*. I used it liberally. There's even grainy footage of me riding a spring-mounted rocking horse in the children's playground at Watson's Bay and uttering the phrase, much to my parents' audible amusement. But what made it most comical was not my forgetfulness but my *accent*, which was distinctly continental – a give-away of all the time spent in my grandparents' home, imbibing the intimacies of that polyglot madhouse where German, Slovak, Czech, Yiddish, Hungarian and English were used interchangeably, sometimes in the same conversation. And although I spoke none fluently myself, retaining only a few lexical morsels from each, still I was indelibly marked by that one phrase as a descendant. *Rrreeee-mem-bearrr*: exposed by the trilling 'r's like exotic bookends; the slightly diphthongized final vowel; the trace of a vowel-shift in *don't*, clipped from a long into a short 'o' sound (as in 'hot'), so that my lips widened instead of closed, as if to belatedly resist the finger of forgetting even as I negated memory. Was there some aura around that phrase *I don't remember*, containing the words in an oral embrace, the lips shaping more than sound but some supra-meaning, transmitted in the rings of silent air fluttering around the faintest image? A foreigner in my mouth, speaking *like* the living – but *for* the dead?

25 March 2011
'You don't get the horror until you go to Birkenau', warns my mother on the phone from Australia a few days before I leave England, referring to the difference between the museum-experience in Auschwitz I and the vast fields containing barracks and crematoria in Auschwitz II. And with this subtle precept, I fantasize an itinerary of pain and pain relief, of witnessing something real and being able to assimilate it. For I suspect that hidden behind the motivations of all thanatourists, however sensitive, is the notion that we go there to *get the horror*. As if horror can be sampled, or even taken home, like some macabre psychic souvenir. Instead, what I feel, even before witnessing the evidence preserved on site, is the weight of absence – the crushing incongruity of travelling to a landscape designed to erase my very existence.

In-between: where the living are entombed in a dreaming with the dead, like lovers asleep with fingertips grazing, I lie still, huddled like a question mark on its side.

The white house on the corner is vast, full of figures and objets d'art. We call it *The Mausoleum*. Under no circumstances are we allowed to touch the walls. Chalky and white, they leave a powdery residue on the fingertips. The sitting room – a place we never sit except when someone dies and we are sitting shiva – is a monument to lost wealth.[6] Antiques, polished silverware and bisque porcelain line the mantels locked in frozen, opulent time. There are four storeys in the house if you include the basement level which features a studio. It's here that my grandmother occasionally sculpts tortured figures, one of which is held in the National Museum of Australia in Canberra. Mostly, they are slim humanoid shapes made from Plaster of Paris and sprayed with bronze. As a child, I used to examine the stark white plaster in the basement before it was polished and etched. Even then, I had an intuitive sense of the distortion at work, the horrible meaning of their facelessness.

Two figures I am sure I remember (don't I?): one tall and bent, one smaller, being held. Which was mother and which was child?

At my family's Passover dinner, I am hungry to embody witness. I set an extra place – not for that truant, the Prophet Elijah, but for Lailah. Tonight we shall feast together. Lailah and I side by side, like old friends, remembrance and forgetting. Together we shall tell stories from absence and loss, finish each other's sentences, until the music and mockery of our tongues has us tripping and lisping over the Seder plate:

You know vhy I don't eat lamb?

– I do the routine for friends, accent and all, my mouth turned down sharply in imitation, we have no need for bitter herbs here –

Because it smells like burning flesh.

Cue laughter: laughter like powdering an old wound.

27 March 2011, 11.15 p.m.

I am on my way to Auschwitz-Birkenau. I am going to a non-place.

Somewhere over Germany, something is wrong. I peer out the window from my aisle seat as the plane begins to dip and bank. A wing is disappearing smoothly. The cabin lights flutter and go out. I can no longer see the front of the plane. I see a wall of night ahead – no moon, no stars, just a red planet. Ground becomes sky and my seat floats back unattached. The jet stream is filled with objets d'art. Inside and out, all is calm, even as things continue to fall away.

I undo my seatbelt and slowly, as if underwater, I swim through the fragments towards the dim red light.

10. Holocaust Survivor, Olga Horak OAM (Medal of the Order of Australia) and her grandson Anthony Levin at the Auschwitz Liberation commemoration service in Sydney, 27 January 2013. Photograph by Henry Benjamin/J-Wire.

NOTES

1. O. Horak, *Auschwitz to Australia: A Holocaust Survivor's Memoir* (Sydney: Kangaroo Press, 2000), p.35.
2. Ibid.
3. The full myth of Lailah and the formation of the embryo can be found in the Judaic text known as the *Midrash Tanhuma Pekude* 3. However, this version is inspired by the account given in H. Schwartz, *Tree of Souls: The Mythology of Judaism* (New York: Oxford University Press, 2004).
4. See Horak, *Auschwitz to Australia*, pp.73–4.
5. See C. Caruth, *Unclaimed Experience: Trauma, Narrative and History* (Baltimore, MD: Johns Hopkins University Press, 1996), p.4.
6. The word shiva means 'seven' in Hebrew. 'Sitting shiva' refers to the seven-day period of mourning observed by a Jewish person after losing a loved one. During the shiva period, mourners traditionally sit on low chairs while they receive condolence calls.

Home, Belonging and Exile

Where to Stay and Where to Go? Ideas of Home and Homelessness amongst Third-Generation Jews Who Grew Up in Germany

DANI KRANZ

> 'Ich bin auch so eine heimatlose Jüdin aus Deutschland.'[1]
> [I am also a homeless Jew from Germany.]
> (Nir, 21, raised in Munich, lives now in Tel Aviv)

Nir, Ella, my daughter, and myself are the beginning and closing characters of this chapter. Ella and I encountered Nir randomly in the summer of 2012, while we were on fieldwork leave in Israel, I as an anthropologist, she as the child of an anthropologist in the field. Yet this is not all there is to say: Ella is, potentially, a Fourth Generation, while I am Third Generation; like Nir, she is a Hebrew native speaker, and an Israeli; I am neither. Having conducted research with Jews and Israelis in Germany, Israel, and the United Kingdom, the turns of this conversations, the themes, the stories of this random encounter felt oddly familiar. By way of gossiping they centred around placing the respective other, belonging, being in and out of place. Yet the encounter struck me on a different, a more visceral level; it unsettled me. I had never had such a conversation with my own child present. I had been trying to shield her, to protect her, to move her away from the shadows of the aftermaths.[2] It is this that this chapter focuses on: the issues of third-generation Jews (hereafter referred to as Third Generations) what they manifest in, and in consequence what comes after the third generation. Will there be a fourth generation?

While I draw on my own – embodied – experience this is not an auto- ethnography. Instead, I approach identity construction of Third Generations, who grew up in Germany as dynamic identity processes. It is my aim to show the diversity of this generation, to point at disjunctures as much as similarities. To follow up on this agenda, I draw on ethnographic data collected since 2003 in Germany, Israel and the United Kingdom; the data consists of more than fifty interviews, hundreds of fieldwork conversations that have been recorded in fieldwork diaries, as well as text messages, emails, Skype or Facebook conversations; all quotes come directly from the Third Generations.

While my undertaking for this chapter lies in presenting identities of Third Generations who grew up in Germany in the wider frame of things, I will duly pay attention to the issue of my own positions in this research, and the stakes I hold. In this sense it is key to note that the Third Generations at the centre share two key parameters of their identity – being Third Generations and being from Germany – but that they deal with being a Third Generation and having grown up in Germany in individually different nuances. In order to present the differences within this generation, I will focus on manifestations of the idea of home/homelessness, being in place/out of place, or remaining in a constant state of transit, which surfaced and resurfaced during fieldwork. The notions of home could stretch from having a physical home – that is, owning property – to being at home amongst specific people, to symbolic rejections of belonging by collecting multiple passports to escape categorization, and to complaints about always remaining somewhat alien in any surrounding. All of these themes – home, homeless, place, transience, physical and symbolic belonging – are interrelated: they form a matrix of possibilities for Third Generations to put words to their embodied identities. These identities are underpinned by the displacement of the grandparents (first generation), or the parents (second generation) who moved with their own displaced parents between countries, and who transmitted their own displacement, homelessness and fractured belongings to their children and grandchildren, respectively. Indeed, in this light it is surprising how many Second Generations raised their children in Germany, as research from the early 1960s had found that 80 per cent of the second generation would much prefer to live outside Germany.[3]

As such, identity configurations of third-generation Jews from Germany in Germany and beyond cannot be understood without reference to the dynamic of intergenerational transmission processes and the long-term effects of the Shoah. In order to personalize identities of Third Generations, and to show their nuances, I will present a select number of third-generation Jews by way of thick descriptions that derive from ethnographic fieldwork, by quotes from formal and informal interviews, and from fieldwork notes.[4]

Some of the Third Generations stayed in Germany, some stayed in the UK and others made aliyah (immigrated to Israel) or became serial migrants. The multi-local focus is necessary to understand just how internally diverse Third Generations are, because the place of residence is underpinned by various other expressions of belonging, identification, de-identification, non-rootedness and attempts to moor oneself, if not to grow roots. In order to allow insights into the identity constructions of Third Generations, I will first give some background to the theoretical, anthropological framework that underpins these deliberations, and relate this directly to my own experiences. Second, I will give a short background of Jewish life in Germany post-1945. Third, I will introduce a number of the Third Generations from my research. The fourth and final part is the conclusion.

Theoretical Background: Anthropology of Experiences, Embodiment and Researching 'One's Own'

My attempts in writing this chapter are as much those of a professional anthropologist who works with Jews in Germany, the UK and Israel as those of a person who has embodied experiences of being a Third Generation from Germany – being German, it should be noted and borne in mind that being 'German' remains a difficult construct for those born 'after'. Ideas of home and homelessness are the focal points of my chapter. I am writing this chapter with both perspectives in mind; that of a professional who has been collecting data since 2003, and who has been discussing, analysing and mulling over the findings with colleagues and friends – amongst them also Third Generations – *and* I am writing the narrative of this chapter in front of my own background, which shapes my awareness context, and which does influence my perceptions as well as interpretations, however much I reflect on either, [5] and how I experience[6] and construct the world.[7] Indeed, the way this research unravelled also reflects my own biography, which is underpinned by moves away from Germany, and returns to Germany. It includes a collection of passports, which betrays my own sense of multiple and fractured belongings, as well as my multilinguality but inability to speak any one language flawlessly. In other words, I express issues of home/homelessness, being in/out of place by way of vehicles I encountered during research work. Yet any of these nuances finds individualized, sometimes shared, sometimes unique, emphases, reflecting the diversity of Third Generations.[8]

Thinking of the relationships between these movements, belongings and (un)homeliness brings to mind that I write with my grandparents and parents as my reference points, but that my daughter holds the key. Is my child – who might be called a Fourth Generation, and who by her very being and questioning forces me to dive into waters which lie outside my comfort zone - to be counted into this generational framework? Do I want to blot out our family history for the sake of the Shoah to become an impersonal meta-narrative, and my child normal, something I never was? What kind of *Heimat* (home in the physical and mental sense, a place one longs for and belongs to) do I offer to this child, a child born with three passports, three different languages, whose mother remains ambiguous, because ambiguity underlies, if it does not constitute the core of my, and by extension, the very third generation identities of many of my research participants and friends? Why did it unsettle me so much that Ella listened to Nir's and my conversation: what do I want for her?

In order to follow this agenda through, I am drawing on anthropology of experience, which was put forward by Renato Rosaldo. Like him, I am not writing an auto-ethnography. I am making use of the ethnographic 'I'[9] and using my own – reflective – self as a resource.[10] In his highly personal piece 'Grief and A Head Hunter's Rage', Rosaldo confronts his own sadness, fury and desperation at his wife's untimely death during fieldwork.[11] His now classic contribution marks a watershed in anthropological writing, because until then anthropologists had hardly been writing with such clarity about how their own experiences impact data generation, drive the analyses and writing process, and, more importantly, how our very experiences in life shape how we experience the world around us. Rosaldo states that in the work that prefigured his wife's death he could analyze the rage of the head hunters, but he could not grapple with the depth of their rage, and he could not grasp the extent of their emotions. His wife's death changed his view on the nexus of mourning and rage, and he argued that he gained a new, a different insight into their – as well as his – emotional depth, abysses and power.

However, Rosaldo's work did not come out of nowhere. Since the early 1970s, strongly influenced by the human rights and women's movements in the United States, anthropologists have been confronting the subject and the 'subjects' of their research,[12] paving the way to the 'reflexive turn' in anthropology. This turn is exemplified in the edited collection *Writing Culture*,[13] which remains a core text that marks the shift in anthropological thinking, away from the anthropologist as neutral observer to the anthropologist as part of the field, an issue that was picked up in later works on anthropological fieldwork, which focussed on the sheer humanity of the anthropologist in the field.[14] Rosaldo's work paved the way for this groundbreaking change: it opened the doors for an emotional anthropology that had not existed previously.

In consequence, the reflexive turn played strongly into the growing literature of topics at close range, such as one's own family and family history,[15] or one's own nativeness in the field.[16] This is to say that my own background is reflected in the interviews, my way into the field, my movements during fieldwork, and of course fieldwork relationships themselves.[17] It furthermore is reflected in my embodied experiences, which is to say that I necessarily remain partial,[18] and that I am a participant as much as an observer.[19]

Concerning the specifics of this chapter, I fully acknowledge these positionalities in the field, and that my research participants and I share specific parameters of our identities, by way of shared (ethnic) descent, similar family histories, as well as similar generational experiences.[20] Furthermore, I acknowledge that sources on the life-worlds of Jews who are survivors or their descendants and which focus on them ethnographically remain rare,[21] and that my access was underpinned, and definitely supported, by way of the shared in-group of my research participants and myself in a field where neutrality does not exist: 'A somehow 'neutral' interview would – if at all – only be possible if it was conducted by a non-Jewish, non-German interviewer. And even then the interview would have been influenced by factors such as ... the positionality of the interviewers native country during the Second World War.'[22]

The psychologist Kathryn Freker remarked upon these issues when reflecting on her own research work with young - third generation - Jews in (West) Germany. She did not conceal her own Jewishness in her research work, and thus repeats what earlier researchers of the second generation had found as well, and which one respondent of the psychoanalyst Kurt Grünberg describes as a strategic placing of the other.[25] In other words, in one way or the other, many – if not most – Jews who are descendants of survivors and who live in Germany attempt to determine if the interlocutor is a Jew too,[26] which reflects the fraught relationships between Jews and non-Jews to date.[27] While the lack of data on the life-worlds of these *living* Jews has been widely lamented,[28] it has been widely acknowledged that a multitude of publications exist on Jewish history, antisemitism and the Holocaust/Shoah, as well as Shoah trauma,[29] and it should be borne in mind that a growing amount focuses on Jews from the Former Soviet Union in Germany, who are commonly referred to as Russian Jews.[30] However, the vast majority of research on post-Shoah history focuses on the immediate post-war period up until the late 1950s, and research on trauma, to date, focuses mainly on the first and second generations. The third generation appears in some (unpublished) master's theses,[31] in very few publications,[32] and Third Generations have only started to write autobiographically infused texts in recent years,[33] but tellingly they do so in English and not in German. Yet these works remain few and far between. This chapter endeavours to fill a gap in the existing canon by adding an ethnographically grounded piece of research on the life-worlds of Third Generations.

Jewish Life in Germany Post-1945

Until 1991, when Russian Jews started to arrive in Germany in vast numbers, the significant majority of the Jewish population in Germany consisted of Shoah survivors and their descendants.[34] The majority of the Jews who formed the post-Shoah community were DPs (displaced persons)[35] from Eastern Europe and their descendants; German Jews formed the minority. DPs came to what was to become West Germany after their liberation from death and work camps, and remained there, because living under the Western Allies seemed the best survival strategy. In 1947 about 200,000 Jewish DPs lived in DP camps in the British, American and French zones.[36] With the creation of the State of Israel in 1948 and changes in American visa regulation only 30,000 Jews remained in West Germany.[37]

It was not until 1950 that the remaining 30,000 Jews founded the Central Council of the Jews of Germany (Zentralrat der Juden in Deutschland).[38] At the core of the problematic foundation lay the different identity configurations of the Eastern European DP majority and the German Jewish minority.[39] The DPs often came from orthodox backgrounds, having been marginalized in their previous countries of residence, and were often Yiddish-speaking outsiders, while German Jews had often been integrated into mainstream German society, German native speakers, liberal in practice and experiencing high rates of intermarriage.[40]

The Central Council to date functions as the official representation of the *Einheitsgemeinde* (unified community) in Germany to the non-Jewish public. The *Einheitsgemeinde* was set up to accommodate all Jews who had remained; its form of religious practice is orthodox, an issue that remains criticized by those German Jews who had survived and who began to feel like outcasts in what used to be *their* communities in *their* country.

Through the Shoah, Jews had been decimated to a tiny minority, traumatized and forced to stick together, which in turn meant that their pre-Shoah identities, their internal divisions and discussions, had been murdered alongside their previous life-worlds. Put succinctly, their identities had first been stolen, then annihilated, forcing them to create new models for a life 'after', which the French psychoanalyst Nadine Fresco describes in reference to phoenix as 'The Diaspora of the Ashes' (*La diaspora des cendres*).[41] Despite these odds, the historian Jael Geis[42] demonstrated that the underlying reason for this fight that surrounded the set-up of the post-Shoah community in Germany was that it was immediately set up to last, although the distinction between German Jews and DPs was to remain a strong inner-Jewish one[43] until the differences to new incoming groups such as Russians or Israelis overruled it, and German Jews and DPs came to see themselves as – uneasy – residents (*Alteingesessene*, literally: long established residents[44]), with burnt-off roots, who created equally homeless, rootless and ambiguous second and third generations.

The 30,000 Jews who formed the *Einheitsgemeinde* were not the only Jews in Germany. Y. Michal Bodemann estimates that in Berlin before the

1991 Russian immigration only 40 per cent of all Jews were members.[45] For Cologne, where I grew up and conducted ethnographic research, the membership is higher. It is likely that 70 per cent of all Jews in the locale were members[46] because the amount of Jewish groups outside the *Einheitsgemeinde* is smaller, and thus in order to remain in contact with other Jews the *Einheitsgemeinde* was a focal point. The non-members were most often German Jews, individuals who had survived through intermarriage, the descendants of these two groups, and Israeli immigrants. Yet, interestingly, these non-members nevertheless self-identified as Jews, or as being of mixed descent, which came with different nuances of self-identification compared to Jews with DP backgrounds, or from fully Jewish families. I am still to find a single person of intermarried descent in and from Germany who did not self-identify as Jewish, partly Jewish or somewhat Jewish,[47] and, tellingly, these non-community Jews all had some relation to other Jews.[48]

The reasons for non-membership of the *Einheitsgemeinde* are manifold. First, only Jews who are Jewish according to the Orthodox interpretation of the Halacha, the Jewish religious law, can be members of the *Einheitsgemeinde*. Halachic Jews, according to this definition, are children born to a Jewish mother, and Orthodox converts. Children of Jewish fathers and non-Jewish mothers are excluded from membership. Second, Jews who had survived through intermarriage had often already been distant from the pre-Shoah communities, and post-Shoah they had no interest in getting involved, or becoming stigmatized. Being Jewish was something dark, something uncanny; as a mixed-decent person (according to the Nuremberg laws) outlined to me in a conversation, “one did not talk about that”. Grabowsky avers this with her findings on ‘mixed individuals of the first degree’.[49] This group of individuals expresses a perpetual non-belonging. They were rather happy about the silence surrounding all matters Jewish of post-war German society: they wished to not talk about their identity, the classificatory system to which they had been subjected, and wished to return to some brittle and ambiguous normalcy. The latter was indeed impossible to achieve for them: more than fifty years after the persecution, their identity remained defined by ambiguity towards Germans and Jews.

Regardless or not if one was a member of a community, or of mixed descent, remaining in Germany begged various questions. The key question, asked by Jews abroad[50] and also by their own children[51] and grandchildren, was why one was in Germany. A telling shift of categorization can be observed here: the children of any of the inner-Jewish groups asked this question because, for them, their ancestry was defined by their Jewishness, and thus survivorness. Often there was no concrete answer, but silence, or seemingly rational reasons because this was the taboo of the family’s history.

If reasons were given, these concerned money, restitution, work, or one was too sick or too old to move, although the difference to the non-Jewish surrounding was pronounced throughout, leading to a self-ghettoization. Even German Jews who were by way of language, culture and socialization German had a hard time coming up with an answer to why they had not left Germany, and that despite all odds they felt German. In West Germany this answer was even more difficult than in East Germany, where some German Jews settled to create a better Germany.[52] The situation was further exacerbated as (close) contact with the non-Jewish majority was inevitable. The apparent solution was to reclassify non-Jewish German friends as very different to 'the Germans'.[53] As opposed to these reclassified, special Germans, unknown Germans were experienced as an amorphous and potentially threatening mass of people, de-individualized, and beset with an equally amorphous fear.[54]

Growing Up and Being in Germany: General Issues of the Second and Third Generation

Given this situation, being Jewish in Germany is an issue for the descendants of survivors; it plays on their minds. The consequences of the questioning of why one is in Germany and the resulting unhomeliness[55] become tangible in the mobility of this group of the Jewish population, which shows non-rootedness, or out-of-placeness, a non-identification with Germany[56] and often any other nation state. Going back and forth between Germany and other countries, longer or shorter intervals abroad and dual or multiple citizenships remain common for descendants. The non-identification with nation states might include Israel, because Jews who have grown up in Germany are aware that they are not Israelis and that Israel is a foreign country. A generational difference exists between the second and third generation: Second Generations saw Israel as a prime country of immigration, while Third Generations are much less likely to see Israel as the country to which they want to move.[57] Regardless of this rational awareness, Israel as an anchor of the identity of Third Generations remains present; it is perceived as a very special place, which is beset by a strong emotional investment. In times of crisis this special connection becomes most visible, because support of Israel is strong, and voiced publicly. Criticism of Israel presents a problem for Second and Third Generations, because it can be taken out of context and used for anti-Israeli endeavours,[58] leading to it being voiced in exclusively Jewish groups, or only privately, and barely in general public situations.

Growing up in Germany as a descendant of survivors comes with various problems that are underpinned by the effects of intergenerationally transmitted trauma.[59] Trauma and trauma transmission are approached differently by different researchers, and there has been no clear definition of what a Shoah trauma consists of since von Baeyer et al.'s 1964[60] groundbreaking publication on the topic, besides the general recognition that it constitutes abnormalities compared to the non-Jewish – German – population.[61] The reasons for the non-definition are many. Firstly, post-Shoah, there was no meta-narrative for those who had survived to tell their story; a cultural script[62] did not exist.[63] Indeed, researchers who work on trauma, (intergenerational) trauma transmission and narrative still refer to the Shoah as the prime example that lacks narratability,[64] because it lies beyond any narrative form and shape that exists, and is not part of any shared narrative.[65] Therefore, the trauma finds expressions through displacement such as an imperative boundary management to the non-Jewish surrounding in certain situations;[66] scenic reliving of the aspects of traumatic memories for survivors;[67] marriage and dating patterns across generations;[68] increased attachment to the parents[69] or the inability to rebel against parents for the second generation;[70] moves in and out of the country for the second and third generations;[71] general anxiety;[72] 'unhomeliness', out of placeness, generally delocalized identification, fractured and/or ambiguous attachments to physical places.[73] The aftermaths of the Shoah are constantly present for survivors and their descendants in Germany, by way of inner-familial dynamics, the lack of specific elements of the families, which are imperatively visible by their very absence at every single holiday, but as well through the multiple memorials around them. Yet, due to the lack of narratability, the communication of trauma remains extremely difficult amongst Jews, and it is even more difficult between Jews and non-Jews.

Third Generations: How is (Un)Homeliness Expressed?

The Shoah was a constant and personal presence for Jews who grew up in Germany, leading to specific (abnormal) expressions. On an impersonal, public level, memorials are abundant; on a personal level, survivors formed part of the family – and (some) perpetrators were still alive, and even if they were dead, their blood and their ideology lived on in their descendants, according to a member of the second generation, psychologist Sammy Speier.[74] Third Generations pondered along similar lines, and wondered what random old people on the street had done '60 years ago', but as well about 'my friends' grandparents. What had they done?' They experienced fear when seeing a German in uniform, going through passport control when leaving or entering Germany, or needed more than one passport 'to feel safe'. Of the six Third Generations I will introduce, three hold multiple citizenships; two of those who do not would preferably obtain a second passport; only one is happy and content as a German citizen only. How I obtained my rather neutral (from her and my point of view) British citizenship was an issue of enquiry for Leah, a third generation who I interviewed in London: 'I am rather a slave to money, than to any nation state.' This need for a second passport exemplifies the non-belonging to Germany and the mistrust held by Third Generations on an obvious, bureaucratic level, and it sets the German framework apart from countries to which surviving Jews immigrated, and where the Shoah was present through survivors, yet not through perpetrators. Descendants of German Jews who immigrated to the US do not have much interested in obtaining a second passport: they feel safe with their US passports, as lawyers who work in the area of re-naturalization stated unanimously.[75] The same goes for the UK, where interest in obtaining a second passport was similarly low amongst descendants of survivors, as my British-born and -raised Jewish interview partners outlined.[76]

The aftermaths shaped the organized Jewish community as well. Third Generations who grew up within the structures of the *Einheitsgemeinde*, and who were exposed to its various clubs, mentioned that 'we were told not to feel like Germans' and that there was the attempt to influence them to make aliyah. This influence was somewhat successful, with a number of Third Generations leaving after finishing school, but not necessarily for Israel, and by no means did all who had made aliyah remain in Israel. Some returned to Germany, others moved on to other countries, exemplifying that forming a lasting sense of belonging and being able to feel settled remained a problematic issue regardless of location. For those who did not want to make aliyah, London became a popular destination but, again, not all emigrants settled in London. Some returned to Germany or moved on to another country, as I found in the course of this long-term ethnography.

The most common reasons for moving once again which specifically applies to Israel includes language problems, a perceived lack of career options, feeling out of place and culturally 'not at home' (which came with the shocking realization for some that one felt at least culturally German), the reluctance to serve in the Israeli army and unhappiness with the state of the State of Israel, but also strong attachment to one's parents who were in Germany, and/or to significant others. The narratives of those who left Israel revealed that it was more important to try out Israel than to stay. During fieldwork it emerged that leaving Israel was in most cases not seen as a failure, while moving there was often seen as 'something I needed to try', based on the ideology to which one adhered, and the process of coping with the transmitted trauma.

However, remaining in Germany, or leaving Israel again for Germany, did not mean that Third Generations do not feel ambiguity towards

German non-Jews, and that they do not require Jewish dominated places and spaces to retreat to.[77] The idea of Germany as *Heimat* is still a rather difficult one for Third Generations, according to Micha Brumlik.[78] Referring to Germany as *zu Hause* (physical home) was not uncommon, but calling Germany *Heimat* was a step too far. Yet Brumlik interviewed Jews of the third generation who had grown up with contact with the *Einheitsgemeinde*. By this token they had been exposed to similar experiences within the *Einheitsgemeinde*, and the vast majority came from Eastern European survivor families, as the quotes from my research indicate: 'Nobody in my family is German. How should I feel as a German? We have no historic roots here [in Germany].' The vast majority of Third Generations show similarities in their attitude towards their German surroundings. It echoed through my interviews and conversations that they felt unable to 'identify with the German surrounding'. This was regardless of German citizenship: 'I don't call myself German. I mean most [pre-1991 resident] Jews I know would not.' Ironically, this interview partner felt very much in tune with German culture when he was abroad, and yet another recounted the shift of her identity in Israel specifically: 'When I am abroad, that is when I feel like a German. I'm a *Yekke*. Can't deny it!'[79] Both come from Eastern European survivor families; their own second-generation parents came to West Germany as children. Ambiguities like this ran like a leitmotif through my fieldwork,[80] when the descendants of German and DP Jews alike attempted to position themselves. This positioning was exacerbated with the rather regularly occurring question concerning where they are actually from. While German was the shared native language used in any interview and fieldwork conversation, it was a specific kind of German, a German that drew on other language reservoirs, and which contained small mistakes that betrayed the 'other' roots. One could say that not only many Second Generations, but also Third Generations are speechless in the face of their own multilinguality. They speak several languages, but they do not own any. This is also reflected in the situation of travelling abroad: attempts to pass as a non-German or to naturalize were thwarted by the German accent, the German cadence and syntax, which resulted in further unwanted questions concerning where one was from.[81]

The situation is further complicated by the absolute minority status of Jews in Germany, which makes inter-ethnic relationships on all levels part of the everyday of any and all Jews in Germany. The majority of Third Generations have many non-Jewish friends, and non-Jewish partners are not that uncommon. In order to bridge the mental gap between Germans as perpetrators and Germans as friends, family or significant others, they are reclassified as 'special Germans',[82] and bestowed with qualities that positively set them apart from the amorphous mass of Germans.[83] The key moment in these relationships and friendships is that the non-Jewish part is willing and able to listen to alienation and pain; they need to be able to realize the anger and frustration of the Jewish part, which resurfaces and is triggered by various stimuli. To name just one example, the circumcision debate of the summer of 2012 triggered various fears amongst Jews across generations, leading to increased tensions between Jews and non-Jews, while at the same time the debate confirmed the all too common non-understanding.[84] This bitter debate brought long-established antisemitism back to the forefront. The ruling of the German supreme court of December 2012 that allows for circumcision for religious reasons, thus confirming the freedom of religion guaranteed by German basic law, was a legal remedy, but it did little to appease the mental turmoil of Jews in Germany. News reports, and to a greater extent, opinion and commentary sections had branded circumcision as violating the rights of a child to an intact body in the name of a primordial religious rite, while often disregarding that circumcision is one of many aspects superimposed on a child by his or her parents. This discussion brought back one issue with full force: the problem of Jewish diversity and the core issue of religious praxis, leading to an increased ethnic bind amongst the Jews of the country, and stymying open, Jewish diversity which otherwise only warfare in Israel does.

This discussion directly affected Jewish/non-Jewish encounters. While non-Jewish contacts have the chance to participate actively in discussions about current affairs, and to explain their personal stance, the issue is more complicated when it comes to the Shoah and its aftermaths or, in this case, Jewish ritual and praxis. Even if they are rather neutral in their opinions, and had not perpetrated any Shoah crimes themselves, they see themselves confronted by the immense aftermaths of events to which they were intrinsically linked but which they cannot undo. Direct Shoah discussion remains problematic too, as Leah recalls:

> We were watching a death camp film in my history class in school. And when we talked about the film, all people talked about were the lighting and the sound effects, not the content. I could feel it build up in me, I was trying to breathe deeply and calm down. But then I decided to speak up and I said 'You're not talking about the content of the film here. I think it's shit that you don't. You're really hurting me. Do you think I have never heard or seen this before? I have grown up with it.' The teacher looked at me all puzzled but then said 'You're right. Let's talk about the content.' And then, that one girl said 'You're making me feel really uncomfortable. I don't think I can talk about it

> with you in the room.' None of the others said anything. I was so furious I left the classroom. I cried with rage.

Stories like this are common stock in the experiences of third generation Jews in Germany. They speak of not fitting in with their German surroundings, and problems with communicating their life-world to non-Jews. Leah's experience happened as late as 2003 and bears witness to the inability of young non-Jewish Germans to deal with the pain, trauma and frustration of their Jewish counterparts; traumas and frustrations they have not caused their Jewish third generation counterparts, but which is embodied through them. At the same time, Third Generations experienced those events as incisive and as the epitome of the abnormality of being Jewish in Germany, which for Leah was the prime reason to leave Germany after she graduated from school. Like other Third Generations, she came to study in London, where I met her. Immigration to London is often not perceived as immigration, because London is so close; one speaks the language; visas are not needed; it is so easy to move there, but also to leave again. The notion that 'I'm not sure I'll stay' was common amongst Third Generations in London. Moving to London has something transient about it to the third generation; staying in London seems to just happen, it is unplanned. Aliyah or moves to the US were perceived as permanent (even when they were often not, in practice), and as a definite statement to leave Germany, and by extension Europe. Leah told me that she had always wanted to leave Germany and had no intention ever to return there. She was not sure if she wanted to stay in London either, but reckoned 'I guess that is what it will come down to. My boyfriend is British [Jewish] … Israel would be an option if I managed to find a job there … I don't speak the language [Hebrew] though … I will never return there [Germany]!' Roni, a Third Generation of Eastern European descent whom I met in Germany, adds a different insight: 'You have to be patient [with your non-Jewish partner].' Yet she realized the difficulties of such a relationship and wished for 'a partner who has a migration background as well. I think that would make things easier.' Another 'immigrant' who presumably had a notion of being out of place[85] seemed easier to communicate with, and Roni believed that this person could empathize with her more easily. Yet, only two years after this assessment, Roni left Germany for Israel, where her sister had already moved. Both hold onto their German passports; they speak German to each other. At the same time, contact with their previous friends in Germany has decreased. Roni went as far as expressing that she has no interest in maintaining any contact; she left completely and totally.

However, not all breaks are as clear as Roni's, and not all Third Generations anchor themselves that much in Israel. David outlined about his time in Israel that 'It's a fallacy that when you go to Israel you relate to Israelis immediately, it's that idiotic Diaspora fallacy that Jews relate to Jews.' He rejects any immediate bond to Israelis based on them being Jews. Roni and her sister felt this very bond existed, which also reflects different family constellations: the father of the two of them is Israeli, granting them access to Hebrew language, and close family in Israel. David, on the other hand, was born into a family of Eastern European origin and was raised as a German native speaker, although he only obtained German citizenship in his late twenties.

Unlike the two of them or Leah, David stressed the ZJD (Zionistische Jugend Deutschland, Zionist Youth of Germany, part of the *Einheitsgemeinde*) in his upbringing, and emphasized that after he graduated from school he went to live in Israel for a year, based on the ideology he was exposed to within the Jewish community, and the ambiguities of his family towards the German surroundings. It is therefore difficult to assess if David's recognition of his foreignness in Israel stems from this experience, or if he had been critically aware of the differences between Israelis and Jews who grew up in Germany before he went to Israel. Regardless of this, David made London his present home, but unlike Leah he actively likes the city. He moved to London to study after leaving Israel, and returned to London after further education in the US. He feels in place in London for the time being; he has a British Jewish girlfriend; he does not rule out a move to the US, and sees Israel as a country to which he could move once he retires. Germany is not off the map, either:

> If I were to go back to Germany I'd go back to my hometown. London's great though. There's so much money to be made, my friends [childhood friends who have immigrated to London] are here. The quality of life is so much better than in Israel ... It's difficult to do business in Israel. And there is a compulsory military service in Israel.

Although David maintained throughout that he is ambiguous about being German, or going back to Germany, he does not rule it out. Unlike Leah, he shows attachment to the town where he grew up in Germany. He demonstrates his attachments with avid support of the local football team and follows its highs and lows together with his childhood friends in the local pub. Similar to Leah, he is pragmatic about moving to Israel. Both are aware that they are foreigners in Israel, and of the difficulties of immigrating to Israel. Their potential aliyah is assessed against the realities of the country, and not measured against idealized notions.

For a significant number of Third Generations the aftermaths of the Shoah take the shape of a superimposed cosmopolitanism that finds expression in a recurrent rootlessness, inability or ambiguity to identify with any nation state, which in turn comes to play a role in personal relationships: neither Roni nor her sister felt able to settle with a German non-Jew, and the same goes for Leah and David.[86] It is indeed the non-German, Jewish partner who offers an anchoring mechanism to Third Generations. Unlike themselves, their British or Israeli Jewish partners are not torn, they are 'something', at least in the perception of the Third Generations for whom they offer solace. These significant other Jews, however critical towards their respective home countries, have something that Third Generations from Germany yearn for: a clear belonging, they speak one language properly and they identify with a country that they criticize but nevertheless relate to because it is *Heimat*.

This *Heimat* is lost on most Third Generations who grew up in Germany. Jews in Germany were part of their German 'host' societies pre-Shoah, to the extent that they defined themselves as German Jews, which still finds reflections in the different identity configurations between German Jews and their descendants, and DPs and their descendants. By way of the Shoah, Eastern European Jews became even more marginal in their countries of residence, and German Jews were redefined as marginal; the Shoah added a new dimension to Jewish marginality. Ilan N. Magat states that it 'is regarded as the ultimate manifestation of non-belonging'.[87] On a verbalized level the inability to identify with Germany, the non-belonging and the feeling of being not understood by non-Jews leads to the emigration of third generation Jews from Germany. On a rarely verbalized level, these are expressions of transmitted trauma, which are reaching further than just being unable to identify with Germany.

And Those Who Stay in Germany?

While most Third Generations are ambiguous about being in Germany, not all leave, or leave for good. Judith left Germany for the US, where she lived for a number of years, but she returned to live in Berlin. Unlike her four contemporaries who left Germany, and unlike her own German-born and -raised parents, she is somewhat religiously practising, and engages professionally with Jews and Judaism, which also means that her engagement with being a Jew runs along different lines to the other four, who are outspoken about being Jews but who did not make it their profession. The four who left Germany want to be Jewish without discussion, effort or a professional engagement; they want the option to be Jews without it becoming a task, project or profession. Regardless of her investment, Judith sometimes thinks about leaving Germany again, for Israel usually, but to date arrives at the conclusion that she prefers to stay in Germany or, more precisely, in Berlin. That she returned to Germany and remains in Berlin does not mean that Judith does not feel ambiguous about being in Germany, yet she found a pragmatic way to deal with this issue: 'In Israel I don't like everybody either!' What first sounds like a defence mechanism is indeed an elaborate argument that Judith puts forward. She does feel that she relates to individuals differently, and that on some level she relates very much to other Jews, while on other levels she might not relate to them. She applies the same to German non-Jews: she individualizes the relationships. Of course, Judith has her own limits; some things lie beyond the pale for her, she admits to losing her patience, or the will to discuss at times. However, it took Judith a significant amount of time, and soul-searching to arrive at that stance. By now she feels settled, despite the recurring pondering of leaving Berlin for Tel Aviv.

Lars proclaimed 'I don't feel out of place here, this is my home!' when asked about his relationship to Germany. He was, and remains, one of the very few Third Generations who has no issue with Germans or being in Germany. Unlike Judith, he does not practise, he is not a member of any Jewish community, yet he does self-identify as a Jew publicly in his professional surrounding; he married his non-Jewish, non-German wife in a liberal Jewish ceremony; their daughter has a traditional Jewish first name.

His upbringing was also very different from the other five: his mother was not a member of any Jewish community, his father is German non-Jewish, his family celebrated Jewish and Christian holidays alike, he is both German and a Jew. His Eastern European survivor grandparents came to Germany in the 1960s. Lars's mother deeply disliked the East European country where she was born; his grandfather was a Germanophile, and his grandmother uneasily submitted to her husband and daughter. The latter remains startled that her own father, who survived a work camp, refused to give up on his stance to be part of the German people and refused to speak anything but German, his native language, with her. She resented it, and replied in Romanian. She also resented being in Germany, and left for Israel in her earlier twenties, but on a visit to her parents met the father-to-be of Lars. Her father approved of her new boyfriend – 'He might be a goy, but he is not an oriental' – expressing a strong preference for this German boyfriend and disapproval of her previous, Israeli Iraqi boyfriend. While Lars's mother is amused about this episode in hindsight, she stresses that her father in particular refused to talk about the Shoah: 'He wanted my children to grow up unencumbered.' He also forbade her to be a member of the Jewish community, and was upset when she had Lars circumcised. For him, being Jewish meant danger, and his daughter marrying a German, her children speaking flawless German, meant safety. Passing as a German or, better, being German was, as he revealed close to death, what he believed ensured his survival – he was too close to the Germans, too similar to the Germans for them to kill him. On the one hand, his Germanophilia conceals a survival strategy; on the other hand, it enabled his daughter to marry a German, and raise two children in Germany, who are neither ambiguous about being Germans, nor Jews. Neither Lars nor his sister feel out of place amongst Germans in Germany, but they are German, and clearly express it. At the same time, they are rare, and constitute the absolute minority of the Third Generation I have grown up with, and encountered as an anthropologist.

Conclusion: of Shadows Closer and Further Away

Depending on family history, upbringing and personality, the Shoah casts different shadows over Third Generations who grew up in Germany. Some cannot stand being in the country; it never became home and it is effectively unbearable because it is beset by the overwhelming feeling of alienation, which is in turn underpinned by transmitted trauma that is too much to overcome. In this case, alienation from German society finds its expression in a non-belonging that culminates in leaving Germany for good, and thus being able to avoid getting stuck in Germany. The temporal relocation to Israel, or any other country, expresses the wish to anchor oneself in a place that one can identify with or, if not identify with, that one is at least not alienated from, a place that is somewhat more neutral. At the same time, these serial moves bear witness to the inability to achieve exactly that, and the multilingualism that comes with it creates an inability to speak any one language flawlessly and without accent; it is an uncanny, audible reminder of fractured belonging. However, this strategy mainly applies to those Third Generations who come from DP families, while the likes of Lars and Judith, with their very different family histories, are comparably anchored in Germany and speak flawless German. Although, having said that, both are able to fully codeswitch, and to litter their German with Yiddishisms and Hebrewisms amongst other Jews.

For those who emigrate, not only psychological or ideological reasons underpin the decision for a specific country, but practical considerations play into the choice of emigration countries, and in underlying the decision of not moving to, or leaving Israel again. As Meron Mendel also outlines, aliyah is not the aim of the majority of Third Generations, which sets them notably apart from the second generation.[88] These considerations are underpinned by the standard of living to which the Third Generations had grown accustomed, by what they aspire to for themselves, and increasing individualism that can be found across all western societies. Just because other individuals are Jews, that is no longer a sufficient reason to bind the third generation together in Germany for longer periods than during acute crisis.[89]

Neither Leah nor David, nor Judith, and in particular not Lars, perceived moving to Israel as a long-term option; they were all too aware that culturally they were Europeans, if not (unwilling and reluctant) Germans by way of socialization such as kindergarten, school and German non-Jewish friends. Their view of Israel was unclouded and assessed against the reality of the country: they all knew that they lacked the language skills to fulfil their ambitions in Israel, and that their being Jewish did not act as an automatic connection to other – Israeli – Jews. All of them have first-hand experiences with Israelis, in as much their statement of the differences within the Jewish in-group should be seen as an assessment of existing differences and not as an assessment of one group being better or worse than the other. Roni and her sister acknowledge these issues as well; they related to Israelis differently due to their own immediate familial ties with them, their cultural and their language skills. They felt homeless in Germany, and non-rooted.

The same applies to Nir. 'I am also a homeless Jew from Germany' were the first words – spoken in German, of course – when she learned that my daughter and I are from Germany too. Although the two of us were speaking English together, Nir asked us where we were from when we entered the shop where she was working. While her question is standard in professional retail, my answer immediately triggered the standard questions that reflect the pattern of communication amongst Jews from Germany: random, as this encounter was in a random shop on Dizengoff Street in the centre of Tel Aviv, it ran along the same patterns as any encounter during fieldwork. Nir and I first traded hometowns, then who we knew, gossiped about individuals we both knew, then we moved to where our respective parents are from; a conversation rendered in German with Yiddishisms and Hebrewisms, which act as the defining proof that the 'other' is indeed of the same in-group, and not just another German.

However, I do not see the heterogeneity of belongings or identities as detrimental to Jewish life in Germany, or beyond. On the contrary, what the key characters show is particularly important concerning the increasingly heterogeneous expressions of being Jewish amongst those who remain in Germany, and, nearly seventy years post-Shoah bears witness to the changing shadow of the Shoah. Indeed, now it makes sense to speak of shadows, which can be closer or further away, and which are dealt with differently compared to previous generations, they are dealt with more individualistically. Third Generations do not necessarily see themselves as part of a *Schicksalsgemeinschaft*, a community of fate, that needs to appear united to the outside,[90] although they still feel compelled to stick together in times of crises. Second Generations were hard pressed to rebel against their parents, the *Einheitsgemeinde* appeared unified to the outside when they were growing up, although it was always very heterogeneous on the inside, much less practicing than it seemed,[91] and most Second Generations had no wish to remain in Germany at all.[92]

Third Generations break with this pattern. Their ways of dealing with the German surroundings, leaving Germany, returning or even staying put, are individually underpinned even though they share specific parameters, and – in their majority – Third Generations show specific abnormalities compared to the non-Jewish German population, such as depression, fear, and hatred,[93] or the fear of hypervisibility: 'I feel like a pink elephant in Germany', mentioned Leah. Thus, while what is normal, and what not is a social construct, normalcy might be too much to ask for in the light of the Shoah and the Second World War. For example, Grünberg stressed the amount of violence in German non-Jewish families as part of the aftermaths of the Second World War.[94] Harald Welzer and colleagues[95] draw attention to the silences surrounding the Nazi regime in general, and Dieter Nelles and colleagues[96] stress the effects of the Nazi terror on children of resistance fighters. For these reasons, I am arguing that the aftermaths of the Shoah need to be appreciated in terms of setting Jews in Germany apart from non-Jews even in the third generation, and that specific issues, in particular non-belonging, out of placeness, the inability to identify with any one place need to be acknowledged as long-term effects of the Shoah for Third Generations who grew up in Germany. It is my believe that only the appreciation of these differences will lead to long-term solution that enables Jews and non-Jews to live together in Germany, and that at the same time what has happened is neither silenced, nor relativized, and the long-term effects on first, second and third generation are not pathologized but accepted as just that – long-term effects of trauma.

Research on Third Generations in Israel showed that the ways of dealing with transmitted Shoah trauma take different shapes, and that some ways are more promising than others. [97] And, more importantly, that Jewish diversity enables different mechanisms of dealing with the trauma, which means that there is a glimmer of hope on the horizon. However, first and foremost it needs to be acknowledged that such transmitted trauma exist by non-Jewish German society. To date, German non-Jewish society hardly acknowledges the trauma-induced abnormalities of third generation Jews, which has been strengthened by the German victim discourse that has gained in importance since the 1990s. In this discourse, non-Jewish Germans distance themselves from their role as perpetrators or as descendants of perpetrators,[98] but define themselves increasingly as victims of the Nazi regime.[99] This change in discourse reflected in the 'discussion' concerning circumcision in Germany in the summer of 2012, and it was underlined by the annually published report Die Mitte im Umbruch (The Centre in Change) of the same year.[100] The report found that antisemitism is well and alive, and indeed increasing, a find that had already been made public by the hotly debated *Antisemitismusbericht* (Antisemitism Report) of the German Ministry for Internal Affairs a year earlier.[101] To Jews, the *Antisemitismusbericht* confirmed their perception, yet, the vitriol surrounding the circumcision debate led to Jews across generations questioning publicly not only if they belonged in Germany, but if 'the Germans' wanted them in their midst. Problematically, Jews are all too aware that various forms of antisemitism run through all societal and educational strata: the criticism of Günther Grass concerning Israeli foreign policy stands in line of shocking examples that even the German intellectual elite compares Israeli foreign policy to Nazi terror, thus discrediting the former, and relativizing the latter (secondary antisemitism). Any Israeli Palestinian conflict, and its problematic media representation corroborated the representation of the 'Jewish country'. Any and all of these debates led to Third Generations who left Germany to feel justified in their decision, while those who stayed or returned are in the uneasy position of justifying their residence, if not existence in the country again, and reassess their (fractured) belonging, despite the growing heterogeneity of this generation. For many Third Generations this culminates in the question: What will I tell my own children? Asked more personally: do I want Ella to have conversations like Nir and I had, or have I already transmitted – am I guilty of transmitting – consciously and unconsciously, a sense of difference that on the surface merely reflects through our multilingualism, our passport collection, and conversations such as the one she, called *chamuda* ('sweetie' in Hebrew), witnessed, participated in, and contributed to? Would us leaving Germany mean giving up on the country that feels homely to me, despite my ambiguities, or would I be just ensuring her 'normalcy'? Can there be normalcy for this fourth generation child, however socially constructed 'normalcy' might be, or is this an issue that I project, and which is mine, but not hers?

Acknowledgements

I am grateful to all those who informed this long-term ethnography. My special gratitude goes to Esther Hertzog, who inspired me to take notes on my own motherhood, and to my daughter, Ella Kranz, who asks fundamental questions. Without either of them this paper would have never come into existence.

11. Ella and Dani during fieldwork in Berlin, January 2014. Copyright, Katja Harbi, who has granted permission for reproduction of photography. (She can be contacted at contact@katjaharbi.com).

NOTES

1. All the quotes are from my research participants. I translated them from German into English. All names, besides my daughter's and my own, are aliases.
2. Conversations about 'the silence' were a regular occurrence in fieldwork and beyond. Second and Third Generations from Germany and from abroad alike mentioned them. While I had been reluctant to accept them when growing up, my own motherhood led to a more empathetic stance towards silence.
3. M. Mendel, 'Jungsein – Judesein – Dasein? Perspektiven für die jüdische Jugendarbeit in einer heterogenen Gemeinschadt' [Being Young, Being Jewish, Being There? Perspectives for Jewish Youth Work in a Heterogeneous Community], in M. Brumlik and Y.M. Bodemann (eds), *Juden in Deutschland – Deutschland in den Juden: Neue Perspektiven* [Jews in Germany, Germany in the Jews: New Perspectives], Göttingen: Wallstein Verlag, 2010), pp.264–70; p.265.
4. C. Geertz, *Thick Description: Toward an Interpretive Theory of Culture* (New York: Basic Books, 1973).
5. B. Glaser and A. Strauss, *Awareness of Dying* (Chicago, IL: Aldine, 1968).
6. R. Rosaldo, *Culture & Truth: The Remaking of Social Analysis* (Boston, MA: Beacon Press, 1988), pp.46–67.
7. M. Hirsch, 'Family Pictures: Maus, Mourning and Post-Memory', *Discourse*, 15, 2 (1992), pp.3–29; M. Hirsch, 'Past-Lives: Postmemories in Exile', *Poetics Today*, 17, 4 (1996), pp.659–86; H. Raczymow, 'La Memoire trouée' [Memory shot through with holes] *Pardès*, 3 (1986), pp.177–82.
8. The language editing of the paper is an experiment. The language editor took out only actual mistakes, but left my odd English as it is to reflect issues of home and homeless that surface in shape of language. The language in turn exemplifies the emotional labour that underpins this

write up. My English in this paper is more German than in other papers, in which I am less emotionally involved.

9. C. Ellis, *The Ethnographic I: An Anthropological Novel About Autoethnography* (Lanham, MD: Altamira Press, 2003).
10. P. Collins and A. Gallinat (eds), *The Ethnographic Self as Resource: Writing Memory and Experience Into Ethnography* (Oxford: Berghahn Books, 2010).
11. R. Rosaldo, *Culture & Truth: The Remaking of Social Analysis* (Boston, MA: Beacon Press, 1988), pp.124.
12. D. Hymes, *Reinventing Anthropology* (Ann Arbor, MI: University of Michigan Press, 1972).
13. J. Clifford and G.E. Marcus (eds), *Writing Culture* (Los Angeles, CA: University of California Press, 1986).
14. Fran Markowitz, 'Blood, Soul, Race, and Suffering: Full-Bodied Ethnography and Expressions of Jewish Belonging', *Anthropology and Humanism*, 31, 1 (2006), pp.41–56; F. Markowitz and M. Ashkenazi, *Sex, Sexuality, and the Anthropologist* (Chicago, IL: University of Chicago Press, 1999).
15. K. Finkler and G. Finkler, *Lives Lived and Lost: East European History Before, During, and After World War II as Experienced by an Anthropologist and Her Mother* (Boston, MA: Academic Studies Press, 2012); A. Waterston and B. Rylko-Bauer, 'Out of the Shadows of History and Memory: Personal Family Narratives and Ethnographies of Rediscovery', *American Ethnologist*, 33, 3 (2006), pp.397–412; A. Waterston, *My Father's Wars: Migration, Memory, and the Violence of a Century* (New York: Routledge, 2014).
16. S.C. Heilman, 'Jewish Sociologist: Native as Stranger', *American Sociologist*, 15 (1980), pp.100–08; M. Shokeid, 'From the Anthropologist's Point of View: Studying Ones Own Tribe', *Anthropology & Humanism Quarterly*, 14, 1 (1989): 23–8.
17. D. Kranz, *Shades of Jewishness: The Creation and Maintenance of a Liberal Jewish Community in Post-Shoah Germany* (unpublished PhD thesis, University of St Andrews, 2009); Markowitz, 'Blood, Soul, Race, and Suffering'.
18. P. Collins, *The Sense of the Meeting: An Anthropology of Vernacular Quakerism* (unpublished PhD thesis, University of Manchester, 1994), p.29.
19. Heilman, 'Jewish Sociologist', p.100.
20. K. Mannheim, *Essays on the Sociology of Knowledge by Karl Mannheim* (New York: Routledge & Kegan Paul, 1952).
21. Kranz, *Shades of Jewishness*, p.96.
22. K. Frerker, *Junge Juden in Deutschland: Lebensentwürfe im Schatten des Holocaust* [Young Jews in Germany: Lifeplans in the Shadow of the Holocaust], (masters thesis, University of Cologne, 1998), p.51; my translation.
23. Freker, *Junge Juden*, p.51.
24. D. Kuschner, *Die jüdische Minderheit in der Bundesrepublik: Eine Analyse* [The Jewish Minority in the Federal Republic: An Analysis], (unpublished PhD thesis) University of Cologne, 1977), p.9.
25. K. Grünberg, 'Folgen des Holocaust bei Kindern von Überlebenden in der Bundesrepublik Deutschland' [Long-Term Effects of the Holocaust for Children of Survivors in the Federal Republic of Germany], in M. Brumlik and P. Kunik, *Reichsprogromnacht: Vergangenheitsbewältigung aus jüdischer Sicht* [Night of the Pogroms: Coming to Terms with the Past from a Jewish Point of View] (Frankfurt am Main: Brandes und Apsel, 1988), pp.59-75, p.65.
26. Kranz, *Shades of Jewishness*, p.142.
27. The relationship of those who immigrated from the Former Soviet Union to the German surrounding is different. Mendel in *Jungsein – Judesein – Dasein?* (see note 3) outlines that the integration of these immigrants into mainstream society is high, and that their children see their future in Germany.
28. Y.M. Bodemann, *In den Wogen der Erinnerung: Jüdische Existenz in Deutschland* [Floating in the Waves of memory: Jewish Existence in Germany] (Munich: DTV, 2002); Y.M. Bodemann, 'A Jewish Cultural Renascence in Germany?', in S. Lustig and I. Levenson (eds), *Turning the Kaleidoscope: Perspectives on European Jewry* (New York and Oxford: Berghahn Books, 2008), pp.164–75; Kranz, *Shades of Jewishness*; P.N. Levinson, 'Religiöse Richtungen und

Entwicklungen in den Gemeinden' [Religious Streams and Developments in the Communities], in M. Brumlik, D. Kiesel, C. Kugelmann and J. Schoeps (eds.), *Jüdisches Leben in Deutschland seit 1945* [Jewish Life in Germany since 1945] , (Frankfurt am Main: Jüdischer Verlag bei Athenäum), pp.140–71; L. Rapaport, 'The Difficulties of Being Jewish in Germany Today', *Trumah*, 3 (1992), 189–215; L. Rapaport, *Jews in Germany after the Holocaust* (Cambridge: Cambridge University Press, 1997).

29. F. Becker, *Ankommen in Deutschland. Einwanderungspolitik als biographische Erfahrung im Migrationsprozess russischer Juden* [Arriving in Germany. Immigration Policy and Biographical Experiences as Part of the Migration of Russian Jews], (Berlin: Dietrich Reimer Verlag, 2001), pp.16–17.
30. Y.M. Bodemann, 'Introduction: The Return of the European Jewish Diapora', in M. Bodemann (ed.), *The New German Jewry and the European Context* (Basingstoke and New York: Palgrave Macmillan, 2008), pp.1–12.
31. K. Freker, *Junge Juden*; M. Vollrath, *Abgespaltene Anteile traumatischer Erinnerungen* [Split Off Parts of Traumatic Memories], (master's thesis, University of Bremen, 2006).
32. Villigster Foschungsforum zu Nationalsozialismus, Rassismus und Antisemitismus, *Das Unbehagen in der 'dritten Generation'. Reflexionen des Holocaust, Antisemitismus und Nationalsozialismus* [The Anxiety of the 'Third Generation'. Reflections of the Holocaust, Antisemitism and Nationalism] (Münster: LIT Verlag, 2003).
33. V.F. Fogel, *Sag es mir* (Frankfurt: Weissbooks, 2010). Fogel's book was translated from German into English; Y. Mounk, *Stranger in My Own Country: A Jewish Family in Modern Germany* (New York: Farrar, Strauss & Giroux, 2014).
34. Y.M. Bodemann, ' "How can one stand to live there as a Jew ... ": Paradoxes of Jewish Existence in Germany', in Y.M. Bodemann, *Germans, Jews and Memory: Reconstructions of Jewish Life in Germany* (Ann Arbor, MI: University of Michigan Press, 1996), pp.19–46; Y.M. Bodemann, *Gedächtnistheater: Die jüdische Gemeinschaft und ihre deutsche Erfindung* [Theatre of Memory: The Jewish Community and its German Invention] (Hamburg: RotbuchVerlag, 1996); Y.M. Bodemann, *In den Wogen der Erinnerung: Jüdische Existenz in Deutschland* [Floating in the Waves of Memory: Jewish Existence in Germany], Munich: DTV, 2002); M. Brenner, *Nach dem Holocaust: Juden in Deutschland*, [After the Holocaust: Jews in Germany] *1945–1950*] (Munich: C.H. Beck, 1995); J.H. Geller, *Jews in Post-Holocaust Germany, 1945–1953* (Cambridge: Cambridge University Press, 2005); C. Kugelmann, 'Die Identität osteuropäischer Juden in der Bundesrepublik' [The Identity of Eastern European Jews in the Federal Republic] in M. Brumlik et al. (eds), *Jüdisches Leben in Deutschland seit 1945*, pp.177–81.
35. This chapter uses 'DP' to connote Jewish Displaced Persons. Due to the attempt to create ethnically homogenous nation states post-war, and displacements of ethnic minority groups, non-Jewish DPs do exist, of course, as well.
36. Brenner, *Nach dem Holocaust*; J. Geis, *Übrig sein: Leben danach, Deutsche Juden in der Britischen und Amerikanischen Zone* [Left over: Living after, German Jews in the British and American Occupied Zones] (Berlin: Philo, 1999); Geller, *Jews in Post-Holocaust Germany*; A. Königseder and J. Wetzel, *Lebensmut im Wartesaal: Die jüdischen DPs (Displaced Persons) im Nachkriegsdeutschland* [Courage to Face Life in the Waiting Room: Jewish DPs(Displaced Persons) in Post-War Germany], (Frankfurt am Main: Fischer, 1994).
37. Ibid.
38. Geller, *Jews in Post-Holocaust Germany*; Geis, *Übrig sein*.
39. Geller, *Jews in Post-Holocaust Germany*, p.17.
40. K. Meiering, *Die christlich-jüdische Mischehe in Deutschland* , [Christian-Jewish Intermarriages in Germany] *1840–1933* (Hamburg: Dölling & Galitz Verlag, 1998).
41. N. Fresco, 'La Diaspora des cendres' [The Diaspora of the Ashes], *Nouvelle Revue de Psychoanalyse*, 2 (1981), pp.5–20.
42. Geis, *Übrig sein*, p.409–37
43. Bodemann, 'How can one stand to live there as a Jew ... '; Bodemann, *Gedächtnistheater*; Bodemann, *In den Wogen der Erinnerung*; Geller, *Jews in Post-Holocaust Germany*; Kugelmann, 'Die Identität osteuropäischer Juden in der Bundesrepublik'; Kranz, *Shades of Jewishness*.

44. J. Kessler, 'Jüdische Migration aus der früheren Sowjetunion seit 1990. Resumee einer Studie mit 4000 Zuwanderern aus der früheren Sowjetunion in Berlin', [Jewish Migration from the former Soviet Union since 1990: Summary of a study of 4000 Immigrants from the former Soviet Union] *Trumah*, 7 (1998), pp.140–62; J. Kessler, *The Cultural and Religious Self-Image of Berlin Jews: Results of the First Congregational Survey* (Berlin: Umfrage, 2002); Judith Kessler, 'Jüdische Migration aus der früheren Sowjetunion seit 1990. Beispiel Berlin', [XXX Berlin Sample], Hagalil Online, 23 February 2003, http://www.berlin-judentum.de/gemeinde/migration.htm; J. Kessler, 'Homo Sovieticus in Disneyland: The Jewish Communities in Germany Today', in Y. Michal Bodemann (ed.), *The New German Jewry and the European Context* (Basingstoke and New York: Palgrave Macmillan, 2008), pp.131–43.
45. Kranz, *Shades of Jewishness*, p.65
46. Ibid.
47. R. Alba, 'On the Sociological Significance of the American Jewish Experience: Boundary Blurring, Assimilation, and Pluralism', *Sociology of Religion*, 67, 4 (2006), pp.347–58; J. Perlman, 'The American Jewish Periphery: An Overview' Working Paper No. 473 (Levy Economics Institute of Bard College, Annandale, NY, 2006), https://www.econstor.eu/dspace/bitstream/10419/31463/1/570166888.pdf.
48. This finding is indicative for the structures of an organic social network that rests on ethnic bind, and ethnic bond. Cf. D. Kranz, 'Living Local: Some Remarks on the Creation of Social Groups of Young Jews in Present-Day London', *European Review of History: Revue europeenne d'histoire*, 18, 1 (2011), pp.79–88; M. Miller McPherson, L. Smith-Lovin and J. Cook, 'Birds of a Feather: Homophily in Social Networks', *Annual Review of Sociology*, 27 (2001), pp.415–44.
49. S. Grabowsky, *'Meine Identität ist die Zerrissenheit': Halbjüdinnen und Halbjuden im Nationalsozialismus* [My Identity is the State of Being Torn – Half-Jewessnesses and Half-Jews during National Socialism] (Göttingen: Psychosozialverlag, 2012).
50. J.M. Peck, *Being Jewish in the New Germany* (Piscataway, NJ: Rutgers University Press, 2006), p.ix.
51. Grünberg, *Folgen des Holocaust*, p.62
52. J. Borneman and J.M. Peck, *Sojourners: The Return of German Jews and the Question of Identity* (Lincoln, NE: University of Nebraska Press, 1995), pp.81–102.
53. Kranz, *Shades of Jewishness*, p.85; Rapaport, 'Difficulties of Being Jewish'.
54. Kranz, *Shades of Jewishness*, p.322.
55. Ibid., p.276.
56. Ibid.
57. Mendel, 'Jungsein – Judesein – Dasein?', p.265.
58. S. Khasani, 'Eine Minderheit in der Minderheit: Das Engagement der linksorientierten Juden in der Frankfurter Jüdischen Gruppe' [A Minority within a Minority: The Activism of Left-Wing Jews in the Jewish Group in Frankfurt], *Trumah*, 14 (2005), 55–74; Kranz, *Shades of Jewishness*, p.64.
59. D. Bar-On, D.K. Brendler and A.P. Hare (eds), *Da ist etwas kaputt gegangen an den Wurzeln ...: Identitätsformation deutscher und israelischer Jugendlicher im Schatten des Holocaust* [Something is Broken in the Roots: Identity Formation of German and Israeli Youth in the Shadow of the Holocaust], (Frankfurt: Campus Verlag, 1997); Grünberg, 'Folgen des Holocaust'; K. Grünberg, *Liebe nach Auschwitz: Die Zweite Generation* [Love After Auschwitz: The Second Generation], (Frankfurt/Main: Sigmund-Freud-Institut, 2000); Y. Hadar, 'Existentielle Erfahrung oder Krankheitssympton? Überlegungen zum Begriff der "Zweiten Generation" ' [Existential Experience or Symptom of Ill-Health? Contemplations Concerning the Notion of 'Second Generation'] in R.-P. Beigel, N. Freudenberg, N. Schmitt and H. Stoffels (eds), *Schicksale der Verfolgten: Psychische und Somatische Auswirkungen von Terrorherrschaft* [Fates of the Persecuted: Psychological and Somatic Long-Term Effects of the Reign of Terror], (Berlin, Heidelberg and New York: Springer, 1991), pp.160–72.; Kranz, *Shades of Jewishness*; G. Rosenthal, B. Völter and N. Gilad, 'Folgen der Zwansmigration über drei Generationen: Familien mit Großeltern aus Deutschland'[Long-Term Effects of Dispalcements Across Three Generations: Families with Grandparents from Germany], in U. Apitzsch (ed.), *Migration und Traditionsbildung* [Migration and the Making of Traditions] (Opladen/Wiesbaden: Westdeutscher Verlag, 1999), pp.45–75; Vollrath, *Abgespaltene Anteile*.

60. W. R. von Baeyer, H. Haefer and K.P. Kisker, *Psychiatrie der Verfolgten: psychopathologische und gutachtliche Erfahrungen an Opfern der nationalsozialistischen Verfolgung und vergleichbarer Extrembelastungen* [The Psychiatry of the Persecuted: Experiences of Psychopathology and Expert Opinions Concerning Victims of Perecution under National Socialism and Comparable Extreme Sresses] (Berlin: Springer, 1964).
61. Freker, *Junge Juden*, p.32–6; Grünberg, *Liebe nach Auschwitz.*
62. J. Bruner, 'Life as Narrative', *Social Research*, 54, 1 (1987), pp.15–37; Kranz, *Shades of Jewishness*, p.225–32 with reference to the fallacy of cultural scripts.
63. C. Linde, *Life-Stories: The Creation of Coherence* (Oxford: Oxford University Press, 1993); E. Ochs and L. Capps, *Living Narrative: Creating Lives in Everyday Storytelling* (Cambridge, MA: Harvard University Press, 2001).
64. Linde, *Life Stories*; Ochs and Capps, *Living Narrative.*
65. C. Noy, *A Narrative Community: Voices of Israeli Backpackers* (Detroit, MI: Wayne State University, 2007).
66. D. Kranz, 'The Dynamics of the Jewish Space', paper presented at the Annual Conference of the German Studies Association, San Diego, USA, 4–7 October 2007; Kranz, *Shades of Jewishness*; Kuschner, *Die jüdische Minderheit in der Bundesrepublik.*
67. K. Grünberg, 'Szenische Erinnerung der Shoah' [Scenic Memories of the Shoah], paper presented at Szenische Erinnerungen der Shoah, Siegmund Freud Institut, 17–18 November 2007; Vollrath, *Abgespaltene Anteile.*
68. Grünberg, *Liebe nach Auschwitz*; Kranz, *Shades of Jewishness*; Rapaport, *Jews in Post-Holocaust Germany.*
69. Grünberg, *Liebe nach Auschwitz.*
70. M. Löw-Beer, 'From Nowhere to Israel and Back: The Changing Self-Definition of German-Jewish Youth Since 1960', in Bodemann (ed.), *Germans, Jews and Memory*, pp.101–30.
71. D. Kranz, 'Leaving, Sojourning, Returning: Young Jews from Germany in London', paper presented at an international workshop, 'German Migrants and European Development: In-Migration, Acculturation and Identity from the Eighteenth Century to the Present Day', Liverpool, 5–6 September 2008.
72. Freker, *Junge Juden*, p.126
73. Kranz, 'Leaving, Sojourning, Returning'; Kranz, *Shades of Jewishness.*
74. S. Speier, 'Von der Pubertät zum Erwachsenendasein: Bericht einer Bewußtwerdung'[From Puberty to Adulthood: A Report on Becoming Conscious], in M. Brumlik et al. (eds), *Jüdisches Leben in Deutschland seit 1945*, pp.182–88.
75. As citizenship is one of my main research areas, I interviewed lawyers who work in this area, and I cooperate with them. The lack of interest in re-naturalization in the US was a point they unanimously raised, and it can be corroborated by general data on naturalizations of German authorities. Cf. D. Kranz and A. Margalith, 'The German Citizenship of Yekkes: Legal and Anthropological Perspectives', paper presented at the Citizenship in Question Symposium, Boston University, MA, 19–21 April 2012.
76. I conducted ethnographic research amongst young Jews in London in 2008 and 2009, to understand the increasing amount of social groups of young Jews (Kranz, Living Local, 2011). Strikingly, the interview partners stressed their identification with the locale London if they were from London, as well as their identification as British Jews (ibid). This strong national identification runs contrary to my finds on the Third Generations who are at the centre of this paper.
77. Kranz, 'Dynamics of the Jewish Space'; Kranz, *Shades of Jewishness*, p.91.
78. M. Brumlik, *Zuhause, keine Heimat? Junge Juden und ihre Zukunft in Deutschland* [Home but note homely? Young Jews and Their Future in Germany] (Gerlingen: Bleicher Verlag, 1998).
79. *Yekke* is the nickname given to German-speaking Jews in Israel. The term comes from the Yiddish jacket, and plays on the – alleged – inability and unwillingness of German-speaking Jews to integrate into Israel mainstream society. The term was negatively connoted, and only in recent years has its connotation changed Interestingly, this interview partner and the one before come from Eastern European families: the first one left Israel again, the second one stays on, to date; D. Kranz, 'Being a Yekke is a really big deal for my mum!', *Austausch*, 2, 1 (2013), http://www.psa.ac.uk/sites/default/files/Being%20a%20Yekke%20-%20Dani%20Kranz.pdf; D.

Diner, 'Jeckes – Ursprung und Wandel einer Zuschreibung' [Yekkes – Origins and Change of its Meaning], in M. Zimmermann and Y. Hotam (eds), Zweimal Heimat: Die Jeckes Zwischen Mitteleuropa und Nahost [Dual Homeland: The Yekkes Between Middle Europe and the Near East] (Frankfurt/M: Beerenverlag, 2005), pp.100–03.
80. Cf. Bodemann, 'A Jewish Cultural Renascence in Germany'; Cf. Brumlik, *Zuhause, keine Heimat.*
81. I see the inability to speak any one language flawlessly as a specific expressions of the rootlessness of Third Generations, which bases on the displacement of the grandparents, the entering of German language into the family home in Germany, and recurrent moves in a out of Germany. While we spoke German amongst each other in fieldwork situations, the language was littered with idioms that draw on Yiddish, and it furthermore commonly contained Hebrewisms, Anglicisms, as well as any other, ancestral, or adopted language. The only exception were monolingually raised descendants of German Jews in Germany, who form an extremely small group.
82. Rapaport, 'The Difficulties of Being Jewish'; Rapaport, *Jews in Germany after the Holocaust.*
83. D. Kranz, '*Nora: Narrative Re/Konstruktion einer jüdischen Identität – Ein Fallbeispiel*', [Nora: The Narrative Re/Construction of a Jewish Identity – A Case Study] in B. Gensch and S. Grabowsky (eds), *Der halbe Stern: Verfolgungsgeschichte und Identitätsproblematik von Personen und Familien teiljüdischer Herkunft* [Half a Star: Persecution and Identity of Individuals and Families of Part Jewish Descent], Giessen: Haland & Wirth im Psychosozialverlag, 2010), pp.205–22.
84. A. Grossmann, *Jews, Germans, and Allies: Close Encounters in Occupied Germany* (Princeton, NJ: Princeton University Press, 2007).
85. Kranz, *Shades of Jewishness*, p.261
86. Grünberg, *Liebe nach Auschwitz*; Rapaport, *Difficulties of Being Jewish.*
87. I.N. Magat, 'Israeli and Japanese Immigrants to Canada: Home, Belonging, and the Territorialization of Identity', *Ethos* 22, 2 (1999), pp.119–44; p.127.
88. M. Mendel, 'Jungsein – Judesein – Dasein?', p.266
89. Ibid, p.267.
90. Kugelmann, 'Die Identität osteuropäischer Juden in der Bundesrepublik'.
91. H. Maor, *Über den Wiederaufbau der jüdischen Gemeinden in Deutschland seit 1945* [About the Reconstruction of Jewish Communities in Germany since 1945], (unpublished PhD thesis, University of Mainz, 1961), http://harrymaor.com/download.htm#item1; Levinson, 'Religiöse Richtungen und Entwicklungen'.
92. Mendel, 'Jungsein – Judesein – Dasein?', p.265
93. Freker, *Junge Juden*, pp.126–36.
94. Grünberg, 'Szenische Erinnerungen der Shoah'.
95. H. Welzer, S. Möller and K. Tschuggnall, *'Opa war kein Nazi': Nationalsozialismus und Holocaust im Familiengedächtnis* [Opa wasn't a Nazi: National Socialism and Holocaust in Family Memory] (Frankfurt am Main: Fischer Taschenbuch Verlag, 2002).
96. D. Nelles, H. Rübner and H. Sünker, 'Die "Kinder des Widerstands": Lebensbedingungen und Sozialisation der Kinder von politisch und religiös Verfolgten des NS-Regimes', [The Children of Resistance Fighters: Living Conditions and Socialisation of Children of the Politically and Religiously Persecuted of the Nazi Regime], *Neue Praxis*, 33 (2003), http://nrw.vvn-bda.de/bilder/neue_praxis.pdf; D. Nelles, A. Nolzen and H. Sünker, 'Kinder des Widerstands" im Nationalsozialismus: Familiale und politische Sozialisationsprozesse' [Children of Resistance Fighters during National Socialisim: Socialisation], *Widersprüche: Zeitschrift für sozialistische Politik im Bildungs-, Gesundheits- und Sozialbereich*, 99, 1 (2006), pp.67–83, http://www.nrw.vvn-bda.de/bilder/widersprueche.pdf; D. Nelles, A. Nolzen and H. Sünker, 'Kinder des Widerstands" und Politik nach 1945: Die Kinder kommunistischer Widerstandskämpfer gegen das NS- Regime und deren Verhältnis zur Politik nach dem Zweiten Weltkrieg' ['Children of the Resistance' and Politics since 1945: Communist Children of Resistance Fighters against the NS – its Relationship to post-World Two Politics], *BIOS*, 21, 2 (2008), http://nrw.vvn-bda.de/bilder/bios.pdf.
97. T. Litvak-Hirsch and J. Chaitin, 'The Shoah Runs Through Our Veins: The Relevance of the Holocaust for Jewish-Israeli Young Adults', *IDEA: A Journal of Social Issues*, 14 (2010),

http://www.ideajournal.com/articles.php?id=49; T. Litvak-Hirsch, D. Bar-On and J. Chaitin, 'Constructing Self, Constructing Others: Jewish–Israeli Perceptions of Palestinians and Germans', *Israel Studies Forum* 22 (2007), pp.3–27; T. Litvak-Hirsch and D. Bar-On, 'To Rebuild Life: A Longitudinal Study of the Influences of the Holocaust on the Following Generations', *Family Process*, 45 (2006), pp.465–83.

98. It is beyond the scope of this paper to go into the problematic of restitution. Only one case should be mentioned here, the one of Cornelius Gurlitt. He was the son of a Nazi official who confiscated or rescued art and kept it – depending on the perspective. The Israeli German lawyer Joel Levy outlined in detail how German bureaucracy across all levels failed for more than two years to deal with this case appropriately, and how the restitution of art is often stymied (cf. Peter Münch, 'Eine Blamage für die deutschen Behörden' [An Embarrassment for the German Authorities], 28 December 2013, http://www.sueddeutsche.de/kultur/zu-besuch-bei-israels-bekanntestem-raubkunst-anwalt-eine-blamage-fuer-die-deutschen-behoerden-1.185 2233.

99. Welzer et al., *Opa war kein Nazi*; M. Klundt (ed.), *Heldenmythos und Opfertaumel: Der Zweite Weltkrieg und seine Folgen im deutschen Geschichtsdiskurs* [Between Heroic Myt and Sacrifical Frenzy: The Second World War and its Aftermaths within German Historical Discourse], (Cologne: PapyRossa, 2004). The recent TV series, *Unsere Mütter, unsere Väter* (English title: *Generation War*) exemplifies this discourse. While it was received positively from the side of many non-Jewish Germans, it garnered major criticisms from the side of critical German scholars, Jews in Germany, and across the spectrum abroad (cf. Hannes Stein, Amerika entrüstet sich über deutsche Lebenslügen, [America is Outraged about German Life-Time Lies] 28 January 2014, http://www.welt.de/kultur/kino/article124291935/Amerika-entruestet-sich-ueber-deutsche-Lebensluegen.html).

100. R. Melzer, O. Decker, J. Kless and E. Brähler, *Die Mitte im Umbruch: Rechtsextreme Einstellungen in Deutschland 2012* [The Centre in Change: Extreme Right- Wing Attitudes in Germany 2012], (Bonn: Dietz, 2012).

101. Bundesministerium des Inneren, *Antisemitismus in Deutschland: Erscheinungsformen, Bedingungen, Präventionsansätze. Bericht des unabhängigen Expertenkreises Antisemitismus* [Antisemitism in Germany: Shapes, Conditions, Prevention. Report of the Independent Expert Commission on Antisemitism], (Berlin: Bundesministerium des Inneren, 2011).

Performance, Memory and Identity: The Israeli Third Generation in Yael Ronen's *Third Generation* Play (2009)

DIANA I. POPESCU

Introduction

Young Israeli director Yael Ronen's theatre play *Third Generation* (2009), a co-production by the Schaubühne Theatre in Berlin with the Habima National Theatre of Israel, gathers Israeli, German and Palestinian actors raised in the shadows of Holocaust memory, and is meant to bring into public discussion the similarities and the differences that either unite or separate them. By offering the actors the freedom to construct their own dialogues and the possibility to interact with a German audience, Ronen proposes a process at the end of which the participants in the play can co-create a new language and a new identity. 'The third generation simply needs its own language', states Ronen, by means of which they can build a story that represents them.[1]

This chapter will primarily investigate Israeli third-generation identities as they emerge within the context of this theatrical performance. Notably, the term 'third generation' giving the title of this performance is employed generically to refer to all the participants in the play, regardless of their divergent personal and national backgrounds. The term, hence, includes grandchildren of Holocaust survivors, Nazi perpetrators and of Palestinians forced to leave their homes in the early years of the state of Israel. The use of the term may appear problematic, given that thus far it has been employed mainly to refer to the Jewish descendants of survivors, and in some studies to the German descendants,[2] and only seldom to the Palestinians.[3] This open and inclusive use of the term 'third generation', I shall argue, denotes a sense of shared awareness among all participants that the history of the Holocaust has significantly shaped their identities and world views, albeit differently; and to a large extent it determines how they interact with each other. My interest is with the Israeli third generation as it is represented in Ronen's performance. I shall engage to a lesser degree with the German and the Palestinian members of the third generation, as these groups, and the complex relationships they develop, deserve a lengthier discussion. In the course of my analysis, I will, however, stress the significance of the interdependent relationship formed by these groups, whose very definition as a 'third generation' is linked to the Holocaust.

Aiming to reveal how Israeli members of the youngest generation relate to the familial and the collective past of victimization, I shall draw a parallel between Ronen's play and the well-known 1991 production *Arbeit macht frei vom Toitland Europa* (Work makes free from the death-land of Europe) at the Acco Theatre Center in Israel, which explores the Holocaust legacy of the second generation. While underlining similarities between the two theatrical performances, I would like to point especially to how these cultural productions contribute to a trans-generational dialogue and, hence, expose the developments in the processes of memory transmission and the attitudes that distinguish the Israeli third generation from their parents. In particular, I will look at the third generation's acts of discursive rebellion against the second generation and ask whether and how third-generation members refuse to walk in the footsteps of their parents.

Understanding the Israeli Third Generation

Psychological studies undertaken by therapist Eva Fogelman have stressed the interest that third-generation Israeli members continue to show in the experiences of their grandparent survivors. The Demjanjuk Trial in 1986 in Israel is one such example. John Demjanjuk was identified by Holocaust survivors as 'Ivan the Terrible', a Ukrainian guard accused of torturing and killing many inmates at Treblinka extermination camp. He was brought to court, judged and sentenced to death, a conviction later overturned due to lack of evidence. Fogelman recalls how 'teenagers flocked to the Court House, and lined up at dawn to get a seat to watch the Trial' and to hear the testimonies of survivors. Also, they are the first generation to have consistently studied the Holocaust at school, therefore 'imbibing a language in which to talk to their grandparents'. Moreover, argues Fogelman, due to them, 'a phenomenon of intergenerational dialogue' surfaced in Israel and became 'a national sensation and was recorded in documentaries and television discussion programs'.[4]

A point of separation from the second generation is, according to Fogelman, 'the [third generation's] awareness that the suffering that [their] grandparents endured is part of the fabric of their lives, [which is especially] channelled into empathy, political activism, a greater consciousness of others'.[5] Indeed, sensitivity to other victimized groups also seems to be a characteristic of the plays under discussion here. However, it is further problematized in the context of third-generation Germans and Palestinians. As shall be shown in my investigation of the *Third Generation* performance, the three groups bring their own 'victimization' into play and discuss it critically, and not without making use of humour with its ironic, sarcastic and therapeutic undertones.

The relevance of the Holocaust to the Israeli third generation is explored in further depth by sociologist Dan Bar-On whose extensive research has revealed a variety of understandings. Bar-On coined the concept 'paradoxical relevance' to refer to those individuals who react either with emotion, even though they have no detailed knowledge of their grandparents' experiences or, on the contrary, possess sufficient knowledge but have no emotional responses whatsoever. At the very opposite end is the phenomenon of 'over generalisation' which centres on the third generation's perception of events in their lives predominantly through the prism of the Holocaust. A more measured reaction and allegedly the most dominant one, comes from those for whom the Holocaust has 'partial relevance'.[6] Following Bar-On's investigation, Tal Litvak Hirsch and Julia Chaitin came to observe that young adults 'appear to be coming to terms with their families' traumatic past in a healthy manner'.[7] Fogelman, too, seems to agree with this, as she argues that, indeed, the third generation 'did not grow up with the concept of Jews who went to the slaughter like sheep', which characterized the identity of their parents. She even goes on to suggest that the majority of grandchildren lack fears, such as that of antisemitism, which are more pervasive in the lives of survivors and their children.[8] Other studies focusing on the behaviour of highschool students during excursions to Auschwitz are especially interested to observe the teenagers' responses to narratives which place them in the victims' shoes.[9] Jackie Feldman has argued convincingly that the trips to Poland are a deliberate re-enactment of Jewish history as perceived through the lens of Israeli nationalist narratives. He demonstrates how each and every aspect of the trip is designed as a process in which the Israeli young people are manipulated to experience themselves as victims, survivors, and finally as witnesses for whom Israel is the only response to the Holocaust. Feldman doubts whether this strategy is in reality effective, as he suggests that as they mature, some of the participants in the commemoration trips recall their trips as manipulative. Furthermore, he argues that the trips may in fact weaken rather than strengthen Israeli national feeling.[10] This latter idea re-emerges in a recent critical inquiry into the ideological dimension of Israeli educational programmes, and which resulted in a praised as well as criticized documentary film called *Defamation* (2009).[11] Israeli journalist and film-maker Yoav Shamir offers a portrayal of Israeli younger generations' relationship with the Holocaust, worthy of presenting in some detail. As part of the documentary, he accompanies a group of Israeli teenagers and their teachers to Poland, and closely observes their behaviour and emotional responses to what they learn about the concentration camps. Throughout their stay in Poland, the teenagers are confronted with stories of victimization which compel them to react emotionally. Nevertheless, some of them find it difficult to respond in this manner and feel guilty about this. A pertinent example is given by two teenagers who, after their visit to the Majdanek camp, state the following: 'We are disappointed with ourselves. We can't comprehend. We feel guilty for not having any feelings or emotions.'[12] The teenagers' sense of guilt for not being able to be emotional seems to be a response to the external pressure put on them by their teachers.

Shamir shows how during their preparation for the visits to Auschwitz and Majdanek the teenagers are made to believe that the external environment is hostile towards them. Moreover, they are told by the secret service officer who accompanies them that it would be dangerous for them to leave the group. As a response to this preparation, the teenagers misinterpret comments made by Polish individuals as being anti-Semitic. However, the teachers' efforts seem to pay off as many teenagers do react in a very emotional manner when they finally get to visit Auschwitz. They are touched by what they experience and admit that the visit permanently changed the way they view themselves as Jews. During their visits, the teenagers are made to feel that the victimization of European Jews can happen again, and that they must act to prevent becoming victims again. Faced with the suffering of the Jewish people during the Holocaust, some teenagers become desensitized to other people's suffering. One teenager admits that he feels that the destruction of Palestinians' homes, which they view on Israeli television, pales in comparison with the victimization to which Jews had been subjected.[13]

Shamir's film attests to how the 'victim identity' of the European Jews becomes a central part of Israeli national ideology and continues to shape this youngest generation's mentality. Given this, the inevitable question that arises is what it means to develop a 'normal' relationship with the past. Shamir concludes with the statement: 'maybe it is about time to live in the present and look to the future'.[14] The notion of normalization, to which Shamir alludes at the end of his film, also intrigued Litvak Hirsch and Julia Chaitin, who attempted to define it as 'the balance between the need to connect to the trauma and the fear of being overwhelmed by it, and the need to keep the significance of the Holocaust alive, without creating a new generation of victims'.[15]

It is only since the 1990s that the 'nationalized memory' approach, hitherto the dominant way in which the Israeli society dealt with Holocaust memory, has started to be challenged. This process was triggered mainly by a generational shift, through the writings of a new generation of historians, and more broadly through a post-Zionist approach. Israeli so-called 'new historians' such as Idith Zertal, Moshe Zuckermann and Daniel Gutwein pitted against what they regarded as the Israeli state's monopoly over Holocaust memory. Zertal questioned the consequences of the centrality of the Holocaust in Israel, arguing that Israel's national identity is rooted in a culture of death and victimhood.[16] Gutwein held that, indeed, post-Zionism played an essential role in 'privatizing Holocaust memory, by depicting Zionist ideology and Israeli politics that portrayed the nationalised memory as oppressive'.[17]

In the period after the Lebanon War (1982), for example, the Israeli public sphere witnessed how an increasing number of public figures expressed their doubts about the social-psychological consequences of the nationalized narrative of Holocaust memory. A representative case is historian and Auschwitz survivor, Yehuda Elkana. His article 'The Need to Forget', in the national daily newspaper *Ha-Aretz* on 2 March 1988, triggered a host of public responses. Published at the onset of the first Intifada, Elkana's article aimed to raise awareness of how 'victimhood consciousness' nurtured by Holocaust memory has led to a collective belief that 'the whole world is against us'. This conviction, in Elkana's view, has also dominated Israel's attitude towards the Palestinians. Elkana warned that 'any philosophy of life predicated solely or mostly on the Holocaust would have disastrous consequences'. In order to prevent this, Elkana argued that 'the past is not and must not be allowed to become the dominant element determining the future of society and the destiny of people'. Hence, he declared: 'there is no greater threat to the future of the state of Israel than the fact that the Holocaust systematically and forcefully penetrated the consciousness of the Israeli public'. Elkana's alternative to the nationalization of Holocaust memory was a call for 'the need to forget'. His demand was to privatize Holocaust memory, adopting 'forgetting' as its aim. Elkana concluded:

> We must learn to forget! Today I see no more important political and educational task for the leaders of this nation than to take their stand on the side of life, to dedicate themselves to creating our future, and not to be preoccupied from morning to night with symbols, ceremonies, and lessons of the Holocaust. They must uproot the domination of that historical 'remember' over our lives.[18]

Elkana shows that Holocaust memory also acts as a vehicle by means of which individuals can adopt critical standpoints vis-à-vis the role of commemoration in shaping collective perceptions of the past. This line of argument – already a part of the post-Zionist discourse which encouraged an individual stance to Holocaust memory and showed a critical stance towards the nationalized approach – re-emerges in *Third Generation* play, as the performers openly discuss how the national approach to memory has affected their individual identities as members of the third generation. Moreover, I shall argue that Ronen's play offers an awareness of the perils of an inherited victimization and explores whether and how a sense of normality can be reached in the aftermath of the historical trauma.

Third Generation, the Play

The *Third Generation* project started with a workshop that took place in June 2008 in Israel and in Germany. The actors Yishai Golan, Ayelet Robinson, Orit Nachmias and Roi Miller from the Habimah theatre; German actors Nils Bormann, Karsten Dahlem, Patrick Güldenberg and Judith Strößenreuter from the Schaubühne Theatre; and Palestinian-Israeli actors Rauda Sliman, Muhuammad Dabdub, Rabia Khouri and George Iskander were invited to come together on stage to discuss how they understood their relationship to history, what they have in common and what separates them. After the workshop, and a public showing in Halle, Germany in the summer of 2008, the Schaubühne and the Habimah decided to mount a joint production that was included in both theatres' performance schedules in 2009. The performers' identities were further complicated by their specific personal and family history and included German actors born on opposite sides of the divided country, Palestinians of either Muslim or Christian background, and Israelis with roots in Europe, the Middle East or North Africa.

Described as a 'Gordian knot' that binds together the three nations, the Holocaust is the prevalent subject of this performance staged as a 'group therapy'.[19] However, unlike real therapy where participants discuss the direct consequences of the traumas they experienced personally, in the 'group therapy' setting organized by Ronen, members of the third generation speak about how national foundational myths are firmly rooted in their personal stories as individuals and shape their interactions with other groups. The participants actively interrogate dominant identity stances such as that of the victim and the perpetrator, dare to open a space beyond this dichotomy and start a conversation about how the memory of the Holocaust should be treated appropriately.

The dialogues between the three groups aim to make room for the many nuances hidden behind the Holocaust-informed metanarratives, by means of which the world is divided into good and evil. The play brings into discussion the fact that even though the Jewish victims and the German victimizers are gradually passing away, the categories 'victim' and 'victimizer' remain dominant for both German and Israeli individuals and the societies in which they live. These categories and the ways they define third-generation interactions are being unravelled in *Third Generation* play. The actors, all in their thirties, ask the public to reflect upon how they – the third generation – live today with the heavy past which is always a part of their present, define themselves in relation to the national narratives of their countries, and are made to regard the 'other' through the prism imposed by the Holocaust.

The play begins with an introductory note by German actor Niels Brosman who appeared on the stage to address the public in German. He asked: 'Are there any Jews out there?' A few timidly raised their hands. 'In the name of the German people', he said, hand over heart, 'I apologize.' He was only getting started, argues journalist Gal Beckerman. 'Any Gypsies in the audience?' No one responded. 'Well, they must be on the way.' More nervous giggles. 'Homosexuals? Sorry. How about Turkish emigrants?' He felt terrible for how the government had treated them in the 1990s.[20] As he apologized, the rest of the cast made its way onto stage, behind him. 'Oh, here's Ishay', Niels said suddenly, turning to one of the Israeli actors. 'To you, Ishay, I would like to personally apologize. Your grandfather was electrocuted on the gate of the Sachsenhausen concentration camp. My apologies. I'm very sorry.' Ishay emitted an awkward, 'Forget about it!' and a relieved smile spread across Niels's face. 'If only it was always so easy', he told the now hysterical audience, as Beckerman observed for the Jewish journal the *Forward*.[21] Indeed, one can argue that political correctness seems to be one of the main preoccupations of the young German, and this political stance becomes the driving force of the play.

On stage, ten chairs placed in a semicircle make it easier for the actors to see and hear each other. When the words become too harsh, some actors leave this setting, turning their backs towards the audience, or covering their faces with their hands. However, the arguments, which frequently ignite, end with a joke or a gesture that takes the tension away. Some actors impersonate national stereotypes such as in the case of Brosman who assumes the role of the German scapegoat, or Ayelet Robinson, the Israeli teenager who sings tunes that glorify the courage of the Israeli soldiers.[22] All actors on stage wear red t-shirts marked with a '3G' stamp which points to how the three national groups are a part of a collective that is united by the historical past. The actors play themselves or a variation of themselves, and the script is based on their own personal histories or draws on their shared reflections of sites such as the Sachsenhausen concentration camp and of a checkpoint crossing in the West Bank, which they had previously visited. Through these common experiences, argued Amit Epstein, the play's dramaturge, they were meant to reach together a 'new terminology' and a new relationship to history and its burdensome legacy. 'So raw was the result of the emotional processing that the shape of the resulting play was actually just the strung-together improvised scenes and monologues that the workshop produced', argued Epstein interviewed by Beckerman.[23]

Performance and Performing Identities

The main objective of the theatrical encounter organized by Ronen is to enhance the expression of a distinct third-generation identity. But is performance instrumental to creating identity? How does it become relevant for the construction of a third-generation identity stance? The Israeli, Palestinian and German actors' interactions on stage resist the prescribed rules of traditional theatre. Ronen describes the play as a 'work in process' since it is through their very presence on stage that the actors come to know who they are. In other words, in being performed, their identities are being shaped into a third-generation collective. Identity, as it is understood through the prism of theatre theory, draws on Lacanian concept of the 'mirror phase', the moment of reflection in the mirror of one's image, which becomes a defining moment of one's acquisition of a sense of identity.[24] German theatre scholar Erika Fischer-Lichte, for example, views theatre as the act of 'self-representation and self-reflection of a society'.[25] Furthermore, she understands identity as the condition which allows a person to develop self-consciousness, and which is firmly rooted in a person's ability to distance herself/himself from his or her self and to relate to relate to this him/herself as another. 'By viewing oneself in the mirror as the other, or within the mirror of another, one creates an image of oneself', argues Fisher-Lichte.[26] Within the theatrical performance, the identities of the characters are shaped in the interaction with the audience. Heike Pearson-Roms further links identity with theatrical performance, arguing that 'it is the experience of identity, articulated through theatrical means that forms an essential part of the history of the theatre'.[27] She thus suggests that there is an inherent theatricality in the construction of identity itself, since it is the theatrical performance that 'materializes in the body of the performer the identity that is prefigured within the dramatic text'.[28]

In Ronen's *Third Generation* play, however, the distinction between the identity of the artist and that of the character in the play disappears entirely, making room for a new understanding of the theatrical performance as a mirror to the self. Ronen departs from the predominant idea that theatre mirrors society. Instead, *Third Generation* is rather a social experiment which takes place on stage, where the audience is there to assist in the formation of a third-generation identity and to confirm its existence. On this occasion, the audience, much like the psychoanalyst, plays the passive role of listener and observer, and acts as a mirror to the third-generation participants.

Through its focus on the identity of the actors on stage, Ronen's experimental play is highly reminiscent of David Maayan's 1991 theatrical tour de force, *Arbeit macht frei vom Toitland Europa*. Indeed, there are remarkable similarities in regard to subject matter, format and setting between these plays. The following parallel with Maayan's play will make apparent what is specific about the third-generation identities of the participants in Ronen's project. The comparison will further probe the relevance of the Holocaust in the construction of the third-generation identities of Israeli participants and shed some light upon the particular perspectives on the role of Holocaust memory for future generations of Jews. Does the *Third Generation* play reveal continuity with the Holocaust-centred Jewish identity narrative in Israel or rather a break away from it? For what purposes is the memory of the Holocaust transmitted to future generations? How do members of the youngest generation view their connection to the Holocaust?

Mirroring Third Generation Identity

Arbeit macht frei premiered at the Acco Theatre Center and remained in its repertoire for more than seven years, during which time it travelled in other countries including Germany, where the script and staging were adapted to address the German public. The play offers a self-critical portrayal of the connection that Jews of the second generation in Israel develop with the traumatic legacy of the Holocaust, and the contemporary grip that the Holocaust continues to have on the Israeli–Palestinian relationship. In Germany, the play opened up a new discursive space, as it triggered a direct confrontation between the Israeli performers and the German spectators. The play adapted during the performances in Germany by investigating a triangular relationship, and hence the similarities with the *Third Generation* play, which followed a similar travelling itinerary by going to Germany. The iterative nature of these performances is rightly highlighted by theatre critic Elin Diamond:

> A performance embeds traces of other performances, it also produces experiences whose interpretation only partially depends on previous experiences. This creates the terminology of 're' in discussions of performance as in re-embody, re-inscribe, re-configure, re-signify. 'Re'

> acknowledges the pre-existing discursive field, the repetition – and the desire to repeat – within the performative present, while 'embody', 'configure', 'inscribe', 'signify' assert the possibility of materializing something that exceeds our knowledge, that alters the shape of sites and imagines others as yet unsuspected modes of being.[29]

It is indeed through the experience of déjà vu that the co-creators of the *Third Generation* play endeavour – while walking alongside the performative lines drawn by the second-generation actors in *Arbeit macht frei* – to reopen a discussion about generational transfer of memories. In this sense, *Third Generation* marks a continuation with *Arbeit macht frei* through its similarly obsessive interrogation of the triangular relationship between the Germans, the Israelis and the Palestinians – the three chain-links of a vicious cycle of victimization and persecution – but also departs from it, through the apparent lightness, humour, self-irony and self-criticism that it is willing to engage in.

Ronen's conceptualization of the play follows closely the one adopted by David Maayan. Both seem to have been strongly influenced by the aesthetics, social politics and work ethics of Eugenio Barba, whose manifesto called 'Third Theatre' included the following statement:

> The third theatre lives on the fringe ... It is theatre created by people who define themselves as actors, directors, theatre workers although they have seldom undergone a traditional theatrical education and therefore are not recognised as professionals. But they are not amateurs. Their entire day is filled with theatrical experience, sometimes by what they call training, or by preparation of performances for which they must fight to find an audience.[30]

Both Israeli directors emphasize the detailed research and the reliance on the autobiography and family histories of the performers, not all having a traditional theatrical education, which served as a starting point for the plays' structures.

Unlike the *Third Generation* play, *Arbeit macht frei* puts more emphasis on the working process, seen to be as important as the final product, a fact further emphasized in the programme notes of the play. The process that led to its production is made known to the audience through a leaflet handed out at the end of the performance, which contains a paragraph written without spaces between the words. This form of written imitation of breathlessness gives a rather poetic account of this process. Furthermore, in *Arbeit macht frei*, historical processes and theatrical processes overlay one another. For example, the statement 'the three years we spend in the living machine of death' that appears in the leaflet could refer both to the three year-long rehearsal but also to the 1942–45 years of the death camps. Hence, the play draws attention to processes of re-enactment, by daringly conflating the 'hell' of the historical pasts with that of the theatrical present. Also, the main protagonist, actress Smadar Yaaron and daughter of a Holocaust survivor in real life, plays the role of Zelma Greenwald – an Ashkenazi Holocaust survivor – and becomes, as Freddie Rokem explains, 'a witness able to testify for the survivors, the real witnesses'.[31] This transference of witnessing as an identificatory process includes the spectators who also become witnesses to the Holocaust, argues Pearson-Roms.[32] The intention to overcome the distance of spectatorship and to create identification with the catastrophe and its aftermath is clearly expressed in other statements made by the Acco Theatre Center, such as this:

> The work of Acco Theater Center deals with the situation of the present Israeli generation and the Israeli existence in the shadow of the Holocaust. The event manifests the intention of its creators to reach a symbolic gate of Auschwitz which bore the heading, *Arbeit macht frei*, enter the personal/collective camp and exit afterwards through the same gate towards a new road. The idea is to keep walking along this road, contrary to the accepted Israeli conception that all stopped there – in front of the gate, and inside the camp.[33]

The term *Arbeit* in the sense of physical labour, a means by which the Nazis intended to kill the Jewish prisoners, is given another interpretation in the context of the performance. Its Hebrew equivalent, *avodah*, relates to a spiritual concept of the emancipatory emotional struggle undergone by the descendants of the Holocaust survivors to 'work through' the inherited trauma.

This attempt to 'work through' the past through the performance is, however, missing from Ronen's *Third Generation*. I would like to argue that *Third Generation* lacks the emotional struggle present in *Arbeit macht frei*. Instead, the stress falls on how tension emerging from the ideological clashes between the three national groups – and which almost always is grounded in the history of the Holocaust – is readily resolved through the use of laughter and humour. It is up to the audience to decide whether laughter is a way of addressing the real issues that are causing the tension, or, on the contrary, whether it remains a way of avoiding the confrontation.

Nevertheless, it is suggested that the performers of *Third Generation* have already walked on the 'new road' opened up by *Arbeit macht frei*, and that they have found a 'new language' in the shadows of Holocaust memory. Like *Arbeit macht frei*, *Third Generation* explores the connection between identity, biography and history, and the relationship between the individual and collective memory. However, a distinct mark of separation emerges from the ways in which the performers relate to past traumas. While a predominant element of *Arbeit macht frei* is the 'working through' and the process of mourning, *Third Generation* rather showcases third-generation members who acknowledge the trauma but they no longer feel compelled to enter the process of 'working through'. For the Israeli members of the third generation, what is more prevalent is the intellectual encounter with the effects of the inherited trauma. They rather prefer to make a critical comment about the ways in which the Holocaust has been appropriated at the national level, and how it continues to fuel a certain identity stance such as that of the victim in relation to the Palestinian. There are, however, other ways in which the *Third Generation* play acknowledges and continues the *avodah* initiated by *Arbeit macht frei*. Mainly, this is seen in Ronen's awareness that when dealing with the consequences of the trauma, one has to include not only the descendants of the victims, but also those of the perpetrators. Maayan came to this realization only through *Arbeit macht frei* play. He explained:

> From our experiences of meeting audiences in Europe, particularly in Germany, and lately in Austria too, we understood that this story has two sides, partners if you like. The descendants of the victims of the Holocaust and the descendants of the Holocaust generators, the Second and Third Generation on both sides. The direct interaction between Acco Theatre Center through its work and individuals from these generations in Europe, have created a new reality and a channel of hope to the present generation in Germany and Austria.[34]

Ronen further explores this 'new reality' by pointing to the differences in the ways in which the German members of the third generation deal with the ritual of guilt and atonement that define German–Israeli relations. Thus, a new reality is made apparent, through the performance of the young German actor who apologizes to all persecuted groups in Germany and provokes laughter on the part of the audience. With this gesture of 'political correctness', he enacts the national stereotype of a German nation that continues to feel shame and guilt towards the Jews. However, what the young member of the third generation actually points to is that this attitude of national atonement has already become an overused cliché which lacks real meaning.

Another trait common to both plays is the fact that the performers are encouraged to transform their individual biographies into fictional characters; hence on one level the characters are grounded in reality, on the other in fiction. Ronen follows the tradition of Israeli performances dealing with the Holocaust as she adopts a 'meta-theatrical approach'.[35] At the core of this approach is the blurring of boundaries between the fictional character and the performer's real self. Through this practice, the actors create a deliberate confusion about the status of what the spectators are watching. This can be best described using the term 'believed-in theatre'.[36] It refers to an experimental theatre technique by means of which its creators explore and express feelings and ideas at the point where the personal, the historical and the political intersect, or coincide, and thus can create confusion among the spectators. The symbolic 'not for real' and what is 'actual' can no longer be distinguished. According to Richard Schechner, it is the real autobiographical identity of the performers that allows for the creation of the contents of the work.[37] Hence, it is the autobiography of the German, Israeli and Palestinian performers that becomes the driving force for both *Arbeit macht frei* and *Third Generation*. The performers – through their personal histories – embody a full range of problematics, and they come to epitomize societal realities.

Whilst tension often arises between the members of the three groups on stage, this is almost always resolved through humour. Humour, in this case, is used as a means to create distance from the processes of 'working through' undertaken by the second generation. It is meant to show that the members of the third generation have achieved a form of detachment from the past that allows them to investigate it with a critical eye. The sense of distance intensifies in time. Israeli philosopher Adi Ophir refers to this as follows: 'Without the blood-transfusion bond to sensations of death and cessation, which silently flow with mother's milk, and with no inner melancholy of hidden anxiety to dampen the torrent of youth, how should the historic memory continue to feed the Holocaust trauma for many a days, dozens, perhaps hundreds?'[38] Distance was not a relevant issue for members of the second generation, who were too intimately connected to the trauma, and did not have the chance to disconnect themselves from the past. This generation is seen by Tali Tamir to have lived in 'the shade of silence and vacuum', and in a world 'full of black holes and taboos', being burdened by anxiety and absorbed by death.[39] This does not seem to characterize the third generation represented in Ronen's play. What is characteristic of their approach is the rejection of what Yael Feldman defines as 'the collective model of representation that they inherited from their parents and cultural mentors'. Younger generations of artists, she argues, look for a 'close subjective encounter' with the past.[40] Ronen, considered an enfant terrible of the Israeli stage, creates this 'encounter' using laughter to draw attention to the ritualized ways in which the Holocaust is being discussed and continues to affect younger generations. The source of the humour proposed by *Third Generation* is, according to Beckerman, 'the stale ways in which we talk about the past'.[41]

Several examples shed light upon this approach, which seems valid in the case of all three national groups. One scene, described by Beckerman as 'one of the most uncomfortable and funny', mocks the dominant place that the Holocaust continues to maintain for younger Israeli generations. Several Israeli actors impersonate teenagers who are pleading for money to fund a programme that offers tours of the Nazi concentration and death camps in Europe. However, the teenagers do not show the seriousness and reverence of their parents when visiting such sites, as, Beckerman suggests, 'they are flip and unthinking about the history, talking about how Auschwitz was much cooler than Majdanek'. One of the female teenagers strums a guitar, while the others sing a jingle titled 'Don't Stop Sending Us to Auschwitz'. Beckerman further suggests that the 'self-indulgence of their inherited victimhood is painfully obvious in their breaking voices'.[42]

It is through ritualized visits to the European sites of Jewish victimization that the sense of being perpetual victims is reinforced and becomes an identity-marker for Israeli teenagers of the third generation. Feldman's writings and, at an empirical level, Yoav Shamir's documentary film *Defamation* confirm this narrative by showing how deeply the possibility of being victims is rooted in the teenagers' education. The image of the victim projects itself in many aspects of the Israeli current understanding of the Israeli–Palestinian relationship. Israeli historian Moshe Zimmermann points out that 'the treatment of the Shoah in the context of the Arab–Israeli or the Palestinian–Israeli conflict underlines an important element of memory: being a victim'.[43] He goes on to argue that 'Jews and Israel naturally deduct their eternal victimhood from the Jewish fate during the Shoah. The Palestinians, on the other hand, not only try to form a correlating victimhood for their collective, but also refer to the history of the Shoah in this process by specifically portraying themselves as victims of the victims.'[44]

The Palestinian perceived sense of victimization is subtly made apparent in *Third Generation* when a young Palestinian actor tells the story of his family's displacement in 1948. This scene is presented to us, however, not in a serious manner that asks the audience to empathize, but rather in a playful way, as one Palestinian actor uses a puppet to represent his grandfather, thus robbing him of a real voice. In glaring contrast, Maayan's play shows the Palestinian actor Haled Abu Ali assuming the underdog roles more clearly, such as that of the servant to an Israeli young woman, and that of a victim and martyr, appearing in the closing part of the play in Zelma's arms in a sacrificial stance that is reminiscent of Michelangelo's sculpture *Pieta*.

Ronen's idea of 'completing a triangle of historical suffering by bringing together the three groups'[45] was received with some criticism from older members of the German-Jewish community, who feared that the play morally equates the Palestinian suffering with the Jewish one. In response, Ronen argued that 'it was just that type of debilitating fear of comparison – of somehow undermining the Holocaust's sacred uniqueness – that I was trying to move beyond'.[46] Indeed, the interdiction of comparison surfaces in an ironic manner in the play, when an actor's monologue contains as a refrain the expression 'don't compare'. This seems to point to the heightened awareness these members have of what is legitimate or not in their discourse about the past. A sense of having stepped over the line of what is appropriate and over the imposed limits on the public discourse about the Holocaust is made apparent when the Israeli performers express their worries about the negative criticism that their play might trigger. Reflecting upon the scene of the Israeli teenagers bidding to raise funds to visit Auschwitz, Ayelet laments: 'We shouldn't have done that teenager scene. They are going to use it against us. They'll say we're self-hating traitors.'[47] It is unclear whether opposition is expected to come from the Israeli government, Israeli public opinion or rather from the established German-Jewish community. What is undoubtedly certain is a sense of rebellion against some views which, for this generation of Israelis, no longer hold true. The young members of the *Third Generation* play construct a sense of being different by departing from a consensus or pre-established set of rules about how to relate to the Holocaust. Instead, they rely on laughter and humour as a way of drawing a line between themselves and the others. However, aside from this rebellion from the dominant discourse, the 'new language' that Ronen and her cast seek does not appear to have been found. In fact, the entire attempt at a third-generation self-definition disintegrates in the final minutes of the performance, when, explains Beckerman,

> The cast members, who listen to each other so patiently throughout, begin brawling wildly. Having arrived at the limit of laughter, they don't come up with anything else to say. Instead, Ayelet, frustrated that the exercise has all been for naught, that the Israelis still look like aggressors and the Palestinians like victims, and that the Germans are adequately repentant, screams at the audience, using words that are still sure to silence any conversation: 'You are all Nazis!'[48]

Conclusion

With this rather disappointing ending, Ronen seems to admit that the dialogue among these groups cannot be fully realized, and that, inevitably, their identities as individuals cannot escape the dominant memory narratives of their nations. Nevertheless, there is a common agreement upon the notion that there are many things one can share. Amit Epstein and Irina Szodruch, the play's dramaturges, see it as the beginning of a 'constant discussion, a constant excavation of the past'. In this discussion, however, all need to agree that 'some things can't be made right again'. The Holocaust, they argue, 'can't be made right again. But we can keep a dialogue going and see the human in those we call enemies; we can accept the suffering of others and understand that we don't lose anything through their suffering.'[49] .

If Ronen's goal was to use laugher as a way to criticize predictable and overused narratives, then the audience's full participation in the laugher proves that this has been well achieved. Still, one cannot refrain from asking what the real alternatives that Ronen is proposing are. Indeed, a 'new language' or discourse should admittedly enable its users to draw a new direction and way of approaching the past. Whether the play has achieved its second goal, as Beckerman argues, 'of pushing us beyond the clichés'[50] is doubtful. The comparison with *Arbeit macht frei* reveals that while the 'new language' may not be yet discovered, 'the new road' opened by this performance has definitely been walked. Indeed, the Israeli members of *Third Generation* seem more likely to be looking for a certain sense of balance, as it is explained by Chaitin, 'between the need to connect to the trauma and the fear of being overwhelmed by it, and the need to keep the significance of the Holocaust alive, without creating a new generation of victims'.[51]

NOTES

1. Christine Lötsch 'Israel-German Theatre: The Holocaust, Nazi and Palestinian "Third Generation" ', 30 April 2009, http://www.cafebabel.co.uk/article/30030/third-generation-germany-theatre-auschwitz.html.
2. For example, the anthology edited by G. Rosenthal, *The Holocaust in Three Generations: Families of Victims and Perpetrators of the Nazi Regime* (London: Cassell, 1998); see also D. Bar-On, *Fear and Hope: Three Generations of the Holocaust* (Cambridge, MA: Harvard University Press, 1995) pp 1-15 and L. Hirsch and J. Chaitin, "The Shoah runs through our veins": The Relevance of the Holocaust for Jewish-Israeli Young Adults', *Idea*, 14 (1 May 2010).
3. See B.N. Schiff, *Refugees unto the Third Generation: UN Aid to Palestinians* (Syracuse: Syracuse University Press, 1995).
4. E. Fogelman, 'Psychological Dynamics in the Lives of Third-Generation Holocaust Survivors', in *Hidden Child*, 16 (2008), pp.10–12, http://www.drevafogelman.com/_psychological_dynamics_in_the_lives_of_third_generation_holocaust_survivors_94110.htm.
5. Ibid.
6. D. Bar-On, *Fear and Hope: Three Generations of the Holocaust* (Cambridge, MA: Harvard University Press, 1995), pp.1–15.
7. L. Hirsch and J. Chaitin, ' "The Shoah runs through our veins": The Relevance of the Holocaust for Jewish-Israeli Young Adults', *Idea*, 14, 1 (May 2010), n.p., http://www.ideajournal.com/articles.php?id=49.
8. See Fogelman, 'Psychological Dynamics'.
9. Articles dealing with these issues include J. Feldman, 'Marking the Boundaries of the Enclave: Defining the Israeli Collective through the Poland "Experience" ', *Israel Studies*, 7, 2 (Summer

2002), pp.84–114; L. Alon, J. Chaitin, T. Gross and D. Bar-On, 'Jewish Israeli Teenagers, National Identity, and the Lessons of the Holocaust', *Holocaust and Genocide Studies* 18, 2 (Fall 2002), pp.188–204.

10. See J. Feldman's study *Above the Death Pits, Beneath the Flag: Youth Voyages to Poland and the Performance of Israeli National Identity* (New York and Oxford: Berghahn Books, 2008).
11. See H. Feinstein, 'Defamation', 6 February 2009, http://www.screendaily.com/defamation/4043007.article.
12. Statement by teenagers in Y. Shamir's film *Defamation* (in Hebrew, *Hashmatsa*), 2009.
13. Ibid.
14. Shamir, in *Defamation*.
15. Hirsch and Chaitin, ' "Shoah runs through our veins" '.
16. Argument developed by I. Zertal in *Israel's Holocaust and the Politics of Nationhood* (Cambridge: Cambridge University Press, 2005).
17. D. Gutwein, 'The Privatization of the Holocaust: Memory, Historiography, and Politics', *Israel Studies*, 14, 1 (Spring 2009), p.36.
18. Y. Elkana 'The Need to Forget', *Ha-Aretz*, 2 March 1988.
19. Term employed by Ronen; C. Lotsch, 'German-Israeli Theatre: The Holocaust, Nazi and Palestinian Third Generation', http://www.cafebabel.co.uk/article/30030/third-generation-germany-theatre-auschwitz.html; and G. Beckerman, 'An Israeli, a German and a Palestinian Walk into a Theatre', *Forward*, 1 May 2009, http://forward.com/articles/105024/an-israeli-a-german-and-a-palestinian-walk-into-a/.
20. G. Beckerman, 'An Israeli, a German and a Palestinian Walk into a Theatre', *Forward*, 1 May 2009, n.p., http://galbeckerman.com/crit3/.
21. Ibid.
22. Ibid.
23. Ibid.
24. J. Lacan, *Ecrits: The First Complete Edition in English*, translated by Bruce Fink in collaboration with H. Fink and R. Grigg (New York: W.W. Norton, 2006).
25. E. Fischer-Lichte, 'New Concepts of Spectatorship: Toward a Postmodern Theory of Theatricality', *Semiotica*, 101, 1–2 (1994), pp.113–23.
26. Ibid.
27. H. Pearson-Roms, *Identifying (with) Performance: Representations and Constructions of Cultural Identity in Contemporary Theatre Practice – Three Case Studies*, (unpublished PhD thesis, Aberystwyth University, Aberystwyth, 2001), p.61.
28. Ibid., p.64.
29. E. Diamond, *Performance and Cultural Politics* (London and New York: Routledge, 1996), pp.1–12.
30. E. Barba, *The Floating Land* (Holstebro: Odin, 1979), p.145.
31. F. Rokem, 'On the Fantastic in Holocaust Performances', in Claude Schumacher (ed.), *Staging the Holocaust: The Shoah in Drama and Performance* (Cambridge: Cambridge University Press, 1998), p.51.
32. See Pearson-Roms, *Identifying (with) Performance*, p.312.
33. Statement by Acco Theatre Center 1994, quoted in ibid., p.315.
34. D. Mayaan, cited in Pearson-Roms, *Identifying (with) Performance*, p.316.
35. See F. Rokem, *Performing History: Theatrical Representations of the Past in Contemporary Theatre* (Iowa, IA: Iowa University Press, 2000).
36. R. Schechner, 'Believed-In Theatre', *Performance Research*, 2, 2 (1997), pp.76–91.
37. Ibid., p.80.
38. A. Ophir, 'Working for the Present: Essays on Contemporary Israeli Culture', in *On the Renewal of God: An Anti-Theological Tractate* (Am Oved: Tel Aviv, 2001), p.12.
39. T. Tamir, 'The Shadow of Evil: To the Third and Fourth Generation', in the art catalogue *Wonderyears* (Berlin: NGBK, 2003), p.78.
40. Y. Feldman, quoted by Y. Loshitzky, in B. Zelizer (ed.), *Visual Culture and the Holocaust* (New Brunswick, NJ: Rutgers University Press, 2001), p.156.
41. Beckerman, 'An Israeli, a German and a Palestinian'.
42. Ibid.

43. M. Zimmermann, 'The Collective Memory of the Victimhood', in *Wonderyears*, p.36.
44. Ibid.
45. Beckerman, 'An Israeli, a German and a Palestinian'.
46. Ibid.
47. Ibid.
48. Ibid.
49. C. Lotsch, 'German-Israeli Theatre: The Holocaust, Nazi and Palestinian Third Generation', 30 April 2009
50. Beckerman, 'An Israeli, a German and a Palestinian'.
51. Hirsch and Chaitin, ' "Shoah runs through our veins" '.

Legitimate Sadness?
Life at the Edge of the Shadows

LEA WOHL-VON HASELBERG

Translated From The German By Esther Jilovsky

I'm not Jewish but I have Jewish grandparents, who fled from Poland toward the east in 1939. They survived. Other family members were murdered. If the third generation dwells in the shadows of Holocaust memory, then I stand at the edge of these shadows. I don't know my father's parents personally, only as small, black-and-white square photographs that I've seen amongst my father's things, who then murmurs something like 'my parents' or 'my father'. But it's not about these grandparents, small, two-dimensional, black and white, who died before I was born, that I wish to write. Instead I want to write about what life at the edge of these shadows is like. My life at the edge of the shadows is shaped by three main things in addition to everything else which shapes the life of a young, female, European doctoral student and as a woman, scholar and mother at the beginning of this millennium.

Firstly there's the uncertainty of belonging, which always leads me to question how legitimate my feelings about this family history actually are. To be – Halachically – Jewish is to be the child of a Jewish mother or to have converted. But that doesn't cover me. And I've so often heard, thought or read this between the lines that I no longer challenge the authority of this position. That the Nazis had another definition of who is Jewish and the consequences that would have had for me was something I must have started to imagine at some point during my schooldays. But even today I often realize that the understanding of who is Jewish and what it means to be Jewish varies considerably in different social circles in Germany. Non-Jewish Germans frequently perceive me as Jewish, or at least *more* Jewish than most Germans. If only there were such a thing as 'Jewisher'!

But something like this can hardly be explained in the atmosphere of paralysing inhibition in the handling of Jewish issues in Germany. Ultimately this situation with the definitions also influences how I am affected by the persecution history of my Jewish family. I ask myself, to what extent can and may I claim their experience of persecution as my family story - particularly when I find myself in the company of Jews whom

I regard as 'really' or 'actually' affected. The affectedness seems probably – and I know this line of thought is rather simple – more strongly linked to being affected as a Jew than to the actual events. That leads to me being cut off from my own family history. How can I explain this difficult access to my family history to non-Jews, and particularly to Germans, without betraying my grandparents or cowardly avoiding taking a position?

The second thing which shapes my life on the edge of the shadows, and which I probably share with many members of the third generation, is that I hardly know anything. The map of my family memory is almost completely blank. When I seem to know stories, fragments or events, I am highly unsure. When I want to tell them in some kind of context, it feels as if I'm trying to speak about events from a dream, which dissolve and evaporate at translation into words. Then I'm no longer sure where I know it from, whether it was told to me, by whom, or whether I've dreamt it up myself. Perhaps that's because I can remember hardly any concrete moments in my childhood when my family history was discussed. I know anecdotes from my father's childhood, funny short stories about both chow-chows Prinzi and Lumpi or childlike pranks in a holiday home for Jewish children. But my grandparents generally appear only on the edge.

I cannot remember learning about the events of the Shoah as a child, yet somehow I knew about it. I know that I was affected differently from the other children when we read *Damals war es Friedrich*, a novel by Hans Peter Richter about a Jewish boy during the Third Reich (the title of the English translation is *Friedrich*), in sixth grade. The exclusion of Jewish Friedrich made me sad but the class's handling of the book made me increasingly angry. And a similar thing happened when we learnt about Nazi persecution of the Jews for the first time in history class in middle school. But none of that was spoken about in our family. Nothing was mentioned about what happened, and nothing about what it means for us today. It was and is a strange situation: the Holocaust was neither concealed nor openly talked about. It is there but may only be touched carefully, which more often than not it is not. I can't remember my father ever saying that the history of his parents or family made him sad or even feel touched in any way. That is of course self-evident. But I've never heard him say that the Shoah has robbed him of something. That it robbed him, as someone born in the aftermath, of something: to grow up with this absent, dispersed family, with sad and overwhelmed parents. But what do I know? Maybe it wasn't like this, and I only mean that they were sad people. Or maybe I can only remember when we were told about this at home. And so once again I'm made aware of the uncertainty of memory. The power of our memory is not just in what it remembers, but also what it forgets.

In the last few years I've had a few conversations with my father's older sister in Israel. Born a few years before him, as a child survivor she has been rather differently affected. She speaks a lot about her childhood, perhaps not with the clarity of memory, as the events took place long ago and are shaped by their frequent retelling as stories. But it surprises me that she speaks and is obviously pleased that I listen, that I want to know. In this way I've discovered more, most notably about what happened to my grandmother, who was on the run with her baby, my aunt. However, these things that I've learnt tell me nothing about the meaning which the persecution of his parents, their life afterwards shaped by loss and otherness, and the murder of distant relatives have for my father. He who I lived with, who was so often mysterious, complicated and distant to me – maybe I could have understood him better. There also remains the question of where I know this from, which always separated me from my non-Jewish friends and has solidified in my memory to a diffuse, dark feeling. I can't reconstruct it. My reaction to being confronted by the Holocaust at school or in conversations with friends was polarized: withdrawn and silent or irascible and full of outrage at the injustice that others could encounter less pain with this history than me.

These days I am occupied academically with the topic and so am on more solid ground. The mode of discussion is set, the objective tone leaves little room for individual affectedness and it does not mean denial to be silent about it. It doesn't occur to anyone to ask about my personal position in this darkness which hides behind the word 'Holocaust', nor about my family history. Although I do, of course, sense the assumptions which certainly occur, often unconsciously because of various clues like my name, my research topics and perhaps also my appearance. They hide between the lines when I'm regarded as Jewish in a professional context, even by Jewish academics. This assumption is expressed by surprise that I don't speak Hebrew, but otherwise they generally remained subtle and unvoiced. The unvoiced assumptions which surround me and my identity simultaneously please me a bit and shame me. But on the whole, the distant, professional conduct of the academy gives me space, and means I don't need to explain myself.

The third thing which I experience defining my place on the edge of these shadows and as a member of the third generation is myself moving in a kind of meta-discourse. The second generation, a generation of traumatized children who inherited the traumatic experience of their parents, who were hurt rather than protected by the silence of their parents, aren't just familiar to me from the relevant academic literature. They laugh or cry to me from feature pages or the radio, or greet me as beloved topos in film and literature. How many novels by Jewish writers of the second generation revolve around the difficult relationship to even more difficult parents? That means I know the subject and the more I'm familiar with it, the less trustful I become of my own perception of it. Am I projecting onto my father what I expect? Am I laying him on the couch and ascribing him a second-generation syndrome? Am I merely seeing what I expect to see? Is that not all too simple: to see our complicated father–daughter relationship against the background of the difficult generational relationship, rather than to acknowledge that it's individually difficult because he's himself and I am myself and that, perhaps, will always be the case? Am I interpreting my older sister's nightmares, in which she desperately tries to rescue us all and always has to decide in the end and who she rescues and sometimes fails to rescue, falsely against the background of our grandparents' experience of persecution? Is the dislike I have of complaining people because I find that it's not really that bad for them and they should be more content – no, more humble – actually a consequence of the fact that I know how much more I have than my family of seventy years ago?

The societal and academic discourse and my knowledge about it protrude here between me and my feelings and obstruct my emotional access to the history of my family and the Holocaust. When my husband asks me something – and he can ask me because I do know my way around the history of the Holocaust – then I find myself answering in an objective tone, presenting facts and lecturing on their meaning. Only sometimes, in small moments which catch me unawares, do I feel the desperate sadness which I sensed as a 16-year-old when visiting Auschwitz-Birkenau.

These three aspects constantly intertwine, determine and strengthen each other and are sometimes nearly impossible to separate. My mistrust of my feelings awakened by the meta-discursive level amalgamates with the uncertainty of how legitimate it really is that I feel affected by the Holocaust experience of my grandparents. In such moments I not only doubt that I am moved and don't only believe that I must be affected, but instead I'm not sure myself whether my sadness is allowed to show, in light of the invisible sadness of my father. It is less about if I have the right to be sad or not, than whether and how I may express my affectedness. A visible affectedness means making a claim and I don't know in which situations and to whom this would be legitimate. It would be a claim which I don't dare to make. Once again I'm caught between a rock and a hard place. My outrage about the lack of affectedness that non-Jewish Germans show about the past stands opposite another extreme when I'm ashamed of my own affectedness in the presence of the second generation. It feels like an illegitimate over-identification, a misappropriated reliving of a foreign experience.

So that is that. Or perhaps I can say: so that was that. Because in the meantime my daughter Toscha was born. A still very small fourth generation, who forces me to grapple with my entanglement and my distanced, highly reserved academic position – if I don't want to pass a similar ghost onto her, invisible but ever-present.

A Politics of the Third Generation: Two Siblings Converse

BEN SILVERSTEIN AND JORDANA SILVERSTEIN

Introduction

For many members of the third generation, the (post)memory of the Holocaust – those memories of our grandparents' experiences that we carry – stands as an ethical call. For Marianne Hirsch this comprises 'an ethical relation to the oppressed or persecuted: as I can "remember" my [grand]parents' memories, I can also "remember" the suffering of others'.[1] Locating the universal in the particular, and exploring the tensions between these perspectives, seems to us to be critical to the development of a broader politics of being third generation descendants of survivors.

We wanted to discuss these issues, to explore the conflicts, politics and identities to which we find ourselves led as members of the third generation. In the conversation that follows, we raise questions about belonging, solidarity and memory as we relate to the Holocaust and the many shadows it casts. We hope that in doing so we point to the open-endedness of the conversations produced by being of this third generation, the Jewish grandchildren of survivors of the Holocaust.

Belonging after the Holocaust

Jordana Silverstein: A question I keep coming back to, when I think about my relationship to my Holocaust-surviving grandparents and to the lives (I imagine) they lived, is to ponder how they felt they fitted-in where they lived. And then I find myself pondering how those feelings have been passed on to us. So, a good place for us to jump into this conversation – a conversation that I think we, like many other members of the third generation, have been having for a long time – might be for me to ask: where do you feel you belong? Is being an exile part of the Jewish condition?

Ben Silverstein: Let's begin with the second question you've posed. In some ways, I think an exilic sensibility is central to the way we are Jewish. But

Jewish exile is, I think, more a sense of a story we tell of ourselves than a migratory state. Because, really, our lives are not defined by being out of place. We become in place. We are transformed by movement, we change to adapt, and we change in unexpected ways. So, even if we are exiles, we can never 'go back' and, I suspect, we wouldn't want to.

I'm not interested in exile inasmuch as it leads us to a story of origin, of looking for a Jewish essence that we can recall as Jewishness changes into what we are today; an archetype against which we can only be measured and found lacking. A people has no invariable essence. What interests me, instead, are stories of production. How did we come to be the way we are? In looking to the past we look not for the real we have lost, but to approach a tradition with an unpredictably dynamic history.

To be in exile is to be out of place, and as migrants or the children of migrants I don't think that is what we are. We have been made by the experience of living in Melbourne, of living as Jews in Melbourne. But this is accompanied by a continued awareness – one that comes from being, in some sense, marginal, but also from being definitively non-Indigenous to the land we live on – that I am not from here.

However secure we may be here where we write, we reproduce that exilic sensibility. But the question was also *where* do you feel you belong? It is curious that belonging is so often tied to place, implying a sense that to be exiled – to be cast out of a place – is to belong no longer. Isn't one of the lessons of Jewish diasporism that one can belong in a way not circumscribed by space? And you ask where I *feel* I belong, suggesting an interest in belonging as sensation, rather than as an objective state. I want to ask you about the affective elements of this Jewish condition. How does this feeling manifest?

JS: It interests me that you bring up this question of place: there's nothing in the question I asked that inherently (only) refers to place. I think I unconsciously formulated it that way, hoping to ask a question about Poland/Europe/Melbourne, but also about a relationship to belonging to being Jewish, or belonging to being a descendant of Holocaust survivors, or belonging to this idea of the third generation.

I think the question of belonging is one which is necessarily raised by the Holocaust, and by the effects of the Holocaust for those who went through it: displacement, being made into a refugee, becoming a citizen again in another place. The emotions which would accompany being produced as non-citizen and then as citizen are, for those of us who have not undergone this experience, impossible to imagine.[2] So in that way – materially, discursively, emotionally – there is no sense in which I am an exile. It's not entirely precise to equate the loss of citizenship with being an exile, but I think the parallels are there.

But then there is the question of exile from what? If it's from a 'common community' of people, then in some ways I would say yes.[3] I'm pondering here a couple of things. Firstly, the question (again) of citizenship, as expressed through access to a passport. We both, through Mum, have access to a Polish passport. Your response – if I remember correctly – to the idea of acquiring a Polish passport is refusal. In that way, you express, I think, some experience of being expelled, pushed out, not wanted. My response to the idea is to embrace it. If they want to expel my family they can, but I'm going to try to exploit them now (in order to gain the rights across Europe that an EU passport offers): I'm going to try to, in some way, reverse the expulsion (while also recognizing that the expulsion can't be reversed, and that for me to carry a Polish passport now is merely simulacra). A passport, of course, does not ensure any sense of a common community: it is one mode of legal belonging, but it does not carry with it the inevitability that one will socially belong.

And secondly, a sense that Jews do not fit in the West. In other research I have looked at the ways that memories of the Holocaust can mobilize feelings of exclusion, and I've critiqued the types of conservative politics that this often produces (for instance, the idea that Jews are facing a security threat and thus must respond with some sort of security or military action; or that if we are being excluded, we should exclude all others in return, so that we cannot be excluded).[4] But I think that memories of being excluded, of our ancestors being exiled, has the possibility of producing different feelings, and different responses. It's absolutely true to say, for instance, that the unstable version of Western modernity in which we dwell in this settler colony we call home, is – as Aileen Moreton-Robinson has written – based around the disavowal of Indigeneity (but also, I would add, the exclusion of all racialized Others. This occurs in very different ways – I don't want to suggest equating the ways in which this is done, or the ideologies behind it – but it sits alongside).[5] This is true, too, of the Holocaust: it was based on exclusion and it makes sense that some of the effects of that exclusion would reverberate through the generations. Another response then, as opposed to bunkering down and excluding others, is to look for ways of being that reject exclusion. So, in short: no, I don't think I'm an exile, but I think one of the inherited memories of the Holocaust is of being exiled, of a radical un-belonging produced by this system of Western nation states, and so I think that this notion of exile informs my familial and collective memories of the Holocaust, in a politically productive way. That is, it produces a distrust of the forms of exclusion and inclusion offered (to anyone) by the nation state.

BS: I think that sense of distrust and scepticism is both useful and productive, and certainly an effect of the inherited or collective memories to which you refer. Edward Said once suggested that the exile 'knows that in a secular and contingent world, homes are always provisional. Borders and barriers, which enclose us within the safety of familiar territory, can also become prisons, and are often defended beyond reason or necessity. Exiles cross borders, break barriers of thought and experience.'[6] Your characterization of the ways exile can frame sensibility suggests something similar.

I wonder, though, about the 'sense that Jews do not fit in the West' that you mention above. You've written of something similar elsewhere, suggesting it is characteristic of the 'liminal position which Jews occupy, as they are simultaneously fundamental to, separate from, and persecuted within, western modernity'.[7] I think the ambivalence of this position is concretized in the symbolic memory of the Holocaust and the ways it is used to frame contemporary Ashkenazi Jewish experience. In many ways, as you point out, working through the traumas of the Holocaust has not done away with a sense of exclusion, even as we 'dwell' in substantial social comfort, sharing many of the normative social prejudices in our new homelands, materially settling within those dominant communities with our Australian citizenship that you mentioned above. And still the spectre of the Holocaust looms as a source of this emphasis on exclusion.

That we are citizens is itself a marker of the change that has taken place over the past seventy years. The 'Jew' is no longer 'alien' to the British or settler colonial world.[8] We are, now, becoming no longer a race apart. And we are, here, becoming included, an inclusion that doesn't erase our Jewishness.

Elsewhere, the 'Jewish state' is placed firmly within the West, materially and ideologically if not geographically. The advertisements controversially placed by a reactionary anti-Islam organization in various cities across the USA in 2012 (see Figure 12) firmly identified the new Jewish archetype as 'the civilized man', that definitive symbol of modernity, deserving of support in his fight against the 'savage' Muslim.[9] I say Jewish, here, rather than Israeli, as the 'war' they refer to is clearly one of religion: the result of a mythically united Judeo-Christian civilization besieged by an even more mythically savage Islam, embodied by Palestinians regardless of their actual religion. This was clearly pushing the point to an extreme but, in so doing, it laid bare an important transition that took place in the second half of the twentieth century. With the advent of a specifically Jewish colonialism in the Middle East, and alongside the post-Holocaust distaste for open demonstrations of antisemitism in the West, to make the argument that 'Jews do not fit in the west' seems dissembling. A preoccupation with Jewish victimhood can occlude the occupation and suffering of others, particularly those who suffer at the hands of 'the State of the Jewish people'.

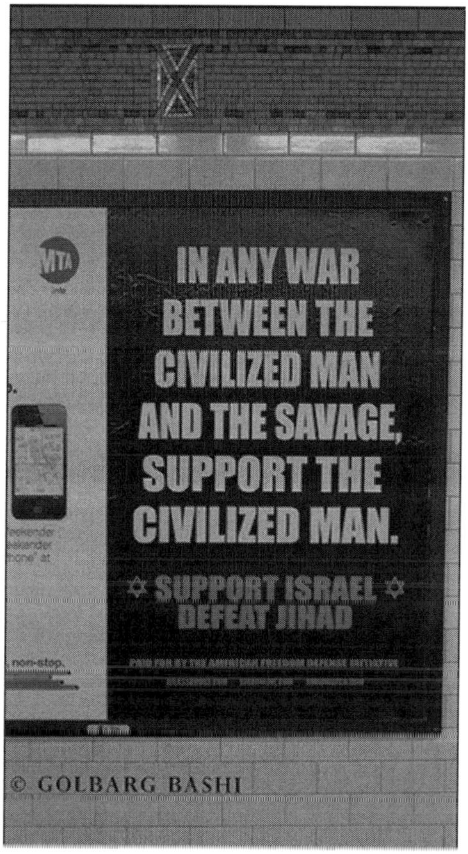

12. American Freedom Defense Initiative advertisement, as seen in one subway station in New York, 2012. Copyright/permission granted by Golbarg Bashi, New York, 26 September 2012, via flickr: https://www.flickr.com/photos/golbargbashi/8028520437.

How can we seriously address Jewish marginalization within the 'West' in a historically informed manner? How, in other words, can we take Jewish marginalization not as ontologically prior (the Jews are always already excluded), but as historically specific (the Jews are included or excluded in certain times and places, changing in relation to the material and ideological needs of the social formation manifesting in Jewish and non-Jewish action)? Of course, Jews have been victims. But this can't be the whole story, for all Jews, everywhere. Even if a state of marginalization might seem fundamental to Jewishness, how can we avoid falling into the trap of naturalizing this as the Jewish condition?

JS: You make a really important point here. It's always necessary not to write of the category of Jews as though we are only European or Western. The effacing of Middle Eastern, North African and Iberian Peninsula Jews – of Mizrahim and Sephardim – is a real problem in Jewish communities in the West that is exacerbated when one writes about the Holocaust. It becomes easy to think only of the experiences of European Jews (and to forget the Holocaust experiences of Mizrahi and Sephardi Jews), and to write clumsily as though one can extrapolate from these experiences to indicate something about Jews generally (or even to infer that the experiences of European Jews are, or have been, homogenous). And Jews have been included in different ways throughout the world, across time and place. So, as you say, Jewish marginalization is historically produced, and historically specific. We need to avoid naturalizing it.

I wonder if I say that Jews do not fit into the West because I don't want the opposite to be true. I want to disavow those aspects of Jewishness that take from the worst of what the West has to offer. I reject the idea that the way to manage marginalization, and its attendant anxieties, is to exclude others, discursively or materially. And while the West is not only its exclusions and its marginalizations – it's too reductive and simplistic (as well as ahistoric) to say the West is completely bad – I'd rather align myself with those who are rejected. This is, for me, an ethical imperative that comes from being a member of the third generation: that I align myself with those pushed out. But it only becomes possible to say that, perhaps, from a position of some sort of inclusion.

I think here of the words of Irena Klepfisz – who was born in the Warsaw Ghetto, survived in hiding, and moved to the US in 1949 with her mother – who writes: 'Only by placing the Holocaust in a larger framework, by insisting on moving toward a Jewish future that is informed, but not defined, by the Holocaust, can we develop a productive way of relating to each other and the rest of the world. Such an approach guarantees memory, without sacrificing the present or future.'[10]

What she writes here seems to echo the point you just made: we need to hold the Holocaust in our memories, but not be defined by it. We need to locate the Holocaust within a history, and try to understand the possibilities for an ethical futurity opened up by that past. In this way, marginalization can offer us the possibility of working with others, of standing alongside those who are excluded, and taking advantage of our own inclusions to create new spaces of belonging.

BS: Your argument on the unfortunate centrality of European Jewish experiences marks a particular problem, one that effaces Mizrahim and Sephardim, but which also, and I think primarily, constitutes Islam as fundamentally other to European-dominated modernity.[11] It's registered in the term 'Judeo-Christian', almost unheard of prior to the Holocaust but now commonplace. The notion of Judeo-Christian values, or a Judeo-Christian morality or tradition, is a false unity; there is no such thing. But, as a performative, it has an important function in the survival of racism after the Holocaust. Today, it primarily represents the recruitment of Judaism (and sometimes Jewishness) to a redefined West that rejects Islam.

Now, there is obviously a long history of European Islamophobia, just as there is a long history of European antisemitism. Each rejection constituted, in different ways, modern Europe as Christendom. But the novel inclusion of Judaism into project Europe reminds us of the important difference between internalized and externalized others, of the importance of tracking the distinct ways groups are constituted through particular strategies of racialization, as they have been mobilized over the past two centuries.

The imaginary Jewishness we are speaking of, then, is categorically European. And it is thus rendered recruitable to the exclusion of others, with all we know that this brings. The problem of anti-Islamic bigotry in the Jewish community is symptomatic, here, of a post-Holocaust accumulation of whiteness. In a way we might attribute your desire not to be included to the persistence of Holocaust postmemory. In seeing yourself in that particular relation to practices of exclusion you cannot recognize yourself in the reactionary communal call to position ourselves as perpetrators of this kind of racism; this manifests as a vehement rejection of amenability to this agenda. This is, if you'll allow me to ventriloquize, a symbolic desire that ought not to be taken literally. No one seriously wants to be excluded, rejected, rendered stateless in a condition of terminal loss. It is rather an attempt to live and express a third generation subjectivity and to push political voluntarism as far as possible in order to realign solidarities.

Solidarity

JS: Rabbi Brant Rosen, in a 2012 interview, said: 'I have personally come to the very painful realization that Jewish nation-statism comes at a very real cost to our Jewish soul – compromising sacred values that teach us that all human beings are created in the image of God, that one law must be extended to all who live on the land, that we must love our neighbors as ourselves.'[12]

I wonder how you position yourself in relation to this question. You once wrote that you learned from our Holocaust survivor grandparents,

Zosia (Sophie) and Vovek (Wolf) Stawski, 'the force of an unconditional solidarity with the persecuted and exterminated' and that through them you had 'been made to consider the complexity and contingency of making solidarities real while living and working on stolen land' in Australia.[13]

Could you could expand on this, in relation to the ways that postmemories of the Holocaust inflect your relationship to both the settler colony where we live, and where our family seems to be planting some solid roots – Australia – and that other settler colony that I think we are both in a constant process of decolonizing our relations with – Israel.

BS: That dedication I wrote was my attempt to describe a meaningful Jewish identity produced in, and in dialogue with, post-Holocaust Melbourne. I was playing with and misquoting Isaac Deutscher's very well-known declaration on Jewishness in the mid-1960s.[14] Reading him, several years ago, I was struck by his deployment of solidarity as a practice that was not voluntaristic, but rather based on feeling the pulse of a history. For Deutscher, I think, to be Jewish represented an affective identification with the historical experience of persecution. He expressed disappointment in the tendency of western Jewish intellectuals towards an extraordinary conformism: political, ideological and social. To this list we might add parochial. His kind of solidarity is based not on a racial or ethnic tie across the 'Jewish community', but on something simultaneously more substantial and more abstract. It involves asking 'Who are *we*?' as Sarah Schulman does so provocatively and usefully in her 2012 book, *Israel/Palestine and the Queer International*.[15]

I think it is helpful to explore this 'pulse of Jewish history' in more detail. Deutscher's is something of a universalist claim, or at least one that rejects the particularity of Jewish experience. It is based in that ambivalent embrace of exclusion, marginality, and exile that is a part of diasporic experience. But it also insists on denaturalizing this experience, on historicizing it, situating exclusion as a constitutive process, not as an eternal state.

The sad privilege that I suggested was an element of Jewishness was, then, born of this process. James Baldwin made a similar argument, based on an African-American past of suffering. For him, such a past, with its 'endless struggle to achieve and reveal and confirm a human identity, human authority ... contains, for all its horror, something beautiful'. Suffering was not to be sought out, but nevertheless a 'people who cannot suffer can never discover who they are'. Something is gained through the struggle: an injunction 'to look beyond appearances, to take nothing for granted, to hear the meaning behind the words'.[16]

Here I'm thinking, in part, of my reaction to reading the notation on the travel documents (see Figures 13 and 14) that allowed our grandparents to travel to Australia, recording their nationality as 'Stateless (formerly Polish)'.[17] These few words obscure, but hint at, a process and experience of great brutality and trauma. Something had been stolen from them. I don't know that they were ever, really, Polish. Maybe they were Polish Jews; maybe Tshenstokhover or Sosnovitzer Yidn. But these words tell us that something had nonetheless been taken away. They record a declaration, made in 1939, that our grandparents will not have been Polish.

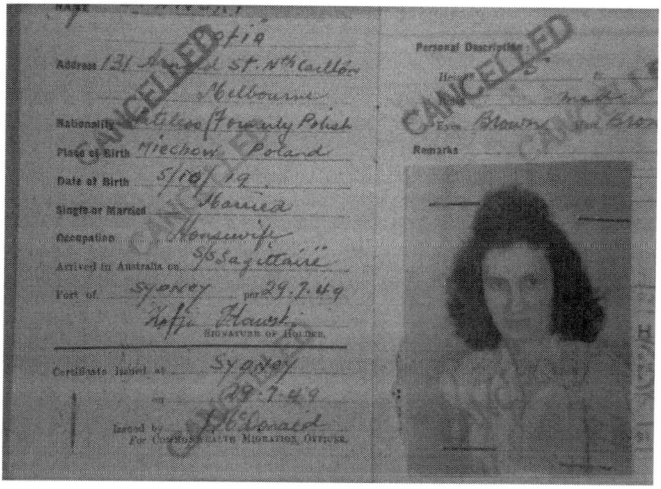

13. Sofia Stawski's travel documents, 1949. National Archives of Australia [NAA]: B78, 1957/STAWSKI S. From the Collection of the NAA.

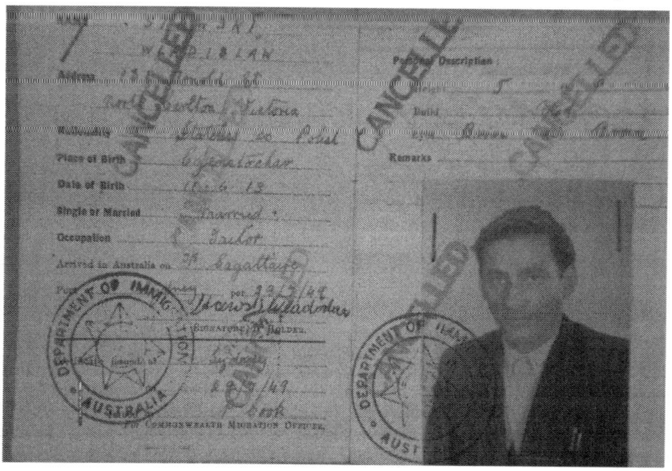

14. Wladislaw Stawski's travel documents, 1949. NAA: B78, 1957/STAWSKI W. From the Collection of the NAA.

JS: The photos on those travel documents evoke to me specific Holocaust experiences. I look at them and think of different experiences of survival. Vovek looks to me like someone who was incredibly charismatic, who made his way from 1939 to 1949 by charming anyone he could. Zosia looks to me steely-eyed, as though she made her way through with horror and sheer determination.

I don't really know, though. That's a problematic of survival, particularly of something like the Holocaust: it is mostly unknown. But a photo seems to give access to something that mere words cannot. A photo seems to bring relations closer. Hirsch has written about photos of the Holocaust and of families within the context of her idea of postmemory. This seems to me to provide an important schema for thinking through the production of solidarity, after the Holocaust.

Hirsch explains that 'postmemory is a powerful form of memory precisely because its connection to its object or source is mediated not through recollection but through representation, projection, and creation – often based on silence rather than speech, on the invisible rather than the visible'. She further writes that postmemory, as we commented in the introduction, is about an ethical relationship of 'remembering' one's family's experiences alongside 'the suffering of others'.[18]

Gazing at photos produces memory produces solidarity. These images which are so filled with meaning to us, because they refer to the particular histories of our family, are also just two more sets of travel documents attained by refugees. Countless other such documents were produced that year, and have been produced both before and since. To look at my grandparents' photos on these documents, to see this after-effect of the Holocaust, is, for me, to think about the ongoing creation of refugees. And to argue for a holding of them in my memory. This seems to me, following Hirsch, to be a condition of holding an ethical postmemory of the Holocaust.

BS: So remembering ethically entails a sense of substitutability, seeing the universal in the particular; the unloved in the loved. It means remembering through broadening the prism of recognition beyond those we recognize as our own. But I think it also needs to resist the tendency to universalize experience, to remember that the ways we are formed, the ways we become subjects, the ways we remember, are both related and distinct. I'm reminded of Vinay Lal's observation, made in a different context, that the 'ontology of the vanquished ... always has room for the vanquisher; the same cannot be said for the vanquisher'. Achille Mbembe identified something similar as a characteristic of Jewish thought, writing of the way post-Holocaust Jewish criticism 'has unveiled the profound connection that ties any ethical practice of freedom to a moral concern with vulnerability – especially as manifested in the figure of the stranger and, to a lesser extent, of the enemy'. Drawing on Levinas, he suggests that to be human is to be vulnerable, and in 'vulnerability lies a relation to the other', a way of being through duty and responsibility.[19]

As part of the third generation, our relationship to the Holocaust is different to that of our parents, and fundamentally different to that of our survivor grandparents. But while we haven't necessarily experienced being robbed of our citizenship, being transported or enslaved or having our families murdered, we are nonetheless the product of these histories. We are brought up in houses of mourning, we feel the loss not only of our family, but of a whole world, of a past and a future. We mourn the theft of this world and we do so, as Judith Butler has so beautifully written, as we accept that this loss changes us forever:

> [W]hen we are dispossessed from a place, or a community, we may simply feel that we are undergoing something temporary, that mourning will be over and some restoration of prior order will be achieved. But, instead, when we undergo what we do undergo, is something about who we are revealed, something that delineates the ties we have to others, that shows us that these ties constitute what we are, ties or bonds that compose us? ... Who 'am' I, without you? When we lose some of these ties by which we are constituted, we do not know who we are or what to do. On one level, I think I have lost 'you' only to discover that 'I' have gone missing as well. At another level, perhaps what I have lost 'in' you, that for which I have no ready vocabulary, is a relationality that is neither merely myself nor you, but the tie by which those terms are differentiated and related.[20]

We do lose some sense of ourselves, but I think we are made by and through this tradition of mourning, as the experience of loss offers new relations to our sense of those we remember; we fabricate an inextinguishable, albeit transformed and transforming, relation to the people, language and worlds taken from us. So we mourn the loss of nationality, the stripping of place and of belonging, we retain a sense of the precarious and a trembling suspicion, we doubt everything because we know everything is unstable. And we know this not only of ourselves, but of ourselves as Others. We know enough.

But drawing conclusions of solidarity shouldn't elide difference, neither in the generational sense nor in relation to others. It needs also to acknowledge the dissimilarities that produce fissures between us and those with whom we proclaim solidarity. To return to the context you introduced in your initial question on solidarity, our material interests as non-Indigenous Australian citizens are plainly antagonistic to those of Indigenous people. At a fundamental level, our Jewishness doesn't matter. We are, as Shaista Patel has suggested of post-conquest settlers, 'marginalized and yet [we] participate in the ongoing dispossession of Indigenous peoples on whose [stolen or occupied] lands' we live. We are complicit. From this perspective, we are those who might be described as gubbas, or whitefellas, or however we might be defined. As a visitor, you can't demand to be respected on your own terms.[21] At the same time, a possessive order of whiteness positions us differently to non-Jewish British settlers or migrants.

So there is a complexity, a necessity and an impossibility to the claim of solidarity; something that we struggle with and struggle through. I know there's an element of self-indulgence to this kind of thinking: I find myself wondering (amidst our earnestness) whether this discussion could be titled 'Settler Colonialism and the Jewish Question'? But, at the same time, I do think that a position of contingent marginality is a good place from which to explore these questions, to seek out ways of embracing decolonizing solidarities that deny neither one's own position nor those of Indigenous people.

History and Memory

JS: I read once that all the people from Sosnowitz, where Zosia came from, were transported to Auschwitz. Reading that in a book, flat on the page, made me short of breath. This came a year or so after I had really looked at a map of Poland and realized how close Sosnowitz and Czestochowa (where Vovek was from) are to Auschwitz. But she wasn't tattooed, so I keep telling myself that she wasn't there. I don't know why that is important to me. If she wasn't there, some of our family probably was. That, in all likelihood, is for some of our ancestors their gravesite.

It makes me want to go.

And it repels me.

This seems to me to be illustrative of the intertwining of personal memory and collective memory, personal history and collective history, produced by being a descendant of Holocaust survivors. For it is important to remember and integrate into our family narratives the particularities of our family's experiences of the Holocaust – as has become quite clear through our conversation, they make us who we are – but also to remember that the Holocaust was made up of so many multitudes, of so many different peoples with their own histories and, in some cases, futures. For instance, I think that a Jewish memory of the Holocaust that forgets that Jews were not the only victims of the Holocaust is a memory which is bereft. And a memory that says that all Jews were treated in the same way – that does not recognize, for instance, the range of particular horrors that women faced, and does not speak of the gendered ways in which Nazi violence was enacted – is itself a mode of forgetting.[22] It's interesting to watch the different battles over memories of the Holocaust, and the ways that notions of what the Holocaust can thereby be are constrained or opened up. Who was a survivor? How were different groups of people treated? Can we say that what was done to the other persecuted groups – Roma, Sinti, homosexuals, political prisoners, the disabled – formed part of the Holocaust?

BS: To include all this as 'part of the Holocaust' is, I think, to insist upon that tense universalism to which we have already referred. It is to situate the Holocaust as a crime against humanity that was not committed only against the Jewish people; its history thus provides a lesson that is universal (exclusion) as well as particular (antisemitism). This articulation represents a productive dissonance, one whose legacy impels us to acknowledge our position but not remain confined by it.

I think there's something to this ethic of remembrance that is reflected in the tensions that structure our lives as members of the third generation here in Melbourne. We act as Jews, made so historically, claiming solidarities but refusing to position ourselves only within an abstract humanity. We have been speaking of identity as an ongoing process, not as a thing to be possessed and displayed; a dynamic and open negotiation rather than an indelible and unchangeable template whose performance closes down the possibility of communication with apparently threatening others.[23] Remembering the multiple Holocausts of 1939–45 and beyond can be a basis for fabricating an open Jewishness; one that, in its multiplicity, represents a diasporic ethic.

This combination of heterogeneity and ambivalence, difference and neurosis, is unmistakably and fundamentally Jewish and usefully universal in an affective sense. The pulse of our history is one of fear and of vulnerability, these are constitutive of modernity, and of our Jewishness, after the Holocaust.[24] So embracing Jewishness as a condition, in this sense, is a positioning gesture. When we seize upon these affects born of moments of danger, we articulate the Jewish past historically. It is this that gives our third generation Jewishness life and meaning.

NOTES

1. M. Hirsch, 'Surviving Images: Holocaust Photographs and the Work of Postmemory', *Yale Journal of Criticism*, 14, 1 (2001), pp.10–11.
2. Jean Améry makes this point in a more expansive sense in his *At the Mind's Limits* (Bloomington, IN: Indiana University Press, 1980), p.93.
3. I take the term 'common community' (slightly out of context) from Dennis Altman, 'On Being Jewish, 1973', in *Coming Out in the Seventies* (Sydney: Wild & Woolley, 1979), p.202.
4. J. Silverstein, *Anxious Histories: Narrating the Holocaust in Jewish Communities at the Beginning of the Twenty First Century* (New York: Berghahn Books, 2015).
5. A. Moreton-Robinson, 'The Possessive Logic of Patriarchal White Sovereignty: The High Court and the Yorta Yorta Decision', *borderlands e-journal*, 3, 2 (2004).
6. E.W. Said, 'Reflections on Exile', in *Reflections on Exile and other Literary and Cultural Essays* (New Delhi: Penguin Books, 2001), p.185.

7. J. Silverstein, '"We're dealing with how we live and work with this memory and what are we supposed to do with it": Making Use of Jewish Liminality', *borderlands e-journal*, 9, 1 (2010), p.2.
8. On the conflation of 'the alien' and 'the Jew' as the pre-eminent non-national figure in Britain in 1905, see D. Glover, *Literature, Immigration and Diaspora in Fin-de-Siècle England: A Cultural History of the 1905 Aliens Act* (Cambridge: Cambridge University Press, 2012).
9. That this description bears almost no resemblance to the historical conditions in Palestine/Israel should go without saying. This does not mean it has no power. In many ways, narrating the history of that region in this way licenses imagining, and then committing, atrocities like 'Operation Cast Lead' in 2008–09.
10. I. Klepfisz, *Dreams of an Insomniac: Jewish Feminist Essays, Speeches and Diatribes* (Portland, OR: Eighth Mountain Press, 1990), p.205, cited in J. Schamp, 'Beyond Assimilation: Difference and Reconfiguration in the Works of Irena Klepfisz, Jyl Lynn Felman, and Rebecca Goldstein', *ZAA*, 47, 3 (1999), p.235.
11. To speak of European Jewish experience is itself a mythic conflation. Amidst the myriad histories, there is a world of difference between the Jewish subjects of German citizenship and the Polish Jews from whom we are descended. That all were, to an extent, unified in camps during the Holocaust does not erase the multiple paths each community took to get there, or the different experiences once they were there.
12. M. Karlin, 'A Rabbi's Path to Palestinian Solidarity: An Interview with Rabbi Brant Rosen', *Truthout* (10 October 2012), http://truth-out.org/opinion/item/12009-a-rabbis-path-to-palestinian-solidarity.
13. B. Silverstein, 'Indirect Rule in a Settler Colony: Race, Indigeneity, Government' (unpublished PhD thesis, School of Humanities and Social Sciences, La Trobe University, Melbourne, Australia, 2012), p.viii.
14. I. Deutscher, *The Non-Jewish Jew and Other Essays* (London: Oxford University Press, 1968), p.51.
15. S. Schulman, *Israel/Palestine and the Queer International* (Durham, NC: Duke University Press, 2012).
16. J. Baldwin, *The Fire Next Time* (Harmondsworth: Penguin Books, 1964), p.84.
17. In the case of Sofia Stawski. Wladislaw Stawski was 'Stateless ex Polish'.
18. Hirsch, 'Surviving Images', pp.9–11.
19. V. Lal, 'The Vanquisher and the Vanquished: Nagasaki and Two Uncommon Lives', *Lal Salaam*, 29 August 2010, http://vinaylal.wordpress.com/2010/08/29/the-vanquisher-and-the-vanquished-nagasaki-and-two-uncommon-lives/; A. Mbembe, 'Faces of Freedom: Jewish and Black Experiences', *Interventions*, 7, 3 (2005), p.295.
20. J. Butler, *Precarious Life: The Powers of Mourning and Violence* (New York: Verso, 2003), pp. 11–12.
21. S. Patel, 'Defining Muslim Feminist Politics through Indigenous Solidarity Activism', *Feminist Wire*, 1 August 2012, http://thefeministwire.com/2012/08/defining-muslim-feminist-politics-through-indigenous-solidarity-activism/. The point on 'respect' and identification is taken from Taiaiake Alfred's response to a questioner at a forum at the University of Victoria, British Columbia, on 16 January 2013. See E. Ritskes, 'The Terms of Engagement with Indigenous Nationhood', *Decolonization: Indigeneity, Education & Society*, 17 January 2013, http://decolonization.wordpress.com/2013/01/17/the-terms-of-engagement-with-indigenous-nationhood/.
22. There is now a large body of literature that explores the different experiences that women had during the Holocaust. For an exploration of it, and a discussion of how a category of 'Jewish women' was created through this violence, see my discussion in Silverstein, *Anxious Histories*, chapter 5.
23. See also P. Gilroy, *Against Race: Imagining Political Culture Beyond the Colour Line* (Cambridge, MA: Harvard University Press, 2000), pp.103–04.
24. See F. Jameson, 'History and Class Consciousness as an "Unfinished Project"', *Rethinking Marxism*, 1, 1 (1988), p.70.

A Social Justice Legacy

BETH HERZ

During a recent spring, I was helping my grandparents pack up the contents of the house that they had lived in for more than sixty years. This was the family's epicentre, the home where they had raised four children. It was also a treasure trove of nostalgia for four grandchildren – a quantity of photos and keepsakes that could never fit in their new apartment, less than a quarter of the house's size. In other words, it was the packing and purging project of the century.

After shooing my 91-year-old grandfather away from a shaky ladder in his study, I reached to his highest and most neglected shelves to unearth decades of books, files and dust. Carefully, I helped sort folders of typewritten and yellowed paperwork into two piles: to throw away and to bring to the new apartment.

Leafing through an endless stack, I semi-attentively asked him, 'What are these files marked "Sanctuary"?'

'The Sanctuary movement? That was the effort to provide asylum to Central American refugees', he explained. He went on to remind me that an interfaith group in western New York had hosted refugee families and advocated on their behalf for years. He paused and shook his head. 'But the feds didn't listen. Eventually they had to leave.' Layered with his thick German accent I noticed unmistakable notes of moral outrage and disgust with his government's inaction, stirred two decades later.

'Oh, I ... I didn't know you were involved in that', I said slowly, beginning to focus my attention on the pages of meeting notes and newspaper clippings. 'What would you like me to do with these?' My grandfather had barely formed the words 'Toss them' when I silently created a new pile: reading material for me to take home.

Germany

I should not have been entirely surprised by my grandfather's passionate involvement with the Sanctuary movement supporting refugees. Throughout my life, I had seen both his and my grandmother's devotion to their community, and particularly to supporting those who were struggling in some way. They worked with people with disabilities and helped serve food to those without enough. Beyond that, they worked on improving the social safety net: they were active voters, writing letters when an issue particularly sparked their concern and marching in solidarity with issues dear to them. My grandfather spoke out against the Vietnam War and, even in his eighties, he joined a group of marchers in response to American deployment in Iraq.

I never heard them explain why they participated in these ways. It was simply natural for them. But it is not hard to imagine the experiences that might have helped them to become so community-minded. Like many Jews who left Nazi Germany, my paternal grandparents rarely brought up their background. When they did share their stories, they always gave a self-conscious nod to their successful emigration or mentioned their luck in having contacts abroad who could lend a hand.

Before my grandfather left Berlin in 1937 and my grandmother left Nuremberg in 1938, each of them and their families faced day-to-day signs of antisemitism for years. My grandmother, in particular, recalls being asked to leave her classroom in Nuremberg with two other Jewish students regularly, while the rest of the class had lessons in a new subject called 'race science'. Miles away in Berlin, my grandfather's family received a blow when his father, the breadwinner, lost his senior post in a publishing house because of his religion. Still, both families maintained an attitude of optimism at first, seeing their government as reasonable and believing that the obstacles that they faced were not insurmountable.

Then, as Nazi totalitarianism escalated, their experiences with persecution became more acute, more invasive and more violent. After a family vacation out of the country, my grandmother's father, a lawyer in Nuremberg, was badly beaten and detained for seven weeks. Encountering the same law, my grandfather's mother returned from a family visit abroad and had to spend six months in an 'instructional camp' for women.[1]

Both of my grandparents have spoken about their naivety and unfazed ignorance as German adolescents. Like their classmates, they wanted to fit in and to have fun – to simply be young. In their happy, middle-class lives, they each had the sense that they were utterly normal. At first, the inconvenience of a Jew-hating party in power seemed relatively small. Judaism, after all, was only one part of their identities.

My grandmother's hope for normalcy evaporated on *Kristallnacht*. That night, she awoke as a hanging glass light fixture in her bedroom crashed to the floor. She could hear civilian trespassers ransacking her home and shouting threats at her mother. A 15-year-old, she left her bedroom to call the police. 'Are you Jewish?' the voice at the other end inquired. 'Yes', she answered uncertainly, still unaccustomed to such a question. 'Well, then I can't help you.'

My grandfather's attitude changed in the following year, while awaiting American visas in a series of countries with his parents. After stints in Italy and Switzerland, they arrived in Cuba; he was 18. As they travelled, he began to grasp the gravity of their search for a home and for steady work. He realized that his ability to enrol in college could be their ticket to entry and to a livelihood in the United States. Having an interest in photography, he sent a letter from Cuba addressed to 'Kodak, USA'. With some luck, he was referred to a university in Rochester, New York, where he soon moved with his parents. Immediately upon arrival, he began his campaign to enlist with the Allied forces, contacting both the American and Canadian authorities. It didn't matter to him which flag he donned; he simply knew he wanted to fight back.

Soon after Kristallnacht, my grandmother and her family escaped to Palestine and then settled in Massachusetts; as a young adult she followed a job to Rochester, New York. Once they were both living there, it was not long before my grandparents were introduced through the German-Jewish refugee community. They married, raised four children, and watched their urban surroundings change over several decades. Eventually, their son and daughter-in-law put down roots there as well; my sister and I grew up less than a mile down the road.

Rochester

Following the pattern of many former manufacturing towns in the US, Rochester's racial and ethnic landscape underwent significant transitions between the 1970s and 1990s. My father and aunts went to a neighbourhood grade school filled with students who looked similar to them. Thirty years later, a bussing system bringing students across neighbourhood boundaries and racially integrating schools was in full effect. By then, thousands of middle-class white families had sold their city homes, moving to higher-value suburban areas where the stronger tax base ensured better-resourced schools. Of those who remained in the city, many opted for expensive private schools.

As a result, my classmates in the same urban public schools came from a wide variety of backgrounds. We were a human rainbow of skin tones – the vast majority being darker than mine. Most were in working-class families; about three-quarters lived near or below the poverty line. My sister and I were among about one-tenth of the school district's student body who identified as white.

Like my grandparents in their early childhoods, I was generally comfortable and happy. I valued my diverse, multilingual, urban surroundings and would not have imagined living anywhere else. When I was young, I could not have named many problems in my community. But little by little, I began to notice differences. The public school buildings a stone's throw away from my home, just outside the city limits, were newly renovated and had full athletic facilities – a stark contrast from the schools I attended. When we participated in region-wide sports and music competitions, it became apparent that my city school peers and I never stood a chance; the resources that our instructors and coaches had at their disposal made us the clear underdog every time.

Among my classmates, the inequality was also extreme. I could see that my family's spacious house and yard were not the norm. Few of my classmates could walk from their home to an active business district or a large, well-kept park, as I could. Much of what I had access to – from new clothes to summer camp – was out of reach for most of my peers in school. In third grade, my classmates and I were separated out into two academic tracks, which would guide our coursework through high school. Quickly, I accumulated more and more access to academic support and extra-curricular activities designed to prepare me for post-secondary education. My peers across the hall had notably fewer of these resources. Through my adolescence, I puzzled over how these gross inequalities could exist in a country that promised 'liberty and justice for all'.

Preston

It is the day before my seventeenth birthday and my father and I are arriving at the funeral of a young man my age. The church is buzzing with people, but it feels like it is shrouded in a gloomy haze. We sit together on a back row pew. We listen to a series of unfamiliar Bible readings, joining in with gospel songs when we can follow along. When the pastor begins the eulogy, though, we can barely hear his remarks. The sustained, high-pitched wails of a few relatives in the front row pierce the room. I feel chilled, wishing there was something I could do for them. I turn to my dad, noticing his misty eyes.

The service concludes and we approach the immediate family. 'I was a classmate of Preston's, in elementary school', I say quietly, by way of introduction. 'We are so sorry to hear about your loss.' Our condolences are met, at first, with subtle nods and the glazed-over eyes of mourners. We begin to leave. But before we reach the door, a friend of the family stops us for an important introduction: 'This is Preston Junior,' she tells us, with another nod – this time motioning toward my former classmate's toddler son.

Preston was truly a nice kid. The night before he died, he was standing outside a convenience store with his brother and two friends, sharing snacks. An acquaintance, angry with one of the other young men in the group, crossed the street toward them, holding a paper bag that obscured a gun. As he approached, he broke into a run and began shooting at them indiscriminately. Both Preston and the friend next to him suffered multiple gunshot wounds; Preston died shortly after.

Two generations later

When they shared their stories about Nazi Germany – about persecution and discrimination based on a particular group identity – my grandparents were handing me a lens through which I saw my own environs. I observed the stark inequalities around me in sharp relief through their perspectives. Viewing Rochester alongside them, I noticed that health and wellness, education and employment, wealth and political power – even death – were largely defined by where you lived and what you looked like.

As a young, white high school student from a middle-class family, I could not immediately name these social inequalities. And I had a valuable privilege that many of my classmates did not have: if I wanted, I could ignore the existence of these injustices altogether.

My grandparents both described doing something extremely natural as German-Jewish young people in the mid-1930s: going on with their daily lives. They simply wished the political nuisances around them would evaporate. For a while, at least, that seemed plausible.

But at some point in their lives, they each transformed the painful experiences of their early years into action – through countless acts of community service and civic participation. While looking at my world through my grandparents' stories, I also spent my childhood watching their diligent endeavours to improve their society. With their experiences and example in front of me, it became a clear next step to explore the social factors that contributed to Preston's death and help to improve them. I went on to study urban trends in the US and, eventually, to work to change them.

Tragically, Preston's story is not particularly exceptional. He was among 7,522 black homicide victims in the US that year, a victimization rate over six times higher than that for whites. For a range of reasons, many of my classmates and peers became involved in high-risk encounters with each other and with law enforcement. Almost everyone I knew in school was probably affected – through someone they knew well – by violence or incarceration or both. (The chance of being incarcerated at some point in life is 32 per cent for black men in the US, compared with less than 6 per cent for white men.) While there was some bad luck that led Preston to stand outside that particular store that particular night, the deck had clearly been stacked against him long before.

When I began to explore how sociologists measure inequality among neighbourhoods and schools, I saw that these numbers, too, strikingly highlight the discrepancies my classmates and I had seen in Rochester. They also revealed the exact same phenomenon across the country.

Now, in various ways, I strive to build equal access to opportunities in cities like my hometown, especially in communities of colour. Working in a network of inspiring movement builders, community researchers and policymakers, I feel that there is an attainable goal on the horizon: a society in which access to health, education, livelihood and happiness looks the same for everyone. In other words, a place where no one is born to find the deck already stacked against them.

Martin Niemöller famously recounted how he had observed the persecution of various groups of people passively:

> First they came for the Socialists, and I did not speak out –
> Because I was not a Socialist ...
> Then they came for the Jews, and I did not speak out –
> Because I was not a Jew.

He listed various groups in this way and then revealed that eventually he, too, was targeted and it was too late for him to protect himself. The poem concludes with the memorable phrase 'and there was no one left to speak for me'. Through these words, Niemöller underscored the value of seeking justice from wherever you sit, through empathy or, in some cases, through civil disobedience.

This lesson was even brighter and clearer when I saw it living in front of me, day to day. I have seen my grandparents speaking out in moral indignation when a war seemed unnecessary; encouraging their government to better serve everyone; and supporting refugees and others in need of allies. Rather than telling me, they showed me: they valued human rights and civic participation, building alliances across differences and speaking up against wrongs. My grandfather's efforts, in an interfaith partnership, to support asylum seekers in his community was just one more example in a long list.

As I now strive to be an active participant in developing a more just and equitable society, I am surrounded by insightful and ambitious change makers. Countless trailblazers have improved their communities or spoken out in the past, and countless others continue to guide today's efforts. Amidst all of this inspiration, the roots of my passion remain unquestionable: my family's history and the values that emerged from it are what brought me here.

15. Hildegard Blum Herz and Arthur Herz, Beth Herz's paternal grandparents. Copyright/permission granted by Joshua Herz.

NOTE

1. Gabriele Herz, the author's great-grandmother, wrote a memoir on her experience at Moringen, a camp that held women primarily due to their political affiliation. It was published posthumously in both English and German: G. Herz, *The Women's Camp in Moringen: A Memoir of Imprisonment in Germany, 1936–1937*, translated by H. Herz and H. Hartig (New York: Berghahn Books, 2006).

Representations

Holocaust Music, Nazi Songs and Everyday Angst: Cultural Memory in Young Generations of Roma

PETRA GELBART

It has become something of a cliché to label Romani (Gypsy) suffering during the Holocaust as 'the forgotten genocide'. Indeed, a number of authors have noted the reluctance of Romani Holocaust survivors to pass on memories of concentration camps and other methods of persecution. While reticence regarding the legacy of genocide is certainly a factor among many East European Jewish and, more tenaciously, Romani surviving families, in the case of Roma and Sinti the 'forgetting' is enacted much more strikingly by non-Roma in the public sphere. There is a continued, epistemologically and educationally dangerous interplay between the historical lack of Romani participation (academic as well as political) and the difficulty faced by Romanies who *do* wish to speak, write or perform publicly in the context of Holocaust commemorations.

The struggle to convey to the outside world the anxieties experienced by survivor families residing in or tied to modern-day Europe has been taken up by the third surviving generation of Roma and Sinti.[1] Both these names refer to an ethnic group that, like Jews, was scheduled for complete extermination during the Second World War; the victims numbered around half a million or more,[2] and were proportionally similar to the percentages of Jews killed.[3] "Gypsies" were subject to the Nuremburg race laws, and even persons with very little Romani "blood" could be rounded up, including some soldiers in the German army.[4] In the United States alone, there is a small but growing movement of young Romani or part-Romani students, scholars and other community members who have revived older activists' (energetic, organized, yet in many ways surprisingly unsuccessful) efforts for self-representation in public Holocaust education.[5] To date, would-be Romani representatives in their twenties, thirties and forties (I among them) who are relatively new to the cause are faring no better than their more senior counterparts. Thus, when descendants of the Romani wartime generations attend United Nations Holocaust commemoration ceremonies, for example, they find entire swathes of the audience unaware that anything like the genocide of Roma and Sinti ever took place.

I conducted fieldwork among surviving Romani communities, primarily in the Czech Republic, intermittently between 2000 and 2013. Based on this fieldwork and my ongoing activity in Romani communities, as well as on written sources, this chapter considers the experiences of college-educated American Roma, and focuses on the testimonies of Central European Roma of all strata. It situates the third-generation experience of post-Holocaust Romanies in the dual contexts of a lack of access to participation in large-scale public commemorations or written materials on the one hand, and life in the age of Neo-Nazis and 'Gypsy reality TV' on the other. These issues intensify both the psychological impact of the Holocaust legacy for rank-and-file Romanies and the urgency felt by those in the Romani rights movement for improved Holocaust education. Even those public figures whose primary work is not Holocaust-related tend to be keenly aware of the Holocaust experience as a motivating background for what they do. For example, noted Romani-speaking film-maker and sociologist Katalin Bársony, who heads the Romedia Foundation, is part of the subgroup of third-generation Romani survivors who are descended from both Jewish and Romani victims of the Holocaust in Hungary. Her parents are published authors on genocide-related subjects, and her work in human rights and cultural representation is logically influenced by this background.

The number of European and American Roma who also have some Jewish ancestry is significant enough to complicate the seeming dichotomy between Romani and Jewish Holocaust survivors, however they may be distinguished in terms of victimhood and generational identity. Several of my acquaintances and fieldwork respondents fall into this mixed category, among them a woman in her late twenties who was born in America to a Jewish mother and a part-Romani, part-Jewish concentration camp survivor, and a Hungarian woman in her forties who considers herself Romani but whose father – orphaned but rescued from the threat of deportation as a small child – was ethnically Jewish. She expresses a profound sense of loss: 'I feel cheated, because my father was always depressed about his parents and turned to alcohol to ease his pain. I feel cheated and angry that my father's side of the family was completely wiped out. As the result, I ha[d] to grow up almost like an orphan, without … parental guidance or love.' Interestingly, since this woman married a South Asian man, her children are heirs to a Romani and Jewish heritage, but also, more prominently, to roots in the Indian subcontinent, the ancestral homeland of Roma.

And yet, despite historical and current Jewish-Romani marriages (e.g. some wartime couples or my own marriage) and strong support from many Jewish individuals, the Romani Holocaust experience is most often still represented as something quite apart from the Jewish genocide. This conceptualization runs parallel to stereotypical ideas about 'Gypsies' and Jews as incompatible groups; the former is seen as socially problematic, entirely uneducated or even, absurdly, as still mostly nomadic in the third millennium, while the latter is hardly subject to any of the same associations with crime and poverty. It is thus easier to believe that the Nazis and their collaborators targeted Jews solely for racial reasons and Gypsies for their behaviour – which in reality ranged from the then more common itinerancy to socially integrated and middle-class lifestyles. Ian Hancock, a university professor and leading Romani scholar, writes:

> In an article published in 1996 I listed several of the arguments that have been made for diminishing the Porrajmos, or Romani Holocaust, addressing each one in turn. In practically every case, statements were made which were simply wrong – the result of assuming a situation to have existed or not existed without bothering to check the historical record. Several writers have written that there was no Final Solution of the Gypsy Question.[6]

Indeed, in what is arguably the most widely influential, if historiographically selective English-language monograph on Romanies in the Second World War, Guenter Lewy concludes that not only were Romanies not victims of the Holocaust, but that their large-scale extermination did not amount to genocide.[7] Similar examples abound – for example, the 'Holocaust and the United Nations' office at the UN headquarters in New York has hosted a speaker who claims that while the number of Romani victims was higher than previously thought, their suffering was separate from the Holocaust.[8] No Romani person was invited to the event as a speaker or respondent, just as no Roma or Sinti are permitted to appear in commemorations organized by the dozens-strong United States Holocaust Memorial Council, which has included members of various ethnicities, none of them Romani. (After years of petitioning and brief service by the Rom William Duna, Ian Hancock was appointed to the council for several years, but was neither reappointed nor replaced by another Rom after 2000.) As we will see, the common separation of Romanies from Jews in rhetoric, publications and memorials – the Berlin memorial being the most salient in recent memory – stands in stark contrast to the lived reality of Holocaust survivors and their families.

The wartime Protectorate of Bohemia and Moravia, largely corresponding to what is now the Czech Republic, was one of the countries in which some 90 per cent of Roma and Sinti perished during the Holocaust. In neighbouring Slovakia, by contrast, the war ended before the regime was able to shoot or deport large numbers of Roma, and most of them survived, albeit with fundamental imposed restrictions that made it difficult to obtain food and impossible to attend school (this is why my grandmother, for example, is illiterate). Czech and Slovak scholars have documented the sometimes staggering long-term economic impact of Roma suddenly losing homes, local employment, and other aspects of their pre-war integration levels.[9] The partial extermination of Hungarian Roma, meanwhile, fell somewhere in between the Czech and the Slovak situation with regard to final numbers. The Czech Republic's pre-war Romani population virtually ceased to exist, and was replaced after the war by an influx of Roma from the Slovak part of Czechoslovakia. People often assume that no one is left to bear witness to the large-scale persecution. Two factors complicate this received wisdom, however: a few families of 'original' Bohemian (Czech) and Moravian Roma as well as Sinti remain, and thus some individuals pass on first-hand knowledge of concentration camps either privately or (in only a handful of cases) publicly; also, many of the Slovak Roma experienced their own wartime horrors, both in and out of camps.

In 2000, the non-profit organization R-Mosty surveyed a large number of young, mostly third-generation Holocaust survivors, who were then guided to write down stories passed to them by relatives. The respondents were all older children or adolescents of Slovak Romani descent, although the book's academically informed section was penned by Jana Horváthová, a third-generation survivor of Czech/Moravian Romani extraction. There is much truth to the assertion that Romani survivor families do not necessarily speak openly about the Holocaust, even among their own

16. Petra Gelbart's grandfather and daughter in 2007, photographed in rural Moravia. Copyright/permission granted by Petra Gelbart.

members. The project's results, however, help to dispel the notion that the subject is taboo and that Roma as a rule are still opposed to sharing stories of wartime suffering.[10] Much like parallel scholarly accounts of how Roma were treated in Slovakia, the Czech-language collection published by R-Mosty includes varied examples of murder, torture and/or rape outside of camps, usually by 'Germans', the horrors of concentration/work camps or extralegal internment, conditions of hiding in the woods that made survival difficult (e.g. starvation), and tales of heroism in connection with Romani fighters in the Slovak resistance.[11]

The accounts frequently demonstrate detailed knowledge of suffering that took place in multiple modalities:

> In the end, the Germans settled in Slovakia. They liked to be entertained, so they sought out musicians. Most of the good musicians were of Romani origin. My grandmother's father, too, joined the musicians. In order to save their and their families' lives, they had to play for them [the Germans] every day. The Germans would just drink and eat. Many times the Romani musicians were humiliated – they would mock them. And the others outside were starving. While they [these Germans] were having fun, the others were catching children and women. They put the men into gas chambers and also abused them. Also, one family was taken to the Dubnice nad Váhom concentration camp. They burned villages to ashes, they tortured people by making them lie on bare boards with no blanket and even naked. It was freezing outside and they let them freeze. If someone had a gold tooth cap, they would rip it out of his mouth. Whoever helped the partisans or tried to escape, they would tear his nails from his hands and shave their heads, [and] they burned their bodies and eyes. The Germans behaved like animals. I don't understand why they tortured and abused and terrorized them like that, [considering] they themselves had families. Miroslava, *Co mi doma vyprávěli*, p. 32.

A similar account is given by a girl named Renata:

> It would also happen that the German soldiers were celebrating, at which point they'd come into a Romani house where a musician lived[;] everyone including the children had to get up, the father had to play the violin, the children had to dance and the Germans were amused and drank alcohol. In the end, they raped the wife and they shot the whole family. They behaved worse than animal predators Renata, *Co mi doma vyprávěli*, p. 34.

Musicianship, then, could be both a saving grace (a Czech Romani musician, for example, was once saved from a transport that took away nearly all of his fellow Roma) and a death sentence.[12] Although a meaningful comparison can hardly be made, one is tempted to draw a parallel between the unique experiences of Romani musicians during the war and the fact that present-day performances of Romani musicians sometimes attract violent neo-Nazis.

A number of the young contributors to the collection included psychologically harrowing descriptions of anguish as their older relatives have experienced it, as well as their own reactions to hearing about the events:

> Three weeks after returning, she died. The whole family was very sad. Auntie's mommy hanged herself in the attic, [the] daddy had an attack. The brother (my daddy) wanted to take his own life, too. When my father recounted this, we cried. Lucie, *Co mi doma vyprávěli*, p. 14.
>
> Grandma doesn't like to recall all this. She cries and says, 'Pray you never have to live through war! I am glad that there's peace!' Rostislav, *Co mi doma vyprávěli*, p. 18.
>
> [H]er voice would sometimes shake ... there were tears ... Did it have to be? Did it have to end up that way? How many innocent people had to die. When I listened to these stories, I wanted to cry. War is something that we only see as clips on television, and none of us can imagine the horror. Miroslava, *Co mi doma vyprávěli*, p. 31-2.

Pavel, who was 11 years old, conveyed his grandmother's assessment of wartime conditions as 'unbearable', so intense that when she described them to her children, they found her experiences impossible to believe and laughed as a result. Now the adults weep with her and the grandchildren listen, not yet comprehending the meaning. R-Mosty, *Co mi doma vyprávěli*, p. 14.

One wonders if the experiential knowledge, transmitted in these families and showing how extreme racism can be, sometimes has the effect of relativizing the current discrimination experienced by most Roma in the former Czechoslovakia. This would explain why many Roma can be angry about the slurs hurled at their children or about the harassing behaviour of policemen while at the same time finding these phenomena 'normal' – bearable in comparison to that which, in recent enough memory, was unbearable. The derision of a policeman who dismisses a report of neo-Nazi activity or crimes (something I experienced myself when attempting to report imminent danger related to a skinhead) is hardly comparable to fascists who set light to houses and 'shot first at the children while their [the shooters'] faces laughed, and then they murdered the whole family'. Renata, *Co mi doma vyprávěli*, p. 34.

While the third-generation Roma who are exposed to graphic Holocaust recollections presumably have a sense of gratitude for the far greater safety of their own lives, a knowledge of the vast differences between the 1940s and today in degrees of discrimination does little to assuage cross-generational fears and psychological (as well as physical) trauma from contemporary far-right extremism. One teenager relayed her grandmother's words thus:

> After all this suffering, following the war we went to live in Prague. Daddy found work, we lived better, we weren't very demanding, war taught us humility and love for all living things. That is why I condemn the youth of today who promote fascism, [because] they did not live through the horrors of war, which leave indelible marks your whole life long. Alena, *Co mi doma vyprávěli*, p. 41.

Of the incomprehensible reasons for the Holocaust's unleashing, third-generation survivor and historian Jana Horváthová writes: 'Who can explain it??? [sic] Apparently none of us living today, but considering that the perpetrators were members of the same biological species as all the rest of us – humans – it is important to keep in mind that perverse ideas will occur within society constantly; it is only necessary for us to count on this and to be well-prepared.'[13]

One of my respondents spoke in Czech about his grandmother, who was born in Auschwitz following the rape of her mother by a German guard. Based on her family's experiences, however, her understanding has been that 'the Slovaks were worse than the Germans'. Predictably, the grandson has heightened concerns about the neo-Nazi movement:

> When I think about what effect [the Holocaust] has on my life, I have to admit that even as a member of the third generation, I'm terrified by any mention of growing neo-Nazism. And that I'm not satisfied with the fight against it. I'm afraid of the financial crisis because I see in it the possibility of making such a movement explode. But at the same time my grandma and her stories have made me want to try to forgive, in life, to come to terms with the past, to be open to every culture, every religion, because today, thanks to the particular fate of one life I know what effects it has when a person has prejudices.

A number of other respondents in my fieldwork, as well as countless Roma or Sinti whose opinions I have noted casually over the years, echo similar fears of what may lie just around the corner. Virtually all of them are related to someone who has been physically attacked in the past three decades for his or her skin colour or for some other marker of 'Gypsiness'. 'The Holocaust must never be forgotten ... its memory must be spread among entire generations of Roma and non-Roma', a woman wrote to me in Slovak. 'This memory is very important especially at this tense time, when there is so much prejudice around the status of Roma, not just in Slovakia', she explained. 'Can something similar [to the Holocaust] even be repeated?', one male respondent wondered in a letter. 'I'd like to say no, it can't, but personally I don't believe that.'

Still, there is generally an important distinction between Romanies whose families were spared from the Holocaust or who have not had access to family-based testimony and those who have had the affective, often embodied (e.g. through weeping with relatives or from the original physical suffering) experience of understanding the details of genocide and torture. While both groups of European Romanies are more or less haunted by the visual and other similarities between the Third Reich and current extremist movements – swastikas, pseudoscientific tracts about racial inferiority, etc. – those with a more vague image of Holocaust realities may be quicker to conflate the two time periods. Thus, as a volunteer with asylum seekers in London over a decade ago, I willingly took part in demonstrations against the violence that Roma face all over central and eastern Europe, but was made uncomfortable by pronouncements and signs such as 'STOP SECOND HOLOCAUST! [sic]'. Even a painted sheet asking Bulgaria to stop 'murdering the Gypsies' seemed to refer to something happening on a much larger scale than the actual series of legally unpunished racially motivated attacks in question.

By that point in my life, I had come to know the intense paranoia permeating the remnants of an extended family that had been all but exterminated, so I understood the impulse toward cautionary statements. I also knew the difference between current everyday persecution and actual genocide, with the ethnic cleansing of Kosovar Roma (beginning in the late 1990s and generally ignored by the international community while its echoes of genocide remained hidden to most politicians) falling somewhere in between. Pogrom-like attacks, too, made one more sympathetic to exaggerated warnings of a second Holocaust, as when a Romanian Romani co-worker in London told me how large-scale arson had claimed the lives of her husband and brother. With the exception of scuffles and humiliating encounters with skinheads, my Romani family had experienced nowhere near that level of violence since the war, and yet the fear for one's safety and livelihood always hung in the air.

During the Second World War, my great-grandfather, who would later be a primary parent figure to my mother, had the family's obviously Romani name changed in an effort to save himself and his relatives from being deported. He thought the new name would make them less visible in government records, but it was to no avail. Official numbers say that he was one of only about 500 or 600 Czech Roma and Sinti to survive the Holocaust. My mother tells me he made it because he was still in a German labour camp when he injured himself in a rather gruesome manner and then escaped from the infirmary. Meanwhile, his mother died during the night in one of the two concentration camps set up especially for Romanies by the Czech protectorate government, after the Czech guards forced her to freeze outside the barracks, apparently intending to kill or at least torture her with the lethal temperatures.

Members of my great-grandfather's immediate family, including his children, were briefly interned in a gathering camp, but according to my great-aunt they were released thanks to the romantic interest of one of the German guards, who was later shot for this. After the war, the surviving members of my grandfather's family waited for dozens of relatives to come home from the camps, but most of them never did. My great-grandfather, who committed suicide in the end, had a particular way of reminding younger people of the losses he had suffered. Whereas cremation is normally strictly forbidden by our Romani subgroup's laws, he let his funeral wishes be known quite clearly by repeating one instruction: 'They burned my whole family, so let *me* be burned, too.'

For the majority of Czech- and Slovak-Romani families, songs rather than pronouncements are an important vehicle for the transmission of Holocaust-era images to the third surviving generation and sometimes beyond. My grandmother, who was born in a Slovak Romani settlement, orphaned during the war and later adopted by a surviving Czech-Romani family, sings two Holocaust songs, one with a text I have never encountered elsewhere. Along with another verse or two in Romani, she sings this wartime Slovak-language text to the most anthemic of Czechoslovak Romani melodies, which is usually entitled 'Čhajori romaňi' (Romani Girl) – or, in Czech, 'Cigánský pláč' – the Gypsy lament. Its translation is as follows:

> You Romani women, what have you done
> that you got all your hair cut off?
>
> They cut our hair, they took our men
> They took them and made them work for the Germans
>
> Whenever something happens, they investigate the Gypsy
> They investigate him and whip him to death.

In contrast to this well-hidden Slovak rendition of the very old 'Čhajori romaňi' tune, hundreds of thousands of post-war Czechoslovak and other Roma, including third-generation survivors, have been exposed to one or more of the song's other Holocaust-related variants, usually beginning with the line 'andr'oda taboris' – in that camp.[14] I have selected two examples of the various stanzas that are sung about the camps using this same melody.[15] The first is in Romani and the second is in Slovak.

Example 1

Andr'oda taboris, joj,	In the camp, oh
phares buči kerav.	I do hard work
Ňič na chav, na pijav, joj,	I eat nothing, I drink nothing, oh,
de le trepenca kerav.	I work in misery.

Example 2

Neraz už to býva, hej,	It is not uncommon these days, hey,
že sa Cigán skrýva	that a Gypsy is in hiding
Za čierným lesom	Hiding [in] the black forest, oh,
sa skrýva, jaj,	
veľká bída ide.	great misery is coming.

In contrast to the above widespread melody with its Holocaust-themed variants, fewer Romanies of any generation are familiar with *Aušvicate*, the more elaborate account of concentration camp trauma that has been passed down, incompletely, within my family. The song is, however, a mainstay of cultural representation by activists, many of whom can be counted as part of the third surviving generation. Its text begins with the simple statement 'There is a big house [or building] in Auschwitz' ('Aušvicate hi kher baro' or 'hi baro kher'). The text then muses on the separation of a husband and wife, and goes on to depict some of the harsh realities of camp life. My grandmother most likely learned the song from her sister Zofina, who had survived Auschwitz.[16] I have chosen three published verses as examples:

Ó tu kalo čiriklóro,	Oh you dear black bird,
lidža mange mro lilóro,	take my letter for me,
lidža, lidža mra romňake,	take it, take it to my wife
hoj som phandlo Aušvicate.	[it says] that I'm locked up in Auschwitz
Aušvicate bokha báre,	In Auschwitz there is great hunger,
the so te chal amen náne,	and we don't have food,
ani oda koter máro,	not even a piece of bread,
o blokáris bibachtálo.	[and] the block elder is evil.
Sako ďives amen márel,	Every day, he beats us,
andre búťi amen trádel,	pushes us into work,

the kas kamel, mukel khére,	and whomever he desires to stay inside,
phenel lake: Pášlov téle.	he says to her: Lie down.[17]

One of my respondents spoke of his relationship to the two most common Romani Holocaust songs in the former Czechoslovakia:

> The song *Čhajori romani*, almost everyone knows that one. And because my grandmother is around ninety years old, of course she survived World War II and I know the song *Aušvicate* because, well, she sang it to us as a lullaby or something like that. Or not a lullaby but when she'd be, like, sad, then she'd just sing this type of song ... When I was younger I didn't realize this so much, [but] after I learned about what the Holocaust is, it goes without saying – these days, when she sings the song, or whenever I hear the song, I feel, like, very tense/anxious inside [je mi jako hodně úzko]. I know that for sure, that the mood immediately drops, because I imagine the stories of those people.

If the music of Czech Roma and Sinti is closely linked to the Romani language, and if the language develops in the context of acculturation, then all three – acculturation, language, music – are inseparable from experiences of violence, oppression and marginalization. Third-generation survivors, in the Bohemian/Moravian Romani subgroup especially, are far less likely than their elders to know the songs, or to be capable of translating them from Romanes (Romani). Marie K., a Sinti Holocaust survivor, had much to say on this subject when I visited her in an ethnographic capacity. Her Romani skills are respectable, from what I could judge by our conversations, but the Romanes of the granddaughter she has raised is only skeletal. 'Oh, we knew the language, all right', Mrs K. said bitterly, referring to her youth before and during the war. 'I know Sinti and Czech Romani, too. But what good did it do us? Tell me, what good did it do us?', she demanded. 'That's why we don't teach it to the young ones – it won't do them any good ... it can only get them into trouble.' Her granddaughter, then, is the recipient of a post-war family philosophy that is more common among the decimated Czech Romanies than among the more intact Slovak Roma: being Romani is fundamentally dangerous and thus something to be hidden – an option for those with lighter skin or the ability to dissimulate consistently – or at least downplayed. Terror, rather than any inherent lack of cultural pride, has kept Mrs K. from teaching her granddaughter the family's ancient Indic language. However the young woman feels about her language abilities, fear is a large part of the message she has received.

The anticipation of violence by neo-Nazi groups, in particular, is commonly shared by all Romanies in Central Europe, regardless of their age or level of knowledge about historical fascism. And whereas young Roma collectively have a potential playlist of songs conveying the terror felt by anyone who could potentially be subject to genocide or ethnic cleansing, the right-wing extremists have an even longer playlist of tracks that legitimize murderous or otherwise violent processes. In the Czech Republic, one need look no further than the band Orlík. It is now defunct but was headed by Daniel Landa, a singer of continued mainstream fame, owing to his heavy involvement with high-budget musicals. The band's lyrics include verses such as the following: 'The same blood runs through our veins ... / May our singing keep ringing in your ears / The skinhead is here, the skinhead is everywhere' ('Skinhead'); 'Damn, Jára, and what about those Gypsies / There's problems with them' ('Ty vole, Láďo'); 'A Gypsy with a knife somewhere else / Momentarily succumbed to a girl's beauty / He slit the woman's throat / I can't laugh at that' ('Dvojí metr'). In addition to songs performed by neo-Nazi bands and musicians who openly sympathize with them, two unmistakably anti-Romani texts, referencing skin colour and criminality, have recently been released by the singer Jaromír Nohavica. He is considered the Czech Republic's answer to a figure such as Bob Dylan, and is thus part of the country's widely recognized 'moral' compass.

It is precisely this pervasive acceptance of racialized anti-Gypsy sentiments that forms a feedback loop of increased unease for those, even in the youngest generations, whose family fabric constantly reminds them where hate speech can ultimately lead. It is not only Romani and other darker-skinned or 'foreign' adults (occasionally Jews) who are targeted by skinheads, it is at times small children, and very often teenagers as well. I know several minors who have been attacked, and not all of the perpetrators were official members of any extremist group. Threats of violence can come from people with any affiliation. My own children, from a very young age, have been subjected to treatment during visits to the Czech Republic that would be difficult for a non-European to comprehend. I also have a photo of my then 1-year-old son next to swastikas scrawled onto a playground structure along with an anti-Gypsy slogan. Meanwhile, I am frequently reminded of current dangers by family members who are chronologically much closer than I am to the original context for Nazi insignia.

Here, then, lies the crux of the glaring disconnect felt by current generations of activists and other Romanies on both sides of the Atlantic. On one hand, the continuity of Nazi ideology against 'Gypsies' is increasingly apparent and sometimes impossible to escape (violent paramilitary units in Hungary are perhaps the starkest physical example). On the other hand, the public for the most part still lacks meaningful access to education about the Romani experience in the Holocaust, and about the epistemological misconceptions (such as tremendously exaggerated nomadism) regarding 'Gypsy culture' that continue to seep into public opinion.[18] Third-generation Holocaust survivors and Romani activists in general have therefore coalesced in part around efforts toward greater dignity and accuracy in the representation of genocide. In the Czech Republic, the focal point is Lety, a concentration camp that was populated by Romanies and whose site, mass graves and all, later became dominated by a pig farm. Romani journalist Jarmila Balážová, whose grandparents lived through the Second World War, writes:

> I first went to Lety in 1995 on the day a modest memorial to the victims was unveiled. I remember that it was pouring, and my heels sank so deep into the mud that I could hardly walk. It rained, and the gray atmosphere was unbearably heightened by two facts. The night before, a group of skinheads with baseball bats had burst into the apartment of an unsuspecting Romani family in Zdar nad Sazavou and, before the eyes of his wife and five children, had beaten Tibor Berki to death. The second devastating fact was even nearer at hand and lingers like a stench to this day: the stink of the large pig farm that still stands on the site where there really was a 'Gypsy camp.'[19]

The author's sentiments about the indignity of the pig farm are shared by William Bila, a Slovak-Canadian third-generation survivor of the Romani Holocaust, as well as by the majority of young Czech Roma one might informally poll.

The situation among American Roma is different, as there is no memorial in this country for Romani victims, however modest. Although the US is home to Romani musicians who are able to use references to the Holocaust, or to persecution in general, in their music, there are far fewer Romani Holocaust survivors with permanent American residence than there are in Europe.[20] Efforts at commemoration are thus sparse (although increasingly organized) and not well connected to first-hand testimony. As mentioned earlier, two of the most influential remembrance events have refused to allow regular Romani representation (commemoration produced by the US Holocaust Memorial Museum features no Romanies whatsoever and generally eschews any mention of Romani Holocaust victims, amounting to a form of denialism). However, the organizers of some smaller-scale ceremonies and Holocaust conferences, most consistently in Cambridge, MA, have reached out with an interest in Romani participation that reflects the weight of the wartime experience. In these cases, it is the second- and third-generation survivors – for example, the young Jewish-Romani film-maker and author, Rabbi Galina Trefil – who are called upon to bear witness, in addition to Romani scholars, including Ian Hancock,

Rutgers University sociologist Ethel Brooks (Romani), author Jud Nirenberg (half-Jewish, half-Romani and corresponding in age to the third generation of survivors) and non-Romani researchers such as Krista Hegburg and Michaela Groebbel.

Thanks to the Internet (mailing lists, Facebook groups and international Romani news sites with English translations) the third generation of Romani Holocaust survivors in America has regular access to news of rising and increasingly violent anti-Gypsyism in Europe, as do their activist counterparts who have no personal connection to the genocide. Community discussions therefore often turn to the need to educate the public about the continuities between Nazi practices, neo-Nazi ideologies and structural violence (e.g. police brutality or the segregation of Romani children into schools for those with mental retardation in Central/East Europe). There is an overriding theme of frustration – sometimes mixed with initial incredulity until the Romani person experiences rejection first-hand – stemming from the extreme difficulty of convincing commemoration organizers, college professors and other gatekeepers of Holocaust education that Roma and Sinti should have an active voice in the process. The frustration has become much more urgent in recent years as some American Romanies who were previously content with slow-moving attempts at public self-representation suddenly realize that reality television is moving much more quickly. While schoolchildren and college students continue to learn virtually nothing about Romanies as an ethnic group, programmes such as 'My Big Fat Gypsy Wedding' (which heavily conflates ethnic Romanies with non-Romani Travellers) or 'Gypsy Sisters' are filling in the blanks with some of the worst imaginable caricatures of 'Gypsy lifestyles'.

Romani members of a recent Central European delegation to the United States quickly picked up on this collective disillusionment, referencing their own region's unfulfilled need for the dissemination of socially relevant information about the Nazi legacy. I interviewed two of them – third-generation Holocaust survivors – and they gave something of a trans-Atlantic analysis reflecting a sense of betrayal by those who are charged with Holocaust education:

> I've said in the past that I thank my grandma and grandpa for surviving the Second World War, because they lived through the period in Slovak forests, and part [of my family] – some of my uncles – were resistance fighters and I consider that a big deal. And the paradox is that the Slovak state was a mess, but thanks to that the major part of Roma survived there. And when I was at the [United States Holocaust Memorial] museum just now, it occurred to me what a serious thing it really is, I mean the Romani Holocaust, because while it's nice that

> the Holocaust Museum has a place where a person can find out that it involve[d] Roma, too, the *way* it's done, well, I don't like that, that it's stereotypical and it's a *žebřiňák* [a type of wagon]; it's just – one video, that's not really enough. And in this respect I think that a number of European countries [also] owe a lot to Roma, and they should just do something in this area, definitely, because that's simply [a form of] justice that should come automatically, and it's sad that we have to keep asking for it. It's very sad.

The respondent, David Beňák, refers to an often criticized feature of the museum's small display about Roma and Sinti: rather than providing culturally sensitive information, it is dominated by a large wagon, misleadingly suggesting that the primary characteristic of being Romani is nomadism – a misconception that the vast majority of Americans hold in the first place.

I will quote my interview with the next respondent, David Tišer, at length because it encapsulates not only the activist community's intellectual working out of Holocaust-related issues (including the duality of Jews as sometimes a source of pro-Romani support and sometimes a source of exclusion), but also the emotionally charged musings of many third-generation survivors:

> I was very disappointed, I mean by the museum in Washington [DC], where we have one corner, and of that the largest space is dedicated to a wagon. So – a total catastrophe. And then on top of that when I found out from people at the museum why it's so – because basically it's sponsored by Jews, and so they didn't want other groups to disturb [their space], then I felt even worse. And when I open that up … And another thing is just that our children don't find out about the Romani Holocaust in schools. Or maybe [they do]. Like in my day it was, there was the sentence 'The Roma also went through the Holocaust,' and that was all I found out [from textbooks]. Today, when I look at my sister's history textbook, there's a tiny little paragraph there, so let's hope that in three hundred years there will be maybe one page dedicated to Roma. I'm laughing at it right now, but it's a tragedy. It's as if we didn't exist, as if we weren't [alive], or as if we weren't important, just because we can't finance something – that we don't have the funds, so the issue won't be dealt with. So thank God for those people, Roma and non-Roma, who work on this, who constantly want to inform the public about the fact that Roma went through the Holocaust; that they want to convey to the public the particular stories, and that up until today a few people are alive who survived the Second World War, who are

> engaged, who go into the schools and give their time to the youth. But how it will be when those people are gone, I don't know.

Efforts to be included in widely accessible public commemorations and Holocaust education result in incremental successes, but also in discrimination experienced by members of surviving Romani families and their various allies, particularly in North America. For example, when I wrote to the United States Holocaust Memorial Museum in an attempt to get even a single Romani leader invited to the annual Days of Remembrance – not even as a speaker but as one among hundreds of audience members – the response was decidedly negative. Some time later, thanks to an impressive amount of string-pulling by a government connection, I received a ticket for a standing-room space at the event. This year, finally, more than one Romani person was invited to sit in the audience and, in a small move toward access to the decision-making process, the invitation recipients were allowed to bring one guest each, resulting in a modest Romani delegation. Since efforts to secure a productive, publicly reflected working relationship with the Holocaust Council and Museum staff are now three decades old, it is difficult to estimate when an invitation for a Romani speaker or musician might be extended, or even when Roma and Sinti might be mentioned at all, rather than lumped namelessly into 'others' and rhetorically separated from the Holocaust proper by the event's orators.

In an age of tremendously popular television shows that either lead off-screen 'Gypsies' to hide their ethnic identity or, because of reckless stereotyping, open up American Romani children to some of the bullying they would face in Europe, the Holocaust has taken on new significance in the Romani movement for self-representation. Experiences of exclusion from the public narrative have led to a growing unification of young people, emerging from widely disparate Romani subgroups, who can loosely be defined as activists. Members from the community of Macedonian Roma in New York and New Jersey, for example, are showing an incipient interest in genocide commemoration, in part because some young people are finding previously secret information about Holocaust victims in their own extended families. In another subgroup of American Roma, a member of the third generation of Romani survivors expressed a process of connecting to one's heritage, much as many Jews do, in part through lessons from the Holocaust:

> Up until the age of thirteen [when I learned of my mother's ethnicity], I saw the Holocaust as solely a Jewish experience – sympathizing in whatever way was natural, but not quite understanding what it was like to be in their shoes or be a descendant, and why some descendants seemed 'stuck' on their family's past. Then after learning about my family's ethnicity and Holocaust history, I think about the

> historical event very differently now. It's with a sort of sadness or grief, thinking about what my family members experienced, and that many of them died; and yet also with a sense of triumph – because my family exists and is thriving today. It's like I can look back on the stories and picture family members there at concentration camps, as opposed to the Holocaust being this thing that happened to an 'other'. Knowing that the majority of my ancestors died in the Holocaust, I wonder how different things would have been if we were closer to the extended family.[21]

As the testimony of virtually any Romani Holocaust survivor makes clear, there were no perceptible differences in the suffering of Roma and Sinti during the Holocaust as compared to Jewish victims. Both groups were singled out for their 'racial' background, a motivation that ended up overshadowing any specific grievances against individual Jews or Romanies. A similar dread must therefore necessarily be felt by Jewish or Romani descendants of Holocaust victims and survivors, in particular when confronted with lived, graphic or auditory evidence of how Nazi ideology continues to influence certain societies. When my mother frets that a Czech doctor's recording of my son's ethnicity is akin to 'the Gestapo', she does not expect an imminent raid by members of a fascist regime (although my son did end up mistreated by members of the Czech medical profession because of his skin colour). She is anxious because of an internalized narrative that forever places 'Gypsies' on the lowest rung of the social ladder, whether it is understood by outsiders in terms of 'culture' or, more popularly in Eastern Europe, through the pseudoscientific lens of racialized 'genetics'. As a member of the third generation to be alive despite the Holocaust, in my adolescence I internalized large portions of the self-talk in question, having been taught that 'Gypsiness' is something of a taboo – and not taught more than a few words of Romani until my late teens. I have not always appreciated the logic of the obsession with being on alert at all times in relation to non Roma, but as the years go by, my older family members' analyses of how Romanies are 'kept in their place' ring more and more true.

NOTES

1. Here, 'third surviving generation' refers to individuals corresponding in descent or age to the grandchildren of those whose lives were threatened by the Holocaust.
2. There is a wide discrepancy in the numbers claimed. See, for example, S. Wiesenthal, *Justice Not Vengeance* (New York: Grove Weidenfeld, 1989), p.219; G. Tyrnauer, 'The Fate of the Gypsies During the Holocaust', report to the United States Holocaust Memorial Council, February 1985, cited in O. Linenthal, *Preserving Memory: The Struggle to Create America's Holocaust Museum* (New York and London, Penguin, 1995), p.243; I. Hancock, ' "Uniqueness" of the Victims: Gypsies, Jews, and the Holocaust', *Without Prejudice: The EAFORD International Review of Racial Discrimination*, 1–2 (1988), pp.45–67; and S. Miton, 'Nazi Policies Toward Roma and Sinti, 1933–1945', *Journal of the Gypsy Lore Society*, series 5, 2, 1 (1992), pp.1–18.

3. S. Wiesenthal, cited in I. Hancock, 'Elie Wiesel, Simon Wiesenthal, Romanies and the US Holocaust Memorial Council', at RADOC (Romani Archives and Documentation Center), n.p., http://www.radoc.net/radoc.php?doc=art_e_holocaust_wiesenthal&lang=en&articles=true.
4. United States Holocaust Memorial Museum, "Genocide of European Roma (Gypsies), 1939-1945, http://www.ushmm.org/wlc/en/article.php?ModuleId=10005219. See also Hancock, I."Romani History in Germany and Neighboring Lands: A Chronology to the Holocaust and Beyond. The Romani Archives and Documentation Center, http://radoc.net/radoc.php?doc=art_e_holocaust_chronology&lang=en&articles=true.
4. Linenthal, *Preserving Memory*, pp.240–8, 314–16; Hancock, in personal correspondence to me, has stressed the lack of success of the older activists.
5. Hancock, posted response to the Google group Romano Liloro, 8 December 2006, https://groups.google.com/forum/?fromgroups#!forum/romano_liloro.
6. G. Lewy, *The Nazi Persecution of the Gypsies* (Oxford and New York: Oxford University Press, 2000), p.223. Lewy is known for his denial of the Armenian genocide as well.
7. Event entitled 'The Holocaust by Bullets' in November 2012, featuring Father Patrick Dubois.
8. For example, M. Hubschmannova (ed.), *Po Židoch Cigáni*: *Svědectví Romů ze Slovenska, 1939–1945* [After the Jews, The Gypsies: Witness Accounts of Roma in Slovakia, 1939-45], (Prague: Triáda, 2005).
9. *Co mi doma vyprávěli: Rodinné příběhy Romů z druhé světové války vyprávěné romskými dětmi*, [What They Told Me at Home: Family Stories of Roma from World War Two as Recounted by Romani Children], collection in a series put out by Fenomén holocaust/The Holocaust Phenomenon (Prague: R-Mosty, 2001).
10. Hubschmannova, *Po Židoch Cigáni*. R-Mosty, *Co mi doma vyprávěli.*
11. D. Holý (ed.), *Mudrosloví primáše Jožky Kubíka* [The Wisdom of First Violinist/Ensemble Leader Jožky Kubíka (Prague: Supraphon, 1984).
12. In R-Mosty, *Co mi doma vyprávěli*, p.78.
13. See, for example, D. Holý and C. Nečas, *Žalující píseň: o osudu Romů v nacistických koncerntračních táborech* [Accusatory Song: On the Fate of Roma in Nazi Concentration Camps] (Strážnice: Ústav lidové kultury, 1993), p.121, where it is also mentioned that one version of many was collected in 1950 by the Polish ethnographer Jerzy Ficowski.
14. J. Belišová, *Phurikane Gila* [Old-time Songs] (Bratislava: Občanské Združenie Žudro, 2002), Vol 2, pp.104–05.
15. Various other, sometimes more graphic versions of this and related songs have been collected. See Holý and Nečas, *Žalující píseň*, including the following verse, sung by Polish Roma in a Polish- and Russian-Romani dialect that is notably different from the Czech- and Slovak-Romani dialects (p.98, my translation):

Vligirde men vudarenca,	They dragged us in through the gates
vymekhen men kominenca.	They will let us out through the chimneys
Do lagrostyr na vydžava,	I will never leave this camp
pheńen, pšalem na dykhava.	I will not see my sisters or brothers

16. Holý and Nečas, *Žalující píseň*, p.12.
17. J. Smith, 'The Marginalization of Shadow Minorities (Roma) and its Impact on Opportunities' (unpublished PhD thesis, Purdue University, Indiana, USA, 2008).
18. See http://www.tol.org/client/article/14411-the-lessons-of-lety.html.
19. There are a number of American and Canadian cities in which there are hundreds or thousands of Roma, although the frequently cited number of 'one million American Roma' is a very rough estimate. American Romanies began immigrating centuries ago, with new waves coming after the abolition of Romani slavery in the 19th century within what is now Romania, and more recent sub-populations arriving largely from communist or post-communist Europe. Ian Hancock – the British-American Rom who has been instrumental in the little public recognition the Romani Holocaust receives – has worked with American Romani groups. Certain sub-populations in the US have been documented extensively by Anne Sutherland and Carol Silverman.
20. Email to the author, 2012.

Knowing the Third Generation: Representations of Trauma

RIVA GODFRIED

Before My Time

What I know is that my mother's father, Shlomo, shovelled bodies in the camps. The corpses of those who died in the trains were shovelled out by my grandfather. The heat had made the skin of the dead come off and stick to the bottom of the van, so it had to be scraped off the train floor. I know that my grandfather saved his own life in a death march by making up an excuse. In the death march there were three guards; one at the front, one in the middle and one in the back. If a prisoner sat down and the last guard reached him, he would be shot. My grandfather saw a corn field and thought about escaping. He sat down thinking that from the middle to the last guard, he would have enough time to get up and run away. However, sooner than he expected, there was a gun pointing at him. He said to the guard: 'Man kann doch nicht mit ungeputzten Schuhen laufen' (One cannot walk with unpolished shoes). The guard answered: 'Ach so' (Ah, right).

What I know is that my grandmother, Aliza, went into a Nazi office in Budapest to get identity papers under false pretences. She had braided her blonde hair and made two knots, the German fashion. She spoke to the woman behind the counter in flawless German and told her that she was a Hungarian farm girl who had lost all her family and papers in a bombing. Now she needed new identity papers. The woman at the counter looked at her and said she'd take an oath to say that my grandmother was 'a true Aryan'. I know that my grandmother lived in an orphanage of the Jewish Bond in Budapest until it was bombed to the ground by the Americans. The bomb killed half of the girls and caretakers there; my grandmother was standing on the right side when it hit. I know that she lived in one of the Wallenberg houses, where Jews would be safe. However, one day some older boys told the children in the house to run away if they could, because the Nazis were going to take them away from there as well. My grandmother climbed out of the window. She roamed the streets looking for a place to hide, looking for a house to live in. Doors closed shut on her. I know that she came to a convent, where one of the nuns quickly pulled her inside. She stayed there for the rest of the wartime pretending to be

Catholic. The nuns told her that if she ate the Eucharist without believing it was the body of Christ, she would go to hell. I know she was scared to be discovered. She was also scared that their warning about hell would be true. There were other people hiding there, who were equally afraid of getting caught. As my grandmother was blonde and blue-eyed, they all thought she was a real Christian.

What I know is that my great-grandmother Regina was sent to Auschwitz. I know she hid an illegal paper in the palm of her closed hand, whilst the Nazis searched her house. When they came to get her, she sent my grandmother out through the backdoor to the neighbours. My grandmother Aliza was 13 then. I know that when my great-grandmother came back from Auschwitz, she went to the orphanage in Budapest. Neighbours said that all the girls died in the bombing. She nonetheless kept coming to the same spot every day. She and my grandmother found each other again one day on the ruins where the orphanage had stood. They could not have agreed to meet there at that exact day and time, because neither one even knew whether the other was alive. But both of them were there one day, at the same time. The first thing my grandmother saw my great-grandmother do, was pick up a potato lying on the ground. My great-grandmother Regina said: 'It's such a waste.'

What I know is that my grandmother's current husband Arthur was also in Auschwitz. In a year and a half, they nearly killed his entire family. The prisoners built their barrack in the camp on barren ground. They made their shelter as a wigwam of wooden poles with bunk beds. They slept on wood chips and shared their bed with about ten people. During the day they worked to make a railroad leading to the camp. They dug and placed explosives, going deeper into the ground. I know that one day an explosive hit Arthur's leg. A large open flesh wound was the effect. He was brought to the camp doctor, who said he would be taken to another part of the camp. Then a different doctor came in. Arthur knew him from before the war. This doctor said to him that he should go to work. He told him he needed to get in line for the daily inspection. Even though Arthur was reluctant, the doctor did not take no for an answer. I know that Arthur was carried by two other men to help him remain standing during the inspection. Only later, he heard that the place they would otherwise have sent him to was the crematorium. After being liberated, he received clean water from the Red Cross for the first time. When telling me this, he says: 'Do you know what that is, clean water?' I know that he had horribly swollen feet. He got on a train not sure of its destination. Most of all, he didn't know what to do of his feet. These feet stared at him, his feet, swollen and inhuman like two large fish.

I know my father's mother Kitty worked with the Dutch 'underground' resistance in Amsterdam. She spread secret messages and newspapers. She hid the papers on her belly, pretending to be pregnant. One day she was caught and thrown into prison. She sat there in a cell with other women, mostly prostitutes, who loved her thick long black hair, brushed and braided it with so much pleasure, that my grandmother could not refuse them. After a week of interrogation she was released by a Nazi officer. He was the father of a disabled child that Kitty took care of in day-care. She came home however with a head full of lice. The only way to get rid of them was to either cut her hair or to put petrol into it, which burned horribly on the skin. She chose the latter.

What I know is that my father's aunt Caroline was deported to Sobibor. When they summoned her to a 'work camp somewhere in Eastern Europe', she answered the call even though her former neighbours in Amsterdam had offered to hide her. She did this to make sure that the Nazis would not retaliate for her disappearance by deporting her brother, my grandfather Emanuel. She could not have known what awaited her. She thought her brother would be needed, because he was a doctor. After being fired from a general hospital my grandfather Emanuel worked in an all-Jewish hospital with Jewish patients, and Jewish nurses and doctors. Here he also taught in an 'underground' school for Jewish medicine students. At the hospital one day he was assigned to select patients who were 'fit to travel to Eastern Europe and work there in the camps'. He refused. He realized that the Nazis would deport the Jews anyhow, whether he would report them to be healthy or not. My grandfather went into hiding and spent the next year and a half in a small room without windows. He was not allowed to leave even for a single moment. His sister Caroline never came back. Upon arrival in Sobibor she was sent to the gas chamber.

I know all this. At least I think I do. I am almost sure that I know. Do I really know? The necessity to write these stories forces itself upon me. The stories are perhaps not mine to tell, since I have not lived through them. I am not even sure if all the details are correct. When speaking of truth here, historical occurrence is not the main issue. We are dealing with a different type of history, that of representation of trauma.

The sources of this history are of a personal nature, passed on across generations orally. Astrid Erll argues that these sources form a type of 'generational memory'.[1] The stories are not easily told, nor clearly defined into a narrative. In the introduction of *Recapturing the Past*, Cathy Caruth writes that the experience of trauma denies common modes of access to it.[2] The essays in her book ask: 'How is it possible…to gain access to a traumatic history?' Moral issues arise when we embark on representing traumatic stories. Theodor Adorno sparked the debate, when he wrote in *Prisms*: 'To write poetry after Auschwitz is barbaric.'[3] Fragmentary and short as this sentence may have been, this statement has led (and continues to lead) to many questions. What is this barbaric aspect? Is it barbaric to represent suffering in art forms such as poetry? After being written down, the experience is no longer what it was before; it has been incorporated into an art form. At the very beginning of her book *Auschwitz and After*, Charlotte Delbo says: 'Today I am not sure that what I wrote is true, I am certain it is truthful.'[4] How can we represent trauma while staying 'truthful' to the experience of suffering? When the trauma is represented, there is the issue of understanding. How should the reader who was not there, understand it? In this contribution, I address these questions with a theoretical framework of memory studies. Michael Rothberg's *Traumatic Realism: The Demands of Holocaust Representation* will mainly be used as explanatory material to Adorno's statement.[5] In addition I draw on ideas about traumatic memory from Caruth's introduction of *Recapturing the Past*.[6] An excerpt from a poem by Charlotte Delbo in her autobiographical book *Auschwitz and After* serves as a case study for my analysis.[7] Furthermore, I analyse Primo Levi's poem *'If This is a Man'*, which appeared in his book of the same name.[8] I connect the theoretical background to my family narratives. Finally, I incorporate into the argument my personal experience as a member of the third generation after the Holocaust.

Narrative Memory

The complexity of representing trauma resides paradoxically in the experience itself, in its traumatized nature. As Cathy Caruth states in her introduction, the ability to access and recover the past is tied up in trauma.[9] Caruth continues by saying that because the trauma was never fully understood, it has no place in the 'narrative memory' which is part of a 'completed story' of the past.[10] From the narrative memory, one would be able to form an understandable representation of past events. However, due to the incomprehensibility of traumatic events, their memory cannot be integrated into this representation. The lack of means to understand the experience leads us back to the initial trauma. The cycle seems endless, as the trauma resurfaces to find a place in the narrative memory and fails every time again. Is there no way out of this cycle? Representing trauma forms the crux to the complexity of finding a place for it. Caruth expands on how Claude Lanzmann dealt with this complexity in his documentary *Shoah*. She quotes Lanzmann, who says: 'Not to understand was my iron law during all the eleven years of the production *Shoah*. I had clung to this refusal of understanding as the only possible ethical and at the same time the only possible operative attitude.'[11]

Central to Lanzmann's making the film was the unwillingness to understand. Lanzmann has chosen here for the refusal to understand as a modus operandi. He used it as the only possible ethical position towards his project. It seems as though this was a protective shield, to retain the appropriate distance from the Holocaust survivors he interviewed. Yet, Caruth argues that we can learn something from Lanzmann's refusal to understand. Caruth says: 'It is precisely in the struggle to make sense of this refusal that a truly pedagogical encounter, an encounter that, by breaking with traditional modes of understanding, creates new ways of gaining access to a historical catastrophe for those who witness it from afar.'[12]

Caruth interprets this 'act of refusal' as a way of gaining access to knowledge of 'a historical catastrophe'. The refusal of Lanzmann creates new ways of understanding a past event. There is a 'pedagogical encounter' in the 'struggle to make sense of this refusal'. Refusing to engage in traditional modes of understanding generates new ways of 'access'. It may seem contradictory to gain knowledge by deliberate non-understanding. Yet, precisely through this refusal, some parts of the experience might become intelligible for those who have not had the immediate experience of the event. By refusing to adhere to traditional modes, the experience could be authentically represented. If we draw this idea further, we can look into how this would work for literature. How can literary works break with traditional modes of representation?

Discussing modes of representation, the fragmentary sentence by Adorno quoted earlier comes to mind. As it has often been misunderstood, misquoted and finally rephrased by Adorno himself to concern only lyric poetry, there can be confusion about the meaning of this statement.[13] Rothberg's interpretation can be helpful: 'The barbarian or irrationality of "poetry after Auschwitz" is that against its implicit intentions, it cannot produce knowledge of its own impossible social status ... As a form of ostensibly free individual expression, the mystifying 'semblance of freedom [that] makes reflection upon one's own unfreedom incomparably more difficult.'[14]

According to Rothberg, the barbaric aspect of 'poetry after Auschwitz' lies in its incapability to represent the poet's actual position of 'unfreedom'. The poem takes on the guise of freedom, when in fact it is not free. Adorno belongs to the Marxist school of thought. In line with Marxist theory, poetry has been taken over by culture industry, wherein lies its 'unfreedom'. The mystifying 'semblance of freedom' makes it almost impossible for the poet to be critical. Contemplating about the 'unfreedom' of the writer however does not touch the most painful issue in this sentence. What does Auschwitz have to do with it? To delve deeper into this statement it is fruitful to look into the original context of the sentence. Adorno writes in *Prisms*: 'Cultural criticism finds itself faced with the dialectic of culture and barbarism. To write poetry after Auschwitz is barbaric. And this corrodes even the knowledge of why it has become impossible to write poetry today.'[15]

Opposite to culture stands its negation, which is barbarism. Criticism of culture 'finds itself faced' with 'the dialectic of culture and barbarism.' The demise of culture has even damaged our thinking about this 'impossible' position of poetry. However, Adorno describes this as a 'challenge'.[16] It is not the end of poetry, but more so a call for critical thought. Poetry is a form of critique and a cultural expression. Auschwitz stands on the side of barbarism, at the denial of critical thought. In the wake of this atrocity, poetry is 'caught' in the aftermath of barbarism. It is in the contradiction between poetry as a cultural expression and Auschwitz as the ultimate form of barbarism, that the barbarity of writing poetry after Auschwitz arises.

Yet, this interpretation might grant (capitalist) society too much power and the poet, not enough agency. When representing the trauma of an event there is a risk of continuing the violence in the work. This is in the poet's hands, but also in those of the audience. Rothberg expresses this concern as follows: 'representational art creates the possibility for sadistic identification in members of the audience because it contains a surplus of pleasure'.[17] This would imply a disturbing pitfall for the audience, furthermore, a risk lies in repeating the atrocity in a literary form. A possibility of immorality is then inherent in poetry about atrocity. The representation could continue the violence in an art work. How can we represent horrific events and avoid perpetuating their violence? As Rothberg states, the issue at hand is how to 'remain true to suffering'.[18] He explains that Adorno finds successful examples in the works of Beckett, because of his refusal to write a realistic setting.[19] Through this refusal, the work avoids identification and the possibility of 'surplus of pleasure'. In the absurdist plays of Samuel Beckett, we are taken into a world where the main characters wait, suffer, talk to avoid silence, and fall without reason. In *Waiting for Godot* the interaction between Pozzo and Lucky is exemplary: 'Lucky falls, drops everything and brings down Pozzo with him. They lie helpless among scattered baggage.'[20] We can hardly relate to them, because the setting is not realistic, nor does their suffering sweep us away in a dramatic manner. There is no glorious storyline, only the pains of two men endlessly waiting and helplessly falling into decay.

I feel suddenly insecure and almost fearful about telling the stories of my family. My grandfather Shlomo continues to march through my written words. My grandmother Aliza's fear of the Nazis resurfaces on paper. My great-grandmother Regina is taken away to Auschwitz and Arthur's feet are swollen again in my piece. My grandmother Kitty is taken into prison again in my story. The death of my grandfather's sister Caroline happens again in thought as I write of her. Am I repeating their suffering by retelling the stories? Without being conclusive here, I think it is fruitful to delve deeper into refusal to establish understanding for the audience.

A Nameless Place

The refusal to show a realistic and understandable form might be at the core of representing trauma. As we saw in Caruth's theory, the refusal to use traditional modes of telling is part of creating new ways of understanding. In line with the discussion of Adorno, we can state that countering barbarity is the challenge of poetry on atrocity. If we take this background as a starting point for the question of representation, it is interesting to look further into a specific literary work. Delbo's *Auschwitz and After* is a testimony and a literary work which tries to represent suffering truthfully. Therefore it is fruitful to look closer into her work. I quote here an excerpt of a poem from her book:

> *Untitled*
>
> This dot on the map
> This black spot at the core of Europe
> this red spot
> this spot of fire this spot of soot
> this spot of blood this spot of ashes
> for millions
> a nameless place.
> ...
> Today people know
> have known for several years
> that this dot on the map
> is Auschwitz
> This much they know
> as for the rest
> they think they know.[21]

In this poem, we read about the dot on the map; in geography it is just a dot. However, it is not just a dot, it is a 'black spot at the core of Europe' – meaning, the dark history of Europe. On this spot, blood was shed of millions who did not know where they died. It is a spot of fire and ashes. It was 'a nameless place' for the millions who were deported there. The closing line is directed towards those who were not there: 'Today people know.' This knowing however only applies to the extent of the 'dot on the map.' Everything else 'they think they know'. The relation between the geographical place and the place of the experience of Auschwitz here is intriguing. Perhaps it is not even a placement, but more a 'dis-placement' as Rothberg suggests: 'This placing, or more accurately dis-placing, of the sites of death is not just a metaphorical attempt to evade "the common places" through which those who were not there try to evoke the unimaginable. Rather, for Delbo, Auschwitz is in essence an "un-named", uncommon place, because of the concrete experiences of some of its victims upon arrival.'[22]

From the above we can draw that in Delbo's representation, Auschwitz might be a spot on the map with a name, but the true Auschwitz is the 'nameless place'. As Rothberg states here, there is conscious 'dis-placing' of the location. The Auschwitz of those who were there is not on the map, cannot be found by others, because it consists of personal experiences. Those who know this place by name can never know it as those who were there when it did not have a name. The dot on the map gains a different dimension which cannot be visited or seen. The true space of Auschwitz resides in the experience of its victims.

By refusing to share the experience of place through the understandable framework of a map or a geographical spot, we gain access to a part of traumatic history. We come to understand the impossibility for those who were not there to find the place called Auschwitz. Does the poem adhere to Adorno's preference for absurdist representation? I am not so sure. It refuses to comply with the conventionality of a point on a map and with the thought that those who were not there would be able to understand. However, the imagery of Auschwitz is realistic and the setting is not absurdist. It is palpable in the specificity of the event. We do not find ourselves in a space that could be anywhere; it is the 'dark spot of Europe'. It is a space of experience only really known by those who actually were there.

In this line of thought, I will never know what the trains were like that my grandfather had to face. I do not know how it is to shovel corpses. Nor do I know the place where Arthur slept in Auschwitz. The clean water I drink is not the same as the water he drank after being liberated. I think I have never known what clean water really is. When I visit Budapest, it is not at all the same as the city in which my grandmother Aliza lived during the war. I do not know how it is to roam the streets for shelter; to be hunted down or having to hide my identity in order to survive. I do not know how it is to risk my life to spread secret messages like my grandmother Kitty did. The space of experience of the resistance movement is something I need to imagine, where it resides I do not know. I do not know how it is to lose a sister to murder like my grandfather

Emanuel lost his sister Caroline. Nor do I know the place called Sobibor. The tension in poetry on atrocity lies in knowing and not knowing; understanding and not understanding. Perhaps these oppositions are not necessarily mutually exclusive. We progress by acknowledging exactly this contradiction.

(Un)Knowing

In regard to my family's stories, I am a part of the chain of telling. Imagination comes in to fill the gaps of memories. The stories still have something to do with me; I carry them with me like internal baggage. They became an inevitable part of me and my youth. This baggage is composed of feelings of guilt about luxury and the difficulty of throwing away food. It carries the feeling of necessity to hear Holocaust stories, to feel and show grief about them. Family memories can be categorized as what Erll calls 'intergenerational memory', which is a 'type of collective memory [that] is constituted through social interaction and communication.'[23] It is thus a communicative exchange, where the memory of an experience is transferred unto another generation. Memory in this form is upheld by passing on stories from one generation to the next. Individual and group identity is then formed along generational lines. In the moment of passing memory from one generation to the next, Geoffrey H. Hartman suggests that there is a kind of 'memory-envy' on the part of the later generations. Hartman states in 'Public Memory Discontents': 'Memory-envy also touches a generation that feels belated: the "generation after" which did not participate directly in a great event that determined their parents' and perhaps grandparents' life.'[24]

The word 'memory-envy' does not refer to envy of the actual suffering. Rather it relates to the envy of not having been there, at this 'great event' of significance to their parents. The suffering of the post-war generation, who escaped prosecution and who lost family members, is the suffering of 'not having suffered enough'.[25] This feeling transferred onto the children born after the war and perhaps also to my generation. It is in this chain of telling from one generation to the next, that memory is preserved. The social aspect of memory is also emphasized in Paul Ricoeur's 'Memory – History – Forgetting'. Ricoeur says that 'people do not remember in isolation … [they] preserve their own memories with help from the commemorations and other public celebrations of striking events in the history of their group'.[26] There is thus a public nature to remembrances in order to preserve memories. Telling the stories of memories takes in a central position. In the case of Holocaust memory, there is a feeling of absolute necessity to keep telling these stories.

Why do we have to preserve the memory? Primo Levi writes about this necessity in his introductory poem 'If This Is a Man' appearing in his book of the same name.[27] In his first sentences, Levi calls out to those who have comfortable lives: 'You who live safe, in your warm houses'. Levi asks those people to think about what happened, to consider 'if this is a man', 'who dies because of a yes or a no'. Levi asks to 'consider if this is a woman, without hair and without name'. The arbitrary nature of survival during the Holocaust is expressed here, as well as the anonymity of death in concentration camps. Dehumanization of these victims is brought forward, by the continuing question 'if this is a man'. With a pressing voice Levi urges that 'if this is a man', the stories of what happened should continue to be told. He expresses this urgency saying: 'I commend these words to you.' In the closing lines of the poem, the voice takes on an even more dire tone:

> Repeat them to your children,
> Or may your house fall apart,
> May illness impede you,
> May your children turn their faces from you.[28]

A threatening command speaks through these final lines. If those who have comfort, do not 'repeat' the stories to their children, ill-fate should befall on them. Levi expresses here that this comfort should not be theirs, if they do not consider this suffering. Continuing the remembrance is what the suffering from the Holocaust perhaps most urgently calls out for.

I was a teenager when I said to my mother ironically: 'Could we please not talk about the Holocaust before breakfast?' My mother laughed in her particular way and said 'You're absolutely right.' She agreed to keep the stories until after I had finished my bowl of cornflakes. I was never very talkative before breakfast. However, in this particular moment, a wringing sense of responsibility quickly crept over me. I owed it to everyone in my family to listen. I had to hear these narratives of the past. What if they were forgotten? If they were not told and listened to, they would surely be forgotten. And how would I be able to eat my breakfast then? Before I had finished my cornflakes, I asked my mother to continue with her stories.

I was very young when I first heard about our family history. I do not remember how old I was, but my sister and I were still playing with dolls. My sister told my father when we played that the Barbie dolls were being gassed in their open cabriolet-car. I remember that we actually were in a car and in my mental picture of the moment it was also an open cabriolet-car (which we never had). At that point I did not even know what 'being gassed' was. From my father's reaction I understood soon enough that it was not something to joke about. Some of our family members had died that way, it was horrid and we were not allowed to play-pretend it was happening to the Barbie dolls.

When we had our first history lesson about the Holocaust in primary school, I cried. I was the only one who cried and I remember that I felt the absolute necessity to cry in the public space of the classroom. Everyone would see that this was my heritage; this had happened to my family and concerned me personally. One of my friends told her mother with a mixture of excitement and shock that I had cried in class. The crying seemed perhaps even more shocking than the actual content of the history lesson. It was an event, theatrical in its performance. Yet, somehow a feeling of horror dawned on me in learning that the mass destruction had also been directed towards my family. I felt that someone needed to cry about this. I felt it had to be me.

On a high-school trip to Berlin, I was struck by the same feeling of necessity to display grief when we were at the underground gallery of the 'Memorial to the Murdered Jews of Europe'. I forced myself to look at all the pictures and hear all the stories, identify with the victims' pain and put myself in their position. It could have been me, I was only so lucky to be born in another time. It was so arbitrary that I was born in this present time and not in the time that I would have been hunted down. I felt as if I needed to see and know everything about those people, because they were in some distant or yet not so distant way related to me and my family. If I failed to read one biographical note or look into another file, it was as if I had let them die in anonymity all over again. After an hour or two, when my class mates sat down tired, I still kept on searching for more knowledge. More stories. More. More. What did I miss? Did I see everything? Did I get to know all there is to know? Suddenly, I felt a sickening feeling in my stomach, my head turning dizzy. I would either cry or throw up. I ran to my best friend and cried my eyes out on her lap.

My sister and I still dread the thought of *ktsitsot*, meaning something like 'pastries'. My mother would turn all the leftover food from the week, everything that we did not eat because we did not feel like it, into round flat pastries. For us it was as if she made all the food that we had rejected reappear from the dead in a grey-green form. We were never sure what we would find inside, it could be anything. It was a kind of Frankenstein cooking that we did not appreciate at all. Only later did I realize that this was part of my mother's traumatic inheritance as the second generation after the Holocaust. The fear to throw food away was based on the fear of hunger inherited from her mother and grandmother. This 'inheritance' did not stop with my mother. My sister and I both keep little scraps of food in small bowls in the fridge in case 'we could use it'. In a way, we are still picking up potatoes out of ruins.

Now a student, when I come to my mother's house for the weekend, I know I should polish my shoes beforehand. More often than not, I have to hurry for the train and whilst I bike to the station I look down to my neglected shoes. I sense a foreboding of how she will react. With a concerned and sad face she looks at my shoes as if they are two living beings. She asks me whether I ever take care of them. I say 'Yes, I do' and she half believes me. Before I leave again, the hallway smells of shoe-spray. My boots are standing there polished. I hear her thinking: 'Man kann doch nicht mit ungeputzten Schuhen laufen' (One cannot walk with unpolished shoes).

A phone call with my father before I travel abroad:

> 'Be careful, tell the pilot to fly carefully in the curves will you?'
> 'I will tell him when I see him, OK dad?'

We both chuckle. Implicit in having family you love is the fear of losing them. It is tacit and possible. Death looms in the corner of the street. I know this is true, but I do not want to be afraid to live.

During a master's course on cultural memory, we talk about the Holocaust. Even though I do not feel the necessity to display a type of public grief, I somehow need to add something to the discussion. It is impossible to sit back and just listen to others talk about the Holocaust. Everyone is tiptoeing, afraid to say something wrong. I read Delbo's book, when I am in Israel at my grandmother's house. Her husband picks up the book, turns it around a bit, but does not read one sentence. He does not need to, he has lived through it. I, on the other hand, have to read it. I have nightmares of being hunted down and deported to a camp. When I start writing an essay about the book, I work through the night and notice myself falling asleep while typing, and dreaming while thinking. I am still painstakingly choosing and considering every word, as I want to stay true to the suffering I seek to represent. However, I learn more and more that I know very little; my knowledge is fragmentary and incomplete.

Conclusion

My family's Holocaust stories are intertwined with my own experience. The presence of previous generations retains its strength in our daily routines and thoughts, through the act of retelling. These stories take on form in the feeling of responsibility for those who should not be forgotten, the need to display grief, a search for more knowledge, and the subconscious fear of hunger and of losing a loved one. Intermixed with 'memory-envy' is a sense of pride, that some of my family members have had their great moments where they did the right thing. I see these stories as part of my inheritance. They are stories of suffering and recovery, interwoven with bloodshed and fear of death. Secret messages can be spread. Language can be a saviour. Water is clean after liberation.

We gain more knowledge about traumatic history by acknowledging exactly the incomprehensibility of some of its events. The place of Auschwitz is represented through 'displacement', which cannot be understood by those who haven't been there. The most 'truthful' representation of trauma then consists of personal experiences. The struggle of trying to make sense of what happened is inherent in the continuation of narratives of atrocity. The difficulty of 'poetry after Auschwitz' lies in the contradiction between the cultural character of poetry and the absolute barbarity of Auschwitz. This continues to be a challenge of unrelenting force for those who write about atrocity. Personal narratives counter the threat of anonymity, rather than continue violence. Across generations they are preserved through family stories; they often urgently ask to be retold. The tension between knowing and 'not knowing' their space of experience is part of their complexity. I realize that I know more, about what I do not know at all.

17. Aliza Gor, grandmother of Riva Godfried, Haifa, July 2013, Photograph by Riva Godfried. Copyright/permission granted by Riva Godfried.

NOTES

I dedicate this contribution to my family: to my grandmother Aliza, her husband Arthur, my mother Thalia and father Herman, and my sister Shira. In memory of my grandmother Kitty, my grandfather Emanuel, my great-aunt Caroline, my grandfather Shlomo and my great-grandmother Regina.

1. A. Erll, *Memory in Culture*, translated by Sara B. Young (New York: Palgrave Macmillan, 2011), p.17.
2. C. Caruth, 'Recapturing the Past', introduction to *Trauma Explorations in Memory*, edited by C. Caruth (Baltimore, MD: Johns Hopkins University Press, 1995), pp.151–58.
3. T. Adorno, *Prisms* (Cambridge, MA: MIT Press, 1981; first published 1967), p.34.
4. C. Delbo, *Auschwitz and After*, translated by Rosette Lamont (New Haven, CT, and London: Yale University Press, 1995), p.1.
5. M. Rothberg, *Traumatic Realism: The Demands of Holocaust Representation*, (Minneapolis, MN: Regents of the University of Minnesota, 2000).
6. Caruth, 'Recapturing the Past'.
7. Delbo, *Auschwitz and After*.
8. P. Levi, *If This Is a Man; The Truce* (London: Abacus, 1960), p.17.
9. Caruth, 'Recapturing the Past', p.152.
10. Ibid., p.153.
11. Ibid., p.155.
12. Ibid.
13. Rothberg, *Traumatic Realism*, p.25.
14. Ibid., p.36.
15. Adorno, *Prisms*, p.34.
16. Ibid.
17. Rothberg, *Traumatic Realism*, p.41.
18. Ibid., p.40.
19. Ibid., p.41.
20. S. Beckett, *Waiting for Godot* (London: Faber & Faber, 1965), p.77.
21. Delbo, *Auschwitz and After*, pp.137–8.
22. Rothberg, *Traumatic Realism*, p.151.
23. Erll, *Memory in Culture*, p.17.
24. G. H. Hartman, 'Public Memory and its Discontents', in *The Uses of Literary History*, edited by Marshall Brown (Durham, NC: Duke University Press, 2003), p.90.
25. Hartman, 'Public Memory', p.88.
26. P. Ricoeur, 'Memory – History – Forgetting', in *The Collective Memory Reader*, edited by J. K. Olick, Vered Vinitzky-Seroussi and Daniel Levy (Oxford: Oxford University Press, 2011), p.476.
27. Levi, *If This Is a Man*.
28. Ibid.

Dead Ends

DANNY M. COHEN

Flashes of memories wake me, even though I'm already awake. Like a punch to my stomach, it's the startling recognition that an upsetting event from my adolescence is linked to a blurred moment from my childhood. I hadn't connected these incidents until now and, as soon as I do, I can see their collective significance. As I struggle to make sense of my story, I know that it doesn't belong only to me. My inherited memories of my grandfather, Maurice, are filtered through and framed by fragments told to me by my mother and my uncle. But as I begin to write down my family's Holocaust story, I find myself disconnecting, removing myself, and I create a character – her name is Rachel – who shares my questions and my quest, my beliefs and doubts. Rachel knows the books I once read. She remembers the same violent films and the same familial conversations, the same places, the same horrifying photographs. But she is different. She's not me. And so writing Rachel's story feels easier, safer, than finding the words for my own. Rachel is fiction and her narrative, which overlaps with my realities and fills gaps between my memories, leads me to discover a moment I never experienced, but perhaps once imagined I would.

Stolen bicycles. Stolen uniforms. Throughout her youth, Rachel overheard her mother and uncle relate snippets of a story to their friends. They recited scenes of her grandfather's escape from Nazi-occupied Holland, reduced to family lore, no end, no beginning.

Rachel was sitting on her mother's lap, watching television. 'What were the names of Grandpa's Mummy and Daddy?' Rachel asked.

Rachel's mother shrugged. That she didn't know the names of her own grandparents led to Rachel's mirrored silence, a kind of inherited obstruction, as if such questions had to be swallowed rather than spoken.

Later, when Rachel was much older, she asked again.

'He was born in Amsterdam', Rachel's mother said, thumbing through a television magazine, 'but he never talked about all that. Ask your uncle.'

'No', her uncle said. 'He was born in Antwerp and raised in Holland. In the end, the drink killed him.'

Rachel had just graduated from university and was about to leave for a summer of study and volunteering in Israel. Yet it was the first she had heard of her grandfather's alcoholism; an unexpected divergence from the simple stories her mother and uncle repeated. Rachel's silence indicated her surprise. Her uncle softened his tone.

'He lost everyone.'

With London's suburbs as its backdrop, Rachel remembered her 1980s childhood as a series of afternoons with friends, watching British children's television and collecting stickers of pop singers and Australian soap opera stars. At the weekends, she and her parents visited her uncle and his wife.

At her aunt and uncle's flat, 7-year-old Rachel loved playing with the cats and drinking Dr Pepper. She would sit on the rug in the living room, sipping her fizzy drink through a curly straw, staring up at framed film posters hanging next to pretty black and white photographs.

'Who's that?' Rachel asked.

Her aunt laughed. 'You don't know? That's Elizabeth Taylor. She's Jewish. Just like us.'

In one photograph, the Jewish film star was seated at a microphone. Her aunt's old friend in America, a Hollywood movie director, stood in the background.

One April evening, Rachel's family drove across London to visit her mother's childhood friend. As they travelled through the rain-soaked city, Rachel's mother shared her memories of playing on her street as a child in 1960s Britain and of taking trips to the cinema with her father, Rachel's Grandpa.

Rachel's mother sighed and smiled. 'My friends loved my Dad. You would have loved him, too.'

Thinking of her mother as a young girl gave 9-year-old Rachel the giggles. Rachel adored her mother, so she imagined they would have made the best of friends.

Rachel had never met her grandfather. He had died of a heart attack before her mother was a teenager. Her Grandpa was the kindest man you could ever hope to meet, everyone told her. The hand-me-down memories Rachel had of him included a list of unrelated facts and anecdotes. She knew that he went bald early. She saw photographs of him on his wedding day and with her mother as a baby. She knew how to pronounce his unusual Dutch surname. It was her mother's maiden name. She overheard pieces of his story, whispered at family events, when the adults thought Rachel wasn't listening. Rachel deduced that her grandfather had escaped Nazi-occupied Europe before the rest of his family – all Jewish – had been sent away.

As they arrived at the home of her mother's childhood friend, Rachel's mother was busy uttering her usual clichés. 'We must never forget', she said in a sombre tone. Then she shook her head. 'He lost everyone.'

She said it as if Rachel's grandfather had misplaced his family somewhere just before wandering off in the wrong direction. But Rachel knew that 'lost' meant they'd been murdered.

Nine-year-old Rachel and her parents climbed out of the car and walked up the flower-bordered gravel path. At first, Rachel was nervous about meeting her mother's friend and her daughters. But the hugs and hellos were warm and, within minutes, the children had gone through their lists of favourite television shows, swapping stickers and celebrity gossip. It helped that one of the girls shared her name, and Rachel was pleased when, because she was older, Rachel was given the title 'Rachel-number-one'.

After dinner, Rachel and the girls headed upstairs and settled down in front of the television. Rachel-number-two zapped the remote, landing in the middle of an evening film. The children couldn't look away. With her eyes fixed to the television, Rachel could hear the adults talking in the kitchen. She wanted to call down to them. Her mother needed to see what she was seeing. Rachel didn't know how exactly, but she knew that the film was connected to her grandfather's story of escape. The images on the screen forced her eyes open and her mouth shut.

On the drive home, Rachel could do nothing but replay the film's images in her head.

The *bat chayil* gifts Rachel received from relatives and friends included four Stars of David on silver chains, over £1,000 in cash, and at least two dozen books on Jewish history, humour and culture. On rainy afternoons, Rachel lay on her stomach on the springy carpet, thumbing through them. Always drawn to one coffee-table book, with its glossy dark-blue dustcover, Rachel read again and again its centre pages of maps and texts. And the photographs. Black and white, grainy. Of people in rags or nothing at all. One moment of Rachel's gaze was followed by a quick look away. She turned the pages. Crowds by railcars. Children behind barbwire. Sunken eyes and exposed ribcages. Women. The dead. The nearly dead. Piled on top of one another. Rachel read the captions on each photograph. Words, unfamiliar and frightening, repeated themselves on the pages and in her head. *Extermination. Auschwitz. Gas. Never again. Shoah. Sobibor.*

Six years later, at Manchester University, a meandering search through library books for a project on Holocaust history led Rachel to the writings of Primo Levi and Charlotte Delbo. She watched film after film, both mainstream and obscure. She browsed encyclopaedia entries and attended talks by local Holocaust survivors. Its name both haunting and familiar, she came across an encyclopaedia entry on the Sobibor camp. Rachel read how the Nazis murdered over 150,000 Jews at Sobibor, along with unknown numbers of Roma, Soviet prisoners of war, and Poles. The film she had seen as a young girl, which aired on British television in April 1987, had dramatized the successful revolt of Sobibor prisoners that led the Nazis to dismantle the camp.

Rachel took out books on the rise of Nazism and the development of their murderous policies and methods. She studied the actions against Jews and Roma in the East at the hands of the *Einsatzgruppen*. Rachel learned about Polish Jews ghettoized and starved before deportation. She shook her head at the idea of Western European Jews being sent directly from their comfortable homes in Paris and Amsterdam to the camps. When Rachel read about the mass shooting of Jews in the shtetl of Eishyshock in 1942, which was overseen by a member of the Gestapo by the name of Kopke, she bookmarked a particular passage, partly because the unpronounceable name of a Jewish family reminded Rachel of her grandfather's surname:

> Suddenly there was an order to stop the shooting. Kopke announced over the loudspeaker that all gravediggers with yellow permits could now call out the names of their wives and two of their children … Israel Szczuczynski shouted, 'Shoshana Szczuczynski!' Two naked women jumped out of the grave, his wife and his unmarried sister, both named Shoshana, and both of course bearing the same last name. Kopke told him he could save only one. He chose his wife. Kopke shot the other Shoshana at her brother's feet.[1]

'Why are you reading all this?' Rachel's mother snapped at her during a weekend visit to her parents' home. 'You'll give yourself nightmares.'

Ancient ruins and binge drinking. Learning basic Hebrew with a hangover, followed by waterfall hikes and day trips to air-conditioned museums. Rachel used the money saved from her bat chayil to help fund her gap year to Israel before starting university.

The group's educator went over the itinerary for the following day. 'Tomorrow, Yad Vashem. Get an early night. It'll be a difficult day.'

Rachel couldn't fall asleep. Staring into the darkness of the Jerusalem youth hostel, she remembered being 9 years old, watching that film at the home of her mother's friend.

On the television screen, she recalled, a frightened Jewish boy walked between dried-out orange hedges and through a wooden gate. Women and children stood in lines, naked in the beating sun. Soldiers in black uniforms shouted and the women screamed as a dog mauled a naked boy who tried to run away. Rachel didn't want to watch, but Rachel-number-two, who sat there on the sofa clutching the remote control in silence, didn't change the channel. The frozen picture, before and after the television advertisements, told them that the prison camp was called Sobibor.

After graduating from university, Rachel secured a summer internship in Jerusalem. While packing for the trip, Rachel and her mother sat on the floor of the living room, sorting through old clothes and piles of university files and coursebooks.

Her mother sighed and she tucked Rachel's hair behind her ear, as if Rachel was still a little girl. 'You're all grown up.'

Rachel looked down at the book in her hands, the book containing the account of the women with the same name from the Eishyshock shtetl.

'Did you ever read this?' Rachel asked her mother.

Rachel's mother stood up. 'I'd rather make us some tea.'

Rachel felt a sense of relief. It was better that her mother was uninterested – her mother couldn't bear to hear such stories.

Rachel didn't open the book again until she was alone in her bedroom. Sitting on her bed, she read the story of Shoshana and Shoshana Szczuczynski once again. She gasped when she saw an image at the top of the page. She had read the story of the Szczuczynski sisters-in-law many times, but until this moment she had never noticed the black-and-white photograph accompanying the story. Two women in short-sleeved dresses stood smiling on the front steps of what looked like their home. Reading the caption made Rachel feel as if she had been slapped across the face: '*The two sisters-in-law* named Shoshana Szczuczynski ... In the inscription on the back of the photo is written in Hebrew, "Shoshana with Shoshana, can you tell us apart?" Israel and his wife were murdered in the forest on June 16, 1943, by local collaborators, Lithuanians, Byelorussians, Ukrainians, and Poles.'[2] Rachel remembered her first trip to Yad Vashem.

When she was 8 years old, her parents took Rachel on a fortnight's holiday to Tel Aviv. While her father spent most of his time at the beach, Rachel and her mother explored the city and surrounding towns. Rachel's mother let her daughter take the lead. Hand-in-hand, Rachel led her mother through Tel Aviv's colourful streets and jewellery markets. They climbed Jaffa's ancient steps and bought Rachel's father a new baseball cap. And they arranged day trips to Netanya and Jerusalem.

'My Dad worked in the diamond trade', her mother told their Netanya guide.

Walking toward the Western Wall, Rachel listened to her father's familiar story of how her parents met. At a café in the centre of London in the 1970s, her father, a Sephardi Jew in his late twenties, flirted with an 18-year-old Ashkenazi girl with a Cockney accent. Rachel's family on her father's side was made up of Jews from Iran and Iraq. Rachel's maternal grandparents had moved from Poland to Britain after the First World War. Her grandfather, who had died many years earlier, was from Holland.

Rachel wanted to know more about her Grandpa, but she wasn't sure what questions to ask.

Later that day, at Yad Vashem, 8-year-old Rachel walked through a candlelit room, the names and ages of Jewish children ringing in her ears. In the main exhibition, she looked up at colourless photographs. Women and children stood naked, crying, covering their breasts and genitals with their hands, the camera keeping them in a frozen scream.

'We should leave', Rachel's father said.

They didn't see the rest of the museum.

Her parents didn't realize that Rachel had seen those same images before.

With film posters and photographs of Hollywood stars lining the walls, Rachel, aged seven, sat in her aunt and uncle's flat, sipping Dr Pepper, a cat curled up in her lap. They were watching the Hollywood documentary her aunt's American friend had directed.

'It won an Academy Award', Rachel's aunt said, proudly.[3]

But when Elizabeth Taylor began to narrate images of naked women standing in front of mass graves, her uncle switched the television off.

'When you're older.'

Rachel stood, aged 19 and independent, at Yad Vashem. The official tour had just ended.

'You have an hour to look around', the educator said.

The crowd of young adults split into smaller groups. Most of them headed to the Children's Memorial. Rachel had been there before, a pitch-black room containing candles reflected by mirrors an infinite number of times while a tape-recorded voice read aloud the names of murdered Jewish children. Her friends ran off, almost excitedly, as if they were daring each other not to cry.

Rachel wandered around the Yad Vashem complex, playing her own game of dare. On a map of the grounds, she found the museum's resource centre. Standing outside the centre's doors, Rachel hesitated. Almost every part of her wanted to walk inside, to search through books for her grandfather's family. Instead, she walked away.

Not once did Rachel's mother or uncle refer to her grandfather as a Holocaust survivor. Survivors had been in the camps. They had tattoos on their arms and horrific stories on their lips. Rachel's grandfather had escaped Amsterdam before the round-ups. 'On that stolen bicycle.' 'In that stolen uniform.' 'He escaped the gas chambers.' 'He escaped the camps.' And so he escaped the label of 'survivor'. Details of his story had been distorted and remembered by his children in different ways. Rachel's mother and uncle argued about it. 'He escaped in 1942.' 'No, it was '43.' But they agreed about one thing: he never talked about his murdered family – his grandparents, his parents. Nobody knew if he had siblings, or cousins, or nephews and nieces, or aunts and uncles. A learned familial legend, unexplained.

Each book Rachel read again and again, each piece of film, every museum exhibition, each photograph seeped into the gaps between those disjointed, unreliable memories. But most of the time, when her mother and uncle talked about him, her grandfather's story began in England, in the middle of his life, as he if had no youth, no sense of who he was before 1945, no girlfriends, no ambitions. There were certainly no photographs. He met Rachel's grandmother in London. 'In the last month of the war.' 'He was 26 when they met.' 'No, he was 25.' When it came to the year of his birth, nobody could be certain. After he married Rachel's grandmother, he worked in the diamond business, cutting jewels in Hatton Garden. He ate fried sausages and eggs every morning. He listened to opera. He died at home aged 52. 'No, he was 53.'

Now a young woman, Rachel walked through the doors of the resource centre at Yad Vashem. Her heart racing, she was ready to search the records for her grandfather's family – her family.

The woman behind the reception desk laughed, 'You'll never find them.' Finding information about Rachel's murdered family would be unlikely, the woman warned, as if trying to prepare Rachel for disappointment.

Rachel felt stupid for asking. Clearly, she wasn't the first person to ask for help in finding 'lost' or murdered relatives. Ignoring the woman's sarcasm, Rachel unfolded her arms and waited for the woman to become more helpful.

'Unless they were from the Netherlands', the woman said.

'Yes, they were Dutch.'

'Still, you won't find them', the woman laughed again. She paused. 'Unless they had an unusual last name.'

Perfectly, Rachel pronounced her grandfather's four-syllable tongue-twisting surname. The woman laughed a different kind of laugh and led Rachel to the books of the dead.

'Who – how did these names come to be here?' Rachel asked. 'In these books.'

The woman cleared her throat. 'Nazi lists, mostly. The Germans kept excellent records on the Dutch Jews.'

Unlike the Jews of Eishyshock, Rachel thought.

The dead were arranged in alphabetical order over several volumes, although Rachel knew that was not the order in which the Nazis had murdered them. Rachel searched through the volume most likely to contain her grandfather's family name. She handled each page as if it could dissolve between her fingers. The book was a graveyard, each name a headstone, arranged one after the other. Birthdays, places of residence, dates of deportation to specific Nazi camps, dates of murder. No photographs. Black ink on thick paper. For a moment, Rachel held her breath as she found the names of men and women who shared the surname of her Grandpa. She wanted to close the book, to tell the woman that she was right to laugh. But Rachel's eyes continued to scan the entries. The laughing woman was quiet now, watching Rachel read the names of the people she had found. Each person had been deported from Amsterdam and other Dutch cities and towns. Each person had been murdered at either Auschwitz-Birkenau or Sobibor.

Words escaped Rachel's mouth without any thought. 'I need a copy.'

The woman carried the heavy book across the room. She held the volume as if cradling an infant. As the photocopier glowed and whirred, Rachel wondered how her mother and uncle would respond to her discovery. Would they recognize any of the names? Might this new information trigger rusted memories of her grandfather's past? The woman who laughed didn't wait for a thank you – she nodded her head and walked away.

The machine spat out the two pages Rachel had requested. On warm paper, the printed list of names and dates. Either these men and women were strangers – someone else's family, Rachel thought – or they belonged to the memories drowned in her grandfather's whisky.

Days later, at the airport, tired and waiting patiently for her flight back to London, Rachel found herself reaching into her bag and pulling out the list of names. Half way down the first printed page, she saw a name that she hadn't noticed earlier, a name followed by her grandfather's unusual surname. *Rachel*. A maiden name was listed, too; this woman – another Rachel – had married into the family. Rachel. Born in Amsterdam in 1921. Precise dates. Of Rachel's birth. Of Rachel's deportation. Of Rachel's death. Rachel. Again and again, she scanned her eyes across the entry. Rachel. Murdered at Sobibor in 1943. Rachel. She was 22.

NOTES

With acknowledgement and my sincere thanks to Bernard Cherkasov, Elizabeth Lassner and Phyllis Lassner.

1. The account of Shoshana, Shoshana and Israel Szczuczynski is told in the book by Yaffa Eliach, *There Once Was A World: A 900-Year Chronicle of The Shtetl of Eishyshok* (Boston, New York, Toronto and London: Little, Brown, 1998). The Szczuczynski story and the photograph of Shoshana and Shoshana appear on page 604.
2. Ibid.
3. Elizabeth Taylor and Orson Welles narrated the film *Genocide*, directed by Arnold Schwartzman. Produced by Moriah Films, the film won an Academy Award for Best Documentary Feature in 1981.

The Third Generation and the Responsibility to Remember

DAVID SLUCKI

> *Gedenk di zeks milyon vos zaynen umgekumen al-kidush hashem.*
> Remember the six million who died sanctifying the name of God.
> (Invocation at the annual Warsaw Ghetto Uprising Commemoration of the Jewish Labor Bund in Melbourne)

The most important ritual in my life has been the Warsaw Ghetto Uprising commemoration (*geto akademye* in Yiddish), held annually on 19 April.[1] The *akademyes* are the centrepieces of Holocaust remembrance in the small Bundist community in which I was raised, and 19 April the single most important date on its calendar. The commemoration was our opportunity to reflect, to remember, to weep, and to mourn for family we had not met and those that we were denied. The Jewish Labor Bund in Melbourne is the last remaining vestige of a once influential political, social and cultural movement in Jewish Eastern Europe.[2] Centred in Poland immediately before the war, the Bund was decimated by the Holocaust, and so the Holocaust became a pivotal – perhaps *the* pivotal – episode in its historical narrative. For its followers, almost exclusively Polish-Jewish refugees and their descendants, the Holocaust was the defining event in their lives and their family history.

The Bund's Holocaust commemoration always played to a script: survivors or their grandchildren would light candles, speeches from a survivor and a representative from the Bund's youth movement, SKIF, would follow; and then there would be an artistic programme, including Yiddish poems and Yiddish songs performed by members of SKIF and an ad hoc SKIF choir.[3] It was through these yearly performances that we were reminded over and over of our responsibility to carry on our grandparents' legacies, to ensure the Holocaust would never be forgotten. These commemorations were a critical tool in inculcating the next generation with a sense of the magnitude of the Holocaust, of what was lost, and what was at stake. In the preparation, rehearsal and presentation, we, the young members of SKIF, were constantly reminded of our duty to counteract the dangers of Holocaust deniers such as David Irving.[4] Through these rituals, we were taught about the events of the Holocaust, but even more importantly about our own responsibilities as Jews in the late twentieth century. From the age of around 7, I began to participate in the *akademye*, usually reading a Yiddish poem and singing with the choir of the Bund's youth movement. When I was 16, I began co-convening the evening, which I did several times until I was in my mid-twenties.

The date itself was set immediately after the war, as Bundists took part in a global discussion over the most appropriate date on which to honour the memory of the victims of the Holocaust and, even more so, of the heroism of partisans.[5] The date was as important as the commemoration itself. Some years, when 19 April fell on one of the Seder nights of Passover, a fierce debate would ensue over how to deal with the schedule clash. Should we move it to a day later (impossible – 20 April was Hitler's birthday) or a day earlier? For many, the very idea of moving the commemoration was a desecration. After all, the brave souls who fought in the Warsaw Ghetto did so on Seder night. Usually, a compromise was worked out where the *akademye* would take place in the late afternoon, before the Seder. Those discussions were always very heated, with members split between moving the event to allow for greater inclusion, and those who maintained the holiness of the date. This debate typified the way that remembering the Holocaust was imagined as a sacred, almost religious duty. The date could not be moved; to do so was nothing less than a desecration, an abomination. Here, my father and I often disagreed: I felt it important to be flexible to ensure greater inclusivity; he was steadfast that '19 April is a *heylige date* [a holy date]'.

That 19 April was a holy date was just the tip of the iceberg. During my years as convenor of the commemoration, I began to think deeply about the challenge that my parents' generation posed: how would we remember the Holocaust into the future? How would we, leaders of a Jewish children's movement, teach our youth about the Holocaust and its meaning, its gravity and its centrality? Having been inculcated with the idea that it was my generation's responsibility to ensure the perpetuation of the memory of the Holocaust, I was very preoccupied with the idea that the commemoration needed to reflect the changing demographic nature of the Jewish community. I tried to compile a programme that would speak to young Jews in their own vernacular. Eyebrows were raised when I included a dance to a hip-hop song (we changed the song at the last minute to something considered more conventional, a solo piano rendition of Mordechai Gebirtig's stirring *Es Brent* [Our Town is Burning]); even more so the last time I wrote the script in 2010 and included readings and poems describing genocides and atrocities in Cambodia, Rwanda and Australia. These were eventually removed. If we were going to teach young Jews about the significance of remembering the Holocaust, I argued to the Bund's committee, then our constant incantation of the mantra 'Never Again' needed to be more than an empty statement. But to include that material alongside the traditional Yiddish poems was seen by some as a bridge too far.

It was a speech I gave that year though that sparked the Bund to organize a public forum several months later to discuss the most 'appropriate' or 'respectful' way of commemorating the Holocaust. That year, 19 April coincided with Yom Ha'atzmaut, when thousands of Melbourne's Jews were gathered across town to celebrate the establishment of the State of Israel. It was also the first *akademye* since the death of the Polish Bundist Marek Edelman, an outspoken opponent of Polish communism who had been a commander in the Warsaw Ghetto Uprising. In this context, my speech challenged the audience to think about the ethical implications of carrying the survivors' legacy. I asked the audience: what did it mean to be Jews in the post-Holocaust world? How do we come to terms with the changing place of Jews, the majority of whom now live in western countries? The question I raised that was seen to be most controversial, though, was about the meaning and nature of Jewish political and military power in the wake of the Holocaust. I asked: what were the responsibilities of a Jewish state towards its own minorities, after millennia of Jews living as a minority? This question was particularly pertinent, given that it was also Yom Ha'atzmaut that evening.[6] There was a distinct air of discomfort in the room, and I received a hostile response in the aftermath. The Bund committee received complaints from members and non-members, and I received emails, mainly from those in the second generation, complaining about my lack of propriety in raising 'political' issues, and of impacting negatively on the reputation of other Yiddish institutions. I was accused of 'generat[ing] anger and division' rather than 'helping to bring our community together to pay respect to the 6 million'.[7]

The communal discussion that followed the last *geto akademye* in which I was involved was an opportunity for the Bund's members to discuss the role of commemoration in our lives and in our community. What transpired was an overwhelming feeling that Holocaust memorialization was not to be tampered with, or experimented with; that *geto akademye* was a certain set of known rituals, providing comfort for the audience of survivors, their children and grandchildren. Remembering the Holocaust was not 'political' or 'academic', but was 'emotional', above politics or intellectual engagement, purer. I was accused of having tainted the sanctity of the date.[8] I was told that commemorating was 'simple', that the 19 April ceremony was like standing at the grave of those who do not have graves. I was told that I had been disrespectful to survivors and victims alike.

This was the first time that I had realized how the Holocaust has taken on a kind of religious function for those around me. Its centrality to Melbourne's Jews had always been something of which I was aware, having been surrounded by so many who were so profoundly physically and mentally scarred by their experiences. But the religious overtones of those who claimed that commemorating the Holocaust should follow a set ritual, that it was akin to a funeral (and all the religious implications that had), was truly confronting for me in the role that had been handed to me and every member of my generation: that of assuming memories that would, within a decade or two, be primarily carried by us.

This was a challenge for me: the *geto akademye* was an event that had been non-negotiable for me for nearly two-and-a-half decades. Now, I was told that I was disrespecting it, that I must follow certain conventions of remembrance, certain rituals, as though a Holocaust commemoration was as tightly regulated as a Kol Nidre service. Although I, a member of the third generation, was being forever reminded about my obligation to remember and to transmit the memories and stories of my grandparents, I, along with my generation, was not being entrusted to do so, except within the narrow parameters set by the second generation. How, then, to make sense of the vexed question of how to memorialize the dead, and honour the still living, whilst carrying on the legacy that we have been constantly reminded is ours? Who decides what form Holocaust memorialization should take? Who

18. David Slucki's father, Charles Slucki, as a teenager with his father, Yakub Slucki, in the mid-1960s, about a decade before Yakub passed away. David Slucki's father keeps this photo in his wallet. With the permission of Charles Slucki.

decides what the lessons of the Holocaust are, or if indeed there are lessons? How could I continue to participate in a ritual from which I had begun to feel disconnected? Could remembering the Holocaust be as simple as singing a few Yiddish songs and reciting a few poems, and maybe shedding a few tears as we sang the *Partizaner Hymn* together?

My father, *Shmulik* in Yiddish, was named after either his grandfather, who died in 1916 in Warsaw, or his father's 12-year-old son who was murdered, probably at Chelmno.[9] It almost doesn't matter now which of them he was named after; that he has carried the name of his dead half-brother his whole life has meant that he has always lived with a sense of absence and, stemming from that, a sense of responsibility. It must also inform his own understanding of the Holocaust, even though it's not something he talks about often. He has often said to me that for him, 19 April is 'a *heylige date*. It is my Yom Kippur.' The narrative of the Warsaw Ghetto Uprising has become a pivotal episode in how Jews remember the Holocaust.[10] With our roots in Warsaw, I think that the Uprising has been particularly important in our family, even though we don't have relatives who participated, although my father has always told me that an aunt of his lived before the war at Mila 18, the famed headquarters of the Jewish Fighting Organization. It seems almost natural, then, that the Bund's annual Warsaw Ghetto Uprising commemoration would be the sacred ritual through which we mourned. This sanctification of the Holocaust, replete with the language of holiness and martyrdom, has shaped my own understanding of the Holocaust throughout my life, even if I wasn't consciously aware.

I didn't appreciate the meaning of all this until I recently came across a 1987 article from the Israeli philosopher Adi Ophir, who wrote an explosive critique of what he described as the sacralization of the Holocaust. In his treatise, which appeared in an early issue of the progressive American Jewish magazine *Tikkun*, he identified four 'commandments' which had come to dominate Holocaust discourse in Israel particularly, but which were applicable more broadly.[11] These commandments formed a new 'religious consciousness built around the Holocaust'. They were: 'Thou shalt have no other holocaust before the Holocaust of the Jews of Europe; Thou shalt not make unto thee any graven image or any likeness; Thou shalt not take the name of the Holocaust in vain; Remember.' This last commandment, Ophir argued, is the most important:

> [It is] the burden whose shirking is the archetype of sin. Not only the organized drive to forget, but also the innocent forgetting, the result of assimilation or simple lack of interest in the remnants of the Jewish possessions which a person carries with him or herself is an act of terrible renunciation. Those who cause forgetting, to say nothing of

> those who deny, cooperate with the enemy. Those who assimilate complete the Nazis' work. (pp.62-3)

Ophir warned against the danger of enforcing these commandments, which, he claimed, sought to 'establish the boundaries of Jewish legitimacy; they establish the Holocaust as a transcendent event which precedes and qualifies any attempt to fashion a modern Jewish identity'.[12] The commandments also reinforced the impossibility of representing and understanding the Holocaust, and warned against drawing parallels with the Holocaust. The greatest danger in all this, according to Ophir, was the way that such rules had the reverse effect of what they intended to do: instead of preserving the memory of victims and learning important lessons, sanctification only 'blurs the humanness of the Holocaust', and encourages us to be preoccupied with the past without understanding its implications for the future. Sanctification insists on the Holocaust as specifically a Jewish tragedy, when, as Ophir forcefully claims, it is much more than that. These commandments, enforced and reinforced by many Jewish historians, politicians and educators worldwide, still dominate Holocaust discourse today.[13]

When I first came across this article while researching a piece on the use of Holocaust tropes in popular culture, I recognized each of Ophir's commandments. This sense of piety, of the Holocaust as outside history, has been a constant in my life as a Jew growing up in Melbourne, and had only been reinforced as I tried to fulfil my responsibilities to remember. Although my grandparents, all four of whom lived out the war years in the Soviet Union, probably did not consider themselves to be survivors, we nonetheless always carried an almost sacred burden to remember, given what they had lost. The absence that for them was always present became central to us. My connection to the Holocaust was fostered not only through them, however, but also through my parents, my youth movement, and my community more broadly. In each of these settings – family, school, community – the mandate to remember the Holocaust, and to do so in a prescribed manner, has been a constant.

For Melbourne Jewry, the Holocaust remains a crucial part of the collective foundational narrative. Melbourne, more than most other locations, was profoundly shaped by the influx of European, and particularly Polish, Jews in the post-war decades. Many of these migrants had survived Nazi-occupied Europe; many had escaped to the Soviet Union in the early months of the war. We hear often (although I'm not sure about the veracity of this claim – I've heard similar claims of Skokie and Montreal) that Melbourne has the highest per capita Holocaust survivor population outside Israel. The Holocaust forms part of the curriculum in Jewish schools.[14] These schools have their own commemorative events and their students – at least when I was growing up – formed a combined schools choir that performed at the annual community commemoration. Some youth movements also emphasize the importance of Holocaust remembrance, so that children as young as 8 begin to be taught not only about the history of the Holocaust, but about our responsibility to ensure that it continues to be remembered beyond the lives of survivors. The Jewish Holocaust Museum, established in 1984, is a central communal institution, the leading arbiter of Holocaust memory in Australia, through which thousands of Jewish and non-Jewish schools connect to the Holocaust. The commemorative events are many – whether the large community commemoration, or the smaller ceremonies that take place at *landsmanshaft* memorials in cemeteries.[15] The Holocaust is also regularly instrumentalized by communal leaders and institutions for a variety of purposes: in defence of the State of Israel; in emphasizing the ongoing dangers of anti-Semitism; to try to ensure that future generations of Jews don't marry non-Jews. At the same time, those community leaders warn against it being exploited by others, such as those who compare the Holocaust to contemporary genocides, or those who draw analogies between Israel and Nazi Germany.[16]

For a young Jew, then, growing up in a Yiddish-speaking, socialist family, in a Jewish community that was deeply marked by the Holocaust, this sense of the Holocaust as holy penetrated deeply into my psyche. I was intellectually, spiritually and physically surrounded by Holocaust memories. For me, the story of my relationship with the Holocaust is not one of absence, but of an overwhelming presence. There was never any doubt about its meaning, nor about my role in inheriting and passing on the stories. That is not to say that the Holocaust consumed me all day, every day, but it was an important part of the landscape of my childhood. It shaped my family in ways I wouldn't understand until I was an adult, but which were profound: my grandmother's constant fear of us travelling, knowing that when she left her family in 1939 she would never see them again; the closeness of even distant cousins, a relic of the fact that my father's mother survived only because her own father insisted that the family must stay together at all costs (he literally dragged her by her pigtails so that she would escape Stary Sącz with them); our seemingly genetic predisposition to the telephone, a way to constantly keep tabs on one another, as they had to do in Siberia. These are all psychological scars of wartime, yet to heal, and passed on to future generations. Not only my immediate family, but my uncles, aunts, cousins, even those who were 'like family', shared these foundational narratives, and the curious habits that stemmed from them.

I can't now remember when I first learned that my father's father lost his wife and two sons in a death camp, or that my maternal grandmother was the only one left in the Minc family of Warsaw. I don't remember when I could first sing the *Partizaner Hymn*, the Yiddish anthem of the Partisans in the Vilna ghetto, by heart. Nor do I remember when I became desensitized to images of the Warsaw Ghetto, or of the concentration camps.

I do remember the annual Holocaust commemorations at my Yiddish day school, founded by Bundists in 1975, with the blackened windows in the assembly hall, the large scale maps of wartime Europe, and the oversized images of the Warsaw Ghetto and its inhabitants. I remember the survivors, accompanied by their grandchildren lighting six candles, one for each million. I remember in my pre-teen years hoping that I too might one day accompany my grandparents on stage to light the candles, not then understanding that because they survived in the Soviet Union, they weren't considered by the local community to be Holocaust survivors. I remember the survivors telling us – students, members of a youth movement – their remarkable tales of how they lived through the ghettos and camps. I remember those Holocaust memorial days on SKIF camp – *khurbn tog*, as they would come to be known – when the leaders would run activities simulating death marches and the trains to Auschwitz. I remember the six permanent candles at the Kadimah, Melbourne's Yiddish cultural centre, which, in our family's visual record, have been immortalized as part of the background for our bar mitzvah portraits.

I also remember my grandmothers' amazing stories of survival in Siberia and in the Ural Mountains and Uzbekistan; their ingenuity and resourcefulness as teenagers that helped family and friends survive the harsh Russian winters. I remember the stories of my father's father, who died six years before I was born, leading the Jews from his Siberian deportee settlement in Minor, just outside Yakutsk, on the long journey back to Poland, where they all discovered they had lost everything: their homes, their communities, their families. The Holocaust has always been present, prominent, in my life. In my Jewish primary school, in my socialist Jewish youth movement, within my family, in the community sphere more broadly, the Holocaust was not something from which I, or my peers, were shielded. That we should remember it, that it is a central event in Jewish history, has never been anything we dared to question.

The question of how to carry and transmit the memories of our grandparents and their contemporaries – both the living and the dead – has not, however, been so simple. The third generation relates to the Holocaust very differently to our parents' generation. Our understanding of its significance is shaped by different historical factors, and mediated by our parents' relationship with their parents, by our relationship with our grandparents, and by a world in which Holocaust memory proliferates more widely than ever.

So, can 19 April be moved? Can it be rethought to become more inclusive? Can it be used to reflect on the broader significance of the Holocaust in contemporary society? Is there space to remember different victims of Nazism, or to commemorate victims of other genocides? Is there space for more contemporary artistic expression? How can we commemorate the Holocaust in a way that is meaningful for all generations, and is not confined to a routine established by survivors and expanded upon by their children?

These are questions that I'm still navigating. What I do know is that there is nothing simple about how we remember the Holocaust or what we remember of it. I am more than ever convinced, though, that to reduce Holocaust remembrance to a static, religious ritual, to pronounce its sanctity, will only obscure the memories of those who perished and those who lived. Members of the third generation face a difficult task as inheritors of their grandparents' and their parents' memories. Whether in a family setting or a communal setting, we are continually reminded of the responsibility we carry, yet it is never clear what it means to carry on this responsibility, or what that looks like. Perhaps there is no answer, and we simply need to improvise as our parents did, and as their parents, the survivors, did before them.

A Postscript

In between drafts of this chapter I attended the 2014 communal Holocaust commemoration in Charleston, South Carolina, where I had been living for nearly a year teaching Jewish studies at the historic College of Charleston. Charleston is a city of some 6,000 Jews, with a rich Jewish history.[17] It is considered the birthplace of American Reform Judaism and, as a major port, was an important Jewish centre in the early years of the nineteenth century; since the Civil War, however, it has remained peripheral to American Jewish life.[18] In the aftermath of the war, no more than a couple of dozen survivors settled in Charleston, although they have been active in promoting Holocaust education and the founding of an award-winning Holocaust memorial in a central city square.

I went to the annual Yom HaShoah commemoration because as a grandson of survivors, as a historian, and as someone who has been a participant and organizer of Holocaust remembrance rituals for most of my life, I was curious to see how a small Jewish community commemorated the Holocaust. Perhaps the most significant reason I felt I had to go was the voice of my father in my head telling me that 19 April is a *heylige date*. Although the Charleston memorial correlates with Yom HaShoah, rather than 19 April, the correlation was clear: it was my obligation to participate in such rituals.

The ceremony included familiar aspects, such as lighting memorial candles, a survivor telling his story, and an artistic performance from a local Jewish choir, more noteworthy, to me at least, were those aspects of the commemoration that were unfamiliar. For one, the ceremony took place in the local Reform temple, a site chosen, I was told, because of its proximity to the local Holocaust memorial. I was much more accustomed to attending theatres, auditoriums or even Holocaust museums, but this site seemed to lend the ritual more religious or spiritual significance. This was probably at the heart of what made the event so foreign to me: that the ceremony was dependent on religious Jewish rituals and vernacular for making sense of the Holocaust. Apart from the venue, three of the city's five rabbis and a local cantor played a central role in proceedings, dividing between them the introductory and concluding remarks, recitation of Kaddish as well as a prayer for the six million, and the recitation of the funeral prayer *El Male Rachamim*. It was the rabbis who bookended the event, not only responsible for the formal religious components, but also for framing the remembrance ritual. Instead of the kind of sanctification I was used to, in which religious significance was imposed upon cultural and secular representations (poetry, songs, narratives), here, participants and organizers redirected existing Jewish symbols and rituals towards commemorating the Holocaust. This isn't novel, certainly, but in contrast to the annual re-enactment of a Bundist version of Holocaust commemorative rituals to which I was accustomed, it was as though another event were being remembered. In my experience, the Holocaust had itself become a kind of stand-in for religion; now, however, the boundaries were being blurred in a very different way.

Another new ritual to me was that at the beginning of the ceremony, local descendants of survivors read the names of their family members who perished during the war. This was perhaps the lengthiest portion of the ceremony and, at times, the most moving. Any Charleston resident who lost family during the war was invited to come up on stage with their families and read out the names of those family members who perished, before lighting a candle (I didn't participate). Simultaneously, a slide show ticked over with the names. The thought that I couldn't escape was that if a community Holocaust commemoration in Melbourne included this in its programme, the service would likely take weeks. That this simple and poignant ceremony would not have been possible in Melbourne hammered home the extent to which Melbourne Jewry, and my own life, my own family and my own social circles, have been shaped by the presence of Holocaust survivors.

Two more things that left an impression: at the end of the formal proceedings, the audience of several hundred gathered outside, in front of the temple and marched silently the half a mile to the city's Holocaust memorial, led by members of the local chapter of the Knights of Columbus, a worldwide Catholic fraternal order, dressed in their ceremonial regalia and carrying American flags. No explanation was given as to why this group led the silent march, and although there should be no problem in principle for a Catholic organization participating in a Holocaust commemoration, there was something about the aesthetic of the Knights of Columbus leading the march that I found disquieting.

Finally, I was unsettled when the audience applauded twice during the survivor's talk. They applauded wildly when the survivor described the United States as 'the greatest country in the world', and he received a standing ovation after he had finished. In my whole life, I had never heard applause at a Holocaust commemoration. In Melbourne, it was always the accepted convention that these events were solemn and applause was taboo. It was here I first felt the pang that the moment lacked solemnity, gravity; that those present were not treating the affair with the requisite reverence.

All this simply confirmed to me the malleable and messy nature of remembrance, and that even though I tried to resist the impulse to lay claim to what was the 'best' or 'most appropriate' way to commemorate, I still fell into the trap of judging or censuring those forms that are different and unfamiliar. Despite the inner struggle over how the Third Generation needs to find its own voice in carrying the Holocaust legacy of our grandparents, I still defaulted, against my better judgement, to insisting on particular modes of remembrance. I still demanded solemnity, reverence.

The Charleston ceremony highlighted to me that questions of language, ritual and memory are contingent on so many different factors, such the backgrounds of the participants (including their family backgrounds and their relationship to the Holocaust); the local contexts (it shouldn't have been so surprising that a Holocaust commemoration in Charleston should be so different from one in Melbourne); and the geopolitical contexts in which memories and ideas are fashioned (of course American Jews relate to the Holocaust differently from how Australian Jews do). Just as survivors' experiences are heterogeneous, and their children's (our parents') lives marked by the broad and diverse shadows of the Holocaust, so too does the Third Generation face myriad ways of relating to the Holocaust. We bear a burden and a responsibility that will never be simply defined, and which we may never be able to realize. Perhaps recognizing this fact, though, is the beginning.

NOTES

1. On the history and politics of Holocaust commemorations in Australia, see Judith Berman, *Holocaust Remembrance in Australian Jewish Communities, 1945–2000* (Nedlands: University of Western Australia Press, 2001).
2. The Bund was historically socialist, Yiddishist and anti-Zionist, although in recent years the organization would characterize itself as non-Zionist. On the post-war decline of the Bund, see David Slucki, *The International Jewish Labor Bund after 1945: Toward a Global History* (New Brunswick, NJ: Rutgers University Press, 2012).
3. SKIF stands for *Sotsyalistisher Kinder Farband*, or Socialist Children's Union. First founded in Poland in 1926, SKIF in Melbourne was established by refugees and survivors in 1950. There were also attempts to re-establish SKIF organizations in other cities to which Bundists migrated. On SKIF's founding, see J.S. Hertz, *Di geshikhte fun a yugnt: der kleyner Bund-Yugnt-Bund Tsukunft in Polyn* [The History of a Youth: the Little Bund-Youth Bund *Tsukunft* (Future) in Poland], (New York: Farlag Unzer Tsayt, 1946); on the post-war Bundist youth movements in Melbourne, New York, and Paris, see Slucki, *International Jewish Labor Bund after 1945*, pp.96–101, 131–6, 159–64.
4. David Irving is perhaps the most notorious Holocaust denier, his infamy sealed when he unsuccessfully tried to sue historian Deborah Lipstadt, who accused him of denying the Holocaust. On Irving's libel trial against Lipstadt, see Deborah Lipstadt, *History on Trial: My Day in Court with David Irving* (New York: Ecco, 2005). In Australia, Irving became particularly prominent after the government denied him an entry visa in 1993, sparking a public debate about free speech. He famously debated a local Holocaust survivor on the news programme, *A Current Affair*. On the government's refusal to allow him entry to Australia, see Tzvi Fleischer, 'The End: Issues Surrounding the Denial of a Visa to David Irving', *Australia/Israel Review*, 21, 19 (1996), pp.18–20; Lawrence W. Maher, 'Migration Act Visitor Entry Controls and Free Speech: The Case of David Irving', *Sydney Law Review*, 16, 3 (1993), pp.358–93.
5. See, for example, Idith Zertal, *Israel's Holocaust and the Politics of Nationhood* (Cambridge and New York: Cambridge University Press, 2005); Tom Segev, *The Seventh Million: The Israelis and the Holocaust* (New York: Hill & Wang, 1993); Dina Porat, *Israel, the Holocaust, and its Survivors* (London and Portland, OR: Vallentine Mitchell, 2008); Hanna Yablonka, *Survivors of the Holocaust: Israel after the War* (New York: New York University Press, 1999).
6. For the text of this speech, see tobybee, 'Reflecting on the Holocaust', *Jew On This* (blog), 20 April 2010, http://jewonthis.wordpress.com/2010/04/20/reflecting-on-the-holocaust/.
7. Email communication to author, 25 April 2010.
8. For an account of this evening, see tobybee, 'let's just commemorate', *Jew On This* (blog), 13 August 2010, http://jewonthis.wordpress.com/2010/08/13/lets-just-commemorate/.
9. My grandfather's other son, Chaim, 8 years old, was also killed, while his first wife, Gitl Wiszniewski-Slucki, was murdered in the gas chambers at Chelmno on 28 April 1942, shortly after the liquidation of the Włocławek Ghetto. See Katriel Thursh and Meir Korzen, *Wloclawek un umgegnt yizker bukh* [Wloclawek and Surrounding Region Memorial Book](Association from Wloclawek and Surrounding Region in Israel and the USA, Tel Aviv, 1967), p. 254.
10. In a 2013 *New York Times* op-ed, Holocaust historian Marci Shore summarizes the ways in which this narrative has been instrumentalized: Marci Shore, 'The Jewish Hero History Forgot', *The New York Times*, 18 April 2013, http://www.nytimes.com/2013/04/19/opinion/the-jewish-hero-history-forgot.html?pagewanted=all&_r=0.
11. Adi Ophir, 'On Sanctifying the Holocaust: An Anti-Theological Treatise', *Tikkun* 2, 1 (1987), pp.61–7.
12. Ibid., pp.62–3.
13. Two years later, *Tikkun* carried a similar critique from essayist Phillip Lopate, who decried the proliferation of memorials and museums throughout the United States as nothing more than 'ethnic muscle flexing', and protested the major American, Israeli and European Holocaust museums, which he likened to 'a Tunnel of Horrors or a Disneyland park devoted to Jewish suffering'. See Phillip Lopate, 'Resistance to the Holocaust', in *Getting Personal: Selected Essays* (New York: Basic Books, 2005), pp.263–79. Lopate's angry critique drew equally fiery responses from leading Holocaust historians Yehuda Bauer and Deborah Lipstadt, with Bauer

objecting to Lopate's demand to look at the Holocaust 'from an ironic distance', and Lipstadt most troubled by what she sees as his 'lack of kinship'. Yehuda Bauer, 'Don't Resist', *Tikkun* 4, 3 (1989), pp. 65–7; Deborah Lipstadt, 'What Does This Mean to You?' *Tikkun* 4, 3 (1989), pp. 67–9.

14. Historian Jordana Silverstein provides an excellent account of contemporary Holocaust education in both Melbourne and New York. See Jordana Silverstein, ' "From the Utter Depth of Degredation to the Apogee of Bliss": The Genderings of Diasporic Zionism and Jewish Holocaust Education', *Journal of Modern Jewish Studies* 11, 3 (2012), pp. 377–398.
15. *Landsmanshaftn* are hometown, mutual aid organizations in which migrants from the same town in Eastern Europe would come together for a range of purposes. In Melbourne, they served an important commemorative function for communities that had been destroyed. Not much has been written about *landmanshaftn* in Australia, although there are many volumes on those in the United States. For an excellent volume that looks at the transnational connections of the Bialystok *landsmanshaft*, including in Australia, see Rebecca Kobrin, *Jewish Bialystok and its Diaspora* (Bloomington, IN: Indiana University Press, 2010).
16. For further commentary on this issue, see my forthcoming article: David Slucki, 'Trivialization or Commemoration? Holocaust Humor in Australia', *Humor in Jewish Culture*, Studies in Contemporary Jewry: An Annual, vol. 29, edited by Eli Lederhendler and Gabriel N. Finder (New York: Oxford University Press, forthcoming 2016).
17. Ira Sheskin and Arnold Dashefsky, 'Jewish Population in the United States, 2013', in Dordrecht et al., (eds), *The American Jewish Year Book, 2013*, vol. 113 (2013), Appendix A. Springer
18. On the history of Jews in Charleston, see James Hagy, *This Happy Land: The Jews of Colonial and Antebellum Charleston* (Tuscaloosa, AL: University of Alabama Press, 1993); Charles Reznikoff and Uriah Z. Engelman, *The Jews of Charleston: A History of an American Jewish community* (Philadelphia, PA: Jewish Publication Society, 1950); Theodore Rosengarten and Dale Rosengarten (eds), *A Portion of the People: Three Hundred Years of Southern Jewish Life* (Columbia, SC: University of South Carolina Press, 2002).

Conclusion: The Third Generation and the Future of the Holocaust

ESTHER JILOVSKY, JORDANA SILVERSTEIN AND DAVID SLUCKI

At the beginning of 2012, we sent out a call for papers for a book that would explore the narratives, histories and memories of the third generation. In return, we received an overwhelming number of responses from around the world. It was clear in that moment – if it had not been before – that there exists a multitude of people who feel themselves to be part of this sometimes amorphous mass that can be grouped together under the name of 'third generation'. Indeed, it has been evident for some time that as the third generation gradually comes of age – this is a generation, after all, which has a very wide age range – its members seek to make meaning from their experiences and memories as the grandchildren of Holocaust survivors.

It is perhaps hard to pinpoint exactly what it was that made this moment particularly filled with conversations by and about the third generation. Some have pinned it on the emergence at that time of new films, such as *Schindler's List* (1993), which brought discussions of the Holocaust to wider audiences and thereby in some senses normalized some narratives of the Holocaust. From this, and from the broader public memorializing of the Holocaust, new forms of interaction between familial memories and public collective memories have occurred, including increased efforts to collect testimonies across the globe. In tandem with these developments evolved the practice of covering the Holocaust in the school curriculum, and thus, for many members of the third generation, navigating the Holocaust as a school subject meant encountering their family history. Others point to broader societal shifts in the late twentieth and early twenty-first centuries, as people work towards building strong communities, identities and histories in what is, in some ways, an increasingly fragmented world. Perhaps it is simply that at this moment in time, members of the third generation are finding new languages through which to speak about their experiences, and have the time and space to grapple with what those personal and communal histories have meant. Perhaps it is that we are finding that the representations which exist – whether it is of the traumas of our grandparents and then our parents, or the sanitized versions of that history which Hollywood produces – are unable to articulate our experiences, and so we recognize the need to lay out our own messy emotions, stories and memories.

Whatever the explanation, it is clear that there has been an emergence of the third generation, and that it can be seen in numerous places, including in conversations, in writings, in internet groups and other groups and in the pieces collected in this volume.

Indeed, perhaps the most obvious, but also most important, contribution of this volume is that it unequivocally shows that the third generation exists; that despite the diversity of grandchildren of Holocaust survivors, there are common threads which stretch invisibly between those whose grandparents endured and ultimately survived the atrocities of Nazi Europe. What precisely makes up these common threads is much more difficult to articulate. But the chapters of this book give us many clues. Firstly, the third generation's relationship to the Holocaust is on the whole not framed by their parents, the second generation, but evolves out of a direct connection with their grandparents. It is important to note this contrast with second-generation writers and educators, who see their position very much as mediating the Holocaust to the third generation. Our chapters show that this is not, in fact, the case. The authors featured here barely mention their parents at all, even when their Holocaust survivor grandparents are no longer alive. The third generation, whether speaking in interviews or writing their own accounts, overwhelmingly emphasize their own relationships with their grandparents, at times not discussing their parents.

The many personal chapters in this book show that members of the third generation write about their grandparents in a loving, sensitive and poignant way. With carefully chosen and delicate language, the third generation communicates the complicated and multifaceted relationship they have, or had, with their grandparents. This may comprise the unconditional love that grandparents can have for their grandchildren but it could also involve a sense of loss, absence and even frustration that this relationship may have been cut short because of their Holocaust experiences (for the Holocaust had very real effects on the bodily and mental health of survivors), and a sense of tragedy and even trauma produced by the presence (or absence) of these stories. But, let us be clear, the trauma, if we may call it that, which is carried by the third generation is not a trauma in the way that the second generation has been traumatized. It is even less tangible, less easy to grasp or to describe. It is to a large extent about not knowing, whether the details of the third generation's grandparents' experiences are known to them or not. It is a sense of loss; the knowledge that everything could change at any moment, the awareness that possessions are transitory. It is a different baggage to that which the second generation carries – a different baggage, but one riddled simultaneously with sadness and with hope.

Making it even more difficult to characterize the third generation is the fact that it is such a diverse group, insofar as it is a 'group' at all. Members of the third generation incorporate a whole array of religious, ethnic, political, national, sexual and gender identities. They are diverse in terms of age ranges. The writers and subjects of this book vary in age from teenagers to those in their forties, and anywhere in between. Even those much younger – grandchildren of those born in the 1930s and 1940s – might be considered part of this third generation. This means that those who we characterize as being within the same generation were raised in wildly different contexts. For those at the younger end of the age range, some were born after the end of the Cold War, and after the emergence of a much more ubiquitous Holocaust consciousness. This was a very different world from the one remembered by those who recall the bipolar and delicate global order that persisted through the 1980s, and who were raised in a world in which the Holocaust was not yet the staple of Hollywood and popular culture that it would become in the 1990s. These different ends of the third generation would likely have had different relationships with, and memories of, their grandparents, with their grandparents likely to have been at different stages of their life.

Another important way in which this book reveals the diversity of the third generation is in geographic and cultural terms. It is perhaps self-evident that those raised in the United States, Israel, Germany and the United Kingdom would have different understandings of the Holocaust that are shaped by their local surroundings. But the chapters in this book allow us to start thinking about what those differences are. For example, in what way does being raised in Melbourne, with its high proportion of survivors, shape the way third generation members understand the Holocaust? How does that differ from those raised in local settings where survivors are much rarer? How much more complex do these issues become for those born in the countries of the perpetrators, Germany and Austria? What about those raised in Israel, where the Holocaust assumes national and mythic importance? What about in the United States, where survivors comprise a tiny proportion of American Jewry, yet the Holocaust narrative takes pride of place on the national mall in Washington, integrated into the national narrative? And what about in the United Kingdom, where 27 January, the date of the liberation of Auschwitz in 1945, has been inaugurated as the national Holocaust Memorial Day?

Finally, this book raises many other questions about how the identities of the third generation influence their understandings of the Holocaust.

How do gender and sexuality play a role in relating not only to the Holocaust, but to one's grandparents? In what ways do ethnicity and religion determine their relationship to their grandparents' experiences? Do politics and ideology contribute to this process, or are they shaped by the Holocaust? Do their grandparents' experiences – whether they were in ghettos, death camps, the Soviet Union, Palestine, in hiding – change their sense of belonging to this generation, or their connection to the Holocaust?

We hope that in this volume we have been able to open up these vital questions for further consideration. This book is, it is clear, just one moment in a beginning of a conversation. And this conversation, it is also clear, is not just about Jewish descendants of survivors, or indeed descendants of Jewish survivors: the Holocaust was not only a Jewish event and those of us who are descendants of other victimized groups have much to add to these conversations. Indeed, we are not complete without them. So this book is offered in the spirit of openness, and in the hope that through writing about their experiences, the third generation will be able to move toward the creation of new vocabularies and new emotional languages of connection.

Index

Please note that page numbers relating to Notes will have the letter 'n' following the page number.